THE SISTERS OF OUR LADY OF THE MISSIONS:

From Ultramontane Origins to a New Cosmology

Warmly,
pro

The Sisters of Our Lady of the Missions

From Ultramontane Origins to a New Cosmology

ROSA BRUNO-JOFRÉ

UNIVERSITY OF TORONTO PRESS
Toronto Buffalo London

ISBN 978-1-4875-0564-6

∞ Printed on acid-free. 100% post-consumer recycled paper with
vegetable-based inks.

Library and Archives Canada Cataloguing in Publication

Title: The Sisters of Our Lady of the Missions : from ultramontane origins
    to a new cosmology / Rosa Bruno-Jofré.
Names: Bruno-Jofré, Rosa del Carmen, 1946– author.
Description: Includes bibliographical references and index.
Identifiers: Canadiana 20190162163 | ISBN 9781487505646 (hardcover)
Subjects: LCSH: Sisters of our Lady of the Missions (Canada) – History. |
    LCSH: Catholic Church – Missions – Canada – History. | LCSH: Missions –
    Educational work – Canada – History. | LCSH: Women – Education –
    Canada – History. | LCSH: Feminist theology – Canada – History. |
    LCSH: Ecotheology – Canada – History.
Classification: LCC BX4485.68.Z5 C3 2019 | DDC 271.9—dc23

University of Toronto Press acknowledges the financial assistance to its
publishing program of the Canada Council for the Arts and the Ontario Arts
Council, an agency of the Government of Ontario.

This book has been published with the help of a grant from the Federation
for the Humanities and Social Sciences, through the Awards to Scholar
Publications Program, using funds provided by the Social Sciences and
Research Council of Canada.

Canada Council   Conseil des Arts
for the Arts   du Canada

ONTARIO ARTS COUNCIL
CONSEIL DES ARTS DE L'ONTARIO

an Ontario government agency
un organisme du gouvernement de l'Ontario

Funded by the   Financé par le
Government   gouvernement
of Canada   du Canada

Canada

MIX
Paper from
responsible sources
FSC® C016245

Contents

Illustrations

Acknowledgments

I would like to express my profound thanks to the Religieuses de Notre Dame des Missions / Our Lady of the Missions for their diligent assistance and their profound commitment to scholarship. Special thanks to former provincial sister Dr Veronica Dunne and to Sister Marilyn Leblanc, to the former superiors who participated in the conversations, to the archivist of the RNDM house in Rome, to the sisters and archivist in Sturry, England, and to my former research assistant, Dr Patricia Quiroga Uceda, who worked with me in the archives in Winnipeg. I acknowledge the invaluable cooperation of Brenda Reed, director of the Education Library at Queen's University, and her team, and the excellent work of Angela Pietrobon, who suffered through footnoting, formatting, and copy-editing. Last, but not least, I thank my loving husband Ricardo, who worked me in the archives for countless days.

THE SISTERS OF OUR LADY OF THE MISSIONS

From Ultramontane Origins to a New Cosmology

Coming to Life at the Intersection of Ultramontanism and Colonialism

This book guides the reader through the journey taken by the Canadian province of the Religieuses de Notre Dame des Missions (RNDM) / Sisters of Our Lady of the Missions, from their establishment in Manitoba, Canada, in 1898, by invitation from the ultramontane Adélard Langevin, archbishop of St Boniface, until 2008, when the congregation as a whole redefined its vision and mission as the RNDM Earth Community, "We are One, We are Love."[1] This vision was placed within the framework of eco-spirituality and inserted in a new cosmology that included the celebration of womanness and social justice.

Euphrasie Barbier founded the congregation in 1861 in Lyon, France, at the time of the Holy See's anti-modernist and anti-liberal positioning. At the macro level of analysis, the new congregation, devoted to the education of young girls and women in "infidel" and non-Catholic countries, carved out a space for itself in the colonial empire. The narrative in the book is placed within the many overlapping historical, ideological, and even intellectual configurations in which the congregation was inserted – configurations that denote figurative spaces taken up by constellations of ideas related to the process of colonization, the increasing importance of the scientific method, the impact of the theory of evolution, the spread of industrial transformation, and the ideology of progress. The concept of configuration brings in a heuristic tool with which to work through contexts and take into account the circulation of ideas.

It is significant that Barbier had developed her own religious self under the influence of a rigorist version of Jansenism, which led her to the practice of self-sacrifice and acceptance of suffering. Barbier placed emphasis on the negation of the self, made the congregation semi-cloistered, cultivated a strong loyalty to Rome, and set a strong authoritarian tone with an accent on obedience and limited contact with the world, thus setting clear parameters for the relational and reflective dimensions of the self.[2] In line with this vision, she built a highly centralized, hierarchical, and bureaucratic organization.

When the congregation came to the province of Manitoba, Canada, the sisters had already established an international network of houses in Europe, Asia, and Oceania. Once in Canada, the RNDM soon expanded their educational work to Saskatchewan (1905) and later to Ontario (1940) and Quebec in the 1950s. They taught in public schools, parish schools, private schools, and the publicly funded Catholic separate school system in Saskatchewan. The RNDMs thus secured their own place in the educational state.

The congregation had as its starting point basic ideas on educational thought from Johann Heinrich Pestalozzi (1746–1827) and Friedrich Froebel (1782–1852) that were quite common among teaching congregations. However, the sisters' educational approach was developed through missionary interaction (including their attendance at normal schools), which in turn intersected with the teachings of the Church (the voice of the Magisterium) and the highly centralized international governance of the congregation. The micro context was equally important. The insertion of the sisters in the communities' "social imaginary" nourished intentionalities and even political agendas.

The details of their work in schools, within the limits set by the sources available, are important to show and explain how the sisters' educational work was related to their interaction with the socio-economic characteristics of the communities, which were often marked by scenarios of demographic changes due to immigration waves and also by political struggles. In the end, I argue that the congregation was part of a major attempt by the Church to place itself in the educational state in formation and to keep among Catholics an adherence to a world view and a doctrine grounded in a neo-scholastic theological framework that confronted modernity and tried to assert a Catholic way of being. Thus, the book seeks to convey the unique characteristics of the various settings: in Manitoba, the schools in Franco-Manitoban communities, the parish and private schools in English-speaking communities, and the work with the children of immigrants; in Saskatchewan, the Catholic separate school system, the private schools for girls including at higher levels of education, and the brief experience in a residential school for Indigenous children; and the moves to Ontario and Quebec. Perhaps the most difficult endeavour in writing this book was the recreation of the spirituality in the schools beyond the formalities, ceremonies, and rituals.

The 1930s opened a challenging period for the congregation, but the post-war era and the "long 1960s," with its overlapping socio-economic and theological shifts, would introduce a new landscape and lead to radical breaks. The RNDM private schools for girls did not survive the changes. The sisters belonging to the Canadian province had developed their own sense of being RNDM religious, and the mission in Peru, an initiative of the province that started in the field in January 1969, had moved them to resignify their understanding of mission, transforming their sense of identity as missionary sisters.

The process of reception of Vatican II (1962–65) would, in fact, lead to epistemic shifts and visionary changes through a difficult undertaking in which residual elements and fear of change coexisted with more radical approaches. The Canadian province played a leading role in the process of renewal that moved from questioning hierarchies in the congregation, through a strong commitment to social justice (exemplified by the province in the work in Peru), to a new cosmology. The congregation as a whole embraced social justice in 1984. However, the adoption of eco-spirituality represented the most powerful break. The sisters, influenced by feminist thea/o/*logies and eco-theologists and cosmologists, moved beyond the boundaries of the modern self to resituate themselves in relation to the universe and the human and non-human world.[3] The province played an inspiring role in the late 1990s and early 2000s. In 2008, the international congregation as a whole formalized the concept of the RNDM Earth Community with "We are One, We are Love," a phrase taken from the foundress. The sisters of the province had developed an elaborated understanding of themselves as individuals and as a community, in relation to the earth, the universe, and the non-human world, that was grounded in a critique of Western cosmology and in ways to respect and revere the interiority and differences of others. The sisters fully repositioned their sense of self as religious women to celebrate womanness, relationship, reflection, and social justice with a great awareness of the limits set by the institutional Church.

This book does not pretend to cover all the complex dimensions of the life of the congregation. The book was designed in relation to the central questions leading the various parts of the research, having as its point of reference the educational work in the prairies and the transformative process related to the long 1960s and the reception of Vatican II. The characteristics of the mission in Peru and its impact on the life of the congregation deserved a special chapter. A spontaneous conversation with former provincial leaders included in an appendix gives an intimate dimension to the analysis.

This book is the first one on the RNDMs in Canada and is grounded in extensive archival research conducted at the Centre du patrimoine, Societé historique de Saint-Boniface, Manitoba; the RNDM United Kingdom Archives in Sturry; and the General Archives of the RNDM in Rome; and also makes use of oral testimonies. There are two books on the RNDMs. Susan Smith, RNDM, wrote an enlightened book about the RNDMs in New Zealand that intersects changes in Catholic spirituality with the story of the Mission Sisters in Aotearoa New Zealand, the New Zealanders of Irish ancestry, and the impact of Vatican II.[4] She also edited a general history of the congregation, more descriptive in character, which served as a point of reference.[5] The historical reality in New Zealand was, of course, very different, an example being the French-Canadian issue in Canada and the very setting of the missionary endeavour. The theoretical framework used in this book marks a difference as well. The conceptual tools used in the analysis of the RNDMs in Canada reflect my attempt to open up a new way of studying women teaching congregations, even in relation to my own work on the Missionary Oblate Sisters of the Sacred Heart and Mary Immaculate, whose educational work was centred, by and large, in Franco-Manitoban communities and in residential schools for Indigenous children. In the study of the Oblates, I moved from an emphasis on agency that is still dominant in the study of women religious congregations to focus on patriarchy to explain the myth of foundations of the Missionary Oblates and the working of the sisters' relation with the Church. This congregation, like many others, asserted the rights of the settlers, in particular the French Canadians, to language and a Catholic education, which generated cultural interconnections unique to the place, while their extensive work in residential schools for Indigenous children was aimed at the obliteration of Indigenous culture and identity.

I took a new direction in writing the history of the RNDMs. This narrative, often wrapped in a Catholic idiom, offers a pinch of critical realism in its attempt to understand – grounded in Quentin Skinner's theory – the intentionality sustaining the educational apostolate and its adaptations and changes, and the intended force – or "illocutionary force" – of the linguistic action that has given meaning to the sisters' narratives and concrete work in the field. Following Skinner, the text, in this case imbued with confessional motivations and an intimate religious call, is placed in context, tracing the relevant characteristics of the societal settings where the sisters opened schools.[6] The use of configuration, as mentioned earlier, allows me to navigate the insertion of the congregation in macro configurations, such as the overall guiding neo-scholastic theological framework imposed by the Holy See and its anti-modernist, patriarchal approach to education; the agenda of educationalization carried out by the state; and the national and regional Church, as well as the international configuration of the governance of the congregation. It also helps in exploring the intersection, adaptation, mediation, and reception of circulating ideas and the interaction with the "social imaginaries"[7] in the spaces where the sisters inhabited and interacted – be it the little French-Canadian village, the English-speaking elementary parish school in Brandon populated by new immigrants, the school in Winnipeg, or the normal school where they had to take courses. The narrative often traces the tension between the rules and regulations in a congregation that was semi-cloistered; in the design of the convent – which often served as the school – with its embedded separation from the world, a source of sin; within the pioneering setting in the Canadian West; and, even later, in the social imaginaries of the communities of which the sisters, the Church, and the school were an integral part, even in many cases when the school was public. The sisters' adaptation in the interaction with the context is fully revealed in the changes made to the curriculum, with the offering of commercial courses for girls in the 1930s and the modernization of schools in the 1950s, which show the variegated ways in which the Church related to modernity.

The exploration of the semantic fields uncovered in the sisters' documents, journals, and narratives and the records of the enculturating celebrations that took place in the schools are useful to understand the place of the congregation at the intersection of theological and social configurations. It also demonstrates the movement from adherence to a language of submission, obedience, pain, silence, fear of God, and sacrifice to a more subdued language in subsequent decades – a language of solidarity, liberation, desire, and selfhood – as part of their adaptation in the wake of the long 1960s and Vatican II.

This book examines at length the shaking up of the long 1960s going into the 2000s and the impact of Vatican II, the dismantling of neo-scholasticism, and the process of the secularization of consciousness. The emerging issues moved me to examine how the province re-worked the bodily, relational, and reflective self – as characterized by Jerrold Seigel – both individually and collectively. I also follow the tensions emerging from the province's commitment to change, displayed in three identifiable fields as per Pierre Bourdieu[8] and constituted by what was going on in the Holy See, the positioning of the congregation's central administration, and the sisters of the Canadian province's desires for more autonomy while being critical of the hierarchical character of the congregation's administration. The reading of the often contradictory process leading to social justice is questioned in light of the Vatican II documents and contextual interactions, such as the province's mission in Peru and the sisters' exposure there to liberation theology and the reading of Vatican II through the Document of Medellín, and their experience in the missionary field. Feminist thea/o/*logy emerged powerfully, particularly from the 1970s and 1980s, and became a point of reference in most women's congregations' rethinking of themselves and their positioning in the Church. Although the RNDMs did not leave written notes on their discussions of various authors, the traces are everywhere and make quite patent their movement to eco-spirituality/eco-theology in dialogue with political, cultural, and environmental theories. Feminist thea/o/*logians questioned the dualist theology and patriarchy, reflected from their own experience, and created new analytical terms. However, secular literatures on feminist political theory and gender have not deconstructed the binary between the secular and the religious. Although the RNDMs did not theorize their approach, their actual praxis and the critical construction of their cosmological view provide a historical case that went beyond the hierarchical, sacred structures to actually put in motion a practical understanding of domination and exploitation that goes beyond that hierarchy.[9] This particular history thus helps to expand the understanding of the feminist movement in the context of religion.

The book thus deals with questions not posed before. There is a paucity of scholarly monographs studying women teaching congregations in the Canadian prairies, and the content and focus of this book and its research questions expand on, add to, and complement excellent contributions on women teaching congregations in English-speaking Canada in the form of articles and chapters on women teaching congregations. Some well-respected scholars in this area include Sheila Ross and Tom Mitchell in Manitoba, Elizabeth Smyth and Christine Lei in Ontario, Heidi MacDonald in the Maritimes, and Jacqueline Gresko in British Columbia, to name only a few related to education.[10] Of course, there is extensive literature dealing with Quebec congregations.

History of education, particularly in the Western world, needs to integrate the analysis of the Catholic Church to fully examine its role in the process of the educationalization of social issues, the building of the educational state, the formation of citizens and the making of the Catholic subject, the construction of genders, the formation of leaders, and the education of girls, especially up to the long 1960s. The building of a French-Canadian identity outside Quebec is not intelligible without considering the network of the clergy, professionals, and institutions in which schools played a central role. The RNDMs, just as other teaching congregations, played an important part in the rural prairies and in the separate school system, particularly in Saskatchewan. The close examination conducted in this book provides unique details of the insertion of women religious in the communities and of the role of the Church in their life.

The processes of colonization cannot be fully understood without considering the messianic spread of Catholic civilization, and thus the notion of mission and the Eurocentric theological positioning and notions of salvation and redemption that configured the "other," while converging with state agendas. The RNDMs were involved in the residential schools for Indigenous children for only a few months, but the sisters aimed at assimilation and conversion of the children. Meanwhile, the sisters, a large number of them Canadian, would develop their own identity working with French-speaking settlers, continental and eastern European Catholic immigrants, and English-speaking Catholics. This mission was part of their progressive adaptation to the milieu, while being part of an international congregation. Locality played a central role in the development of the Canadian province of the RNDMs, but within the parameters of the notion of the Catholic faith as the only truth.

This book intertwines the micro and macro history. It will hopefully enrich the understanding of history of education and the workings of women teaching congregations previous to Vatican II. It will also contribute to the problematization and deconstruction of the persistent modern binary between religion and secularism in discussions of feminist theory by providing as a historical case the dramatic changes of the RNDMs and going beyond gender to include race, age, ethnicity, the neoliberal order, and the positioning of humans regarding the earth and the universe.

PART ONE

Contextualizing the Vision
of the Foundress

1.1 Euphrasie Barbier. Source: Author's collection.

Chapter One

Who Were the RNDMs? Arrival in Canada (1898) and Transnational Ethos

To be in Love with God is One of Life's Greatest Adventures.

– Saint Augustine

Euphrasie – What were you looking for?
A desire to serve?
A taste of adventure…?
A Community of Friends…?
Or was it…
The satisfaction of accomplishment…?
The joy of togetherness…?
The strength of ideals shared…?
Maybe
An urge to change traditions
A streak of independence
A personal vision.

– Barbara Henley[1]

Euphrasie Barbier's Beginnings

The Religieuses de Notre Dame des Missions (RNDM) / Sisters of Our Lady of the Missions was founded in Lyon, France, in 1861 by Euphrasie Barbier, known in religious life as Marie-du-Coeur-de-Jésus / Mary of the Heart of Jesus (1829–93).[2] Who was Euphrasie Barbier? A few lines about her pre-congregational life and her religious life will suffice, since there is an excellent scholarly biography on that era.[3] The focus of this chapter is, rather, on her original spiritual inclinations and, in particular, on the contextual forces and configurations of Church doctrines that gave meaning to her vision.[4]

Euphrasie Barbier was born in Caen, in the Normandy region of France, into a modest, deeply Catholic, working-class family. Her father was a shoemaker who was born in Guadeloupe (West Indies), and her mother a daughter of farmers who lived off their land. At fourteen, she left school, after completing primary education, and became an apprentice in a laundry specializing in doing delicate work for the middle class. She was there from 1843 to 1846, at which time, after receiving further instruction from a family member, she opened her own laundry for fine linen in her parents' home.[5] However, a religious vocation was the underlying drive in her life; she had experienced a strong attraction to missions since childhood, which was reawakened by the preaching of a missionary bishop passing through the parish of Saint-Pierre in Caen in 1846.[6] She then ran to the sacristy and asked for an interview with the bishop, who advised her to consult with her spiritual director.

Barbier found a spiritual guide in Abbé Lefournier, her parish priest. She then followed a strict program based on a rigorist version of Jansenism – according to which our fallen nature needs a special grace to overcome our inclination towards evil – present in the form of self-sacrifice and the acceptance of suffering.[7]

In those early years, she took Communion several times a week and went through confession every Sunday at eight o'clock in the morning; meditation and spiritual readings complemented her program.[8] Barbier cultivated for herself practices of sacrifice and suffering to develop spiritual perfection. In 1848, guided by Lefournier, she entered the Sisters of Calvary (later to become the Sisters of Compassion), a congregation newly founded at Cuves in the Diocese of Lagrange and destined for foreign missions. She applied herself to the rule of the community (the Rule of St Augustine) and became imbued with the spirit of the newly founded congregation with a Marian and Trinitarian spirituality, which would have a lasting influence on the future Mother Mary of the Heart of Jesus.[9]

In 1851, Barbier was sent to England, after which the Sisters of Calvary were dissolved to be reconstituted as the Sisters of Compassion. The new congregation, under the responsibility of the Fathers of the London Oratory, was expected to assist the Oratorian fathers in the conversion of England. That expectation meant a shift away from the original vision of the congregation when it was the Sisters of Calvary: to go to foreign missions. This new purpose was disappointing for Barbier, who nevertheless remained in England serving the poor until 1861. But, by the end of 1860, she had been deposed as both assistant to the superior and mistress of novices of the congregation and was moved to the last bed of the novitiate (the last bed in the bedroom of the novices), an act of demotion. We do not know the reasons for her dismissal, other than suggestions that some kind of altercation took place with the superior of the Oratorians. However, we do know that, after her dismissal, she received a transfer of obedience to the Marist sisters by means of an indult given to her by the Congregation of the Propagation of the Faith. The transfer was not feasible.[10] Instead, the Marist fathers received Barbier in Lyon with a companion, Mary St Wilfrid (Elizabeth Norton), under the assumption that Barbier could gather other French women and work with the Marist fathers in Wellington, New Zealand. The plan failed due to the bishop in Wellington having already found other women religious. But the superior general of the Marists decided to have Barbier (Sister Mary of the Heart of Jesus) start a new foundation in Lyon with the dual purposes of assisting Marist missions wherever needed and of incorporating into religious life a number of tertiaries (members of the Third Order of Mary), who were working in the islands of the Pacific.[11] As a result, the canonical erection of the novitiate in 1861, on Christmas night, gave birth to a new missionary institute, the Religieuses de Notre Dame des Missions (RNDM) / Sisters of Our Lady of the Missions.[12] As stated earlier, the RNDM were initially expected to join with the Sisters of the Third Order of Mary, the latter of whom were supports for the Marist fathers in Oceania. Barbier started working on the constitutions in 1863, as is evidenced in an early document dated 1864.[13] It is clear that, as Susan Smith put it, Barbier instead wanted to found a new congregation with its own spirit that would work with the Marist fathers in Oceania. The Marist fathers believed that the new congregation would be part of the Marist missionary outreach and that they would direct the sisters in their work;[14] the Marist fathers wanted a more active role than Barbier wanted them to have in the life of the young congregation. The resulting tension was in part resolved in June 1869 by the Vatican *Brief of Praise*, which gave the sisters the autonomy Barbier wanted.[15] Barbier, who cultivated an ultramontane ("beyond the mountains beyond Rome lay") papocentric loyalty towards Rome, had found support from the papacy in her struggle with the Society of Mary.[16] Loyalty to Rome would persist as a characteristic of the congregation well beyond the Second Vatican Council (Vatican II; 1962–65).

Susan Smith argues that Barbier's experience in London would influence her approach to the governance of the congregation. Barbier had been affected by the capacity of clerical superiors to deflect the vision and mission of a congregation and its legitimate goals; she therefore would put in place a governance structure capable of protecting her congregation from clerical interference. It was best exemplified in 1900 by the congregation's ability to decide to withdraw from an industrial school for Indigenous children in Manitoba, Canada, run by the Oblate fathers in Lac Croche, due to profound disagreements around the kind of administration that had placed the sisters under the control of the Oblate fathers.

Identifying the original intuition guiding the congregation – its charism, in contemporary terms after Vatican II – is significant, not only for understanding the force behind the foundress's actions and writings. It is also fundamental for comprehending the process of renewal in the congregation following the mandate from *Perfectae Caritatis*, the Second Vatican Council's Decree on the Adaptation and Renewal of Religious Life, promulgated by Paul VI in 1965. The decree mandated that renewal had to take place through a return to the sources of Christian life and the original spirit of the institutes and a move towards their adaptation to the conditions of the time.[17] The RNDM sisters, in looking for their original spirit as present in the process of being approved by the Holy See, would soon discover that something from Barbier's original spiritual vision was missing in their current vision: the reference to divine missions.

Barbier created a mission-sending congregation, understanding mission as primarily the work of the Trinity; hence, mission was not something that people did – it was what the Trinity did through people.[18] (Barbier was a Trinitarian, a spirituality not all that common in the nineteenth century.) Thus, in the early constitutions that she wrote for her sisters, she referred to their apostolic work as "works of charity" rather than of mission.[19]

Very early on, in 1870, Euphrasie Barbier wrote: "The Sisters in placing themselves under the title of Our Lady of the Missions have the desire to honour in a special manner the Divine Missions."[20] The 1888 draft of the constitutions included the wording: "which were the sole object of Mary's deepest aspirations."[21] From the start, the foundress placed the new congregation under the patronage of Mary, writing: "The Spirit of the Congregation is none other than the Spirit of Mary."[22] Barbier designed the habit of the congregation. It was black and white, but with blue braided edging on the full-body scapular and on the big sleeves that were worn in chapel; the blue-trimmed scapular represented the congregation's connection to Our Lady (of the Missions). The large rosary that hung at each sister's side was also a visible connection with Mary; the cincture the sisters wore represented

INTRODUCTION

DEDICATION

A. M. D. G.

O most adorable Trinity, Father, Son and Holy Ghost, we dedicate to Your greater glory and for Your pure love, all the prayers, supplications, praise and adoration of our hearts, our souls and of our whole being, in union with Holy Church in heaven, on earth and in purgatory, through our Lord Jesus Christ, the sole object of our love.

In these sad times when our souls are filled with profound sorrow and steeped in bitter grief at the sight of that satanic impiety which, under all possible forms, perverts and ruins our dear France, nay entire Europe, and even extends its influence to the ends of the earth, blaspheming more than ever Your holy Name, persecuting and pursuing with infernal hate and rage Your holy Spouse, the Church our Mother, and multiplies its incomparable and sacrilegious outrages against the Holy Eucharist, the God of our Exile, our only treasure, our one and only love!... O most adorable Trinity, God, thrice holy, the only

6

INTRODUCTION 7

true life of our souls, permit us to gather together in the adorable Hearts of Jesus, our Divine Spouse, and of Mary our Immaculate Mother, all our dear Daughters, the Religious of this humble Institute, those who have already entered into eternity, those who are still on this earth, as well as those who, later, shall be called to it, and deign to accept us all as perpetual victims and holocausts of reparation, adoration, supplication, holy zeal and love.

Vouchsafe to bestow on us a blessing which will purify, sanctify and consecrate us for Your greater glory. Bless also these books—the MANUAL OF PRAYER and the LITTLE OFFICE OF OUR LADY—destined to aid us in our holy calling, so that we may become more perfect instruments and means of salvation, blessing and sanctification for countless other souls so dear to You, O my God, O God of all purity and all holiness, our only joy and our portion for all eternity!

1.2 *Manual of Prayer and Office Book*, Introduction, 1871. Provided by Sister Veronica Dunne and Sister Carmel, archivist of the General RNDM Archives in Rome. The document was distributed to the sisters along with a circular letter: Lettre circulaire à bien chères filles, Marie-du-Coeur-de-Jésus, supérieure général, Lyon, 27 July 1871, letter 205A, General RNDM Archives in Rome.

the Rule of St Augustine. The sisters said prayers when they put on each piece of the habit.

The introduction to the *Manual of Prayer and Office Book* that Barbier wrote in 1871 provides insights into her spirituality and its insertion in her *époque*. The foundress was committed to "the most abandoned, the poor heretics, and non-Christian nations."[23] The messianic spread of Catholic "civilization" is explicit in an extract of the draft constitutions of 1864: "The Sisters will unite to the work of the mind the humble work of the hands, one being no less necessary than the other for their sanctification and the Christian civilization among the poor people among whom they are sent."[24] From the start, education was the special aim of the newly formed congregation. Barbier wrote in 1870: "After personal sanctification of its members, the special aim of the Congregation is the Christian education of women and young girls in non-Christian and heretical missions. The sisters may accept with the consent of the General Council, other works of charity."[25]

In her communication with Rome regarding the 1888 draft constitutions submitted to Rome, Barbier explains the expression "divine missions":

> By placing themselves under the title Our Lady of the Missions, the Sisters wish to honour in a way altogether special the Divine Missions which were the object of Mary's deepest desires and which this Holy Virgin glorified by the most profound and loving adoration, the most complete fidelity and the most generous devotedness.[26]

This preliminary statement, central to her original inspiration, remained in the constitutions until 1890, when the Holy See requested that it be changed in order to get approval. The congregation received pontifical approbation *ad septennium* in 1890. The Sacred Congregation suppressed the concept of "divine missions"; the reason given was that Barbier's understanding of the missionary nature of God was in the realm of spirituality and not necessary for the constitutions.[27]

Divine mission referred to the Trinitarian vision sustaining Barbier's notion of divine mission as "sent." Divine mission, she explained, referred to "the mission of the incarnate Word [Jesus] sent by God the Father to redeem the human race, and the mission of the Holy Spirit, sent by the Father to redeem the human race, and the mission of the Holy Spirit, sent by the Father and the Son to bring about the sanctification of the Church of Christ."[28] The Church received the means from the Holy Spirit to sanctify the people. The source of the mission was the Trinity, but there was room for Mary (submissive, obedient) in this patriarchal religious world. Barbier, Claire Himbeault writes, perceived Mary as being at the heart of the divine missions, as Mary was conceived as the one who received the divine missions and lived them in perfect love.[29] The sisters continued to build on this understanding during the renewal process following Vatican II, although it was not until the 1980s that they liberated themselves from the ecclesiocentric character of their apostolate. In the 1990s, Claire Himbeault explained to her community:

> The Word of God becomes human in the womb of Mary by the power of the Holy Spirit. There begins the central event in the history of salvation. Mary is at the centre of this event; it is realized in her and through her. Through her free "yes" Mary participates in the Mission of God. Through

that "yes" Mary attains a union with her God that is beyond every human hope. The child in her womb is the Son of God ...

His [Jesus's] mission is marked by the cross. He proclaims the reign of God and calls all to conversion. This proclamation of the Reign of God is the revelation of God's love ...

The mission of the Holy Spirit, the Sanctifier, sent by the Father and the Son, is a movement from God into the world.[30]

Barbier also had to narrow down the aims of the congregation, from commitment to the "most abandoned, poor heretics, and non-Christian nations" to the instruction and Christian education of children and women, above all in "infidel" and non-Catholic countries (article 2 of the 1890 constitutions).[31] The sisters did not have a clear articulation of their charism until they engaged in the process of renewal and recreated their identity during the long 1960s, the period between 1958 and 1974 that historian Marwick marked as an era of cultural revolutions.[32] However, they did have traditions that were passed from one generation to another,[33] so to some extent the sisters managed to maintain a Trinitarian spirituality, though it was heavily mediated by the Church, which institutionalized the Spirit.

What follows is the historical context of place and time in which the educational and theological constructs framing the RNDM sisters were configured. These constructs were often part of the colonial matrix in which the Church carved out its own space, one that nested within anti-modernist stands and residual elements from pre-modern centuries. In some cases, the Church just aimed at asserting the rights of Catholics.

Placing Barbier's Vision and the New Congregation in Global Space and Time

Barbier's way of thinking cannot be fully understood without attending to her subjective ideational world developed at the intersections of spiritual, theological, political, and social configurations of the time. The way Barbier lived those intersections gave many shades to the vision and mission of her religious life and that of her congregation. Let us first understand the historical configurations through which she navigated during her journey. In line with a widespread missionary movement; a renaissance of the old orders like the Carmelites, Benedictines, and Dominicans; the admission in France of the Jesuits (now with a strong papocentric bent); and the emergence of new congregations with an international call – such as the Marists, Marianists, Oblates of Mary Immaculate, and Fathers of the Holy Cross, among others – Barbier's goal was the establishment of an institute for foreign missions and education.[34] She knew this very early on in her religious life.

Barbier's existential life and its historical conditions will help us to understand her profound drive towards foreign missions and later the creation of an institute for foreign missions. Barbier was also drawn by the mysticism surrounding foreign missions and an apostolic zeal that was coupled in France with social and political unrest and waves of anti-clericalism. She was further influenced by the work of the neo-Gothic aesthetician writer François-René Chateaubriand, in particular his *Le génie du Christianisme* (*The Genius of Christianity*), published in 1802, which had great currency among Catholics. Chateaubriand, horrified by post-medieval social inequality and poverty, interpreted the experience of the French revolution and its aftermath and related suffering as a foundation for missionary work; he construed the missioner as a potential martyr and adventurer of the faith.

In nineteenth-century Europe, particularly from the second half on, an explosion of active congregations, especially women's congregations, was taking place. These would go on to disseminate Catholic values in a world that was in the process of modernizing and secularizing.[35] From the time of the first Catholic religious institutes to the twentieth century, 2,360 founders created 2,130 religious institutes; among those, 1,861 were founded in the nineteenth and twentieth centuries, and only 269 were founded in the previous centuries. Half of the 1,861 institutes were founded in Spain, Italy, and France.[36] Out of 100 institutes, 84 were female institutes, while 16 were male. The apostolates' mandates ranged from education (22.2 per cent of the institutes), evangelization, catechesis, health, and assisting missions; the contemplatives among the religious were only 12.5 per cent men and 2.4 per cent women.[37]

A complex configuration of ideas, social unrest, and movements of people nested within the politics of modernity and identity in the second half of the nineteenth century. Several factors were particularly relevant in these emerging configurations into which the congregations were inserted, including the spread of industrial transformation and the widening of world markets, processes of colonization, consolidation of the bourgeoisie as a new political and economic class, profound social disparities, and exploitation of labour and children, to all of which the Church would respond through social Catholicism. Modernity was taking shape alongside the now dominant presence of science, revised views of cognition, critique of knowledge (including Friedrich

Nietzsche's and Ernst March's critiques of the unequivocal knowledge of nature), innovative literature, evolutionism, social reformism, and, towards the fin de siècle, progressive thought of transatlantic dimensions (with race and gender as travelling blind spots).[38] However, the modern world did not erase Christianity and personal piety, which continued to be expressed in many ways, whether it was in its Protestant strands (in many cases in tune with modernity) or in its Catholic traditions that condemned modernity.

The fin de siècle corresponded to what Eric Hobsbawm refers to as the "Age of Empire," the time of a new form of colonial empire between 1880 and 1914.[39] During this age, religious missionaries had a "civilizing" mission and found a space for their vocations both through such missions and by providing educational, social, and health services to colonial settlements. At the time, many women and men religious were sent to England to learn English, since it was the language of the colonies; Barbier was among them, dispatched early during her time at the Congregation of the Sisters of Calvary.[40] The Age of Empire was also a time of changes in the structure of world capitalism. Hobsbawm refers to a global world with "two sectors combined together into one global system: the developed and the lagging, the dominant and the dependent, the rich and the poor."[41] During this time, Christian missions, Protestant and Catholic, moved across the world. The active apostolates of sisters in various parts of the world were part of the increasing intercontinental movement of people and communications (including the electric telegraph). In time, the apostolates and, in our case, school teaching became naturalized in these new spaces. From very early on, in the midst of its own reform after the Protestant Reformation, the Catholic Church had seen in schooling a means to transmit "the truth" and open spaces for a Catholic order.

During these missions, unpredicted elements were to emerge, however: the ways the missionaries experienced their apostolates in time and space generated new meanings, new knowledge, and – in the case of Catholics – new ways of being.

The RNDM was founded at the crossroads of modernity and the Holy See's reaction to it. The nineteenth century had brought to France the positivism of August Comte (1798–1857) and the scientific socialism of Karl Marx and Frederick Engels (*The Communist Manifesto* was published in 1848; *Das Capital* in 1867); the basis of anarchist theory was established, and French libertarian socialism developed through Pierre-Joseph Proudhon (1809–65). The reaction from the Holy See took shape in the encyclical *Quanta Cura* (1864), along with the appended document *Syllabus Errorum* of Pope Pius IX, who took a strong position against the "errors" of the time: socialism, liberalism, rationalism, and the separation of Church and state. These were the doctrines that the pope felt were a threat to the papal monarchy.[42] Although Catholic enterprises of the time were not necessarily a faithful reflection of the anti-liberalism and anti-modernism of the papacy, they were still framed by those positions.

The ultramontane papocentric view dominated the First Vatican Council (1870). It was expressed in the *Pastor Aeternus*, the First Dogmatic Constitution on the Church of Christ, which declared the teaching authority of the pope on faith and morals as infallible, and the constitution *Dei Fillius*, which insisted that the Magisterium (the teaching authority of the Church) was the authentic interpreter of the Bible and rejected the autonomy of reason. Anti-modernist positions continued with Leo XIII (1810–1903) and were fully conveyed in the 1907 Pius X encyclical *Pascendi Dominici Gregis*, in which the pope condemned "modernism" as the "synthesis of all heresies."[43] These positions developed from the defeat of movements such as Jansenism, which championed the role of local bishops and local rule, and Gallicanism, which in its democratic version went as far as asserting that Christ had conferred the power of jurisdiction on the whole ecclesial assembly.[44]

Ultramontanism, which encouraged such non-critical loyalty to Rome and to a hierarchical Church, was dominant in France and in Canada as well. This ideology had serious consequences for the study of theology in general, for the historical study of the Bible, and even for the incorporation of new educational theories. As mentioned earlier, Barbier had cultivated a hierarchical and ultramontane view of Catholicism.

Catholics, in reaction to the abhorrent social conditions of workers, developed the first essays of social Catholicism in France, such as the *Oeuvres des cercles catholiques d'ouvriers* (Society of Catholic Worker Circles), created by Albert de Mun (1841–1914) in 1871. In 1876, Father Aimé Coulomb, parish priest in Armentières, established the Catholic Workers with the support of Christian industrialists and wanted the RNDM to provide education for young working girls.[45] Barbier was sensitive to the plight of the young employees who lived and worked in the textile factories spread along northern France, since she herself had been an apprentice in a laundry establishment at fourteen. The congregation opened a school for girls in Armentières, followed the next year by a school for the children of workers and later by the opening of the Saint Eloi crèche (kindergarten), with spacious accommodation for small children and partly funded with funds raised by a society of workers. In 1889, the sisters extended their work to Houplines, located close to Armentières.

The work in Armentières and Houplines are interesting examples of how Barbier responded to contextual needs and emerging social inter-sections and, in particular, to renewed meaning, values, and new prac-tices among Catholics. This early commitment to the poor became a source of inspiration to which the RNDM sisters would go back when embracing social justice after Vatican II. An 1884 letter from Reverend Marie de la Redemption to the novices described with tenderness the work in Armentières. It said that the Monastery of Saints-Anges (the RNDM convent) was situated in a new neighbourhood inhabited by workers, most of them poor and of Flemish origin, unable to speak French, and with their homes full of little children. "These dear chil-dren run in the street from morning to night ... [U]nder the care of the Sisters, they were moved in in good time and instructed while their parents were in the factories."[46] The sisters' projects in Armentières and Houplines were to end in 1901, when they had to leave France due to anticlerical policies (to be elucidated later).

Modern Catholic social thinking developed as a response to the so-cial conditions of the poor and was nourished by the organizations that clergy and lay Catholics started while recreating the mission of the Church.[47] The idea of educating the poor and serving their needs goes back to the Council of Trent (1545–63), which recognized the power of education to keep the flock in the Church. But the individuals and communities involved in practical action had to deal with the impli-cations of the industrial revolution and the need to critically position the Church in relation to labour and other distressing social issues. In 1891, Pope Leo XIII issued the encyclical *Rerum Novarum* (Rights and Duties of Capital and Labour) in which several streams of thought somewhat converged as it addressed problems emerging from the eco-nomic structure (relationship between capital and labour, employer and employee, the wealthy and the poor), as well as those emerging from the perceived threat of socialism. The encyclical aimed at rais-ing the social consciousness of Catholics and envisioned the creation of a corporativist Christian social order as an alternative to liberalism and socialism.[48] Its impact, however, was uneven; it even produced resistance.

At the time when the RNDM received pontifical approbation in 1890, it had an international network of houses spatially radiated over Eu-rope and Asia to New Zealand. In practice, the congregation went be-yond article 2 of their constitutions, which stated that the sisters would

devote themselves to the instruction and Christian education of children and women, above all in "infidel" and non-Catholic countries,[49]
and did extensive apostolic work among European settlers. Such was
the case of Western Canada.

As stated earlier, in 1851, while she was with the Sisters of Calvary,
the foundress of the RNDM had been sent to England to learn English,
since it was the language of the colonies.[50] The RNDM would consequently have a strong connection to three towns in the county of Kent:
Deal, Hastings, and Sturry. That connection became crucial to the congregation during the time of France's Third Republic, when, in response
to the Associations Bill (under the government of Waldeck-Rousseau),
which subjected religious associations to regulations and ensured the
supremacy of civil power, the congregation left France in September
1901 to establish the motherhouse in Deal. Nonetheless, the congregation had begun its foreign missionary foundations much earlier.

When the first RNDM sisters came to Manitoba, Canada, in 1898, they
had already opened missions in New Zealand (Napier, 1865), Australia
(Sydney, 1867, closed in 1870; Perth, 1897), England (Deal, 1870; Sturry,
1881; Hastings, 1895), the Pacific Islands (Tonga, Apia, Samoa, and Wallis, from 1871, from which they withdrew after a few years, in 1878),
India (Chittagong, 1883; Akiab, 1897), Switzerland (Fribourg, 1896),
and Burma (Sittwe, 1897).[51]

The RNDM sisters were formally invited to Manitoba in 1898 by
the archbishop of the Diocese of St Boniface, Adélard Langevin (1855–
1915), as part of his response to the school crisis (1890–96), known as
the Manitoba School Question, which ended the dual confessional educational system – Catholic and Protestant – and the status of French
as the language of a founding nation in the province.[52] The Manitoba
School Question placed ultramontane Archbishop Langevin vis-à-vis
modernity.[53] The establishment of common schooling was one of the
administrative mechanisms built in the process of developing a modern
state. It was the realization of a project that Ian McKay conceptualized
as one of liberal rule, which, in its articulation, preserved, cancelled, or
transformed many social and political realities.[54] The language of public education was, in fact, rooted in a Protestant view of the world. The
public school had, indeed, a strong assimilationist thrust with a view
to preserving Canadians' heritage as members of the "great British Empire." The Catholic Church did not accept these so-called non-sectarian
schools, which were seen as an irresistible force of de-Christianization –
in other words, an anti-Catholic force.[55] Therefore, Langevin and the
Catholics had to carve out their own space in the educational system.

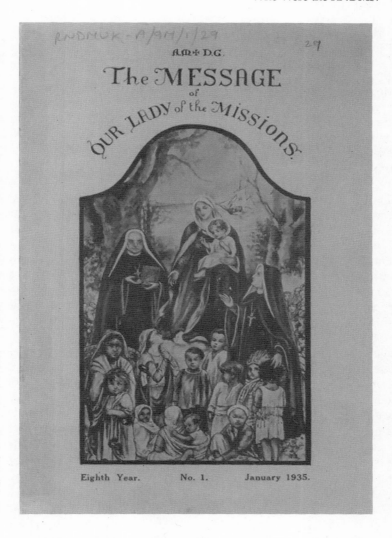

1.3 *The Message* magazine, 1935. This cover of *The Message* magazine from 1935 illustrates the RNDM conception of mission dominant until the 1950s. The foundress is in the centre with the Virgin Mary, child Jesus, and a member of the congregation bringing civilization through Christian education to other cultures. "The Sisters, who were incidentally white, occupy a position closest to God in this hierarchical structure and the children appear abstracted from their culture and history" (see note 51). Source: Author's collection.

Consequently, they recreated dominant cultural meanings and often cultivated opposing practices.[56]

Archbishop Langevin, who believed that the development of the faith was related to Catholic schooling, tried to bring (and succeeded in doing so) as many teaching congregations as he could to his large diocese, which included Manitoba, the district of Keewatin to the north, and northwestern Ontario to the east, down to Lake Superior, as well as the district of Assiniboia to the west, which extended into southern Saskatchewan.[57] He was attempting to answer the linguistic and educational demands of a diverse Catholic congregation, which included not only French Canadians but also Ukrainian, Polish, German, and Italian Catholic immigrants in addition to those of Irish or Scottish descent.[58] He feared the cultural force of anglicization and considered retention of the maternal language as a countermeasure to Protestant proselytizing.

Langevin's protestation and rejection of the Laurier-Greenway Compromise aside,[59] the bilingual system – applied to French or any other language under special conditions – and the provisions for religious exercises gave room for the Franco-Manitobans to function within the public system, given the large number of school districts and their ethnic configurations. As Taillefer nicely demonstrates, the Franco-Manitobans did integrate into the public system.[60] The clergy and the female teaching congregations had a major role in this process, and the presence of the priest was as important as that of the teacher in the one-room, rural schools in francophone Catholic areas. (New challenges emerged when the official bilingual system was eliminated in 1916.)

Langevin expected the French–English bilingual congregations to sustain their French and Catholic heritage and identity. He understood the latter as a collective identity based on the notion of two founding nations with non-territorial cultural duality; however, Quebec was his major point of reference. Langevin thought that the future of the Church in Canada depended upon French-speaking Catholics; he talked of the French race, its distinctive qualities, and the role of the school in maintaining those qualities and the language: "If our people lose their language all those treasures are in peril since they will then acquire the English temperament."[61]

While the French-Canadian identity was a defining component of the mission and identity of the Missionary Oblate Sisters – a diocesan congregation founded by Langevin in Manitoba in 1904 – for the RNDMs, the French issue was not a congregational matter at the core of their identity.[62] Nonetheless, the French RNDM sisters working in those communities were fully engaged with the Franco-Manitoban and

French-Canadian causes, having the support of their congregation. It was typical for Archbishop Langevin to pay visits to the schools and the communities. The sisters recorded in their journal of 1906 that Langevin visited the convent in Ste Rose du Lac, Manitoba, and told them that the school question was very important to him and that he was fighting against the invaders (*envahisseurs*) for the rights of the French Canadians. He then visited their school, a public bilingual one, and blessed the children.[63]

As stated earlier, Archbishop Langevin organized as many private and parochial schools and hired as many certified teaching sisters as possible. He wanted sisters to teach in the public system, particularly in largely Catholic communities, where struggles over values with the Department of Education were waged through the boards of trustees, since schools were under the jurisdiction of elected boards. One of the RNDM sisters wrote that Langevin possessed "the noble end of uniting the settlers according to their respective nationalities, to ensure their religious formation, to help them in encouraging parish organizations such as churches, Catholic schools, etc., and to protect 'the faith against the progressive and threatening invasion of error which surrounded them from all parts.'"[64]

Although the sisters first came to Canada within the context of the French issue in Manitoba, since they came from France, their missionary educational work went beyond that parameter; the prairies (the current provinces of Manitoba, Saskatchewan, and Alberta) – with their waves of Catholic immigrants from various ethnic and cultural backgrounds, who were struggling to keep their identity, and with the colonization of the Indigenous peoples – provided fertile soil for missionary work.

Arrival of the RNDM Sisters in Manitoba

The RNDM sisters' first Canadian foundation in August 1898 was in the Canadian West in rural Manitoba in the village of Grande Clairière, which had been founded ten years earlier when Father Jean Gaire (1853–1925) – a diocesan priest and native of Lorraine, France – arrived in Manitoba and filed a property claim that the government had made available to "homesteaders."[65] He placed the village under the protection of Saint John the Evangelist. At the time, a few Catholic families as well as Métis and French Canadians were dwelling in the neighbouring hills, albeit in precarious conditions and very poor. He started with a hut that served as both school and church. He travelled to Europe to bring settlers back to the village and was successful in France and Belgium.[66]

In the winter of 1898, during one of his trips to northern France, Gaire visited the family of one of the settlers in Armentières. When he expressed his interest in taking sisters to his parish of Grande Clairière, his host directed him to the convents of the RNDM – the Monastery of Saints-Anges in Armentières and the Monastery de la Visitation in Houplines, both on the Route d'Houplines that ran between Armentières and Houplines. Father Gaire went to Saints-Anges and talked to the prioress of the monastery. She suggested that he wait until he could talk to the Reverend Mother General Marie du Saint Rosaire in Lyon, who was at the time visiting missions in New Zealand. He did so.[67] Meanwhile, word of mouth at the monastery kept alive the excitement of the new prospective mission. However, many of the sisters had only an official teaching diploma for France and needed further preparation in English. Gaire put them at ease by telling them that French was spoken and was also a teaching language in Manitoba. "Our aspirations grew stronger than ever," one sister was recorded as saying. Given the intensity of the conversations during recreation time, when the 1898 Lent began, the prioress decided "that we offer to our good God, in a spirit of penance, the mortification of not talking of Canada at all, letting the Divine Providence make her will known to us so we may fulfil her intention."[68]

After being informed by Father Gaire, Archbishop Langevin went himself to the motherhouse. His words were memorialized by the congregation: "Today," he told the reverend assistant general, "I beg you to give me at least four Sisters and within the next ten years I will need more than forty for my archdiocese."[69] The four sisters assigned to the first mission in Canada were French. Mother Marie St Paul (prioress), a novice of the foundress (Euphrasie Barbier), had made profession in 1894 and taught at the convents of Armentières and Houplines. Mother Marie-Madeleine de la Croix, professed for twenty years, had been in Armentières and Sturry, England. Sister Marie de l'Eucharistie, formed as a novice under the direction of the foundress, had made profession in 1894 and had lived in Deal, England, where she had studied English, which she now spoke fluently. The fourth, Sister Marie Ste-Valérie, not yet professed, had spent two years in Fribourg, Switzerland.

The narrations of the trip made by the protagonists, gathered by one of the sisters in a written record, reveal the adventure of the trip as well as the spiritual tenets and beliefs sustaining the travellers. The sisters had begun their journey by going to the motherhouse in Lyon, from where they left for Paris on 22 July 1898, the day of the feast of St Magdalene, "full of confidence in Him, who does not abandon souls who sacrifice parents, friends, and homeland to make his Holy name known across the ocean."[70] The assistant general took them to the Perrache train station for the train to Paris, where they were provided with tickets and said their goodbyes. Once in Paris, a taxi took them to the Little Sisters of the Assumption, where they prayed and had some rest. This account reveals another view of the networks generated by the congregations in providing each other with mutual support and of the role of the priests and brothers in this process, despite the lack of continuing regular connections among congregations at the time.

The four RNDM missionaries were going north to Anvers, Belgium, where Father Gaire would meet them to take them to Canada. The assistant general had bought each of them a second-class express ticket; however, once in the Paris train station, they were told they had to pay for their extra luggage weight. Of course, they did not have any money. One of the missionaries recorded: "What to do? It was unthinkable to leave our possessions behind, and the steamer departed the next day, in the afternoon. It was impossible in Paris to ask a charitable person for the urgent assistance we needed! It was almost ten o'clock p.m.! It was too late! We prayed to all the saints in heaven asking for their help. Mother M. Madeleine of the Cross was crying in a corner of the waiting room."[71] The prioress explained the situation to the ticketmaster, and their second-class tickets for the express train were changed to third-class tickets that would take them to Belgium on an indirect route; with the difference, they were able to pay for the extra weight. Another recorded reflection is revealing of the sisters' understanding of God: "He [God] wanted to prepare us for the inconveniences and humiliations of holy poverty of which we will have our abundant share in our future mission." In Anvers, Father Gaire and the mother prioress's parents had been waiting, and, after two nights on the train, the sisters had some rest. Yet, they still had to secure food for supper and for the next two days without money: "Were we not practicing Our Lord's advice to his disciples: 'Take with you no purse, no staff'? A few friends became instruments of providence and gave us the means to buy what was strictly necessary."

The sisters took a train to the seaport (Father Gaire had taken care of the transportation of the luggage – thirteen cases). The sisters and Father Gaire took a ship to Liverpool, where the agents of the emigration company placed them in their hotel, which had beds full of insects. The next day they embarked for Canada on the *Tunisian*, a boat from the Allan Line Steamship Company; the sisters took a second-class cabin, while Gaire travelled third class. It was 26 July, the day of the feast of St Anne, and on 5 August, the feast of Our Lady of Snows, the group landed in Quebec: "Not without emotion, we entered that beautiful city, and admired the Chateau Frontenac and other ancient monuments."[72] Father Gaire again attended to the sisters' luggage, which was in a pitiful state. Once in Montreal, the travelling sisters were taken to a church of the Oblate Fathers of Mary Immaculate, and some sisters (there is no mention of the name of their congregation) who lived close to the church invited them for lunch.

In the afternoon of Saturday, 6 August, the party took the train to Manitoba. They were in a third-class compartment for forty-eight hours, sitting on a plain board without being able to change positions. They had little food, only some bread, a sausage, and a few dried biscuits left over from the trip from Lyon to Paris. At night, Father Gaire climbed up to sleep in the hanging berths provided for the immigrants. At one of the stops, Gaire bought a loaf of bread and a can of beef with his scant resources. This food only lasted a day, since there were five of them.[73]

At what is now Kenora (at the time, Rat Portage), two Jesuits got on the train. Also on the train was an Oblate, Father Lacasse, with whom the sisters would later work, and who, being unfamiliar with their habit, asked whether the sisters were Anglican nuns. He was duly informed that he was in error. Since they were all getting off the train at Winnipeg, Lacasse invited the sisters and Gaire to share the carriage waiting for him in Winnipeg. Later, he telephoned the Grey Nuns and asked them to receive the sisters and give them hospitality; he also showed them the principal buildings of St Boniface, which the sisters later described as the "Rome of the Canadian West." The record reads:

> We went to see the girls' orphanage, the seniors' home, and the magnificent hospital directed by their Community [the Grey Nuns], the Industrial School for Aboriginal boys and girls [L'école industrielle des enfants sauvages]. We were taken to the large Jesuit College. Everything in these flourishing and well-organized Catholic institutions interested us, everything would be useful given our complete inexperience with the conditions of existence in the new country, where, within our modest sphere, we were to do the work of God.[74]

Back on the train after a day and a half of rest and recreation, the sisters admired the ripened wheat fields along their way. Once again, they were without food and forced to fast the whole day. At about 8 p.m., the train dropped the sisters and Gaire off at Findley, a small village about 5 miles (8 kilometres) north of Grande Clairière and, at the time, the nearest station to it. No one was expecting the group. Gaire had to walk several miles to find vehicles and men to take them and the luggage to their new home. The narration continues:

About 11:30 p.m., Mr Quennelle, one of our drivers, invited us to stop at his home. His wife offered us a hearty dinner, although prepared in a hurry. We gladly accepted since we had had no food since the morning. However, we had to hurry; it was near midnight, and we did not want to miss Communion in the morning. Promptly, we took our place again, two of us in a light carriage called a buggy and the other two perched on the irregular pile of cases packed in a large wagon. The road was rough, and the heavy vehicle was continually being jolted. Poor Mother M. Madeleine of the Cross sat in the highest place on the top of the luggage, and was in constant fear, given the lack of stability. Moreover, she had to keep Father Gaire in his uncomfortable seat. He had a small cask of wine for Mass on his knees and could not grasp onto anything, and was at risk of being thrown out at every jolt.[75]

On 11 August 1898, at 1 a.m., the little group arrived at "the post assigned to us by holy obedience, to the front of the poor rectory of Grande Clairière. There was no one there, but the door was fully open, left open by some unknown stranger."[76] (The charitable priest, Gaire, had the habit of receiving and lodging any passerby in search of shelter.) The house was the picture of destitution. Under the wretched light of a lantern, the interior displayed only poverty and discomfort; the sisters compared it to the stable of Bethlehem. Even the straw was there: the beds consisted of four planks nailed to the wall and covered with a rough straw mattress. Gaire gave the sisters clean sheets. As for himself, he took his fur coat in lieu of a bed and went to the upper storey of the "school." At 4:00 a.m., Father Gaire was already hammering doors, repairing them, and sweeping up the dust; later he took to cleaning an old pot. Then the little group had their first Mass. Early in the morning, two young women, the Misses Lafontaine, came to the rectory to help put the house in order. In the afternoon, a few mothers arrived to greet the sisters. They could not express their happiness enough at the thought that the sisters had come to provide education for their children. The sisters had seen only two or three houses in the surrounding districts and had concluded that the place was uninhabited. What a surprise they had the next Sunday when they found the church filled with people! These were people living in neighbouring districts; they had travelled a long distance. On 28 August 1898, the school opened at the rectory with twenty pupils, both boys and girls.[77]

The original inspiration or illocutionary force behind the sisters' words, and the formation of a Catholic self, acquired complex dimensions in the field. The apostolate in this early public school in Grande Clairière – a setting of colonists and Métis, as the sisters described

1.4 Grande Clairière Convent, 1919. Source: Author's collection.

it – illustrates one of the early steps taken by Franco-Catholic communities in pursuit of achieving their educational aims and retaining their
cultural and political identities. The relations between the French Métis and the Euro-French members of the Franco-Manitoban community
would eventually take their own contours in Manitoba – an issue that
went far beyond the life of the little school.[78]

The foregoing narration also opens a window for an understanding of the nuances of cultural and social interactions that configured
missionary work in time and place, in this case, Western Canada at
the end of the nineteenth and the beginning of the twentieth century.
To give an example, while the foundress of the RNDM was very firm
regarding the contemplative and reflective component of missionary
work and saw the grille as essential, the grille would not be always
feasible. To name another, the international character of the congregation, its foreign missionary experience, and its centralized governance,
located in England since the end of September 1901, had tainted power
relations with the local clergy. The RNDM in the Canadian province
would manage to develop its own profile. The sisters' identity as religious was permeated by their lived experience during the mission, as
we will see later.[79]

FAITH

Unknowing
I stand
Within
"You
who
are"
Blindly rejoicing
to be
naked
and known
and
in my
utter poverty -
loved.

Norah Tobin

Foundational Thoughts on Education and the Interplay of Locality, Congregational Structure, and Church Teachings

Central Questions

This chapter will explore the foundations and references of Barbier's educational views, the intersections of the congregation's vision with the Magisterium, and the educational decisions of a centralized governance and its interplay with the apostolate.

Central questions guiding the chapter are the following: What were the foundress's foundational thoughts on education that informed the initial pedagogical tools the RNDM sisters had when encountering the Canadian prairies and their many scenarios? How did the sisters relate to the framework and directions coming from the local ecclesiastical authorities and the teachings of the Church?

Foundational Educational Theory: A Difficult and Evasive Genealogy

In order to relate Barbier and the RNDM sisters to the framework and directions coming from the local ecclesiastical authorities and the teachings of the Church, we begin by identifying the stand of the Church on education and the intended force of that stand in light of large processes of educationalization from a *longue durée* perspective. From the sixteenth century on, teaching congregations and orders provided organized education – a form of schooling for the poor – in order to address their social issues and educate them into a Catholic world view, while by and large cultivating the upper classes. The educationalized Catholic culture and the preoccupation to educate poor boys and girls found a space at the Council of Trent (1545–63). Meanwhile, the Society of Jesus, approved by Pope Paul III in 1540, as O'Malley put it, inaugurated a new era in Roman Catholicism for formal education.

"If the Jesuits were the first religious order to undertake as a primary and self-standing ministry the operation of full-fledged schools for any students, lay or clerical, who chose to come to them they were in time followed by many other orders, both male and female. Such schools became a hall-mark of modern Catholicism in every part of the world."[1] The Jesuits aimed at forming lay male leaders and established a network of humanist schools throughout the Catholic world, including in their curricula Thomas de Aquinas's work as well as literatures of ancient Greece and Rome and drama and classical rhetoric. In other words, Renaissance humanism had an impact on education and on Catholic education. The Jesuits would work with Indigenous populations, most notably in Spanish colonies in America.

Despite this new direction towards the education of the poor in an active apostolate, the Council of Trent and subsequent papal decrees denied women access to apostolic work.[2] The spiritual renewal of the French School of the seventeenth century, with its debates on Gallicanism and the theological presence of Jansenism, mentioned in the previous chapter,[3] and voices like Vincent de Paul, Pierre Bérulle, and Jean Eudes, among others, brought into the open the needs of the outside world. This understanding led the visionary religious to value active apostolate in a new way and to act to broaden women's involvement. Thus, in 1662, Minim Fray Nicholas Barré (1621–86) founded an Institute of Charitable Teachers in Rouen, France, allowing a community of women teachers to work with poor girls under the direction of a superior, but without vows or cloister, thus avoiding rules and decrees. These teachers would consist of the Sisters of the Infant Jesus, Saint Maur, who became involved in international work and schools for the upper middle classes, and the Sisters of the Infant Jesus, Providence of Rouen, who remained in France.[4] In 1684, Barré's spiritual advisee, Jean Baptiste de LaSalle, founded the Institute of Christian Brothers to provide free elementary teaching and religious instruction to poor boys. The pedagogical methods developed by de LaSalle and Barré – the latter less known – were grounded in principles of modern education.[5] In the last decades of the seventeenth century and the first half of the eighteenth century, Europe saw a movement away from autocracy and towards political democracy. Religious wars of the time generated a weariness around dogmatic theology; realism and a new spirit of philanthropy had gained a place. John Locke's empiricist philosophy provided the background. After the socio-political upheavals of the eighteenth century in France and in Europe, within the context of the transition from Church- to state-controlled education and the building of national educational states, there was an "explosion" of active congregations, in particular of women who were leading a "mixed life" – a way to incorporate women religious in an active apostolate while keeping the cloister. This process was accompanied by the Holy See's production of multiple rules in the nineteenth century; as a result, apostolic women's congregations grounded in gendered ideals and subordination would become institutionalized.

Against this context, the ideas on education of the RNDM's foundress, Euphrasie Barbier, varied between the conservative and the progressive. They included the centrality of the child, the building of a Catholic self (including supernatural destiny) – albeit gendered, teaching as subordinate to catechism, education as both individual and social, engagement instead of punishment, practicalism, and generalism. As for the sources of her educational views, her letters to the sisters, in which she provided substantial instructions about their teaching, contain no references to particular pedagogues or Catholic educators. It can be inferred, however, that Barbier was influenced by the approach of the Sisters of Notre Dame de Namur at the normal school (the name then given to schools that trained teachers) she attended while she was a member of the Sisters of Compassion (formerly the Congregation of the Sisters of Calvary). Our Lady's Training College on Mount Pleasant Street in Liverpool, also known as Mount Pleasant Teachers' College, where Barbier prepared for the state examination that she passed successfully at Christmas in 1857, was run by the Sisters of Notre Dame de Namur, whose avowed mission was to educate girls and women.[6] Julie Billiart, co-foundress of the Sisters of Notre Dame de Namur and a woman of simple origins, is said to have been concerned with universal, free Catholic education relying on well-organized rural schools and trained teachers. Billiart understood education as an individual and social process in line with what was emerging in her time. Instead, her co-foundress, Françoise Blin de Bourdon, an aristocrat, linked the nascent congregation with congregations related to upper classes, thus providing means and connections to the congregation.[7]

At the college of the Sisters of Notre Dame de Namur, the *method*, how to teach, was very important.[8] Barbier, like Billiart, came to strongly believe in teacher preparation and the need to keep the sisters updated on teaching matters, with a proviso. Barbier wrote: "You will be abreast of the times, but without allowing oneself to be influenced by the frivolity of fashion in teaching, as in other matters, e.g., one must not sacrifice solid instruction and Christian Education in order to seek after accomplishment."[9]

Barbier placed children at the centre of the education process, as did Billiart and the Teachers' College from very early on. The roots of this approach went even further back. Since teacher education did not accompany the creation of teaching congregations, the new teachers had to seek advice from the more experienced ones. Anglican congregations like the Anglican Community of the Sisters of the Church (CSOC) were willing to share their experiences with Catholic sisters. The CSOC had found pedagogical inspiration in Johann Heinrich Pestalozzi (1746–1827) and Friedrich Froebel (1782–1852), whose ideas were travelling across Europe in the nineteenth century.[10] Froebel's notion of the intrinsically good and creative nature of the child and his emphasis on love and good teaching were attractive to religious congregations. Pestalozzi's method, quite appealing at the time, focused on the mind of the child and its development (what would be referred to as psychological laws), attention to the senses as a bridge between the external world and the evolutionary principles that shaped the child, and the idea that the world should be presented to the child in an organized fashion. In Pestalozzi's view, cognitive development had to take place along with the child's physical, moral, and religious development.[11] And, as Tröhler argues, education and the solution of social problems through education was for Pestalozzi a maternal question.[12] Pestalozzi also paid great attention to music and vocational practical components, both relevant to teaching congregations like the RNDM.

The idea of the centrality of the child would be at the core of Christian education. The notion of the child Jesus, the spirituality around the infant Jesus, goes back to the seventeenth century. Pius XI would later put it this way in 1929: "But nothing discloses to us the supernatural beauty and excellence of the work of Christian education better than the sublime expression of love of our Blessed Lord, identifying Himself with children, 'Whosoever shall receive one such child as this in my name, receiveth me.'"[13]

Barbier was also not far from Billiart on what was fundamental for students to learn: an accurate knowledge of the catechism and of religion, knowledge of grammar and of the languages used in the missions (following the policies of the British Empire), the "first elements" of liberal arts, and knowledge of the useful arts of life and of domestic economy. It was also important that the sisters prepare their lessons to meet the requirements of the time.[14] Over the years, Barbier conveyed in her letters to the sisters these and more of her ideas on the role of the sister as teacher and on their preparation, educational aims, and relations with the children.[15] The major goal was to teach the Christian doctrine through providing Christian (Catholic) education; it was their mission as religious.[16] This approach was quite dominant in teaching congregations in the second part of the nineteenth century and well into the twentieth century. Whether the student was a Catholic settler or a Maori in New Zealand, the central aim was to build a Catholic self: "to impart to our children an education which would be thoroughly religious, and at the same time very practical so as to help the children to acquire those virtues which will make the young Catholic girls hence women, real treasures both in the Church and in the family." She wanted "valiant women, worthy of God and of the praise of Holy Writ."[17]

Not surprisingly, Barbier's understanding of education followed quite strictly gendered lines in its perception of girls' needs in the social milieu of the foreign mission.

While gendered, the objective was practical. Barbier did not wish her pupils to pursue an accomplishments curriculum that would produce drawing-room ornaments.[18] Education for life was another important principle that Barbier may have received at the college, since it had been extremely important to its foundress Billiart.

The intended force, or intentionality, of Barbier's stress on children acquiring Catholic virtues was, as can be seen, "the salvation of the souls of the children or others entrusted to us." She added: "And for them I sanctify myself." The goal would be achieved by "carrying out faithfully and conscientiously our religious duties, and in practicing the virtues of our state that we shall be able to do any real good to the people who surround us, and help to sanctify and save their souls."[19] Salvation of others was rooted in the example of piety. The sister-teacher was constantly reminded against a spirit of vanity and affection, a spirit of independence that would lead to vanity and levity, and the spirit of self-indulgence. Sisters who exhibited a spirit of insubordination or who questioned the rules were dismissed.[20] This view was nourished by an ultramontane centralist Church and the notion of holy obedience.

Similar ideas had appeared in the lectures given to the Missionary Oblate Sisters of the Sacred Heart and Mary Immaculate, a diocesan congregation founded in Manitoba by the archbishop of St Boniface, Adélard Langevin, who, we will recall, was the person who invited the RNDMs to Manitoba.[21] Langevin did not neglect to stress that religious teaching could only be done under the authority of the Church, for only the Church could provide the true sense of the sacred texts.[22] A Father Beauregard told the Oblate sisters that they should aspire to be catechists, the role of teacher being subordinate, because it was the heart and the soul that they wanted to reach.[23] Beauregard also lectured the RNDM sisters. In 1906, Langevin, who had jurisdiction over the congregation, sent a letter to the superior of the Soeurs de la Croix de Murinais, copied to all the other congregations in his diocese, announcing that the Sisters of Our Lady of the Missions would offer preparatory courses meeting high school diploma requirements in Regina. He admonished that no woman religious would be authorized to take preparatory courses in other schools. He deplored the fact that sisters mixed with young people who were too liberal, as this connection had negative consequences to the point that some sisters adhered to the "detestable" co-educational system, which mixed sexes. He also regretted the "sad need" for sisters to attend normal school (co-educational) in Regina (Saskatchewan), which was led by men who were often hostile to the Church and where the sisters would be exposed to false ideas. It was important, in Langevin's view, that the sisters did not lose sight of their religious life and the spirit of their vocation.[24]

Returning to Barbier's views on education, we see she was keenly aware that what the children "receive" at school reaches the families and makes God and the Catholic religion better known and loved. However, she did not encourage the sister in charge of a class, whether the children were rich or poor, "to make arrangements with their parents" (to contact parents).[25] The distance from the world through semi-cloistered contemplative practices was important to the foundress. She valued good discipline in school, but it was forbidden to beat the children or deprive them of their meals, to impose penances on them outside school hours, or to give them as penance any part of the catechism or Bible to write out. Her approach was to stimulate the children through encouragement and rewards. There was no system of punishment.[26] The sisters who were employed in the kitchen or in other domestic duties had to show respect and charity to the students. Notably, refraining from punishment and showing respect and charity were particularly challenging to the young congregation in New Zealand in the case of the Maori children. The sisters found it difficult to transform young "uncivilized" girls who enjoyed their freedom into disciplined students.[27]

The educational aims of the RNDM would take their original traits from the direction of the foundress, who, to recapitulate, advocated child-centred education, proper teaching training, and an integrative, formative education relating spiritual, academic, and practical aspects – none to the detriment of the other – in addition to their Trinitarian spiritual intuition (mission and vision), articulated in the previous chapter.[28] The following paragraph is nicely illustrative of the sisters' early approach to education and recalls Barbier's original inspiration, the deeper intended force giving life to her congregation, the salvation of souls through the formation of a Catholic self:

There is no need to mention the obligation we have of giving the first and most important place to the practical study of the knowledge and love of

God and of our holy religion. The education which we endeavour to impart to each one must be eminently Christian, whatever the social standing of the children entrusted to us may be. Furthermore, we must strive to make virtue attractive to the children and form them, with God's help, to a love of duty, in the fear of God certainly, but a fear which comes from love. The children will be trained to perform tasks and make the sacrifices which the service of God and the neighbour require, with joy and devotedness in order to please God.[29]

This text was written in 1882, and the central concepts comprising the semantic field of the sisters (not only the RNDM) are there: sacrifice, joy, and devotedness; fear of God; obedience as coming from love; and pleasing God with joy. Barbier construed the notion of spiritual advancement in relation to acts of humility, self-denial, charity, and obedience that the sisters were expected to carry out for the love of God.[30] These components of religious life are also present in the documents related to the missions in Canada, in particular in the first decades of the twentieth century. Thus, the narration of the first missions in Canada, recounted by Sister Mary of the Holy Trinity in 1923, made recurrent references to sacrifices, privations, filial submission, and crosses of all sorts in a language that was not alien to the way the sisters experienced their apostolate at their arrival, as I will demonstrate in chapter three.[31]

The illocutionary force that helps to make sense of the discourse of mission can be easily traced to religious education and to salvation and inspiration in Jesus's teachings and care of the poor. However, there was more than that to the educationalization of the Catholic culture. For some time, the foundresses had been dealing with the political, social, and economic dislocations that came with modernity and capitalist development. As well, the congregations working with the poor offered practical programs in their curricula. Barbier conceived of education as an individual and social process, and thus the congregation took care to educate the child as a member of society and as an individual from a Catholic perspective. This approach was at the root of Catholic educational efforts that also aimed at affecting the social order. By the mid to late nineteenth century, when female teaching congregations flourished, the Western world was by and large involved in the building of the educational state and the modern citizen, which came with various methodologies for the deployment of governmental power through schooling. The Magisterium (the Church teaching authority) took a strong stand against modernity and the "errors" of the time; the congregations played a fundamental role in conveying the position of the Church, albeit mediated by their charism, through their network of schools.

Relation between the Foundress's Thoughts, Local Ecclesiastical Authorities, and the Church's Teachings

The sisters' narrative gains meaning in relation to the doctrine of the Church at the time and its impact on education, in particular because the congregation's apostolate was based on an ecclesiocentric model of mission. In other words, it was based within the intellectual (theological) boundaries of the Church authority and the notion of Catholic education that emphasized indoctrination. Thus, the Trinitarian inspiration (charism) of the congregation, as Susan Smith, RNDM, explained, needs to be understood in line with a Tridentine Catholicism, which institutionalized the projection of the Spirit in the progression from God to Christ to Church and was consolidated by neo-scholasticism (the Magisterium's neo-Thomism, described in detail further on), thus controlling the notion of radical freedom of the Spirit.[32] The work of the sisters and their original Trinitarian intuition to sanctify the people was mediated by obedience to the Church authorities and their interpretations, even as the sisters carved out their own spaces and meanings. The main point here is that the Church had varying needs in particular spaces, and thus it often developed various strands of thought or practical action. Nonetheless, the authority of the Magisterium (see chapter one), the authority of the Church as the authentic interpreter of the Bible, and the principles of the Church permeated the teaching of religious education. Barbier wrote that, whether it be catechism, Church history, or any other subject, the lessons had to be well prepared and well taught: "The syllabus prepared by Ecclesiastical Superiors should be followed faithfully, and you will find that such schemes are a great help. However, if you have not such a syllabus, your Mother Prioress will procure one for you from His Lordship or from the Head of the Committee for Diocesan Schools. If she cannot obtain one, then she should make out a syllabus suitable for our schools."[33]

The sisters had to adapt their educational work to a Catholic philosophy of education based on Thomistic principles as mediated by the Magisterium. Their work acquired official status in the Church with the Thomistic revival that started in 1879 with Leo XIII's encyclical letter *Aeterni Patris*. This revival is known as neo-scholasticism, a speculative dualistic theology that involved a mediated reading of Thomas and a reliance on theological commentary from the sixteenth and seventeenth centuries. Between the 1920s and the 1950s, there was nonetheless an internal pluralization of neo-Thomism, with neo-scholasticism being one of the tendencies. Neo-scholasticism became, by and large, the highest authority, or the only intellectual framework recognized by the Holy See, until the 1950s.[34] Meanwhile, "nouvelle théologie," a theological movement of the 1930s, 1940s, and 1950s that in its various phases engaged historical-critical research, returned to the sources of the faith, and related theology to the modern world, built strength even though it was not accepted by the Vatican until quite late.[35]

The congregation's overall conception of education was necessarily related to an ecclesiocentric model of mission within the boundaries of Church authority, and we can say that, at the end of the nineteenth century and well into the twentieth century, most Catholic schools (there were notable exceptions) pursued indoctrination. The ultimate aim of the congregation's vision and mission within the configuration of religious ideas that nourished the sisters' discourse was certainly to help students to reach a supernatural destiny and – no less important – create or maintain a Catholic order of things in society. The 1925 Minutes of the General Chapter read:

> The Rev. Mothers Provincial and the Prioresses should never lose sight of the fact that our Institute was established for the Foreign Missions, therefore the [congregation] should consider it a duty to develop in the Sisters and young persons aspiring to religious life in our Institute a true missionary spirit, a holy enthusiasm to rescue from the darkness of paganism souls purchased by the Precious Blood of their Divine Spouse, but to whom the benefits of redemption can be brought only by those who are ready to sacrifice themselves to carry out the command of the Divine Master when He said to missionary religious as to His Apostles: "Go Teach all Nations."[36]

The neo-scholastic version of neo-Thomism reached Catholic schools, in particular, through the encyclical on education, *Divini Illius Magistri*, or the Christian Education of Youth, issued by Pius XI in 1929, which underlines the position of the Church with *Aeterni Patris*. The encyclical's article 14 states that education "belongs to all three societies [the family, the civil society, and the Church] in due proportion, corresponding, according to the disposition of Divine Providence, to the co-ordination of their respecting ends."[37] Article 15 reads: "And first of all education belongs preeminently to the Church, by reason of a double title in the supernatural order, conferred exclusively upon her by God Himself; absolutely superior therefore to any other title in the natural order."[38] The notion that the Church has immunity from error is reiterated.[39] Until the changes brought by Vatican II, Catholic philosophers and teachers swore an oath to teach a form of neo-Thomism that ecclesiastical authorities had codified in twenty-four propositions.[40] The bishops became intermediaries in the process of ensuring the application of neo-scholasticism to Catholic religious formation in the schools.

As my examination of the RNDM's work in the Canadian prairies shows, female congregations would carve out their own spaces in the Church, while schooling and non-formal education became for the Church a means to secure or consolidate a place, depending on the setting, within the power structures of the modern educational state.[41] The underlying intended force was to build a Catholic spirituality rooted in salvation mostly through indoctrination and to keep alive a Catholic order as counter to both the dominant Protestant and secularizing ones.

The Congregation's Centralized Governance and Overreaching Educational Decisions

The RNDM sisters' role as teachers took place in a highly regulated space. The minutes of the general chapters provide some glimpses of regulations affecting work in the schools. The General Chapter of 1912, with three mothers representing Canada, included two resolutions with such implications. Resolution (77) reads: "It is forbidden to engage men as teachers in any subject for the Sisters"; and (79) reads: "The reading of every kinds of fiction is strictly forbidden. However, in certain examinations, unfortunately, works of fiction are prescribed for study. In this case, the opinion of the Bishop or of the authorities of a Catholic college should be asked, and a selection of the least harmful books made."[42] The restrictions were accentuated after the Canon Law of 1917, which governed congregations. The General Chapter of 1919 decided that the sisters could not read newspapers and that only the news necessary or useful for their classes would be given to the sister-teacher, as judged by the superior. Catholic publications could not circulate in the community either; the superior would allow sisters to read the articles that could be of interest or were instructive for them.[43] The 1925 Chapter contained a proposal that each province (a category embracing the totality of missionary houses in a country or region) should have a centre to prepare the sisters who would teach. Its director would be in charge of inspections in the province to secure uniformity and efficiency without disregarding local needs; she was expected to keep herself updated on educational matters, read books for the teachers, and visit other good schools. There were no details regarding the objectives of the visits. The Chapter also recommended the circulation of the *Annales de la Propagation de la Foi*, missionary brochures, and the *Messenger of the Sacred Heart* to counterbalance the "profane literature" complying with the official curriculum of the Department of Education that Catholic schools were forced to include in their curriculum.[44] Every house had to maintain a good library, as spiritual readings were seen as a means for spiritual progress. However, there was another dimension, which can be traced in letters, provincial council minutes, and other local documents, that was out of step with heavy rules and regulations, and shows independence and assertiveness in doing business – for example, as we will see later, with the (Catholic) separate school boards in Saskatchewan and even with the clergy (the case of the industrial school in Lac Croche) when it came to non-doctrinal matters and missionary work.

It is interesting to note that secrecy as an official policy of the Church is stated in the Chapters, another restriction on the sisters' lives. The same 1925 Chapter says that, in order to safeguard the reputation of her children, the Holy Church will not allow any record to be kept that could be detrimental to the character of a religious. Further, those who heard such a report would be just as deserving of blame.[45] Later, in 1944, the General Council decided that "when an unsatisfactory Sister is sent from one house to another her new Prioress should make no reference whatever to the past [the Sister's past] or let the Sister feel that she knows of her blunders."[46] The potential implication cannot be neglected here. Restrictions affecting the daily life of the sisters and the relinquishment of any privacy, control by the superior of inner thoughts, prohibition against relations with the students' parents, and the attachment to rules as a means to spiritual perfection were all part of an institutionalized Catholicism that was overstressed in most women's congregations and certainly by the RNDM's foundress. Strict adherence to prohibitions and blind obedience – to the superiors and the authorities of the Church representing God on earth – had a pedagogical impact, although it is difficult to explore, in part because life in the classroom had its own contours.

In 1930, the mission in Canada was divided into two provinces: Sacred Heart Province, covering the geopolitical province of Saskatchewan, and St Mary's Province, which covered the provinces of Manitoba, Ontario, and Quebec. The provinces were unified in 1956. Each RNDM province needed permission from the Council of the General Administration and approval from the general chapters for every decision they made related to their school work, administration, and their own day-to-day necessities. As late as 1943, the Council of the

General Administration was reminding mother provincials that, before they asked for permission to send sisters to a normal school or university, the matter should be discussed in council and "only Sisters possessed with a good spirit and who have good common sense should be chosen. Discontented or disobedient Sisters should never be sent."[47] The same document regrets the shortage of vocations; women were not eager to enter religious life.[48]

The central congregational reports of the 1940s and 1950s contain concerns with weakness in "supernatural" obedience, few vocations (shortage of numbers as a big problem), and sisters moving to secular life, in particular before their perpetual vows. The bureaucracy and the lines of authority are evident in the minutes of the Council of the General Administration, for example, when the provinces had to ask permission to send a sister to normal school, or permission was denied for a summer course in Banff, or a sister with temporary vows was not allowed to attend courses of study during the holidays; permission had to be granted even to replace or repair the roof of a school. The Central Administration and the Central Council, after neglecting to consider the changes coming with the post-war era after 1945, kept reminding the province of the need to build fences and to comply with the cloister.

In 1954, the Canadian RNDM Sacred Heart Province made requests regarding the schools that were approved – but not without discussion. The sisters in government schools would be allowed to attend home and school meetings in the evening once a month and to accompany the children's choir at music festivals and other programs with the permission of the prioress, among other changes.[49] From the late 1950s and the 1960s, documentation shows the General Council approving a variety of university courses as well as other courses for sisters from the two Canadian provinces.[50] The Canadian provinces, meanwhile, developed their own identity and understandings of religious life, including a concern with the bureaucratic centralized approach. This process would all work to make the Canadian provinces strong protagonists during the renewal process in the 1960s and 1970s, and they would form a *field* (à la Bourdieu), with powerful positioning on major issues such as style of governance and the habit.[51]

An ongoing tension between the rules and regulations dominating religious life, the political configurations in which the schools were inserted, and the social imaginaries of the communities with which the sisters worked was constant in the history of the RNDM. The formation acquired in normal schools and universities would inject new approaches. The strict instructions regarding the grating, or grille, the semi-cloistered character of the congregation, and the ambiguous relationship with the world, one that was to be distrusted, were reflected not only in the decisions of the General Administration but also in the design of the convents that often served as schools. Nonetheless, the pioneering milieu of the Canadian West and the field experience would leave its imprint on the process that led to the naturalization of the missions.

Although the Vatican rejected concepts emerging from New Education (present in Canada in the 1920s and especially from the 1930s) and, in particular, from pragmatism and John Dewey's theory of education, given its negation of duality, what the Church called its experimentalism and its fallibilism, the sisters had to obtain certificates and were thus exposed to various ideas and pedagogical methods that they discussed in their meetings.[52] It must be noted, however, that Catholics, out of necessity, "de-pragmatized" Dewey (a term coined by Gonzalo Jover).[53] Despite the Vatican's misgivings, some Catholic schools in Canada and many in the United States embraced progressive education and John Dewey's and William Kilpatrick's methods. A well-known case is the Corpus Christi School, in existence since 1936, located across the street from the Columbia Teachers College in New York. The school was established under the pastoral leadership of Father George Barry Ford and under the teaching leadership of the Dominican Sisters of Sinsinawa, Wisconsin, most of whom studied at Columbia Teachers College. From the design of the new building in 1936, to its Catholic philosophy of life and education, to its very principles of education as involving experience and growth, to the notion of democracy permeating its life, the school embodied Dewey's educational conceptions. Interestingly, the school's documents of the 1930s explain that the school worked within the principles of Pius XI's neo-Thomist *Divini Illius Magistri* (Christian Education of Youth). The context and leadership opened up unexpected ways of engaging with the modern world, even questioning its injustices, while dealing with the rigidity of the Magisterium. Of course, Ford had his quota of conflicts with the ecclesiastical authorities.[54]

The RNDM schools in Canada did not take such an audacious route. However, as we will see, the sisters developed their own profile and vision rooted in their Canadian experience in spite of the conservatism and the hierarchical – often even authoritarian – makeup of the congregation. Former provincial superior Veronica Dunne has said that the sisters came in 1898 to a foreign and difficult mission. "But as time went on, while sending a few Sisters overseas, we gradually 'settled in.'"[55] In 1923, there were ninety-eight sisters in the Canadian province; fifty-one had come from the motherhouse in Lyon, one from New Zealand, and forty-six were Canadians. That year, there were nineteen postulants and novices.[56]

The next chapter deals with the schools and the geographical spaces and configurations in which they were inserted. The account of actual work in schools, while sometimes difficult to follow given the paucity of information kept, helps to articulate nuances of the missionary work and to think about the many ways in which the apostolate was configured in its interactions with the social imaginary in the communities, with the actual living experiences of the families and their socio-economic context, and with the state through the Department of Education.

THE GIFT OF NEW LIFE

I believe
that
Today I was conceived.
In a gentle, warm, loving and
Spirit-filled motion
A seed was laid within me;
The seed of new life.

Life - vibrant, joyful, lightsome
healed, RESURRECTED!

A tiny glow of light
Permeates my darkness

And settles deep within
My innermost being,

Bringing a feeling of peace, tranquillity
Gratitude and hope.

As a flower
Slowly responds to the first touches
Of warmth from the morning sun,
And cautiously opens her petals
To receive
The crystal drops of morning dew;
So am I before you, Lord.

I believe
That
Today I have begun to live.

Theresa McCutcheon

PART TWO

Educational Apostolate in Time and Space: The Schools in Canada

In this part, the schools will be analysed with the process of building the Catholic subject in mind. Quentin Skinner's theoretical framework will be useful to examine meanings and intentionalities as developed by the Church and the congregation itself. Thus, the intentionality, "illocutionary force," or "intended force" of the linguistic action, a concept of J.L. Austin, further developed by Skinner, is as important as the meaning of the utterance itself for understanding the RNDM sisters' narratives and actions, as well as the Church texts, because it constitutes a "force co-ordinate with the meaning of the utterance itself" without being part of it.[1] Furthermore, as Skinner writes, "the text itself is shown to be insufficient as the object of our inquiry and understanding," and so I place the relevant texts in their practical context, the political activity or "relevant characteristics" of the society in which the authors are inserted.[2] Thus, "illocutionary force" and contextualization will be essential to our aim of construing meaning and understanding in relation to various theological, social, and political configurations within which the sisters' apostolates were nested. Examples of the enquiry in question are as follows: What was the intentionality behind the sisters' thinking and practice? How did they make sense of their apostolate?

This apostolate took place in different Canadian communities (for example, those of French-Canadian settlers or of other various origins, the Métis population, European immigrants), first in Manitoba and Saskatchewan, and later on in Ontario and Quebec. The intentionalities of the apostolate will give meaning to the sisters' utterances and actions, not only in relation to the vision of the RNDM and the Church's teachings but also in relation to the local and national context of the apostolate and the place of the national and/or local Church. I understand this context to consist of overlapping historical configurations, be they religious, political, or social. These configurations denote figurative spaces taken up by constellations of ideas and historical phenomena, capable of coexisting even if in opposition.

Charles Taylor's notion of "social imaginaries" is a useful conceptual tool for understanding the building of intentionalities in a particular setting. Taylor defines social imaginaries as "ways in which they [people] imagine their social existence, how they fit together with others, how things go on between them and their fellows, the expectations which are normally met, and the deeper normative notions and images which underlie these expectations."[3]

Here, "social imaginary" will be used to explain and refer to the congregation's understanding and practice of education, and the Catholic construction in situ of the learner as a cultural and political subject within the gendered principles of the Church.

Our examination of life in the missions and the schools will lead us to a complex lifeworld with layers of restrictions and ecclesiastical rules as well as concrete fields where personal aspirations, social imaginaries, political agendas, and intersections nested the sisters' educational work. The approach in the analysis of the RNDM's school work will be situational, and the schools will be then arranged following the overall characteristics of the communities, but they will be introduced by province, since education in Canada is under provincial jurisdiction, and also chronologically. I will begin with the first school in Canada, in Grande Clairière, Manitoba, in 1898, and close with the educational changes and the ruptures of the long 1960s, a time when Vatican II enabled an *aggiornamento* of the congregations with the world around them and a different encounter with the inner self and the collective identity of the sisters. (Occasionally, I will compare the RNDM with the Missionary Oblate Sisters of the Sacred Heart and Mary Immaculate, a diocesan congregation founded in Manitoba by Archbishop Adélard Langevin in 1904.)[4]

From the mid-1800s, English Canada, with its unique and complex educational and cultural identity, forged a modernist path in uneasy tension with traditions at various levels, a path between liberal ideology and political practices and more conservative ideas and institutions; modernity was embraced and then left aside at various times.[5] Schooling was the medium through which to shape, solidify, and perpetuate a dominant culture, but schools were also spaces where values, including traditional, anti-modernist values as well as emergent ones, were negotiated. The secular educational system, often denounced by Catholics as Protestant, had, in fact, underlying Anglican and Methodist elements. The Catholics tried to carve out their space in the educational state while taking part in the social configurations of ideas. Overall, Ian McKay has argued, the period of liberal modernity from the 1840s to the 1940s – based upon the ideals of "liberty, equality and property" – was slowly naturalized through coercion and consent, force and negotiation.[6] Catholic schools, however, pursued an anti-modernist discourse. At the same time, through their praxis, they became part of regional and local Catholic agendas, as well as participants in major political networks; such was their relation to the French-Canadian agenda – with faith and language at the core – outside Quebec.

Chapter Three

Manitoba in the Early Years: Building a French-Canadian Identity with the RNDM Foundations

At Manitoban convents and schools – and to some extent in the Saskatchewan ones – the first of which was established in 1898 in Grande Clairière, spirituality as a set of beliefs and values would be intertwined with language and culture and the Catholic faith. Religious education and expectations of schools acquired their own historical characteristics in the mostly rural, French-Canadian communities, where the parish priest, teaching congregations, and members of the community, working with the trustees, were in charge of the local schools. Language and faith were interwoven for a long time in settings that were able to resist assimilation into the non-Catholic culture. Many school districts had only one school, and the trustees were in charge of hiring, ensuring that the values of the community were upheld.[1] The various parties together formed a configurative space with a common agenda and shared community goals. This situation also held for a number of ethnic communities, including that of the Mennonites and Ukrainians. Teaching congregations were often in charge of public schools, as was the case with the RNDMs in Grande Clairière, Ste Rose du Lac, St Eustache, Letellier, Elie, and St Joseph in Manitoba. The RNDMs were committed to the French language, given their history and origin; for many years, a majority of the sisters were French speaking and worked in francophone areas of Manitoba, in Catholic separate schools, and in their own private schools in Saskatchewan. The French sisters and the French-Canadian sisters were fully involved in the process of keeping the language and faith and building a French-Canadian identity in communities; however, the rest of the congregation did not participate in this manner. The influences of Franco-Manitobans and of the Church on school life, in particular in francophone rural areas, were facilitated by the existing provincial educational structure with its hundreds of school districts, each with rather homogeneous communities. Keeping language and faith was also part of the process of construing the identity of what Martel calls the French-Canadian nation (that is, Quebec and French-speaking communities outside Quebec).[2] Martel argues that, with the support of professionals, the French-Canadian clergy created a national network of institutions, which acted as an instrument of collective action to preserve the identity of French-Canadian communities.[3] These institutions drew upon, by and large, ultramontane and agriculturalist ideologies throughout Canada, particularly Quebec. As was clear in national meetings held in Quebec in 1937 and 1952, language and faith were the central elements of identity and attachment to tradition; this focus continued until the end of the 1950s.

The French-Canadian Catholic identity pursued at the time in the churches and schools in Manitoba was not far from that prevalent in Quebec nationalist circles. However, French-Canadian or Acadian communities outside Quebec worked together to create a provincial body to promote their own particular interests.[4] Thus, l'Association canadienne-française d'éducation de l'Ontario was formed in 1910, two years ahead of the provincial decision to limit the teaching of French to the first two years of elementary school. Shortly thereafter, l'Association catholique franco-canadienne de la Saskatchewan was also founded in 1910; l'Association d'éducation des Canadiens français du Manitoba in 1916; and l'Association canadienne-française de l'Alberta in 1926. The role played by the Catholic Church in the forming of the associations and in the delivery of their programs was not a negligible one: note that the first national congress on the French language that took place in Quebec City at Laval University from 24 to 30 June 1912 was presided over by Monsignor Paul-Eugène Roy.

Adélard Langevin, archbishop of St Boniface, died in 1915. The following year, in 1916, the Manitoban provincial legislature repealed the section of the Public Schools Act that permitted bilingual instruction in schools supported by public funds and unanimously approved the School Attendance Act, making school attendance compulsory and instruction unilingual in English. The sisters quickly submitted to the law of the province and taught in English, in a creative oppositional way, to secure their presence in the classroom and the preservation of Catholic influence on the children.[5] It was also in 1916 that l'Association d'éducation des Canadiens français du Manitoba was created, with its headquarters located in St Boniface and its mandate of protecting the interests of Franco-Manitoban Catholics.[6] The associations of Saskatchewan and Manitoba, where the RNDMs were active, would have a great influence in the classrooms and on the work of the teaching congregations, which played a powerful role in shaping a collective

French-Canadian identity. In Manitoba and Saskatchewan, where the RNDMs carried out their teaching apostolate, the associations were active in developing French and religious educational programs, administering French exams, and inspecting schools. The associations were supported by parish circles, organized local parent groups, trustees' school associations, associations of teachers of French, and, of course, the Church.[7] The *Bulletin des Institutrices* (1924), published by the Ligue des institutrices catholiques de l'Ouest, as well as periodicals such as *La Liberté*, founded in 1913 by the Oblate fathers, were also part of the network.

In 1922, the Manitoban association developed a parallel curriculum in French (programme de français) that was infused with Catholic values, and it was implemented in public schools affiliated with the association and run by a French-Canadian Catholic or in Catholic parish or private schools. Written annual exams (concours de français) had been made available to students in 1921. By 1931, the number of participant schools had reached 82, with 7,220 registered students, representing 4.7 per cent of the total student population in the province. There were 220 teachers, 92.1 per cent of whom were women; of these, 114 were religious, meaning that women religious represented 52.5 per cent of all teachers.[8] Clearly, the association functioned as a parallel Ministry of Education, having an inspectorate, exams, and selection of books (including religious ones), and followed the identitarian agenda mediated by the congregations' teaching apostolate in the field. The ideals and values of the community were therefore fully interwoven with the programs.

Walking to the First Class in Canada: Grande Clairière

The sisters started classes in Grande Clairière on 28 August 1898, with twenty pupils, in a simple public school that was ten years old. Pupils were boys and girls from six to fifteen years of age. Mother M. St Paul, prioress, taught French, and Sister M. de l'Eucharistie taught English. The classroom was one room with four long shaky tables in the centre of it, at which the students were to sit – on benches that were also quite old; there was a desk for the teacher, whose chair was a packing case, and a blackboard that was almost unusable.[9]

The sisters lived temporarily in the impoverished rectory. Meanwhile, Father Gaire, aided by a Métis (as noted in the narrative), built a house for the sisters near the school – their first convent in Canada, called Our Lady of the Snows – which would also serve as a boarding place for students. By October, it was ready. The house consisted of

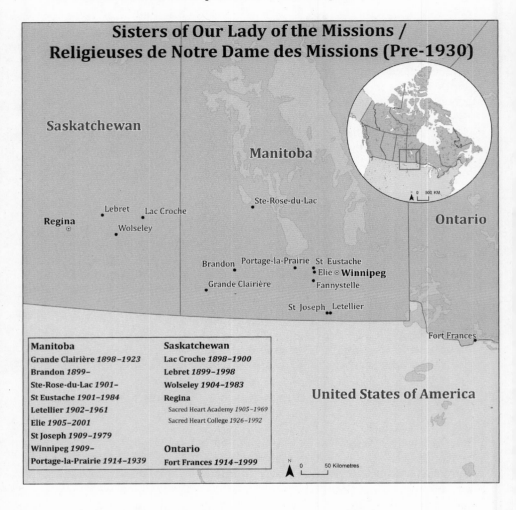

**Sisters of Our Lady of the Missions /
Religieuses de Notre Dame des Missions (Pre-1930)**

Saskatchewan

Manitoba

Ontario

Ste-Rose-du-Lac

Lebret   Lac Croche

Regina

Wolseley

Brandon   Portage-la-Prairie   St Eustache
                                Elie ⊙ **Winnipeg**
Grande Clairière   Fannystelle

St Joseph Letellier

Fort Frances

United States of America

Manitoba	Saskatchewan
Grande Clairière *1898–1923*	Lac Croche *1898–1900*
Brandon *1899–*	Lebret *1899–1998*
Ste-Rose-du-Lac *1901–*	Wolseley *1904–1983*
St Eustache *1901–1984*	Regina
Letellier *1902–1961*	Sacred Heart Academy *1905–1969*
Elie *1905–2001*	Sacred Heart College *1926–1992*
St Joseph *1909–1979*	
Winnipeg *1909–*	Ontario
Portage-la-Prairie *1914–1939*	Fort Frances *1914–1999*

3.1 Map of RNDM early missions in the Canadian prairies. Map designed by Graham Pope for the author.

a large room on the ground floor and an upper storey, and had low ceilings, small windows, plaster on the walls, and lots of cracks that welcomed the sun, the rain, and the icy blasts of winter. The upper storey was the private residence, where four rough boards nailed together served as a bed with a hay-filled mattress; the beds were separated by sheets hanging from a rope. This large room was expected to serve as chapel, refectory, dormitory, community room, laundry room, and whatever else might come up. The ground floor served as a kitchen, parlour, and living room for future boarders, with everything in one room.[10] At the beginning, these and other realities of setting up a life in Western Canada challenged the preoccupation with rules, prohibitions, daily rituals, the grille (or grating), and semi-cloistered life. Material conditions thus set the tone for the sisters' religious life.

The sisters and Father Gaire – who would leave Grande Clairière in 1903 – worked together in their new pioneering life on the Western prairies. They celebrated all the religious feasts with good humour, a scarcity of food, and faith that providence would provide for them – and there were many feasts, including the feasts of the Very Reverend Mother General, the Holy Rosary, the Very Reverend Mother in Heaven, and the Saints. Father Gaire tended to invite guests without much food on the table; the sisters served the guests first, and then there was little left for them. Yet, sometimes they were more fortunate or, as the sisters put it, their faith in providence was answered. The narration left by one of the sisters reads:

> That same evening [they had little food and were making bread without yeast, Métis bread as the Sisters called it], the most holy virgin sent a gracious surprise; an eight-year old girl, Celina Charette, was brought to us as a boarder. She brought us three chickens all ready to be cooked and a delicious cake, so that, thanks to providence, we had an excellent festive supper, a little treat.[11]

The records show that the sisters at Grande Clairière had a close relationship with the community and that the public school was subsumed within the convent. The reverend mother general or her assistant, normally accompanied by another mother, from time to time visited the foundations around the world, which by the end of the century had been established in New Zealand, the British Isles, Switzerland, India, Myanmar, and Western Australia. The record states that a visit from the superior was the most efficacious means through which to ensure complete conformity with the spirit and customs of the congregation. In the spring of 1900, Mother M. St Etienne, the assistant general, visited the houses in Canada. Mother Marie du St Rosaire, superior general, visited the Canadian houses in 1904 to preside over the annual retreat to the Canadian province. After witnessing the living conditions in Grande Clairière, the mother superior general decided that the apostolate there had to be moved. The sisters were in agreement with her and had already packed everything when the parishioners heard the news and united in their efforts to keep the sisters running the school. A Mr Filteau offered the sisters two acres of land east of the Church, and the mother superior general reconsidered. Construction on this convent began in the spring of 1905 and was completed in January 1906. The convent was a compact building, built on a solid cement foundation, with a hot air furnace in a good basement; it had dormitories for the sisters, regular parlours, a dormitory for the girls, a classroom, and a refectory for the children. There was no chapel; instead, a modest wooden altar, painted white, was set up in a small room, forming a sanctuary that adjoined the classroom, from which it was separated by folding doors that could be opened during religious services, allowing the children to attend these from their desks.[12] This building, too, was a public school.

Year after year, the convent – in fact, the public school – was attended not only by young children of the locality but also by many others from the country and from neighbouring villages, where, in the view of the sisters, only Protestant schools (meaning public schools not run by Catholic communities) existed. By the late 1910s, apart from the twenty to thirty children who were boarders, there were around thirty more children from the district who attended the public school. Many of them also lodged at the convent during the winter.[13] It is also interesting that, thanks to the request of the Ordinary, boys under the age of thirteen were admitted as boarders to prepare them for First Communion. The Church and the archbishop opposed co-education, but the public character of the school and the needs in the Catholic community demanded the reception of boys.[14] Boys of that age were not allowed as boarders in the convent, however. At first, the boys slept in the shack adjoining the rectory. Beginning in 1910, the community and the priest began to build a dormitory and a room for the supervising sister at the back of the convent; the boys were thereafter properly lodged.

There is no information about the educational work done in the school, except for mentions of the following: every year, some students passed their official grade eight examinations; the school followed the official program, which was taught both in English and French; and its Christian education and instruction were second to none "of the other

government schools."[15] It is very important to note that the cradle of
the congregation in Canada gave "two vocations" to the RNDM; they
received their formation at the congregation's novitiate at Ste Rose du
Lac. By that time, the number of sisters at the convent had increased
from four to six. There is no specific information available about the
children or on the ethnic composition of the community. Conversions
could not be missed, and three young Protestants were said to "return
to the true faith."[16]

The convent was destroyed by fire in 1923, and the sisters withdrew
from this mission. The members of the parish wrote to Mother General
St Pacôme, promising funding and support, but with no results.

Ste Rose du Lac

Ste Rose du Lac (hereafter Ste Rose) was situated 175 miles (281.6 kilometres) west of Winnipeg.[17] At the beginning, the population was Métis
and made up of those who had moved from St Vital, near Winnipeg.
However, "soon [a] mixture of Canadian, French, Belgian, English and
Irish families settled in the village and the surrounding area. Since all
were Catholics, their worthy pastor desiring to encourage his settlers
and, above all, to provide a Christian education for their children, insisted on bringing the RNDM Sisters to the village."[18]

Oblate Father Joseph Magnan founded the parish in 1892. The Oblate
Missionaries visited the Catholic settlement from Winnipeg and offered
Mass in a private home. In 1895, the parish was canonically erected,
and Oblate Father Lecoq became the priest. Four years later, Lecoq was
returning from Europe when, on the ship, he met some of the RNDM
sisters coming to Canada. He then wrote to the mother superior of the
congregation, Marie du Saint Rosaire, requesting a foundation; in the
following year, in June 1900, an agreement was reached during Mother
M. St Etienne's first visit to the Canadian houses as the assistant general. Father Lecoq himself helped to build a house on the site selected
by the assistant general. The house would give the sisters a home where
they could live according to their constitutions and customs.[19] This
house would be the Monastery – as the sisters called their houses, since
they were semi-cloistered – of Notre Dame de Fourvière, namesake of
the motherhouse located on the slope of the hill of Fourvière in Lyon
during the fall of 1900, when the sisters in Lyon were under duress during the Third Republic, which asserted and defended the republican
spirit, particularly through the country's schools. It is pertinent to note
that, in France the next year, the 1901 Law of Associations prohibited

3.2 Convent at Ste Rose du Lac. Source: Author's collection.

congregation members from serving as teachers.[20] The process culminated with the break-up of relations between France and the Vatican in 1904 and the separation of Church and state in 1905, which led to the exile of thousands of women religious. The RNDMs established the motherhouse in Deal, England, as was mentioned in a previous chapter, and a number of them came to Canada.

On 1 September 1900, Archbishop Langevin, accompanied by other members of the clergy, blessed the convent of Notre Dame de Fourvière and the school (a public school). The sisters taught in the public school, as they would do in St Eustache, Letellier, and Elie, for which they had a contract with the district and were paid. In Ste Rose, the sisters offered a boarding place in the convent and charged fees; the sisters also collected monthly fees for music and drawing lessons.[21] There were similar arrangements in other convents.

On 4 September 1900, the sisters began to offer two bilingual classes in the school, since it was a public school, and the Manitoba Public School Act of 1897 had a provision allowing schools to offer bilingual education when ten or more pupils spoke French or any other language. The act also allowed for religious teaching in public schools, if sufficient numbers wished it, to be provided between 3:30 and

4:00 p.m.[22] Seventy-two boys and girls attended the school, and five of the young girls were taken on as boarders. Before the end of the scholastic year, there were sixteen girls boarding at the convent. During the summer of 1901, Father Lecoq added another floor to the school and built a boarding house. The design of the complex, which had the convent, the church, the school, the boarding house, and, later, the novitiate all in the same space and just a few metres from each other, gives a glimpse of the central place the Church and the congregation had in the village and in the social imaginary of the community.

The RNDM community of Ste Rose was invited in 1901 to teach at a school in the Crooked River school district, which belonged to a parish where a few French and Métis families lived. The number of pupils, the sisters established, would not exceed twenty-five to thirty. The two sisters assigned to the school were financially compensated; however, the school was situated 4 miles (6.4 kilometres) from Ste Rose, and so they had to procure a cart and a horse and also pay a driver. The sisters stayed during the week in a small apartment above the classroom. In 1910, the RNDM withdrew from this school.

The school, as happened with other public schools run by Catholic trustees and congregations, was a fertile ground for vocations. The Ste Rose community was a closed environment, a social imaginary in which the school, the Church, the convent, and family life nourished a world view and a way of life. The situation was similar in other villages and little towns in the Franco-Manitoban areas mentioned earlier, including St Eustache, Letellier, and Elie.

Journals kept by sisters reveal their internal processions honouring Mary and adorning altars, and their expressions of tender feelings of emotion and gratitude for blessings and for celebrations. Those were particular ways in which they could relate to each other – although quite restricted in terms of friendship and intimacy – and to the transcendental world in which they lived. Recruitment of future sisters was central to the work of the priest and the congregation, and the school was a fruitful site. In 1901, the first postulant at Ste Rose, Bertah Ramsay, a young girl of seventeen years of age, received the white veil. It was the beginning of the novitiate in Ste Rose, which was officially erected in 1902 with approval from Rome.[23] Of course, everything had to go through approval from the General Council in England, the archbishop, and the Vatican.

Archbishop Langevin would visit the schools in Franco-Manitoban areas where sisters taught, and the children were always ready to welcome him. He, in turn, recommended obedience and distributed images of saints. The narrative states that the archbishop "made descend from heaven a powerful blessing on the heads of the children. He blessed them in the name of the Pope."[24] These visits, as well as visits from priests, took place rather regularly. On the occasion of perpetual vows, Archbishop Langevin attended the ceremony or sent a delegate. The journal of the convent relates one such visit by Langevin. His presence was celebrated with hyperbolic language that talks of life in a particular mysterious world. The sisters would wait for Langevin's entrance in the most solemn silence: "The moment is near – still a few minutes more, then a few seconds before the arrival of the Spouse. Finally, the soft voice emitted by each one of the consecrated virgins. Who would ignore the goodness of God humbling himself to his poor creature to raise her to the dignity of Spouse, who could recall without trembling that God, so good, is a jealous God who cannot bear any foreign affection in his privileged creature."[25] Langevin would deliver the sermon of eternal alliance; in his address to the new Spouses of Christ, he talked about what constituted religious life, underlining in a vibrant way "the excellence of the vow of obedience being the most perfect of the three vows of religious life, but also the most difficult to practice, bringing the blessing of God to the house where obedience is kept in all its force."[26] Langevin carried an ultramontane message. The environment and the message make sense within the context of a papocentric Church, one that is infallible, hierarchical, and grounded in obedience and belief. Nonetheless, the conceptual space (Bourdieu's *field*) created by the Holy See, with its rules of interaction at every level, was frequently challenged by the sisters when their goals did not coincide.

The language of devotion, submission, and obedience is often quite colourful in the narratives of the sisters, since there was an eagerness to please God and since vocations invited celestial blessings. Father Lecoq built additions for the novitiate and was quoted thusly on the matter: "'Since I brought you the first bird for your aviary,' he said pleasantly, 'let me now give you the cage to shelter her.' (Sister Bertha was his spiritual daughter). He then became the builder of the fresh cage for the divine bird-catcher."[27] By August 1904, there were "seven young souls" from the various sites in the province who were preparing themselves for the apostolate. Very Reverend Mother of the Holy Rosary, superior general, making her regular visit in August 1904, brought three postulants from Letellier for the novitiate in Ste Rose.[28]

What also becomes clear from a reading of the journals is that the situation for the schools changed in 1916, when the bilingual system was eliminated. The inspector of bilingual schools was replaced by "the public school inspector." While the RNDM sisters in Ste Rose – as in all Catholic schools and public schools in Catholic Franco-Manitoban areas – followed the official curriculum, classes in French that were well aligned with the programs of l'Association d'éducation des Canadiens français du Manitoba, created in 1916 as mentioned earlier, continued. The French language examinations, or "concours," and visits from the inspector of the association were recorded in the sisters' journals.

The school, the community, the Church, and the convent were one in dealing with education. In Ste Rose and the other school districts in Manitoba where women teaching congregations taught, the sisters had priests coming to talk to them about pedagogy. One of these priests was Father Boursque, SJ, who, in 1926, organized the League of Catholic Teachers with secular teachers.

The construction of a railway branch line from Ochre River to Ste Rose signalled growth in the business life of the village, which reached a population of 1,200, the majority of whom were of French descent. Thus, in 1918, a fourth classroom was added. However, the trustees were convinced that a new modern school would be in harmony with the changes of the time. At a special assembly of all the taxpayers of the school district, held on 25 January 1918, it was unanimously decided that a new school would be built. The decision was to buy about three acres of the northwest corner of the RNDM's property and build a school that would have at least six classrooms. The trustees of the school district approved a debenture of $25,000 that was approved by the province.[29] The trustees also decided that the new school would only accept children from the district, and were thus opposed to the admission of the convent's boarders who were from other districts.[30] This decision was a local political issue that affected the number of boarders.

In 1923, the school added high school courses to its offerings. The convent was also rebuilt, this time with brick, and was blessed in 1924.[31] The trinity constituted by the school, Church, and convent continued on until the dramatic changes of the long 1960s, a time when opposing intentionalities began to overlap. The Church continued to carve spaces in the system while being imbued in the community, and the sisters played their salvific role and reproduced themselves. The material dimensions of place had modified the sisters' preoccupation with rules at the beginning (as hinted at earlier), but in time this preoccupation returned, playing out in constructions of gendered identities and accomplished through the disciplining of the body and the spatial ordering embodied in the grille that separated the sisters when they were not teaching. The building of a convent that could respond to the demands of the constitutions and the rule was a priority for the congregation, in particular for the central administration.

In January 1922, the novitiate was transferred to St Eustache, also in Manitoba. At that point, fifty-six Canadian sisters had received their religious formation in the convent at Ste Rose.

St Eustache

St Eustache was one of the first parishes established in Manitoba by Bishop Provencher at Bay St Paul, a Métis settlement. The site had previously been abandoned due to frequent floods from the Assiniboine River, but was re-established in 1888. It was decided that the centre of the parish would be in St Eustache, where many French-Canadian families had settled. By 1901, there were around 855 inhabitants, and a church and school had been built. A French-Canadian priest, Arcade Martin, was in charge of the parish at that time.

In September 1901, the RNDM had left France and moved to England, as mentioned before. Twelve sisters were given obediences in Canada; six of them would go to Ste Rose, one to Grande Clairière, one to Brandon, and four to St Eustache. The sisters took a sailing ship from Liverpool to Montreal, accompanied by a priest who was returning to Fannystelle (Manitoba).

It is interesting how, in spite of the isolation in which, by and large, the congregations worked, the various components of the Church functioned as part of a global institution. There was also a feeling of solidarity among congregations. The sisters had been exiled from France, yet they lived the feeling of being persecuted in defence of the true faith – almost as martyrs – with a sense of happiness. This acceptance was in line with the overall discourse and the salvific intentions. In Montreal, two Canadian sisters of the Congregation of Notre Dame went to meet the missionary sisters and offer them hospitality in the motherhouse. The sisters spent the night in the Notre Dame convent, where they were given night attire belonging to the boarders. The outfits were rich with ribbons and bows, engendering a comical situation when they saw each other.[32] The narration of the trip by train from Montreal to the Canadian Pacific Railway station in Winnipeg, Manitoba, reveals their ethnocentric apprehensions and shows that they felt it was rather heroic that they travelled in a train full of immigrant men: "[I]t was filled with all types of men, mostly Negro and Chinese."[33] The sisters first went to St Boniface, where they were hosted by the Grey Nuns and met with Archbishop Langevin.

On the morning of 18 October 1901, the four sisters assigned to St Eustache went by train from Winnipeg to Elie, since there was no station in St Eustache. The sisters were taken by carriage from Elie to St Eustache through an almost deserted countryside; they saw only a few houses at the side of the road until they reached St Eustache with its church, rectory, school, and three or four more houses.[34] When the carriage arrived, the school bells began to ring, and the teacher and students lined up to greet the sisters along their way.

This school was a public school, and so the teachers that the sisters replaced were lay teachers. The sisters praised these former teachers in their narration of the event: "The teachers were very delicate in resigning their posts for us."[35] It was also related similarly in the historical account of the events: "With delicate self-sacrifice, the school teachers, who had been hired for the year, gave up voluntarily their positions to their replacers."[36] On 4 November 1901, the sisters took over the direction of this bilingual public school that served one hundred pupils in only three classrooms. The teaching of English was compulsory and had to go hand in hand with that of French. That requirement was difficult for two of the sisters who did not know English, but they persisted. An inspector visiting a school in Letellier referred to the sisters in St Eustache, saying in a pleasant way: "I admire the zeal of your Sisters in St Eustache; it seemed that one cannot find them without having in hand the Ollendorff book [a short-form method used to study English]."[37] The school was also a site of Catholic formation. Apart from catechism being offered only from 3:30 to 4:30 p.m., in line with the provincial school law, the sisters taught catechism in the school each Sunday after Vespers. Catechism was taught to young children, but they also gave lessons on Catholic matters to young men (who, the sisters wrote, listened with docility) and also to older women. It is not surprising that the school and the community would become a place of recruitment of future sisters.

The sisters took up residence in what had been the rectory of the church, which became the Monastère de Ste Madeleine, an old building similar to the private homes of the country people of the time. The sisters arranged the building to have room for a parlour, a common room, and a refectory for the children. The families in the community gave them small gifts of bread, butter, meat, potatoes, jam, pastries, vegetables, and the like. Again, the church, school, and convent were fully integrated with the community. It was a way of life.

After the 1902 visitation of Mother M. St Etienne, the sisters bought seventy-nine acres of land adjoining the lot on which the school was built, on a corner facing the church, to build a convent without delay. The building where the sisters were living had been deemed inadequate for complying with the expected observance of the constitutions and the customs of the religious in the community. The sisters negotiated a loan with the Archiepiscopal Corporation, and the work began in May 1903 under the direction of architect M. Cinq-Mars from St Boniface. The building would be surrounded by a 7 foot (2.1 metre) fence and would have a perimeter of 1,320 feet (402.3 metres); it would also have grilles. The sisters would have a garden, two or three cows, and poultry. The contracts and specifications for the building of the convent were signed by Father Campeau, parish priest of St Eustache; Langevin and his office negotiated the acquisition of the land.[38] The finished house was heated by hot air from a wood-fuelled furnace, which was placed in the middle of what felt like a vast "cave" (basement) due to the dimensions of the building.[39] The "real" convent was blessed on 13 March 1904 by Archbishop Langevin. It was a beautiful Sunday, and, at the end of the High Mass, all the faithful walked in procession to the new building.

Sisters wrote about their experiences in a mythical way that tells us something about the ethos involved in religious life at the time: "Since the Beloved Master [Maître] is in possession of his home, his humble spouses eagerly came to live, pray, suffer and work in his dear company."[40] That utterance expressed a simple language of faith and submission without much theological background. It is within this context that the sisters would open up their space for agency.

The sisters brought their French religious world to the villages in Manitoba in a way that nourished a common intent to keep a Catholic world view, cultivate vocations to continue their own congregations already rooted in the place, and acquire new ways of doings things. In 1906, the congregation created Gardes d'Honneur (Guards of Honour), a project surrounding the Sacred Heart that would replace the "congregations d'enfants de Marie de France [Congregations of the Children of Mary]." The "Gardes" was started in St Eustache in February 1907. The girls wore a red scarf, and those who had taken Communion, a white veil; the boys occupied the first three rows of chairs in the choir; later, the members wore medallions. The project was aimed at cultivating piety in the children. The sisters registered that, on 31 May at the feast of the Sacred Heart, they enrolled sixty children into the Guards of Honour, twenty-four boys and forty-two girls. The activities took place in the (public) school. During the recreation period, the children were gathered in an assembly and promised God ("Our Lord"), with strong voices, that they would glorify him (sic), and that they would love him on behalf of those who didn't love him and to compensate for the human lack of gratitude. After the act of enrolment, they all sang

"Cantique des Gardes d'Honneur" and "Venez Gardes d'Honneur en-
tourer le Divin Coeur."[41]

Religious processions involved the school children and the entire
community. Thus, on 2 June 1907, the feast of the Très St-Sacrement was
celebrated with a procession that marched in the following order: the
Cross and the two associates; all the men of the parish, in silence and in
perfect order; the women, the Dames of Ste Anne; the boys of the school
who were not members of the Guards of Honour; those of the Guards
of Honour who were members of the choir, holding a torch; the other
members of the Guards, holding their provisional banner; and finally,
the girl members of the Guards of Honour, a group of forty, thirty-six
of them in white, and all of them with their medallion, their crown,
and their scarves made of red silk, out of which those who had made
First Communion also wore their veil. They carried a large heart surrounded by flowers and twelve golden strings that the girls held. The
Coeur (heart) was left in the vestibule of the convent. There were many
processions.[42]

The school was under government regulations and had to follow the
official curriculum, or program, and teach English as well. However,
the Provincial Council of 12 December 1912 recommended that, while
teaching the subjects of the program, the sisters aim at developing children's piety.[43] When the bilingual system was eliminated, like in other
places in Franco-Manitoban districts, life in the school continued to be
bilingual and religious, and French was spoken at home. At the time,
the bilingual inspector was replaced by the public school inspector;
however, l'Association d'éducation des Canadiens français du Manitoba took care that its program of study was also implemented through
its own inspectors. Thus, the sisters had a double program. There are no
references to pedagogy, to methods used in the classrooms. However,
one can find observations, such as regret that at least two sisters were
too severe, to the point of having given the children painful names (in-
sulting the children); there were also recommendations that penances
be given in relation to the age of the children.[44] These practices were not
in line with the congregation's statements on child-centred education
and the letters of the foundress.

Within the context of community life and the dominance of a religious ideology permeating everything, it is not surprising that there
was in that early period, until 1923, "the generous oblation of eight
young souls, who, faithful to the voice of grace, consecrated themselves
to God by entering our dear congregation."[45] The novitiate remained in
St Eustache at the Monastère de Ste Madeleine from 1922 to 1926, when
it was moved to Regina to the Sacred Heart convent.

Letellier

In 1876, many families who had come from Quebec settled on the west side of the Red River, about 56 to 60 miles (90 to 97 kilometres) south of Winnipeg, where they built a church dedicated to St Pius. When the Canadian Northern Railway line that ran from Winnipeg to St Paul, Minnesota, United States, was built, a train station was constructed 5 miles (8 kilometres) from the church. A few Catholic families settled near the railway station; that was the beginning of Letellier. In 1889, the parish of St Pius was canonically erected and its centre transferred to Letellier. A two-storey school was also built in the town.

The situation regarding the school was similar to the one in St Eustache. There were two lay teachers already there, but the families wanted teaching sisters. So, on 13 June 1902, the feast day of St Anthony of Padua, they built a special table at the foot of his statue to ask the saint to send sisters to the community. They also presented their petition to the bishop, who went to the community for a pastoral visit. The bishop conveyed to Visitatrix Reverend Mother M. St Etienne from the Generalate that they wished to establish a foundation in Letellier. The Mother Visitatrix and Mother M. St Paul, prioress of Brandon, visited Letellier and met with the priest and with the school trustees, who requested three teachers for the opening of the school in September. The positioning of forces was clear, as was the place of the Church in the power relations and in the organized structures that gave room to hiring practices and school life. On 13 August 1902, two sisters arrived in Letellier; they were met by young girls and went to the rectory, and then quickly established themselves in the upper storey of the school. They had a small kitchen, a room for themselves, and another large one that served as a bedroom. During the day, the sisters pushed the beds against one another and pulled a curtain to hide them, creating a space for a refectory, a community room, or whatever was needed. On the other side, a bilingual classroom for older students was divided by a folding door, which formed a small oratory at the back and a parlour at the front to be used as a music room as well.[46] With help from the community, the sisters built a small simple altar, a box painted white with two drawers for cloths and everything else that was needed for the chapel. On 20 September, Holy Mass was celebrated for the first time.

At the beginning of September 1902, three classrooms were opened in which the sisters would teach grades one to eight; two were bilingual and one exclusively English. There were eighty-seven students, including boys and girls from six to twenty-three years of age. The sisters recorded that "[a] dozen of them were Protestants and not quite [as]

docile as the Catholic children," who were reportedly models of submission and respect.[47] The sisters' universe of submission to authority,
obedience, and sacrifice seem to be reflected in the expectations that
the sisters had of the students. Inducing the students and members of
the community to become religious was central to the sisters' intentionality, an important aim in their educational work. In Letellier, the
sisters tried to organize the Society of the Children of Mary, remember-
ing the good influence it had had on young people in Armentières and
Houplines in France.[48] The sisters regretted that family gatherings on
Sundays did not allow the initiative to succeed, so the priest asked them
to teach catechism before Mass on Sundays instead.[49] Soon after the sisters established themselves, Reverend Mother M. St Etienne came from
England for another visit. It was then that the name of the convent was
chosen: Virgo Fidelis (Faithful Virgin). The visitatrix talked about "the
marvelous products of the fertile garden of our Sisters of St Eustache,"
and said that the "mission could be called the House of Fertility." The
mother vicar, in turn, wrote: "Very well, my Dear Rev. Mother, we want
that our House here [the one she was visiting] be the house of vocations." In fact, it already was.[50]

The sisters' interaction with the community was intense. Social life
and relations were marked by the Church, and the convent and the
(public) school were the hub of activities. The sisters were able to buy
a piano to give music lessons and accompany hymns during their devotions. Besides the frequent and small donations from members of the
community, they received $518.00 during the first year, half the "profits
of the [community] bazaar."

Illustrative of the place of the convent in the community is the celebration of perpetual vows of one of the sisters in 1903. The bishop ("his
Lordship") wanted to preside over the ceremony, which a number of
sisters from Ste Rose would also attend. The priest wanted to have
the ceremony in the Church for the edification of his parishioners, but
the mother vicar in charge of the mission did not agree. The priest
then asked the school trustees for permission to remove the folding
doors between the chapel parlour and the adjoining classroom so that
more people could assist at the ceremony. The historical record reads:
"A crowd attentive and contemplative gathered not only in the apartment [where the chapel was] but on the stairs and in the corridor.
Without chairs or benches, they remained standing or kneeling for
more than two hours in a profound, respectful attitude. Already a
vocation had blossomed in this humble beginning; Carmélia Loiselle
joined our ranks for that Mass of profession, and did not return to her
family."[51]

Another retrospective memory conveys a simplistic understanding of the theological basis of the sisters' dualistic, hierarchical spirituality, which was diminishing to women and had Jansenist tones, although it was in tune with the hard life of the community in which they were inserted: "The limited space, the poor altar, the low ceiling, a chapel only in name, contrasted with the majestic dignity of the celebrant, the great solemnity of the ceremony and, in particular, the infinite Sanctity of the sacrifice [the Holy Mass]. The contrast symbolized, in some way, the contrast between heaven and earth, between the divine spouse and the bond with the miserable creature to whom he deigned to unite with indissoluble links."[52] This narration is one example of the type of statement persistent at the time (alongside others encountered earlier in this chapter), one that embodied language and practices aiming at the internalized, hierarchical male order of patriarchy.

The narrations of these early times also show a pious, but informal, way of life in the "convent." A case in point is the living experience of the sisters during the week of the ceremony of perpetual vows just mentioned. The story reads: "Such a wonderful week we spent together! We were eleven members of the congregation counting two postulants, and we had only six beds and six blankets, etc.... We practiced common life day and night and very joyfully."[53] In these early experiences of the missionary sisters and the young Canadians who joined them, we find the roots of the sense of being Canadian and of their questioning of the centralized decisions that flourished before Vatican II, following the oral tradition. We find the roots of the "social imaginary" that would characterize the Canadian province.

It is clear that parish priests, together with the trustees, made an effort to have sisters teaching in all public schools of the parish. Beginning in September 1903, two sisters from Letellier had to go to St Joseph, 4 miles (6.4 kilometres) from Letellier, every Monday, returning on Fridays. They had an apartment with three rooms above the school and could go to Mass every morning because the church was very close.

The French sisters needed to submit their French diplomas to the Manitoba Department of Education and obtain a teaching certificate valid in the province, but first the inspector would visit without notice and check, in particular, the teachers' competence in English. Everything was going well, but, nonetheless, the sisters needed a regular convent. When they arrived back in Letellier on Fridays, the two sisters who taught in St Joseph had to climb a ladder up through the narrow attic trapdoor, which was above the sisters' quarters, to bring down mattresses, blankets, and so on to sleep in the classroom until Monday morning. The convent was not adequate.[54]

They found a suitable lot behind the school, facing the road to St Pie, but the owner did not want to sell. The sisters, as they usually did when dealing with money issues, prayed to their protector, St Joseph. The record states:

> One evening, at dusk, Rev. Mother Vicar and Mother Prioress went to the desired place, which was surrounded by a large stable, where, for a fee, families from the village sheltered their cows after they pastured them all together in the surrounding fields. There were piles of manure in a deep pond caused by melting snow where the ground was low. We sank to our knees, we threw the medals of our Holy Protector [St Joseph] here and there. Counting on his help, some time later, we went to see the inflexible owner. After a few attempts, he agreed to sell one acre, then two. Rev. Mother Vicar wanted five acres to have freedom of action when further development would be needed.[55]

The owner requested a deposit from the sisters; knowing that a member of the community had promised a contribution for the convent, the sisters went to see him and received $100, which they gave to the owner of the land.[56]

Once the congregation got the authorization in the fall of 1903, construction began. The sisters continued to give thanks to St Joseph for his protection and for the $300 they had received to pay for the land. The sisters did not want to have the barn facing the convent, and so a fourteen-year-old boy, a student, was hired to drive the horses and help move the barn. During the process of removing the barn to the back of the owner's land, the boy died, shortly after a horrible accident. The boy was rushed to his home, the priest was called immediately, and the boy died "peacefully" after five hours of suffering, the narration tells us. The narration is shocking in its retelling of the incident. The sisters give thanks once more for the protection of St Joseph, which helped the congregation to get the land, and this statement is followed three lines later by a relating of both their desire to remove the barn and the accident.[57] The sisters did not conclude that the boy was not protected by St Joseph. Thus, the narration reflects the sisters' priorities, but also their abstract notion of faith.

The new building was what the sisters called a "regular" convent with a parlour, an entrance according to the rule of the congregation, a grille, private quarters, and so on. The design was meant to create the daily living conditions that would imbue in the sisters the rules and the lifestyle of the congregation, control their emotions, and maintain their separation from the world. The convent was blessed in January

1903 by Archbishop Langevin. All the parishioners, as well as people from other nearby villages and their priests, were there. The people from St-Jean-Baptiste (situated 9 miles [14.5 kilometres] north) arrived with their priest, on sleighs decorated with Canadian and French flags, to join the people of Letellier and celebrate the event. First, there was a Mass at the church and a sermon in which Langevin recommended that the sisters continue, with a spirit of self-sacrifice, the great task of providing a Christian education for youth. In a procession and singing, the people moved towards the convent. After the blessing and the Benediction of the Blessed Sacrament in the chapel of the convent, the people were invited to the school to see a little concert. The Ladies of St Anne had prepared supper for the archbishop; after he left, the sisters sat down to eat the leftovers. The Ladies had displayed the food in silver dishes, were dressed in silk dresses, and followed the rules of "refined etiquette."[58] It was quite novel to the sisters, who in their daily pioneering life, along with their local superior, were involved in heavy cleaning and repairing duties, including planting, painting, cleaning up piles of rubbish, and cleaning up mud during the spring.

Like in other Manitoba districts where the RNDMs were situated, the school, the convent, and the community were closely intertwined in Letellier, creating a common way of being, a mentality, an imaginary. Parents and members of the community sustained the convent by bringing gifts and money they collected through raffles and donations, and by not charging the convent for expenses at the local general store. Again, the school, the church, and the parish converged as sites of recruitment. A "juvenate" for girls was created with a group that met in the convent every Sunday. The sisters recorded that these girls each had an excellent disposition and that, little by little, some of them began to desire a religious life. By 1923, the school "had the privilege of giving three priests to the church and fourteen religious to our Institute," without counting the sisters in other houses.[59]

During her visit to Letellier in 1904, the Reverend Mother Superior General Marie du Saint Rosaire recommended that a regular 7 foot (2.1 metre) fence be built around the convent immediately, although there was opposition from the neighbourhood. Winter snowbanks around the fence and other difficulties later obliged the sisters to change the front fence for a lower iron one that, it was noted, improved visibility.[60]

The sisters had great political awareness of the French issue in Manitoba. In the convent's journal of December 1915, the sisters recorded that the school inspector's visit that month was preceded by the fact

3.3 The convent at Letellier. Source: *Petit Historique*, 107.

that the government wanted to eliminate bilingual schools and needed to find them at fault to do so. The inspector, known as the English inspector, visited the four classes and verified that the sisters and the children were able to speak English.[61] The sisters did not leave French shamefully at the school door. Instead, they wrote: "[W]e followed the instructions of the ecclesiastical authorities, his visit [the inspector] did not trouble us; on the contrary we threw ourselves with full confidence into God's arms and fervent prayers escaped from our hearts."[62] The sisters played out the politics of life along with the community with its militancy on the French issue.

Life in the convent had a routine. More visits from the mother general resulted in her insistence on the particular work the sisters should do to reach perfection in a religious life based on regulated external practices. The recommendations extended to the sisters' practices with the children in the school; for example, in 1913, Mother General S.M. Pacôme advised that the sisters teach children the sign of the cross, how to incline with reverence to the name of Jesus, and all the other habits that would later make them model Christians.[63] In an attempt to generate religious meaning and purpose for the children, the sisters organized them in various ways. There was one group called the Children of Mary, for example, which celebrated the feast of the Immaculate Conception in the chapel of the convent, consecrated themselves to the Virgin, and received ribbons from the priest.[64]

When the sisters celebrated the Golden Jubilee of the congregation in Canada in 1949, the work in Letellier was highlighted as having steadily progressed. It was noted that, in June 1905, eleven students wrote departmental examinations; in 1911, a fourth classroom had to be opened to accommodate the increased number of pupils. In 1929, a new modern school opened its doors to the youth of the parish wishing to obtain senior matriculation. The sisters complied with the requirements of the Department of Education and also with those from l'Association d'éducation des Canadiens français du Manitoba. The school work was the measure of their apostolic success.

Elie

Elie is described by the sisters as a French-Canadian village, situated 6 miles (9.6 kilometres) from St Eustache, which had for many years been part of the parish of St Eustache. Located 31 miles (50 kilometres) from Winnipeg, Elie is conveniently located along the railway line leading from Winnipeg to Portage la Prairie, Brandon, and other communities to the west of the city. In the beginning, only a few families settled near the rail station. A Catholic church was built in 1904, although it did not have a resident priest until 1907; however, there had been a school for a long time. When the sisters arrived, there was a public school with two classrooms. The history gathered by the sisters was that the district was named Elie after an early French settler named Elie, who, anxious to provide education to his children, adopted a number of poor children into his already numerous family so as to have the number of pupils required for the establishment of a school.[65] As often happened in rural areas, teachers did not last long. They were poorly paid and at the mercy of the trustees, and married women could not teach. An interesting example was recorded of the conviction that Catholic schooling would solve disciplinary problems with young people in the village. It was common knowledge that some of the youths stole tobacco and alcohol from the train station and hid these goods in the forest to enjoy later, when they were truant from school. In an effort to address this and other issues, the trustees and their community approached Archbishop Langevin about bringing sisters to the community to teach the children. Langevin approached Reverend Mother M. St Irenée, vicar provincial, saying: "If you do not send sisters to Elie, you will be responsible for the loss of faith and virtue of many souls." This pronouncement was no light pressure coming from the authority, and it essentially represented an order for the sisters to go immediately. The suggestion of a delay due to the lack of sisters was countered by Langevin, saying: "Well, it would be better to close the classroom at St Joseph where there is less danger for the pupils."[66] In other words, he wanted the sisters to leave St Joseph, where the young people were not in moral trouble, and go to Elie. The sisters, caught up in his discourse and power and in view of the greater good, accepted the proposal. Sisters were moved around, and they were ready to start the school year in Elie in September 1905.

The "convent" was established in four small rooms above the school, and the sisters placed themselves under the patronage of St Martha. The sisters brought some furniture from other communities by train, and a local workman made an altar for them to keep their "Beloved Master" in their midst. The tiny chapel was 10 feet (3 metres) long and about the same width. The other rooms – the dormitory, kitchen, and community room (also refectory) – were slanted. A neighbour gave them a plot for a garden, where the sisters began cultivating their own vegetables. Here too, the material living conditions once more defied the rule and created their identity as pioneering sisters.

Daily life intersected with patriarchal ways to complicate things further. When, in 1907, a priest was named for the parish of Elie, the sisters had to serve the priest meals. He lived in the rectory, and, since the convent did not have a reception room outside of making use of a class-room, the logistics were complicated. The sisters would dismiss the students at noon, and they would have hardly enough time to get the table set, dinner decently served, and everything put in order before 1:30 p.m. Then classes began. Of course, the sisters' meals also needed to be served after the priest was done. Quite often, the priest appeared for dinner with another priest and sometimes up to three priests who were visiting the area.[67] However, the sisters considered this duty to be much more manageable than when some of the mothers and sisters would arrive unexpectedly. There was one situation recorded in which the small St Martha community accidentally reached thirteen members, whereas there were beds, dishes, and so on for only four. The language used by the sisters to recall the situation is telling: "Then, quite happily, we crowded together and shared; the hours or the days passed thus, in freedom and pleasant confusion of these sisterly gatherings, were too short."[68]

On 3 September 1905, the public school opened. There were two classrooms for about sixty boys and girls from six to seventeen years of age, and almost all were Catholic; the classes were bilingual. Some of these students had a reputation for lacking discipline, but were, the sisters recorded, docile and affectionate towards the sister-teachers. When the sisters took the students to the Requiem Mass on 2 November, the group filing in two by two in perfect order, it generated "surprise and admiration at this strange sight and such a sudden transformation."[69] The school was a public place, and hence all kinds of political meetings also took place there.

In May 1909, the mothers bought a small private house in the centre of the village, close to the school. The sisters tried to make it a "real" convent, but the house burned down on 1 January 1912, when a candle lit around the child Jesus caused a fire. After taking refuge in St Eustache for a week, the sisters went back to the apartment above the school. A new building was built on a lot on the other side of the river in 1914–15; a new, more modern school was also built. In Elie, we find again the school, the convent, and the church built close together, symbolizing their protagonism in a local political and social configuration that was inserted in a social movement around language and faith, with these being understood as rights issues.

In the new building, the chapel and the parlour grilles were set up according to the congregation's customs. The school trustees agreed in 1916 to hire a third sister-teacher. Meanwhile, the students continued passing their written examinations for grades eight and nine, and then ten. The sisters followed both the English and French programs, being

3.4 The convent in Elie. Source: Author's collection.

closely connected to the association, and also taught religion. They gave music lessons, and the convent sheltered twenty-five to thirty boarders at a time, which provided a source of income. Together with the priest, the sisters revived the sodality of the Children of Mary. Not surprisingly, a number of girls went into the novitiate.[70]

St Joseph

The sisters from Letellier, as indicated earlier, travelled weekly to the village of St Joseph to teach for two years between 1903 and 1905. Situated 4 miles (6.4 kilometres) east of Letellier, St Joseph was an old village, originally inhabited by settlers from Quebec, and had a consistent 400 parishioners over the years; Gretna, a German Protestant (Mennonite) town was 7 miles (11.2 kilometres) to the west. In 1908, the parishioners and the priest insisted that the sisters return to St Joseph. Notably, the parish priest was alarmed that some farmers in the vicinity were selling their land to a group of Mennonites; he thought that the presence of a convent to educate the children would offer his parishioners an advantage appreciated by all Catholic families and thus keep the Catholic people in the parish.[71] In 1909, after the reverend mother vicar agreed to establish a regular community in St Joseph under the patronage of St Martin, two sister-teachers were hired for the bilingual public school. Three sisters became the foundresses of this mission. The parishioners gave the sisters fifteen acres of land and an old house next to the school grounds. The house had served as a chapel, school, rectory, and store, and the parishioners promised to prepare it for the sisters. However, upon their arrival, the sisters found that the work of repairing the house had not yet begun.[72] It was decided they would live with an elderly couple while they waited for the house to be readied. Classes were started, with forty-three students divided into two classes, and the two languages were taught.[73] The students were described as docile, an important virtue for the sisters. The repairs, for which the approval of the priest was required (who at the time of the sisters' arrival was in Quebec), were finished at the end of October, and the sisters moved in. The village at the time was comprised of a church, rectory, school, the house of the elderly couple with whom the sisters had lived, the remains of a dairy farm, the old house of the sisters, now a "convent," and a little store where it was not possible to buy what they needed. The "convent" was named St Martin's Convent, honouring the priest with whom they had been working in the area. The house was small, and again the rule and the congregation's customs could not be fully applied. The school, also in an old building, was not large enough, nor was it in line with the recommendations of the time, as the layout did not meet government regulations. The trustees sold the building, and a new modern school was built that had good air flow, was well lit and heated by a furnace, and included a recreation room in the basement.[74] A new "real" convent was built in 1923.

School Life in French Catholic Areas: Links to a Major French-Canadian Configuration

The emphasis on discipline, obedience to authority, fear of God, notions of otherness, and Christian love and the articulation of a sense of identity that was based on religion, ethnicity, and community history intersected with the official discourse from the Manitoba Department of Education. The latter, amid drastic demographic changes from the late nineteenth century, aimed at generating a common polity based upon a shared identity, loyalty to common institutions, and a homogenizing notion of citizenship. In 1918, a time when there was a growing feeling among Canadians that their country was a distinct national entity, but also an important component of the British Empire, the minister of education, Dr R.S. Thornton, in his address to the Manitoba Educational Association, indicated the need to bring newcomers quickly into Canadian national life and into the life of the province.[75] He said: "Our aim is to plant Canadian schools with Canadian teachers setting forth Canadian ideals and teaching the language of the country."[76] Thornton did not neglect to mention the 1916 census, which showed that 42 per cent of the population of Manitoba represented thirty-eight different nationalities.[77] This context, along with the existence of hundreds of school districts with a degree of ethnic homogeneity, provided the framework for a major Canadian educational issue: while in the official discourse French Canadians were not immigrants in the usual sense, "the problems with regard to education that beset other minorities directly involved French Canadians."[78] With the School Act of 1916, French was now treated as another "foreign" language in the Manitoba curriculum.

As happened in other foundations in French Catholic areas in Manitoba, the RNDM sisters registered in their records a commitment to the French-Canadian cause, including the teaching of French. These little schools in rural Manitoba were a small chain of a larger, national institutional network in which the family was the cell. When enough French-Canadian families occupied a geographical space, a church and a school were built, and – as noted earlier – the convent then became a "bastion of French survival."[79] The schools were linked to organizations involved in the defence and development of these communities. Their local configuration was thus nested in a macro project. L'Association d'éducation des Canadiens français du Manitoba, headquartered in St Boniface and founded after the School Act of 1916, previously mentioned, would have a great influence on classrooms in Franco-Manitoban areas and on the work of the congregations, which played an important role in shaping a French-Canadian identity outside Quebec. (The Catholic Church played a prominent role in the association.) The public schools described earlier participated in the "concours de français," organized by the association starting in 1921, and followed the programme de l'association, created in 1922 (later called the programme d'études françaises). The program included the teaching of Canadian history in French and the history of the Church, apart from catechism, plus advice that all teaching (public and French curricula) be permeated with Catholic values. The program also included accompanying books, annual competitive exams (concours), the hiring of competent teachers, and the creation of an inspectorate.[80] In practice, it was a curriculum parallel to the official one. The *Bulletin des Institutrices* (1924), published by the Ligue des institutrices catholiques de l'Ouest, was the medium for providing curricular and pedagogical information. The Missionary Oblate Fathers founded *La Liberté* in 1913 and – as *Le patriote de l'Ouest*, founded in Saskatchewan in 1910 – played an important role in the educational network. *La Liberté* published the results of the concours (annual competition for French writing) and contained many articles on education. In 1941, *Le patriote de l'Ouest* and *La Liberté* merged. In 1946, French radio station CKSB served as another political tool for Franco-Manitobans. The Letellier journal has a notation indicating that, on 1 February 1959, Reverend Mère Prieure and Sister M. Ste Emilia accompanied the students of higher grades to a CKSB radio post to participate in a French program and that it went very well.[81]

The trustees of the district actually provided input about the workings of the school in Manitoba. Also, from very early on, the sisters attended the meetings of the Manitoba Educational Association, a body that included inspectors, trustees, and departmental officials and held the main role of operating the teachers' convention held annually in Winnipeg during the Easter break.[82] The sisters were not alien to the system, and it is not surprising that, later in the 1920s, they attended not only the meetings sponsored by l'Association d'éducation des Canadiens français du Manitoba, such as the Congrès régional des instituteurs et institutrices catholiques, but also those of the Manitoba Teachers' Federation.

The association's inspectors (known as French inspectors) ensured the implementation of the program. The French inspectors' visits were duly registered by the sisters and indicate the results from the 1920s. A notation dated 17 June 1941 reads: "Rev. Father Fauré S.J., our French inspector, visited our classes [St Eustache]. The students responded well be it the Catechism or questions regarding French. He was happy."[83] The results from the French concours and concours de cathechism, and information regarding the sisters travelling from various locations to St Boniface to help correct the concours, appear in the reports well into the 1960s.[84] The inspectors from the Manitoba Department of Education were expected with some concern. The inspector was responsible for ensuring compliance with the provisions of the Public Schools Act and the regulations of the Department of Education in hundreds of school districts controlled by the local community. The inspector – normally a man, although there was a woman named Eleanor Boyce who served in such a position – reported on the competency of teachers, progress of pupils, and on the conditions of the building, both to the board of trustees and to the Department of Education. The inspector made sure that teachers followed the official curriculum, which was a form of invisible power.[85] There are some vivid memories recorded. For example, Sister Cécile Granger recalled: "We would like to mention a teacher of that time, Sister Marie des Séraphins. She related how the teachers continued teaching French in the school. A child was appointed to watch [for] the arrival of a gentleman with a black serviette, Mr Clarence Moore. Immediately, the child ran to all the classes and the French textbooks were quickly hidden and the teaching of English began. We could tell similar stories experienced by teaching religious in Letellier."[86] Divine Providence was often invoked as a source of favours (being given adequate time and circumstances) when dealing with inspectors. A journal entry from 1937 relates how they breathed easier when Father Fauré, the French inspector, left; the following Monday, Mr Albright, the inspector from the Department of Education, had intended to spend the entire day in the classrooms, but, the sisters reported, the Good Lord intervened (the writer wondered whether someone had prayed more devotedly than usual). The wind started to blow quite strongly in the morning, and, by noon, blowing snow had made the visibility quite bad, and the inspector decided to return another time.[87]

Apprehension of the inspectors was shared by all teachers, particularly in rural areas, as the inspector's position was a source of visible power. The inspective function is key to understanding the political relations between the Department of Education and the rural districts and their trustees and communities. As Hon. W.C. Miller put it, the inspector represented the Department of Education in relations with the school boards. In his words, "You may have heard within your own division, the Inspector is the Department. To a large extent this is true."[88] This depiction makes sense in the context of the over two thousand school districts in rural Manitoba that embodied the social organization of the prairies, which was reflected in the life of the school (including harvest time, seeding time, and so on). As R. Sandwell wrote, "almost all the newcomers [including French-speaking families from Quebec, Europe, and the United States] shared a form of social and economic organization rooted in the family and household."[89]

Although religious teaching took place early in the morning before class, religion was central to the life of the school, both in the overt and hidden curriculum. The association's program was permeated with French Catholic nationalism, Catholic morality, and content from catechism (for example, in the concours). In the 1930s and 1940s, the sisters participated in teaching catechism classes to children and young people in the area, who were intensively recruited by priests so they could be taught the "truths of our St. Religion" and prepared for First

Communion.[90] The Church used various means to develop the Catholic self, such as musical gatherings and little music festivals and the creation of sodalities.

The overall sense of a Catholic self was imbued with a gendered identity that was grounded in the complementarity of the sexes. In the 1950s, things had still not changed in the relationship between the school, Church, and community. Overall, the teachers in rural areas, and those in the one-room schools in particular, saw themselves as embodying the community.

There is no doubt that the Church – the spirit of the Church as the sisters put it – dominated the terms of the social imaginary within the context of the French-Canadian identity being constructed in the rural prairies. This dominance displayed the power of the clergy over the community. However, the records of the congregation show that the language of simple submissive piety changed over time, and this change is evident starting from the late 1910s and even more clearly in the 1930s and 1940s. The change had to do with the progressive adaptation of the French sisters to the milieu and to the large number of Canadian sisters, mostly born in the prairies. The traditions and language from the old country became residual.

Chapter Four

English-Speaking Communities, Immigrants, and the Quest for Social Recognition in Manitoba

The Mission in Brandon: The Quest for Social Recognition

The mission in Brandon, a city 133 miles (214 kilometres) from Winnipeg, Manitoba, was situated in a Protestant and even hostile setting, one that was changing with the presence of immigrants from continental Europe. The Redemptorists of the Belgian province had taken charge of St Augustine's parish in Brandon, and Father Godts had repeatedly asked that the RNDM sisters direct their parish school. On 10 August 1899, eight sisters left the convent at Deal for Canada, escorted by Reverend (Oblate) Father Lecoq, who was returning from France. Four sisters were destined for another new mission at Qu'Appelle, three were going to Brandon, and one was going to Grande Clairière to replace the sister who would become prioress in Brandon.[1] The eight RNDM sisters landed in Montreal on 17 August and were well received by the sisters of the Congregation of Notre Dame with whom they spent Sunday; the next day, they took the train to Winnipeg, where they spent the night with the Grey Nuns in St Boniface. When the sisters arrived at the train station in Brandon, they were received by two sisters and the leading Catholics of the town, who were there with their carriages and conducted them to St Augustine Church, where Father Godts said a Te Deum. The sisters then went to the convent for a reception organized by the women of the parish and attended by two priests and two brothers.

The reverend mother superior of the congregation had agreed to send four sisters to Brandon to teach the Catholic children of the parish and to open a boarding school in the convent left vacant for some years by the sisters of the Faithful Companions of Jesus. Those sisters had been from a French congregation, founded in 1820 and embedded in Ignatian spirituality, which had established foundations in England and

4.1 RNDM sisters at the beginning of the twentieth century, St Michael's
Convent. Source: Author's collection.

Ireland, as well as expanded throughout the world. They had arrived in
1883 and had with great success run the St Joseph Convent School, located on Lorne Avenue and 3rd Street, and had even attracted Protestant families. They left Brandon in 1895. The context of their departure
is important. Tom Mitchell argues that Brandon's Ontario-bred Protestant population had intended to recreate Ontario institutions and
that there was no hostility towards the convent. But, by 1886, the financial situation of the Protestant School Board had deteriorated, and
there were demands from militant Protestants that Protestant student
attendance at the convent school come to an end. The convent and
the sisters were victimized by attacks initiated by members of two
Brandon congregations, Methodist and Presbyterian, combined with
the Orange Lodge. The sisters also went through the crisis known as
the Manitoba School Question, which led to the abolition of the dual
confessional system (Protestant/Catholic) and the setting up of the
common school. Lacking students and experiencing hostility, the sisters left in 1895.[2]

Brandon grew gradually from 1881 to 1901, when it reached 5,620
inhabitants; by 1911, it had 13,893 inhabitants. Most of the new people
were immigrant men from other homelands, as well those driven to
the city by employment in the expanding transportation and building

industries. The British and Protestant character of the city's population changed rapidly at the beginning of the twentieth century, which had repercussions in the Catholic parish. While, in 1901, 83 per cent of the population was British, that percentage declined to 74 per cent by 1911. The proportion of the city's population that was of central and eastern European origin grew from 2 per cent in 1901 to 9 per cent in 1911.[3]

The location of the convent within Brandon, on Lorne Avenue and south of the commercial district in a "good" area, is also important. The city had acquired, as Errol Black and Tom Mitchell point out, a distinctive residential pattern. The most affluent families lived along Princess, Louise, Lorne, and Victoria Avenues to the south and west of the central business district. The homes of workers occupied the rest of the city, particularly to the east of First Street. South of Victoria Avenue, in the area known as the English Ward, there was an expanding working-class neighbourhood to the east of First Street; the area north of the Canadian Pacific Railway, the North End, was populated by manufacturing plants and the overcrowded homes of central and eastern European working-class immigrants.[4]

The convent was a two-storey, wooden framed building with a Mansard roof (a form of curb roof, where each face of the roof has two slopes, the lower one steeper than the other), painted in a drab grey colour. The convent was surrounded by a picket fence, with the portion in the front painted in white by the RNDM sisters themselves. Two rows of maple trees whose branches met above a wide plank walk were planted outside the front door. The convent, built in 1883, was 40 feet by 40 feet (approximately 12 by 12 metres); in 1887, another building of the same size had been built on the east side of the main building.[5] The new occupants – who duly indicated in their narrations that the exterior resembled a monastery, an aspect very important for them – made changes inside to better adapt the convent to their way of life. In the chapel, the sisters adored the "Divine Teacher who seemed to be waiting in his modest tabernacle to give them a welcoming blessing. The St Martha parlour, the grille parlour, the refectory, the dormitory, the cells, and the community room conformed with the regulations."[6] On the top floor of the attached building, there was a large dormitory to be used for boarders; in the basement, there was a refectory and music room; there were two classrooms on the main floor. It is not surprising that the sisters appreciated having electricity, running water, and a hot water furnace.[7] Certainly, the buildings were an improvement in comparison with previous houses, like the one in Grande Clairière.

4.2 St Michael's in Brandon. Source: Author's collection.

The public schools were construed as Protestant by Catholics. Hence, it was urgent that the Faithful Companions of Jesus be replaced, as "Catholic children were forced to attend government schools and were in contact [with] and under the constant influence of heretic companions and teachers."[8] They were, in other words, being drawn away from the intended path of salvation. The St Michael's community opened St Augustine's parish school on 1 September 1899. In 1900, two sisters came from New Zealand to help staff the classrooms.[9] Classes were taught entirely in English, and there were fifty pupils ranging from six to eighteen years of age – according to the community journal[10] – at a time when Brandon had a population of 5,000 that was mostly British and Protestant. Almost all the students – boys and girls – were Catholic, but, the sisters recorded, they were undisciplined and difficult to control, and had little sensitivity towards religious feelings and principles of respect. It would take many years of patient effort and courage, in the sisters' assessment, to erase from the young people's souls bad influences coming from an environment that encouraged independence, amusement, and pleasure.[11] "English" children (a description used by the sisters to refer to British children) attended the school or were boarders along with the children of recent continental European immigrants, resulting in a culturally diverse classroom. Sister Cecile Jordans recalled in a narrative about the old St Augustine school, though not regarding a particular year:

> I must go back to the days we taught in the old convent ... I was assigned the girls' large dormitory with pupils of Polish, Ukrainian, German and Russian origin, some 60 in all. These children received religious instruction daily from two CSSR's [Redemptorists], one Ruthenian Rite, the other, a Polish, [and] both spoke and taught in the language of the pupils.[12]

Catholic teaching was at the core, even as the school followed the provincial curriculum. As discussed earlier, the Manitoba Public School Act of 1897 allowed religious instruction when there were at least ten pupils of the same faith, and bilingual teaching when at least ten pupils spoke French or any other language. In any case, St Augustine was a parish school, and it continued its religious mission. In spite of scanty information, it can be inferred that the school attracted a large number of children from working-class British and central and eastern European families. The sisters did not charge fees since Catholic parents gave what they could afford. There was, however, a boarding and tuition fee that was set from the beginning at $8 a month.[13] One of the sisters recalled, "My pupils never had money to give or spend. However, each morning saw my desk growing under the load of donations. Apples, jams, pickles, etc. These were all carefully carried to St Mike's where they were stored away in the pantry."[14]

There was great cooperation with the French Redemptorists (CSSRs) in charge of the St Augustine Church from 1898 to 1913; there were five priests and some ten brothers in the 1920s. The priests served missions as far as Regina; the brothers looked after the garden, the school, the church, their order's kitchen, and so on. The priests also offered monthly conferences to the sisters. In 1908, the sisters and the fathers signed an agreement in which the sisters committed to providing three teachers for the parish school for an annual payment of $600; the sisters agreed to pay $100 to the fathers for lodging for themselves and the student boarders. The fathers agreed to take care of the school building and the heating; the sisters would take care of washing the priests' clothes for $15 monthly, and look after the "clothing" of the Church in exchange for the fathers' ministry.[15] In its aim to generate a Catholic community, the parish had also created organizations along gendered lines, including The Ladies of Mercy, Ladies of Ste Anne, The Children of Mary, The Catholic Club (for men), and a branch of the Knights of Columbus (for men).[16]

The idea of preserving one's cultural heritage, language, and ethnicity is closely related to how the Church approached the preservation of the faith. The schools in Brandon cultivated the worth of cultural language in the community by rooting it in the way the groups experienced faith. The school thus broke with the universality of the common school and its approach to building a cohesive citizenry through Anglo-conformity. There was also a quest for social recognition in the process of building a community identity on the part of new groups. The "illocutionary force" – salvation of the soul and a Catholic social order – was inserted into the living experience of the community, to which the Church was responsive. There was a powerful dimension in the life of the students in line with the idea that withholding recognition can be a form of oppression. Philosopher Charles Taylor wrote on the matter:

> On the intimate level, we can see how much an original identity needs and is vulnerable to the recognition given or withheld by significant others. It is not surprising that in the culture of authenticity, relationships are seen as the key loci of self-discovery and self-affirmation ... They [love relationships] are also crucial because they are the crucible of inwardly generated identity.[17]

The idea of preserving the cultural language, and not conforming to the dominant culture, was framed by the doctrine of the Church and the attempts at opening spaces in the school system. Within this configuration, the schools cultivated a sort of proto-multiculturalism – but from the standpoint of holding the truth while living in a Protestant milieu. It is interesting to note that, in 1900, the St Augustine parish comprised eighty-three families, including fifteen that were Polish. Four years later, Poles and Ukrainians had formed the most numerous elements in the parish; by 1911, Polish parishioners were the majority, amounting to 392 faithful, and the following year, there were 743 Polish faithful. For a decade, until the 1920s, the Polish were the majority at St Augustine.[18]

In 1904, the sisters had bought a piece of land on Victoria Avenue to build a new convent that was actually built in 1909, and ready on 29 September 1910, the day of St Michael's feast. The convent would also house St Michael's Academy, a senior day school and boarding school for girls offering instruction entirely in English. Two private classrooms were opened immediately for the boarders and day students. The Catholic ladies of the parish prepared a bazaar that brought some funds to defray costs; this fundraising became a practice that continued over time.[19] The convent was blessed by Archbishop Langevin in December 1910.[20]

Music had a powerful place in the schools and the community, and St. Michael's Academy earned a great reputation. The musical teaching and success were not only in piano, but also in theory, violin, and vocal preparation; the latter was showcased in the choirs. There are records of the presence of Trinity College of Music examiners who came from London; later, the students had their music examinations at the University of Manitoba. It is interesting to note that music created a link with the community at large through the students, who took lessons at the St Augustine parish school or at St Michael's. Even St Augustine's Church, pastored by the Redemptorist fathers, acquired a state-of-the-art pipe organ and attracted people of all faiths to a concert by a prestigious artist from Quebec.[21]

In particular, the Church and the St Augustine parish school were powerful forces working towards the quest of recognition and preservation of cultural values in the midst of a hostile environment where the political struggles often acquired anti-immigrant tones and the notion of otherness was conveyed in several expressions, such as "strangers within our gates,"[22] referring to foreigners and others who needed to be assimilated. The school provided a space with a configuration of alternative meanings for immigrants trying to find their place in Canada.[23] The interesting point here is that a special committee of the Brandon Council of the Knights of Columbus submitted a report on St Augustine School in November 1919 about the general tendencies of the school and its organization, teaching methods, and results obtained.[24] The committee's members found the equipment inadequate and interpreted the poverty of parents as requiring investigation, because that poverty, in their view, "could be the result of indifference and of lack of interest in education. We feel that the books purchased should remain the absolute property of the school and they [should] only be loaned to the pupil. In view of the conditions above we feel that the results obtained in the school are fair."[25] Overall, the committee did not represent poor immigrant Catholic families, tried to assert the social status of Catholics, and was very critical of the preoccupation with helping students maintain their own culture. The Knights of Columbus wanted to implant in their co-religionists, many of them Polish, the Catholic values of the English culture – their own culture. The committee's report stated that the school was leading to disintegration of Catholic unity by focusing on the students' culture. The report also questioned the quality of schoolwork, which tended to lower rather than elevate all pupils.[26] There is no doubt that class and ethnic prejudice pervaded the report. The Polish immigrants represented the lowest stratum of the white socio-economic ladder of the city; in 1920, there were around 1,100 people from Poland, of whom only 1 per cent engaged in artisanal activities or were "semi-professional" or owned a small business; there were only two professionals (an engineer and a teacher).[27]

In 1918, a year previous to the Knights of Columbus report, the school had only 151 pupils, two of whom were non-Catholics. It was noted that "many parents seem unscrupulous about sending their children to public schools, without even consulting the priests."[28] In 1920, the creation of St Hedwig's parish in response to requests from Brandon's Polish Catholics, followed by the opening of a parish school run by Benedictine Polish sisters, affected attendance at St Augustine starting in 1921, when its student population was reduced to eighty "English" (meaning British) children. However, the Benedictine sisters left in 1924; the people could not support them, so the archbishop refused to let the sisters stay.[29] St Augustine School continued its work as a parish school until 1968, when it became part of the Brandon School Division. St Michael's high school diversified its curriculum to offer commercial courses (basic accounting, typewriting), and its students excelled in music events. In 1967, the school ended as a missionary enterprise; in 1968, it became part of the public school board as a co-educational junior high school.

Conversions of Protestant students were duly registered in the convent journal (six were counted between 1903 and 1922, inclusive). The sisters, as they did in other schools, actively recruited future members for the congregation; thus, between 1904 and 1923, there were nine new sisters who came from the small city of Brandon. Successful recruitment would in the long run give the Canadian province of the congregation its own characteristics and foster a desire for recognition of its uniqueness.

Winnipeg Foundation, Convent of St Edward's

In Winnipeg, the Church of St Edward was built in 1908 in the midst of a compact population mostly made up of small tradespeople, merchants, and workers. A little later, a large school was built near the church, and Archbishop Langevin invited the sisters to be in charge of the school. On 5 September 1909, the mother superior sent three founding sisters for the school: Mother M. St Gabriel, prioress (New Zealander), Sister M. St Laurence (Irish Canadian), and Sister M. of the Holy Angels

(French Canadian).[30] There was no separate dwelling for the sisters; the priest who occupied part of the ground floor of St Edward's School gave the sisters four small rooms on the same floor. This building was the initial convent of St Adélard honouring Archbishop Adélard Langevin. The sisters described Winnipeg, the capital of Manitoba, as the "hinge" of the province: "[O]n account of the lakes and marshland in the north and the American frontier in the south, all the railway lines and highways pass through Winnipeg."[31] Winnipeg was even at this time a cosmopolitan city; thus, to the skirmish between English-speaking Catholics and French Canadians, we need to add the presence of Catholics from various European countries. St Edward's was one of the parishes created in response to requests made by English-speaking Catholics to the apostolic delegate in Ottawa to have their own bishop.[32] The city of Winnipeg was beautifully described by Gerald Friesen:

> To descend from the train at the CPR station in Winnipeg was to enter an international bazaar: the noise of thousands of voices and a dozen tongues circled the high marble pillars and drifted out into the street, there to mingle with the sounds of construction, delivery wagons, perambulatory vendors, and labour recruiters. The crowds were equally dense on Main Street, just a block away, where shops displayed their wares in a fashion more European than British North American: fruits and vegetables, books and newspapers, coats and jackets stood on side-walk tables and racks, even on the outer walls of buildings when weather permitted. The smell of fresh earth at an excavation site, of concrete being poured and lumber being stacked, reminded the visitor of the newness and vitality of the place. But the smells were mixed with beer and whisky and sweat and horse manure to remind one, too, that this was not a polite and ordered society but rather was customarily described as Little Europe, Babel, New Jerusalem, or the Chicago of the North.[33]

Archbishop Langevin wanted the RNDM sisters, the French congregation, to be in charge of the school in St Edward's parish. On 21 July 1909, St Edward's priest had written a letter to the reverend mother provincial asking her to give him an answer to the question he had put in previous letters: "Are you prepared to send English Sisters for my school, two for this fall and more any time I should want them?"[34] A few days later, the exasperated priest wrote back again to the mother; he was surprised that she did not seem to understand the statement contained in his letter regarding English sisters. The priest clarified what he meant by "English sisters": "sisters of either English,

Scotch, Irish, English-Canadian or English-American descent, or sisters of other nationalities who have obtained certificates to teach not merely in bilingual schools, or country schools, but in exclusively English and city schools, or schools attended exclusively by pupils of English speaking parents."[35] There was obviously some political tension around the English–French issue. In September 1910, the angry priest reminded the sisters of the two letters he had written some time ago regarding the conditions under which the sisters had been asked to come to the school. He wrote: "Notwithstanding we have here a teacher who cannot speak English sufficiently well for our school. I would ask you therefore on my own behalf and on behalf of our school board to send us another teacher in her place, who will answer the requirements of our school."[36] If this were not possible, the priest would engage a lay teacher.[37] The mother provincial responded that she could send a sister by the middle of October.[38]

On 8 November 1909, classes began with two classrooms and about forty children, boys and girls, in grades one to four. In December, Archbishop Langevin blessed the school. One year later, the school had doubled the number of pupils, as children from other parishes also came to the school that now offered grades five and six. In 1912, there were 160 children, and St Edward's was established as an examination centre for grade eight and for music examinations through Trinity College, London.[39] Of the twenty-one pupils who tried their music examinations for the Trinity College that year, eighteen were successful. The number of students in grades one to nine increased from 40 in 1909 to 350 in 1920. The school was enlarged to accommodate the rise in students a number of times.[40]

The sisters did not have their own building serving as a convent until 1923. The superior general approved the building of the new St Adélard Convent in 1922, as the sisters did not have privacy and the school needed the rooms to comply with the law regarding schools. At the time, there were ten sisters, nine of them teachers.[41] Recruitment of future religious was somewhat successful. The number of students was kept more or less steady through the 1950s. A 1970 report from Superior General Mary Gertrude tells us that the St Edward's community had sixteen sisters. Four were teaching in the parochial school, and one sister taught in a public school, while another sister gave music lessons as well as doing part-time studies; four sisters were ill, and the remaining of the sixteen were retired.[42] Over the years, and until it closed in 2007 – and in particular after Vatican II – the convent became the home base for several ministries in Winnipeg.

Today, the school is partially funded by the government, but is not run by the sisters.

Portage la Prairie: Private Elementary School in an "Orange Lodge Setting"

The RNDM community, upon the request of Archbishop Langevin, started a foundation on 16 July 1914, when the sisters took possession of an old and quite large house that they had bought and repaired. This house became the St John the Baptist Convent. Three sisters were the foundresses: Sister M. St Isabelle (French Canadian), in charge of works, Sister M. St Ethelred (English), and Sister M. St Laurence (Irish Canadian).[43]

The city of Portage la Prairie, described by the sisters as a flourishing one, is located 53 miles (85 kilometres) from Winnipeg and 79 miles (127 kilometres) from Brandon (via the Trans-Canada highway). At the time, there was a small minority of Catholics, who, according to the sisters, were somewhat indifferent to matters of religion. The sisters had bought an old house not far from the church, and, on 16 July 1914, took possession of the empty house from the contractor whom they had hired to make repairs. Their first concern was to sprinkle each room with holy water and to place a crucifix in the room destined to become the chapel; the sisters all knelt down, fervently recited the rosary, and asked their mother in heaven (the foundress) to protect them. Their first meal was eaten off an old crate covered with a sheet. They did not have any furniture, so they had the choice of standing or sitting on the floor. The same day, two sisters went to shop for necessities (beds, chairs, utensils), while the others prepared the place. They were invited by the parish priest, Father Baribeau, to have dinner in the rectory; they accepted gratefully. The two reverend mothers who had accompanied the two founding sisters returned to Winnipeg the same night. A third sister promptly joined them. It was written that "[n]o soul came to trouble their solitude."[44]

The first Mass the sisters attended was in a building that had been used temporarily since the church had burned down some time ago. The sisters approached the old ruined cabin in front of them with hesitation; they thought they had the wrong address until they saw the priest entering the shack. It was an indescribable hovel, decorated inside with rubble from old decaying barracks. This building, in their minds, could not be the home of the "King of Kings." It was a place loathsome with misery and filth. The place is described as having a ceiling covered with tar paper that was yellow, torn, patched, ragged, and hanging in more than one place; the walls were colourless and covered with stains, still decorated with worm-eaten shelves that were numbered and probably used in the past to hold the saddles and arms of the soldiers; there were chairs, dirty and broken, and nailed together without any pattern. The sanctuary was a platform of rough wood that could be reached by two coarse steps serving as a communion rail. There was a little lamp lit and flickering in front of a sort of table covered with a white cloth, and on it there was a box, the tabernacle. "Yes, the Good God is there ... This is where He [sic] is night and day waiting." They recorded a fervent adoration during Mass, and back home they worked to prepare a more decent dwelling for the "divine guest" in their chapel.[45]

On Sunday, 19 July, the sisters went to Mass. The priest gave a sermon praising the sisters and the purpose of their establishment in the area. There was general indifference towards them. Contrary to other places, the sisters did not receive visits or any sign of sympathy; people were just polite.[46] There were around 300 Catholics excluding the Polish Catholics, who had their own parish and a school run by Polish religious.[47] The sisters' loneliness in those early summer days was broken up by the stay of two Franciscan sisters on a begging tour, who were received with great hospitality.

Other RNDM houses made contributions to the St John the Baptist Convent in Portage. The sisters had a small number of children in the private elementary school they ran; by 1923, the number had increased to sixty students. Nonetheless, by 1923, the little mission had given three young subjects to the congregation. The sisters wrote: "It is interesting to note that among the pupils there are many nationalities, even Chinese and Negroes who preserve, intact, the characteristics of their race."[48] A profound notion of otherness framed the universal message of salvation. In the late 1920s, the sisters also taught catechism in the Reformatory Training School at Portage la Prairie; eighty-seven of the 137 young people imprisoned (all under twenty) were Catholics. The sisters aimed to "dissipate their blindness and open their minds to the reality of the Eternal Truths, and the loving tenderness of their Saviour in their behalf."[49] In the congregation's historical summary on the occasion of the twenty-fifth anniversary of the Canadian province in 1923, the sisters described Portage la Prairie as a citadel of the Orange Party, which was most hostile to "our holy religion." The school closed in 1939, when the children went to the public school during the Depression.

Fort Frances, Ontario

In 1914, two weeks after opening the house in Portage la Prairie, the congregation started another one in Fort Frances, located at the western edge of the province of Ontario, in the Diocese of St Boniface, near the Canada–US border. The sisters built there the St Jude's Convent and taught in schools of the Catholic separate system, a provision existing in Ontario. The last sister-teacher serving in the system left in 1986. The convent remained involved in various activities until May 1998, when the sisters officially left.

Chapter Five

The RNDM in Saskatchewan: Residential, Parish, Separate, and Private Schools for Girls

Lac Croche, Saskatchewan: Redemption or the Silencing of the Soul?

The "education" of Indigenous children was under federal jurisdiction, and the state and the Church (there were also Protestant churches running residential schools) converged in their intentionalities.[1] The Church aimed at conversion to the new religion and the salvation of a self-disciplined child, while the state pursued assimilation and a governable Indigenous subject. Both converged in the colonization process.

In 1898, the Oblates of Mary Immaculate requested through Archbishop Langevin that the congregation send three sisters to the Marieval Indian Residential School for Indigenous children, situated at Lac Croche (Crooked Lake), Assiniboia, close to a Cree reserve. The school was situated 280 miles (450.6 kilometres) from Winnipeg. A second group of four sisters came to Canada from Deal (England) to work in this mission; two were French, one Irish, and one Belgian. The sisters were accompanied by Monseigneur Émile-Joseph Legal, Oblate of Mary Immaculate (OMI), bishop of St Albert, who was returning to Canada.

The new missionaries visited Grande Clairière before going to their mission in Lac Croche; there, they were affected by the destitution in which the sisters lived at the Our Lady of the Snows Convent. The missionaries left the convent to go to Brandon and travelled in sleighs in the midst of a blizzard, wrapped up together in a large blanket. The sleigh overturned in a ditch hidden under a mantle of snow, but they were not hurt. In Brandon, they were met by Father Campeau, OMI, who went with the sisters to their final destination by train. Campeau had already had a great deal of experience with the residential schools in the area. They all got off at the Broadview station to finish the final leg of their journey to the school by sleigh. The sisters described their arrival at the mission:

> When he [Campeau] arrived at the station in Broadview accompanied by the sisters, they were greeted by a group of Indians on horseback who had come to meet them. They were escorted all the way to the mission, a 20 mile [32 kilometre] journey, which they travelled by sleds. The Indians were all dressed up for the occasion in tanned buckskin clothing, with a coloured shawl on their shoulders, their long black hair hanging on each side in two shiny braids adorned with rings of various colours. On their feet they wore embroidered moccasins and on their head, a kind of crown of long coloured feathers which they wore as a helmet or mane. At intervals they would echo their noisy long-drawn salutes. When they got near the village, they stopped and gathered in a semi-circle to present their official salutations. In conformity with Indian etiquette, the sisters had to shake hands with each of them. They were welcomed with obvious pleasure. Father Campeau served as their interpreter as well as their guide. At the sound of the only bell, all went to the church.[2]

The sisters felt that they were welcomed as the teachers coming to teach the children. They recorded the events that way. The Indigenous peoples had requested that their treaties with the British Crown include schools being set up for their children on the reserves. However, it is important to note that they did not expect residential schools. The children's painful lived experience in these residential schools and its colonizing destructive path were not even considered by the missionaries.

After the ceremony, the sisters were taken to their temporary house, a rather small one-storey log house. It had a place for the sisters and a dormitory for the little "Indian girls," of which there were about ten. One of the sisters was to sleep near them as a supervisor. Instead of beds, there were a few rough boards on which five or six girls, rolled in the same blanket, were to sleep during the night without worrying about the legions of parasites sharing their rustic bed. The place for the sisters consisted of a refectory on one side and a community room, also the dormitory, on the other. A corner with a strip of coloured material hanging from the ceiling was the mother prioress's room. Of course, they did not have a chapel of any sort, and, more seriously for the sisters, there was no space to keep the Eucharistic presence. The appearance of the building was one of destitution, of misery, following the sisters' account; there were vermin everywhere, the roof was so low that it could be touched, and what they called mushrooms grew freely on the walls. The sisters described the unhealthy living conditions as being part of the sacrifices that they had made for God, and not out of a concern for the well-being of the students.[3]

The quality of the meals became part of the expected mortification. The Oblate fathers had a cook for everybody, and, contrary to what happened in the other convents where the sisters had their own financial and in-kind means (donations, lessons, fees, gifts), the sisters of Lac Croche had "to endure the trials of painful privations. For example, on a patronal feast day, they were served as a whole meal, a dish of beans." The narrations are wrapped in a language of sacrifice brought by God and a generosity in being accepting of those sacrifices, as well as a language of devotion, since the sisters were there to take care of "young souls under their care."[4]

Not far from the "convent" was the "maison dite 'des Sauvages'" (in the English version, this name was translated as the "so-called house of the Indians"), which had two storeys: Fathers Campeau and Bousquet and the lay brothers lived on the upper floor.[5] The large lower floor had a large stove in the centre that was surrounded by rustic benches, which were fixed along the walls. On Sundays, before and after Mass, members of the community gathered there to eat the food they had provided for themselves, smoke their pipes, and chat. When the sisters arrived, this lower floor was divided into two parts to make a dormitory for the boys, who spent their days in school in the care of the sisters and nights in the care of the fathers. There was a church as well, which was also divided by a curtain separating the sanctuary. The nave then served as a classroom, where the students, about twenty boys and girls, sat on rough boards. The sisters recorded their impressions of their pupils as being satisfactorily obedient and docile.

> They were still in the most complete ignorance and spoke only their In-dian dialect. Their nature, always yearning for freedom, was often rebel-lious to submitting to a civilization of which they did not understand the advantages. We had to hide the wax candles which they would chew as candy. During the warm season, on the first favourable occasion, swift as young untamed colts, they would escape from their teachers' benevolent supervision; our little savages would quickly remove their clothing and shoes and plunge in the nearby shallow river called "La Coulée," which is only an overflow of the beautiful Crooked Lake. Such escapades were more in line with their dispositions than to apply themselves quietly to the short hours of study.[6]

The sisters joined the Oblates in the goal of providing a "Christian and civilizing education."[7] There is no question that, in the residential school, the learner was the "other" with dramatic overtones, to be redeemed by converting to the "true religion" in line with the doctrine of the Church at the time. This positioning was no different from other Christian churches of the period involved in missionary work.

In the narration written by Sister Mary of the Holy Trinity, there is a poignant story. One day, Father Campeau arrived on horseback, carrying "something" wrapped in a blanket; while dismounting, he asked for a tub of water, quickly. The sister asked if it was a fish.

Yes, a famous fish!

He unrolled his bundle to the great surprise of his questioner, and let a young child, two to three years old, and terribly dirty, fall out into the tub. Here is Moses.

It was Moses whose name in Cree means: "Frog's Leg."

His father, Yellow Calf, and his mother, White Cow, had been raised pagans but had baptized their son. The missionary, anxious to give the child a Christian education, had taken him by force, because these good Indians are very much attached to their children and do not want to be separated voluntarily from them. The mother often came to see her beloved Moses, and trying to adorn herself to give herself more importance, she wore, around her neck, a real harness decorated with copper nails. She seemed proud of this adornment.[8]

There is also another story that the sisters recorded regarding a little girl, about two years old, who Father Bousquet found while making his rounds in the parish. Her mother was ill and destitute, and lived in a kind of hut without even ventilation. The girl, following the sisters' account, would eat all that she could pick up from the ground. She is described as a mass of sores, dirt, and putrefaction from head to toe. Her mother died soon afterwards. The sisters took the child. Her name was Minouche, but she was baptized and became Marie. In the middle of the ceremony "in which she became a child of God," the new Marie grabbed the glass she saw within her reach[9] and, before anyone could stop her, drank, to the last drop, the water that had been prepared for the administration of the sacrament. Marie reportedly improved. When Archbishop Langevin visited the school, the sisters and Reverend Mother M. St Irenée presented her to the prelate to receive his blessing. In a joyful tone, he said, "Oh! What a horror! Yes, yes, my dear Mother you may love her to your pleasure for there is no danger of self-satisfaction."[10] There is no further information about this child or of any extended family that she may have had.

In the dramatic case of Moses, and for the students in the residential schools in general, a Christian (Catholic) education – in other words, the concepts of conversion and salvation that went along with the assimilation of the Indigenous child into Western ways – was the force, the intentionality, behind removing and keeping a child from his or her family. The congregation had an explicit commitment to a child-centred approach and a thorough Christian education, and certainly expressed love towards children, but this commitment was situated in relation to the inculcation of universal truths, one true faith, and a particular way of life. In this case, the notion of child-centredness, so dear to the congregation, goes along with the dehistoricization of the Indigenous child (for example, Moses) and his or her family, in that this notion, if decontextualized, is hollow. Indeed, the editorial page of the first issue of *Les Cloches de Saint-Boniface*, a periodical publication of the Archdiocese of St Boniface, reads: "As Christopher Columbus raised the cross in the new world, these missionaries raised as well the sign of Redemption and all will come to kneel at the foot of this cross to receive the benefits of the Religion. The savage will hear for the first time the sweet word of the Gospel."[11] This belief was the force behind the education of the Indigenous child. The missionaries failed to understand the relationship that Indigenous peoples have with the natural world and how that relationship includes a religious dimension that is distinctive to their culture.[12] Thus, although the churches (Catholic and Protestant alike) aligned with the state policy in the process aimed at the colonization of the Indigenous peoples and their culture, and, as Phillips has argued, in the goal of ending their claims for land that were not compatible with the settlements and the Western economy, it was with different intentionalities.[13]

When Mother St Irenée left Lac Croche, a general meeting was held where, in a farewell speech, an Indian chief said: "Remember that no matter where you direct your steps, you will be treading on soil that is ours, we are the only true masters of this land of our ancestors." The narrator of the story, Sister Mary of the Holy Trinity, added immediately following the recounting: "Most of these savages were still pagans. With their chief 'Chi-Chip,' they adored the sun and, as a symbol of their cult, wore its image painted on the covering thrown over their shoulders. It also decorated the trappings of their horses and even the tents." Then the reader learns that the Indigenous people loved the sisters, although the language barrier and the way the mission was organized did not permit a direct relationship between the two.[14]

The sisters were employees under the "immediate and sole direction of the missionary priests [Missionary Oblates of Mary Immaculate]," who acted as official agents.[15] The priests were in absolute control of all arrangements and of looking after the finances, while the sisters were used to managing and controlling their own missions. The sisters soon concluded that the kind of administration to which they had to submit was neither consistent with their customs nor with the way of life of the congregation. Therefore, the RNDM sisters left the residential school after seventeen months. Given the congregation's pontifical character and structure of governance, they had a degree of autonomy in relation to local authorities and could make the decision to leave.[16] The archbishop, following the Church protocol, proposed that the Lac Croche community be transferred to Ste Rose du Lac. Contrary to the Missionary Oblate sisters, a diocesan congregation, the RNDM sisters did not participate in any other residential school apostolate in Canada.[17]

The sisters did not question their mission with the Indigenous people or its character. Instead, they questioned the subordinated position they had under the Oblate fathers. The sisters stated in their narration of events that they were entirely devoted to their apostolate among "those poor children of nature, new souls for whom so much could be done."[18]

Lebret

Lebret was the first foundation in Saskatchewan. Situated on the shore of Lake Mission, one of a chain of seven lakes in the Qu'Appelle Valley, it is northeast of Regina. Founded by Oblate of Mary Immaculate Monsignor Taché in 1865, Lebret was one of the oldest mission centres in Canada to preach to Indigenous and Métis peoples of the Northwest Territories, and later became the village of Lebret. In 1884, the federal government established and was in charge of operating an industrial school, a major colonizing tool; the school was run by the Oblates with the support of the Grey Nuns, who had been in the district since 1881. Settlers new to the area, particularly French Canadians at first, obtained land grants from the government, while the Indigenous peoples were settled on reserves. There were many Métis families involved in the fur trade and soon also in farming. Father Prisque Magnan, superior of the mission, requested the teaching services of the RNDM sisters for the school, which was in fact a public one. Four sisters arrived on 3 September 1899.

The province of Saskatchewan was not created until 1905. At the time of the sisters' arrival, the Northwest Territories was composed of the Districts of Saskatchewan and Assiniboia, which later were part of the newly created province of Saskatchewan, and the Districts of Alberta and Athabasca, which became the province of Alberta.[19] The territorial ordinances of 1884, 1891, and 1892 regarding education set the legal precedent for the establishment of separate schools: the first school in a district had to be designated a public school, after which area members of the minority faith (be it Protestant or Catholic) could establish their own school district with a school that would be designated as a "separate school." In 1885, the Board of Education centralized the power to licence and hire teachers for both types of schools. There were ordinances from time to time, but the most important were those of 1891 and 1892 creating the Council of Public Instruction, forerunner of the Department of Education, thus placing educational matters in the hands of the government. Although the Lebret school was a public school, being the first in the district, it is not surprising that it appears to be a Catholic public school, as the population was largely Catholic and not Protestant (of course, Indigenous and Métis people's beliefs were not acknowledged).[20] As discussed, there was a substantial difference in Manitoba, where, after the crisis known as the Manitoba School Question, confessional schools were denied public funding. Catholic schools had to be either parish schools or private schools with no public funding. However, the congregations often took charge of public schools in rural districts in Manitoba, a move facilitated by the existence of hundreds of school districts in rather homogeneous communities.

The foundresses of the new mission in Saskatchewan arrived in Canada with those destined for Brandon. The group stopped at Grande Clairière and then had a short visit at Lac Croche before the sisters went on to Lebret. They made the trip of 60 miles (96.5 kilometres) in two heavy wagons with two OMI brothers. Twice during the day, the travellers stopped to let the horses rest. The sisters lit a fire of brushwood and dry branches and made tea, and all had a frugal meal. The group of four sisters (two French and two Irish, with three of them coming from Europe, while the other had been in Lac Croche) and two brothers reached Lebret at midnight.[21] The Oblate fathers accommodated them in the rectory, while they prepared the convent following the sisters' directions. They added an extension to the building; however, there was no chapel. On the ground floor, there were five rooms: a tiny parlour, a classroom, the children's and sisters' refectories, and the kitchen; on the second floor was a second classroom, a cloakroom, two dormitories for the pupils and one for the sisters, and a common room. The fathers took care of the furniture.[22] This building was to be a temporary

5.1 Lebret (Saskatchewan) Community, 1916. Source: Author's collection.

"Angel Gabriel convent" for the sisters; in August 1905, Archbishop Langevin blessed the new convent, built following the regulations of the sisters' constitutions.

As happened in other convents in rural centres, and as planned by Oblate Father Magnan, the sisters were to take charge of the public school immediately. However, the Catholic teacher in charge of the school, supported by the community, kept his position. While waiting for the opening of the public school, the sisters opened a private boarding school for about twenty girls and boys, with the latter sleeping at the rectory; many day pupils came from the district. The sisters indicated in the record that almost all the students were Catholic and most of them were Métis, and described them as docile and respectful of their teachers.[23] The Church indeed influenced the spiritual life and the socio-cultural identity of the Métis; but it is important to note that the Métis people had adapted many components of the Cree social order, grounded in a spiritual and philosophical world view that framed their experience.[24] The congregation's documents are mute about the complexities of their conversion.

5.2 Sioux chief and his family, Lebret. An old Sioux chief, accompanied by his son, comes to see his two daughters, who are being brought up by the Sisters of Our Lady of the Missions in Lebret, Saskatchewan. Source: Author's collection.

In 1900 and 1902, the houses in Canada received a visit from Mother M. St Etienne, and in 1904, from the Reverend Mother General M. St Rosaire. They found that the "convent" in Lebret did not have a grille, and there was no sign of a cloister. The sisters also recorded that, although the sisters' rooms were separated from the others, they could not prevent frequent visits from the "sauvages," who came from the neighbouring reserves and, without much preamble, went into the convent's kitchen and sat there indefinitely. They could not talk given the language barrier, but the sisters construed that the Indigenous people were expressing admiration and kind feelings towards the "women of prayer."[25]

The private boarding school was in operation and going well. From the beginning, the sisters prepared school candidates for the official examinations, according to the age and level of knowledge; the female students were also trained in manual work that the sisters considered essential to a girl's education, thinking that went back to the vision of the foundress in which the learning of practical skills was relevant. It was for these reasons, the sisters explained in their journal, that the school drew so many boarders, even though the convent was 22 miles (35.4 kilometres) from the nearest railway station of South Qu'Appelle on the Canadian Pacific Railway line. Mail came by stage coach from the railway station, but anyone undertaking a train journey had first to go by sleigh or wagon to Qu'Appelle.[26]

At the opening of the school in 1901, Father Magnan, superior of the mission and trustee of the school district, had been able to obtain the appointment of a sister as a teacher in the public school. However, she was able to teach for only a few months. As they had only been in Canada for three years, the sisters did not have a Saskatchewan diploma; the congregation had not realized that Saskatchewan did not have the latitude of Manitoba and that the province did not recognize French teaching certificates. A secular teacher therefore replaced the sister. However, many of the students moved from the public to the private school, and the number of students enrolled in the public school declined dramatically. The important outcome is that Mother M. St Irenée, vicar provincial, decided that it was necessary that the sisters be "trained" to be "efficient teachers." She was happy to comply with the recommendations from the trustees, and, in 1903, the sisters took charge of the public school. The number of pupils increased to thirty by 1905. The boarding school continued its work.[27]

Two years after the sisters took over the public school, Father Magnan began to plan a new convent. The mother provincial was invited to choose a building site for the mission, and she chose a place on the slope of a hill between two groves, close to Lake Mission. The work began in the spring of 1905. The new convent, dedicated to the Angel Gabriel, to whom the sisters invoked, was built with the "aid" of the boys from the "Indian Industrial School," who were under the care of the Grey Nuns.[28] The convent was blessed by the archbishop. No further details were given about the work of the young students nor were any concerns expressed. The principal of the industrial school, Father Hugonard, provided the sisters, until his death in 1917, with fruits and vegetables cultivated by the boys in the gardens of the residential school. In 1912, the railway line was laid through the centre of the village, which allowed for easier communication with urban centres. The sisters were busy teaching and running the private boarding school, teaching in the public school, and teaching music classes. The schools in Lebret produced six Canadian sisters for the congregation between the beginning of the mission in 1899 and 1920.[29] In the early 1920s, the sisters trained the sanctuary boys and the choirs, and moderated sodalities such as the Congregation of the Children of Mary (five members) and the Holy Angels (fifty-five members), and the League of the Sacred Heart for small boys (thirty-five members). In their private school classrooms, the sisters taught grades one to eight in conformity with the Department of Education and prepared the pupils for the official examinations. At the public school, there were two classrooms of the same grades with ninety-one children directed by the sisters.[30]

The 1920s were not easy times for the Catholic Church in Saskatchewan due to the presence of the Ku Klux Klan, which created a fearful environment. In addition, a 1930 law was issued that prohibited religious to teach in public schools in Saskatchewan unless they took off their religious habit and did not allow any religious emblem to be displayed in classrooms.[31] The sisters in Lebret adopted a black overcoat that they wore over the religious habit; this compromise enabled them to continue to teach in the public school, where they taught both the primary and secondary grades.

The parish was dedicated to the Sacred Heart, and the feasts of the Sacred Heart and Corpus Christi were celebrated with magnificent processions involving Catholics who came from well beyond Lebret. By the time of the Jubilee (1948), these processions included one hundred religious from various orders, hundreds of school children in the regalia of their sodalities, and thousands of laypeople from distant places such as Regina, all climbing the steep ascent of the Way of the Cross, which led to a shrine of the Sacred Heart near the summit of the hills above the valley village.[32] The students in both the private and the public school had great success in drama and music, as shown in their performances

5.3 St Gabriel's Convent in Lebret. Source: Author's collection.

at annual local festivals; later, in the 1940s, student accomplishments in athletics brought awards to the school.[33]

St Raphael's Academy, Wolseley, Saskatchewan

On 15 December 1904, the sisters started a parish boarding school in the little town of Wolseley, located on the Canadian Pacific Transcontinental line, 295 miles (474.7 kilometres) from Winnipeg and 63 miles (100.3 kilometres) from Regina (on the Trans-Canada highway). The foundresses were four French sisters and one English sister, two of whom had already been working in Canada. Archbishop Langevin wanted the sisters to run a school for the French-Canadian Catholics who had settled there in a mostly Protestant populated area. A church had been built, St Anne du Loup, in the southeast section of the town near one of the old chapels that was not in use. The concern of Archbishop Langevin, following the sisters' account, was familiar: young people were always in touch with heretical teachers and friends, which would expose them to ideas that might cause their loss of faith. Langevin made the request for a foundation to the Very Reverend Mother Marie du St Rosaire, superior general of the congregation, when she visited the missions in Canada in 1904. A convent, named St Raphael's Convent, was built for the sisters. They moved there in December 1904; on 25 December, the convent was duly blessed by Archbishop Langevin. His sermon, made first in French and then in English, referred to the sacred obligation that parents had to bring up their children in the Christian (Catholic) faith. He also recounted the special advantages of having religious educators "whose self-abnegation, zeal, and devotedness were above praise."[34]

The sisters continued preparing for the opening of the school. They were quite separated from the world, since at first people from the community did not visit them. One day, they received the special visit of two girls who went to the convent to ask how much it would cost to be a nun. The school opened at the beginning of January with a classroom that held twenty to thirty students in the basement of the convent; the students were boys and girls from the parish. Another classroom on the ground floor held fifteen to twenty boarding students during the school term. All the children were Catholics, and the sisters proudly recorded that the students were docile. The teaching was bilingual, in English and French. However, once again, the government did not recognize the school because the sisters did not hold a teaching certificate from Saskatchewan. The resources were very limited. The sisters carried a heavy debt, did not receive gifts or any assistance from the people in the parish, and did not have a salary; there were only small fees from the day pupils and a small profit from the boarders. The sisters successfully organized a concert to raise funds to buy an organ for the chapel that gave solemnity to their service with pious and joyous music.[35] They also planted hundreds of bushes with help from the students and planted a garden, which the gophers enjoyed; the sisters declared a war on the animals, setting traps, putting out poison, and flooding their dwelling places.[36] In 1905, two sisters from New Zealand were, for a short time, helping in this mission, which shows the early movement of sisters in the community. By 1910, the parish school had been transferred to a new building, a former church, and it became a Catholic separate school; this transfer brought financial improvement to the community because the sisters received a salary. In 1917, it was re-categorized as a public school, and the number of pupils had increased to ninety by the early 1920s. The sisters continued having student boarders; in the early 1920s, the number of students varied from twenty-one to forty-four. In those early years between 1908 and 1917, Wolseley also gave three vocations to the RNDM community, another step forward in the creation of a rooted Canadian province. The convent closed in 1983.[37]

Sacred Heart Academy

Six months after opening the mission in Wolseley, the congregation accepted the request to start another foundation in Saskatchewan, this time in Regina. The village of Regina, situated 356 miles (573 kilometres) from Winnipeg (on the Trans-Canada highway), had just become the capital of the newly formed province of Saskatchewan, a promising field for the sisters.[38] In 1883, when the Oblate fathers from Lebret visited the village, a journey of 52 miles (83.6 kilometres) via the current highway, it was a small settlement of only a few families. A small wooden church and school, also of wood, were built, while the parish developed slowly to a population of around 3,000 by 1903. The Catholics in the little town, a minority among the population, were mostly German, as was the Oblate priest.

The four sisters who started the foundation, one originally from New Zealand, two Alsatians, and a Swiss, lived first in a room near the church, in a private house the priest had bought for himself. There were still tenants in the house, which was located near the construction site of a new church, a stone building that would be called St Mary's Church. In their room, the sisters tried to lead their complex and semi-cloistered religious life and hold their community exercises. They had their meals in the rectory of the old church.[39]

The sisters were well received by the lieutenant governor of Saskatchewan, Mr Forget, a Catholic, and his French-Canadian wife, and were invited by the couple to a luxurious dinner that on all accounts made them a bit uncomfortable. The silver dishes and the elegance of the etiquette were not part of their lifestyle. Nonetheless, it is noticeable that, when the sisters were invited by distinguished people, they readily accepted the invitation, recognizing the importance of the connection; but, after providing a detailed description of the event, they would customarily indicate how miserable they felt because they missed the humility and religious simplicity to which they were attached that they felt was central to their being.[40]

When the tenants left, the sisters made of the house a convent that was given the name Sacred Heart. The sisters thought of this name as an encouragement towards the forgetfulness of the self. A school was opened with seven to ten pupils "from the city's best Catholic families"; what they meant by "best" is not explicit in the narrative. They also gave music and painting lessons. The fees helped them to pay rent to the priest and cover their basic expenses. But then, with the construction of the new church, the priests decided to move into the house, their own building, and the sisters were obliged to move. They bought a small wooden house at 1886 Albert Street in which they set aside a room to serve as a chapel, which was very important to them. And, it was written, they felt that "[w]ith their Divine Spouse in their midst, no difficulties could prove insuperable."[41] The notion of the "Divine Spouse" was cultivated as a common bond and a central component of religious identity; it was done in a simplistic manner, an analogy to the notion of a married woman in a patriarchal society. These were core values for the missionaries.

The sisters opened a small day school for boys and girls, and they enlarged the music and painting classes to accommodate more pupils. Archbishop Langevin wanted the sisters to direct the old St Mary's School, which had been functioning for several years with secular teachers, but he was not successful.[42] It was not until the school was moved to a new building in 1909 that the trustees offered to hire a few sisters, but under the direction of a lay principal who would be the only head of the school. The sisters did not accept because they would be immediately dependent on him.[43]

In 1905, the sisters started to attend normal school for the first time in Saskatchewan. This training, in the sisters' view, contributed to the maintenance and success of their public and private schools, since they became competent and legally qualified teachers. It was important for the congregation to prepare students for the departmental examinations, and, in 1907, two students from their little school took the exams.[44] The number of pupils increased at the day school until there were forty to fifty boys and girls. The work spread to all the rooms of the small house, which served various functions: the community room was transformed into a classroom, the kitchen into a music and painting room, and so on.

Meanwhile, Regina, the provincial capital, grew rapidly. With this in view, the sisters bought four lots near their property, but, as a whole, it was a small space in which to undertake any work of importance. St Mary's parish in Regina was mostly German; the sisters thought that, before long, groups of Catholic English-speaking people would form a second parish at the other end of the city, situated along the railway, southwest of the settled area. Speculators were buying land there. It is interesting how the sisters described the place: "Our dear foundresses remembered that when they wanted to show to a visiting Sister the coveted ground for their new convent, they could not determine the place, they could only indicate that in front of the place there was a cabin occupied by a family of negroes [sic] in an open field; there were no roads or demarcation in this solitary district."[45] In 1906, the sisters bought that piece of land, an entire block (about three acres), which would soon be surrounded by four streets. They remained in the old small house with the hope of being called by the only Catholic separate school (Gratton School), since several young professed sisters had passed their examinations. Their difficulties did not pass, but, in 1909, construction of the "real convent" began, although only the east wing was built. Nevertheless, the sisters made clear that it was a real convent with all the regular apartments for the community and the boarding school. The convent, which, of course, had a chapel, was ready in August 1910. The sisters opened the school immediately and began to provide boarding for girls; the number of pupils quickly increased to the point that a third classroom had to be created. It was the beginning of the Sacred Heart Academy, a private day school for girls in grades one to twelve.[46]

Changes in the ecclesiastic structure also took place at the time. The Diocese of Regina was established in 1910, and Monsignor O. Mathieu, bishop elect, was consecrated in Quebec on 5 November 1911. The sisters wrote: "On November 24, the respectful, submissive and devoted Sisters of Our Lady of the Missions of his episcopal town offered him their wishes of welcome and sincere homage. His Grace, on this occasion, blessed the convent."[47] In 1913, Bishop Mathieu asked the sisters to teach children in the basement of the pro-cathedral placed in the newly created and growing parish of the Holy Rosary, whose centre was located opposite the convent. This little school, which started with fifteen boys and girls, was the origin of the Holy Rosary School, whose building was completed in 1915. This school became the separate school of the Cathedral parish to which the Sacred Heart Academy belonged. At the Holy Rosary Separate School, the sisters first taught grades five, six, and seven, and the number of pupils increased.[48] In 1915, the bishopric became an archiepiscopal diocese, the Diocese of Regina, separate from the Diocese of St Boniface.

In February 1914, Reverend Mother M. St Pacôme came to Regina for her regular visitation and authorized the expansion of the convent. Meanwhile, the municipal council had denied a request for exemption from taxes on the congregation's property. The new part of the convent, which would later become the central part of the building, was finished by September 1914. Like the existing wing, it was divided by a large hall. In the basement were the children's refectory and recreation rooms; on the ground floor, the parlours, foyer, music rooms, and two classrooms; on the first floor, the chapel, sacristy, a room for commercial classes, a painting room, and a room for visitors; and on the second floor, dormitories for the older girls, bathrooms, washbasins, and a few private rooms.[49] Marking the separation of the sisters from the outside lay world was important, as was the enculturation of the sisters and students in the life of the convent.[50]

The sisters were active in converting and recruiting for future vocations, and their success was construed as blessings and encouragements that "the divine master lavished on his humble servants." It was noted in 1923 that, over the years, several young Protestants attending the schools had been converted to Catholicism. One of the girls entered the novitiate in 1914, after making her First Communion. For several years, Mother M. Pia of Jesus was in charge of the instruction and preparation for baptism of women and girls of the city.[51]

It is interesting to note that two sisters arrived from New Zealand in December 1916: one, Sister M. St Damien, a true artist, came to Canada to give painting lessons to some of the young sisters; the other, Sister M. St Felix, gave music lessons. At the beginning of 1919, the visiting sisters returned to New Zealand.

The mission continued recruiting vocations in their schools, shaping the Canadian province of the congregation. There is a record indicating that, between 1920 and 1922 inclusive, seven postulants became novices and then sisters.[52] The sisters at the Convent of the Sacred Heart were asked by the archbishop to make the altar breads; the sisters had special knives to cut the hosts and a special electric stove that enabled them to make 15,250 small and 1,600 large hosts each week.[53]

It is also interesting how the sisters intertwined their faith with events linked to the operation of their schools and convents. In 1921, the sisters finally obtained the solicited tax exemption, although only for one year; in each annual session thereafter, when this matter was brought up, the forces hostile to Catholics, one sister wrote, united to oppose the exemption. However, with unshaken confidence, the sisters asked the favour of St Jude, apostle of desperate cases; his feasts were solemnly celebrated, fervent novenas were made, prayers said, and nothing was omitted to obtain the protection of the saint. The sisters noted that their persevering confidence won, but also, on an earthly note, that they were thankful to their good archbishop who gave them the help of his influence. In 1923, the congregation obtained a tax exemption in perpetuity for their current and future buildings. At that point, there were also three colleges of three Protestant denominations, the Jesuit college, and the Grey Nuns Hospital that were not being taxed. The sisters wrote: "Glory to God and thanks to St. Jude for this remarkable victory over the spirit of opposition and injustice."[54]

When the congregation celebrated its twenty-fifth anniversary in 1923, there were twenty sisters at the Sacred Heart Convent. Sacred Heart Academy diversified its offerings in the 1920s and included commercial courses (accounting, administrative skills, typewriting). Certainly, the concern with secondary education for girls was an issue related to wider changes in society that were not alien to the feminist movement; the circulation of new curricular offerings in girls' education and the idea of girls' secondary schools circulated in education circles through the internationalization of ideas coming from teachers' organizations and associations with which the sisters were in touch.[55] English women educators argued for the benefits of girls' secondary education. The RNDMs cultivated from very early on a tradition of educating their sisters with post-graduate education. Since the congregation had the motherhouse in Deal, Kent, many studied in England. Thus, Mary St Domitille (Mary Margaret Hickey) obtained a master's degree in 1916 from the University of Canterbury and a doctorate in 1924 from the same university.[56] She was one of seven sisters from New Zealand who successfully completed graduate work during the inter-war years, and we know that the Canadian province received sisters from New Zealand. We don't have data for those years in Canada, but there are references to sisters obtaining degrees to teach at the high school level. We also know, as indicated before, that the sisters in the Canadian province attended meetings organized by the Ministry of Education, as well as annual meetings organized by teachers' federations in Manitoba and Saskatchewan. In 1924, the academy became a junior college of the University of Saskatchewan; as such, it was able to offer first-year university classes. The students were easily recognized by their uniform, which was a black dress with a blue hat in the winter and a white dress with a straw hat in the summer.[57]

In 1925, another extension was built comprising a spacious chapel, children's refectory and dormitory, and an entire western wing of four storeys for the sisters' apartments. A large gymnasium with a stage was built in order to serve as an auditorium or assembly room. The conception of space in the school was changing in tune with what was happening in the public schools. All the additions enlarged the building to the point that it ran the width of an entire block and could provide room for a modern Sacred Heart Academy. Further changes would take place in the 1930s.

Sacred Heart College, Regina

In 1925, the Canadian province obtained permission to build a new novitiate and a girl's residential junior college at the south entrance to the city, on the main highway, on a block of twenty-five acres of land across town from Sacred Heart Academy. It was called Convent of the Sacred Heart and College (both have the same name) and located close to the Jesuit Campion College. Campion College, named after Jesuit priest and scholar St Edmund Campion, had opened in 1918, known as the Catholic College of Regina, and provided a liberal education in the arts and sciences. In 1923, Campion was recognized as a junior college of the University of Saskatchewan.[58] Given the proximity to the Jesuit college, the sisters would obtain spiritual direction from the Jesuit fathers.[59] The novitiate that was located in St Eustache, Manitoba, was transferred to the Sacred Heart College Convent on 4 November 1926, and the convent was blessed on 26 April 1927 by Archbishop Mathieu. That same evening, a fiery cross, the symbol of the Ku Klux Klan, was burned on the grounds of the Sacred Heart Academy on the other side of the city.[60] The new house, the Sacred Heart Convent, had a chapel where the ceremonies of religious profession took place every year on 25 and 26 July. There was a steady flow of prospective sisters coming from the schools where the sisters taught. When, in 1930, the Canadian province was divided in two to save trips and resources, the Sacred Heart Province was one of them; it comprised Saskatchewan, and the motherhouse was located in the Sacred Heart College.[61] The other was St Mary's Province (Manitoba, Ontario, and later Quebec).

The college opened in September 1927 and admitted a large number of first- and second-year arts students. College classes previously
offered at the Sacred Heart Academy were moved to the new facility.
In 1928, Sacred Heart College became affiliated with the University of
Ottawa, making third- and fourth-year arts courses available to girls
from Western Canada in a Catholic environment that was for girls
only. A number of sisters came with graduate degrees, and sisters in
Canada pursued further education, particularly in Catholic colleges. In
the early days of Sacred Heart College, Sister Cecile Roddy and Sister
M. St Andrew (from New Zealand), both with master's degrees, taught
there. In 1949, the college stopped offering a bachelor of arts degree –
granted through its affiliation with the University of Ottawa – and then
closed the same year; the first-year university classes were transferred
to Sacred Heart Academy for a couple of years, but the second- and
third-year classes were discontinued completely. The college was an
early progressive initiative intertwining Catholic, gendered, and conservative values.

The sisters were aware of the reform movement for girls' education
that had an international dimension along with the feminist movement,
the new education movement. Regrettably, I could not find documentation, but the sisters' statements make clear that the sisters offered a
liberal education that would prepare girls to become Catholic wives
and to enter the work force without compromising the gender duality
sustained by the Church. One can therefore acknowledge that the entire
missionary effort by women sisters and the secondary schools, and particularly the college, represented a contradictory construction of gender
that was emerging out of the Church's and the congregation's interactions with modernity and with emerging socio-economic conditions at
the intersection of locality and internationalism.

In the Canadian prairies, the 1920s were times of changes in education that included the introduction of progressive ideas and the critique
of a bookish education and non-"practical" education expounded by
the rural communities.[62] Normal schools, and other cases, particularly
sisters coming from other countries, exposed the congregation to new
ideas. The congregation was international and had its motherhouse in
England. The interwar years were characterized by a desire for international cooperation that, although not new, reached a high point, not
only in women's organizations (for example, the International Council
of Women; Women's International League for Peace and Freedom; International Woman Suffrage Alliance; and the National Council of Women
of Canada, established in 1893), but also in teachers' organizations

and organizations related to the new education movement.[63] As mentioned earlier, after the Canon Law of 1917 regulating congregations, the RNDM Generalate restricted the readings and tried to centralize educational matters to protect the sisters from the winds of modernity conveyed in "profane literature."[64] However, the Generalate seems to have selected educational ideas that the congregation could work out within prescribed doctrinal limitations. But there is something else of note – locality also played a role. The mission was inserted in a regional configuration of emerging ideologies and experiences often influenced by US social and educational movements. In the processes, the Church, out of necessity, developed a Catholic engagement with modernity. The prairies proved to be fertile soil for social movements and reform. Women's reform in the west carried out the work initiated by their sisters in the east. In the building of a newer society, women, who worked alongside men, developed a sense of equality. The *Grain Growers' Guide* (started in 1908) had included a women's column since 1911, while the Grain Growers' Association of Manitoba, Saskatchewan, and Alberta endorsed women's suffrage. The west also had women who became nationally known, like the five women involved in the Persons' Case of 1929, in which the Supreme Court decreed that women were persons for legal purposes. But there were other important socio-economic changes generated by the Great War and its aftermath. As Friesen put it, "the new realities included a community that was more industrialized than ever before, more than ever plagued by French-English tensions, and as preoccupied by regional problems in the Maritimes as in the west. The era of farm supremacy was over."[65] The sisters responded to the new situation with changes in their programs, including the provision of commercial courses and the creation of a college of liberal arts for women.

Perhaps most importantly, French-Canadian upper-class women embraced feminist causes with philanthropic tones and created the Fédération nationale Saint-Jean-Baptiste, an umbrella organization for religious and secular associations that was concerned with women's activities in charitable associations and emerging issues in education and in the work force. Marie Lacoste Gérin-Lajoie, a distinguished Catholic, directed the fédération for twenty years and collaborated with local branches of the National Council of Women of Canada (the Montreal branch was created in 1893). The important point here is that the fédération and the sisters of the Congrégation Notre-Dame approached Monsignor Bruchési in 1906 to obtain approval for a classical college for women, with courses that would lead to a bachelor of arts degree. When, in 1908, Bruchési learned of the opening of the French lycée, a lay classical college for girls in Montreal, he gave authorization the same year to the congregation to open the École d'enseignement supérieur pour les filles, also in Montreal. Although I have not thus far found references to that école (named collège in 1926) in the documents related to the Sacred Heart College, it is difficult not to associate initiatives of these kinds.[66] Furthermore, the congregation had a committed engagement with the education of women. Was the creation of the college an expression of a feminist endeavour? As mentioned before, Catholic women's colleges created an interesting intersection with the modern world and with socio-economic changes framing the sisters' and the Church's missionary work. Although the sisters worked within the theory of the complementarity of sexes that framed their own religiosity, the RNDM as the Congregation of Notre Dame claimed spaces for women by reason of their gender.[67]

The Great Depression shook the congregation at a point when the various houses were in the process of consolidation. They had gone through the influenza of 1918 that had taken the lives of a few sisters, and, in the first two decades, the congregation had also had many cases of tuberculosis and heart conditions. Subsequently, living conditions had improved. However, the dusty years set a new challenge for the sisters, when once again they encountered difficult material circumstances.

Chapter Six

The Dusty Years to the Post-war Years

The late 1920s and the dusty 1930s were not easy in the Canadian prairies. The 24 October 1929 crash of the US stock market brought poverty and unemployment. In 1929, the crop was poor, especially in the southern part of the prairies, and the pattern of dry weather, dust storms, and poor crops was repeated for ten years. The year 1929 was also the year of the school question in the Saskatchewan provincial election. The school question had taken on many different shapes, from objections against legislation dealing with financial arrangements for separate schools to, by 1914, a shift to attacking the separate school system itself; by late 1915, this hostility had transformed into an attack on the teaching of languages other than English.[1] In the 1920s, the Orange Order and the Saskatchewan School Trustees Association kept the school question alive by calling for the elimination of both the French language and the separate schools. To compound matters further, the presence of Protestant children, albeit in small numbers, in public schools controlled by Catholic ratepayers was used as an example of the reason for religious freedom.[2] The revival of the Ku Klux Klan in the United States after World War I brought an anti-black, anti-Catholic, anti-Jewish, and anti-foreigner ideology; by 1923, the Klan was strong in the urbanized north of the United States, and its reach stretched across the Canadian border.[3] When the Klan's professional organizers became active in Saskatchewan in 1927, the school question was alive and being hotly debated, and the Klan's presence added to the hostility.[4] In 1929, the new Conservative government of J.T.M. Anderson supported national school ideas; in February 1930, Anderson introduced legislation initiatives related to the school question, including some prohibiting religious symbols and religious garb in public schools. In 1931, Anderson introduced an amendment to the School Act abolishing the use of French in the first year of school.[5] The sisters duly registered in their journals the way they coped with the situation. Since most of the sisters

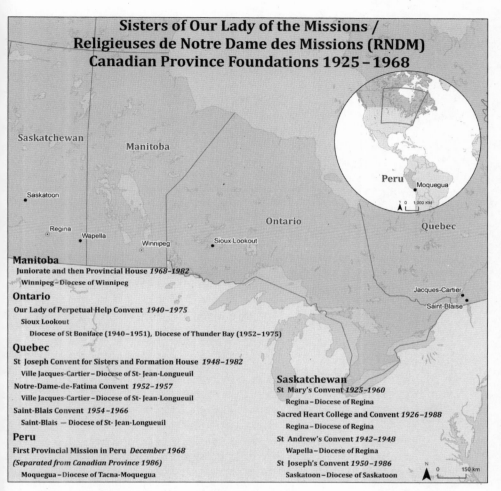

Sisters of Our Lady of the Missions / Religieuses de Notre Dame des Missions (RNDM) Canadian Province Foundations 1925–1968

Saskatchewan

Manitoba

Saskatoon

Peru

Moquegua

N   0   1,000 KM

Regina

Wapella

Winnipeg

Sioux Lookout

Ontario

Quebec

Jacques-Cartier

Saint-Blaise

Manitoba
Juniorate and then Provincial House *1968–1982*
   Winnipeg – Diocese of Winnipeg

Ontario
Our Lady of Perpetual Help Convent *1940–1975*
   Sioux Lookout
      Diocese of St Boniface (1940–1951), Diocese of Thunder Bay (1952–1975)

Quebec
St Joseph Convent for Sisters and Formation House *1948–1982*
   Ville Jacques-Cartier – Diocese of St-Jean-Longueuil
Notre-Dame-de-Fatima Convent *1952–1957*
   Ville Jacques-Cartier – Diocese of St-Jean-Longueuil
Saint-Blais Convent *1954–1966*
   Saint-Blais — Diocese of St-Jean-Longueuil

Peru
First Provincial Mission in Peru *December 1968*
(Separated from Canadian Province 1986)
   Moquegua – Diocese of Tacna-Moquegua

Saskatchewan
St Mary's Convent *1925–1960*
   Regina – Diocese of Regina
Sacred Heart College and Convent *1926–1988*
   Regina – Diocese of Regina
St Andrew's Convent *1942–1948*
   Wapella – Diocese of Regina
St Joseph's Convent *1950–1986*
   Saskatoon – Diocese of Saskatoon

N   0   150 km

6.1 Map of the RNDM Canadian province foundations, 1925 to 1968. Map designed by Graham Pope for the author.

wore a crucifix on the breast, they were ordered to change their manner of dress to continue teaching in public schools; some religious adopted a modified habit. But, in September 1930, the RNDM withdrew from the public school in Lebret and opened three private classrooms in the convent for pupils in grades one to twelve. The sisters were able to attract a large number of students who left the public school to enrol in the convent. After meeting with the minister of education in 1931, the sisters decided to wear a smock to cover the crucifix and rosary, and they returned to teach in the public school. Meanwhile, the convent in Lebret was a centre for Trinity College of London music examinations; the students also participated in the French concours, and, after petitioning the Department of Education in 1931, they were able to restore their centre for the writing of grades ten and twelve departmental examinations.[6] Very soon, the school question faded from the Saskatchewan political scene; the Depression became the centre of the people's focus. Then, in 1934, the Conservative government was defeated by the Liberals, and the situation normalized for the Catholics.[7]

In 1930, Mother M. St Pacôme, superior general of the congregation, made a major organizational change to the government of the Canadian congregation. Up to that point, there had been a local superior in each of the fourteen convents who was under the direction of one provincial superior for the communities in Saskatchewan, Manitoba, and Ontario. There were 129 professed sisters and 16 postulants and novices in training when Mother St Pacôme recommended that the five convents of Saskatchewan form one religious province under the patronage of the Sacred Heart and the nine convents in Manitoba and Ontario become St Mary's Province. Each province was to have a provincial superior with assistants. The changes aimed at simplifying the bureaucratic process and would cut travelling expenses in a time of economic hardship, since sisters were often transferred back and forth.[8] In July 1956, the two Canadian provinces united once again, under the name Province of the Sacred Hearts of Jesus and Mary, with the provincial house at St Edward's in Winnipeg and regional superiors in Saskatchewan and Quebec.[9]

The socio-economic conditions explain relations between the sisters and Catholic families in rural areas, particularly during the 1930s. As Ruth Sandwell explains, despite the dominance of commercial wheat farms, not all of those working on the land were engaged in commercial farming enterprises. Many had modest goals, such as obtaining enough goods for their household while earning a small income from seasonal work and the sale of any surplus products.[10] In normal times, it was a difficult life, but the drought and the Depression aggravated the conditions to extremes. Sandwell writes that the number of farms on the prairies in 1941 was just under 300,000. That year, the author says, there were 60,000 farm families, made up of Métis and Indigenous peoples, immigrants from Ukraine, other European countries, Britain, and those who had come from Central Canada.[11]

Most Canadian sisters had not left for foreign missions, but, in 1930, Mary Agnes Blaquière was sent to French Indo-China. She accompanied Mother M. Imelda, visitatrix to Tonkin, and remained there for forty years, working with the poor and teaching music and regular classes.[12] The Canadian province received sisters coming from other missions in the world, but the Canadians, by and large, did not leave the country for other missions, giving them room to develop a way of living their identity as Canadian RNDMs.

In some of the congregation's houses in Manitoba, the situation was extreme; such was the case in Portage la Prairie (St John the Baptist Convent). People in the parish were impoverished and could not pay fees, but gave the sisters vegetables and other foods they had produced. There were also annual grocery showers that strengthened the relations between the sisters and the community. In 1935, the convent discontinued the phone service to save money, but the taxes could not be paid because most students went to the public school and those who remained could not pay fees. By 1937, the school only had twenty-two students able to pay something. On 24 June, the sisters closed the convent and left Portage la Prairie. In other places in Canada, the sisters continued their work in the midst of hardships.

Still, for the most part, the convents became centres of Catholic activity. Official visits to Regina included the apostolic delegate in June 1935 and Cardinal Villeneuve in May 1936. Both used the venue of Sacred Heart College to meet with delegates from the various congregations in the area. Through the parishes and the clergy, as well as the Jesuits (their neighbours), female congregations were integrated into the Church network, although there were limited relations among the women religious of various congregations.

In February 1934, with the intervention of the sisters and a priest, Reverend and Dr J.E. Cahill, the Alumnae Association of the Sacred Heart was created. As was customary, the language of the document conveyed the idea that the initiative had come from the alumnae and that "Father Cahill voiced his approval for the creation of the association. He stated that it was a means of bringing the Sisters in contact with their own pupils, to whom they could give practical advice and counsel."[13] One of the first tasks was to organize activities to collect funds. By 1938, the economic depression had made a tremendous impact, as very few were able to pay fees to the congregations' Saskatchewan schools, especially at Sacred Heart College. The situation was so bad that the daily exposition of the Blessed Sacrament was discontinued because the sisters could no longer buy candles.

In the mid-1930s, the Sacred Heart Academy discontinued its primary day school at the convent in order to provide more courses in the secondary school; the school started to admit only pupils who had completed grade eight and were ready for commercial or high school.[14] The commercial department of the academy was successful in the 1930s (as well as in the 1940s), and annually turned out a good number of young women who obtained positions as stenographers, accountants, and bookkeepers. The school had a double dimension, being religiously conservative while also trying to adapt to the socio-economic context, including increasing urbanization and financial networks and new trends in education.[15] The spiritual life of the students was cultivated through social activities during the school year and also through the Sodality of the Blessed Virgin Mary, annual retreats, seminary contributions, aid to home and foreign missions, and work for the Holy Childhood Association. Music, art, and drama had a central place in the life of the school. In the 1940s, the school added, with funds from benefactors, a modern and well-equipped household science laboratory to teach domestic arts. By 1948, the school had two hundred students, and there were twenty-six sisters in the community.[16]

Religious Vacation Schools

In 1932, Archbishop C. McGuigan and his priests launched the religious vacation school movement throughout the Regina Archdiocese; it spread to the provinces of Manitoba and Ontario.[17] The archbishop asked the religious communities to send sisters to different districts to teach catechism during the holidays, and the RNDMs became fully engaged in the movement. The January 1933 issue of *The Message of Our Lady of the Missions* includes an article from Canada that made manifest the understanding of mission and the intentionality:

> The vast mission-field of Canada offers ample scope for the ardent zeal of brave missionaries. Still, in spite of their great earnestness, owing to the extensive area of the districts, many people and more especially the Indians, and their children, are deprived of instruction in our Holy Faith.[18]

It was usual that two or three sisters would spend a week in the parish and after that a week in one or more missions connected with the parish. They kept regular hours of instruction for the children and placed great importance on recess, when games in which the sisters participated were played. The sisters collected old catechism books and prepared holy pictures, medals, and prizes for the end of the courses. After school hours, the sisters visited families and took care of the sacristies and whatever needed to be washed and mended. Most of the boarding schools became catechetical centres. Boys and girls would go to live in the convent for a week or two, which allowed many children

6.2 Vacation school, Theodore. First Communion class, July 1953. Source:
Author's collection.

to receive their first Holy Communion; others prepared themselves for
a year or two for confirmation. There were a number of centres running
vacation schools that used Regina as a point of reference; there was a
large one in Ceylon, 75 miles (120.7 kilometres) from Regina, and others
at Bergfield, Bengough, and Big Beaver.

The sisters had a general registry of 405 Catholic children, who came
not only from the villages but also from homes scattered all over the
province. Many who lived too far away to come in every day lived in
tents at the centre during their period of instruction.[19] In a very short
time, the vacation schools had gained ground in Manitoba, supported
by the archbishops. The RNDM quickly organized twelve groups of
sisters, with each group including two or three sisters. The sisters were
required to visit the few scattered families within distances no nearer
than 8 to 12 miles (12 to 20 kilometres), and to live like the Apostles, depending upon strangers for lodging and food. The sisters found themselves face to face with the poverty of the 1930s: many farmers lived
many miles away from a mission; they had not had crops for years; the
children, in many cases, did not have clothes; and the parents had lost
faith in God. The sisters tried hard to make the children realize that God
loved and cared for them. They also encountered communities that

only spoke French, where many had lost their faith; others sent their children to the sisters on the condition that they be taught in French. The sisters, aware that many families did not attend Church or follow Church prescriptions, wrote: "We spoke to them of their obligations, and their duty of obedience to the authority of the Church. Hay making started early in July, and the children are needed at home from the age of eight, when they start to milk the cows and do similar work. Some have to drive them forth and back every morning and evening." "I don't believe I ever saw such workers," exclaimed one of the sisters in the narrative. "The whole thing is making a living; their soul is secondary with them."[20] What the sisters did not fully grasp was that the families were struggling to survive. Indeed, the sisters had difficulties connecting to reality from their binary world. In April 1938, a catechetical conference took place in Regina, with priests, seminarians, and delegates from sisters' congregations coming together to design plans for the summer vacation schools and catechetical work. The summer vacation schools were in operation well into the 1950s.[21]

World War II and Its Aftermath

In spite of World War II and its impacts, new missions were established within Canada. In 1940, five RNDM sisters moved to Sioux Lookout, Ontario, to replace the Sisters of Loretto in a separate school that was already established. Sioux Lookout, a little town built on a hill overlooking Pelican Lake, located 279 miles (449 kilometres) from Winnipeg, was at the time part of the Diocese of St Boniface, until 1952 when it became part of the Diocese of Thunder Bay. There were 110 pupils in four classrooms. Grades one to eight were taught, with two grades in each classroom; there were five sisters and two lay teachers on staff. There were also music lessons, church choirs, drama pieces, and, of course, the Christmas concert.[22] It was a mining region; lumber was the industry, and it was also an outfit point for trappers, fisherman, and hunters. There was a hospital for Indigenous people run by the federal government. Not much information is available about this mission.

In 1942, the sisters were invited to St Andrew's, a Catholic Scottish settlement near Wapella, Saskatchewan, where there was only a cemetery, a church, and a hall. The three sisters who were sent there took up accommodation in the hall, which also served as the school. With the help of volunteers, the sisters built a convent. The school remained small, and the four sisters there at the time closed the convent in 1948 and returned to Regina.[23] In November 1945, the mother provincial had received authorization from the Council of the General Administration to withdraw the sisters from the school due to their difficulties with the parish priest.[24] The sisters had space to assert themselves with the clergy when necessary, given their pontifical character. However, this agency did not translate to a fluid decision-making process in which the sisters could have a voice inside the congregation, given its hierarchical character. The central administration of the congregation – the Generalate – expected the provinces of the congregation to adhere faithfully to the customs established by the foundress. Keeping uniformity was the means to build community, and the language of sacrifice would encourage this "virtue," which was seen as necessary to secure uniformity. The sisters thus cultivated a language of self-denial and obedience that would remain as a residual element for some time, even during the renewal period.[25]

The references to the war in the sisters' journals always contain a touch of mystical vision centred in their truth – the Catholic doctrinal truth – although the bombing of one of the houses in England would affect them badly. In the journal of the Convent of St Martha, from the Elie, Manitoba, Franco-Manitoban setting, a writer conveyed her reflections in January 1942:

Another year has dawned. What shall it bring to individuals, to nations, to the world at large? Shall it be Peace? That lasting Peace based on justice? It is the universal desire but are Rulers and Subjects willing and ready to give the dear Master His undeniable rights? May the loving Emmanuel give each and all light and courage but above all unlimited confidence in His Supreme Power.[26]

The end of the war opened a period of transition to dramatic socio-economic, political, and cultural changes that characterized the "long 1960s." What was the situation in the RNDM schools from post–World War II until the long 1960s? Schools were renewed, and new programs emerged, increasing the number of students, which made the buildings inadequate; to make room for pupils, in 1944, the lower grades were abandoned except for kindergarten. There were not enough nuns for such an expansion in some of the missions, a problem that would be soon accentuated; the crisis of vocations was fully recognized in 1952 by the pope. In 1955, St Michael's in Brandon was renovated, and a new wing was built with modern classrooms and laboratory equipment, as well as a spacious auditorium-gymnasium.[27]

The sisters' regulated life was still fully enforced by the General Council that resided in Hastings, England. It is interesting to see the restrictions from 1945, restrictions that even in the next decade would sound part of the past and unacceptable; this point is in reference to the Sacred Heart Province of the Congregation in Canada. The minutes read:

> The Council does not approve of the Sisters going to the cinema to see the "Song of Bernadette." In a former "Process Verbal" of a few months ago it was mentioned that twelve Sisters went out to the cinema for the same purpose. Although the film was exhibited here with similar concessions – ecclesiastical permissions, etc. – none of our Sisters went, it is not our custom. Even when it was screened for children only, the Sisters did not accompany their pupils, they arranged with some ladies to take their pupils.[28]

The order of the General Council to enforce this restricted world would become disjunctive with values and ways of life after the war. The RNDM sisters became familiar in the 1950s with the work of theologians of the "nouvelle théologie" – who would be the precursors of Vatican II – which aimed at tuning the Church to the modern world; the sisters in the Canadian province were taking courses with theologians in Ottawa, Saskatoon, and St Boniface. The religious formation movement advocating the sisters' theological education reached Canada in the 1950s. They also had higher levels of education, including university degrees.

The post-war era into the 1950s brought changes that started to show the misalignment between the sisters' culture and language of sacrifice, submission, and the evilness of the world and the world around them. In 1947, the General Chapter decided that there would be only one class of sisters, rather than have choir sisters (entrusted mainly with the governance, administration, educational work, and care of the sick), auxiliary sisters (devoted to the manual work of the house; their dress was slightly different, and they did not do the prayers of the Little Office of the Blessed Virgin Mary), and oblate sisters (or, third order; they had no canonical vows and did not wear a religious habit like the one worn by choir or auxiliary sisters; they were illegitimate, aged women, or had been engaged to be married).[29] The sisters started to experience profound contradictions between their own culture, their own universe, and the rest of the world, even at the religious level. Their symbolic universe, particularly as enforced by the Generalate, did not function as a level of legitimation that integrated various layers of meaning.[30] Already in 1950, Pius XII had started to move towards change,[31] inviting both male and female religious and secular institutes in each country to organize themselves into federations and conferences, while also calling on the institutes to adapt themselves by creating a happy alliance between the new and the old.[32] In Canada, the Canadian Religious Conference (CRC) was founded in 1954 and included both male and female congregations, 186 in total, three quarters of which were female.[33] Within a broader context, the war had led to a questioning of racist and ethnocentric ideas, and theories of cultural relativism began to emerge more clearly in the "long 1960s" (1958–74). The certainty of religious truth – still present in Catholic schools until after Vatican II – did not match a world that was moving rapidly towards further secularization and pluralism. After the war, Canada underwent profound political, economic, and demographic changes that increased the call for changes within education. The demographic changes created by the "baby boom," post-war immigration, and the arrival of 160,000 displaced persons between 1946 and 1952 made the expansion of the educational state imperative.[34] The congregations felt the impact in their schools. From the late 1940s to the mid-1960s, Canadian children entered schools in larger numbers and stayed longer; in response, the congregation expanded some of their schools. However, a dramatic change was in the making and was fully revealed in the long 1960s. Immediately after 1945, almost every Canadian province launched reviews of their educational systems and of the "aims and objectives of education."[35] As Stevenson put it, there was a clear realization that Canada could not rely on the educational institutions as they were before the war.[36]

In 1950, the Province of the Sacred Heart (Saskatchewan) established a new house in the city of Saskatoon, located 161 miles (259 kilometres) from Regina via the current highway. The purpose was to provide a house of study for the sisters, since the Basilian fathers conducted university classes on the University of Saskatchewan campus in Saskatoon. This house would give the sisters the opportunity to attend classes offered by Catholic priests. Some of the sisters who lived there taught in the separate school system; those who did not study at the university attended teachers college. A number of sisters came in the summer to take summer courses. There were similar facilities in Regina and Winnipeg, where the sisters attended the Collège de St Boniface, run by the Jesuits.[37]

In 1947, the RNDM delegates to the General Chapter of the Canadian provinces met with Bishop Forget of the Diocese of St Jean-Longueuil, near Montreal, who offered the sisters a school in a newly opened district 12 miles (19.3 kilometres) south of Montreal, later known as Ville Jacques-Cartier. The following year, in 1948, two sisters opened a school with the help of lay teachers. A few years later, the sisters built St Joseph's Convent. The sisters taught among the poor at École Hélène-de-Champlain, a public elementary school for girls. Most importantly for the sisters, in 1952, they opened a novitiate for French-speaking girls; after a while, they realized that a Juvenate was necessary to recruit "vocations" coming from the secondary school. In 1952, they opened another house in Ville Jacques-Cartier, Notre-Dame-de-Fatima, for sisters who were teaching grades one to eight at a nearby public elementary school. They closed this house in 1957. Finally, the congregation opened a house in St Blaise, Quebec, a village situated a 30 mile (48.2 kilometre) drive away from Ville Jacques-Cartier in a rural area. The sisters wrote:

> In 1954 the Education Authorities, who in the province of Quebec are all Catholic, thank God, decided to build in St Blaise a central school which would be large enough to accommodate the children from the surrounding districts as well as those from the village itself. The higher authorities in the County granted the permission on condition that a religious Community would assume the direction of the new school.[38]

The building would have classrooms on the lower floors, and the entire second floor would be for the use of the sisters and included a chapel. They had "the Divine Master present in the Tabernacle," and there was a community room, refectory, kitchen, laundry, and ten "cells" (small personal rooms for the sisters). There were four sisters who were also in charge of the sacristy, the children's choir, and altar boys; they also took charge of visits to the sick and poor in the parish and taught music lessons. The school opened in 1954 with 218 pupils, many of them bused in from surrounding areas, and there were eight classes for those in grades one to ten. The students were involved in Catholic Action. The sisters left St Blaise in 1966.[39]

In 1955, Sacred Heart College (the bachelor of arts program had closed in 1949) had also started a secondary school of the same name as an offshoot of Sacred Heart Academy, which had been located in another part of the city since 1905. During the 1950s, the sisters continued their work in their schools across the prairies, although there was a degree of unevenness in their financial situation. The situation will further unravel in the 1960s and 1970s.

Religious Education in the Pre–Vatican II Period

The Catholic Church's official language of education – the modality of thinking and talking about education – and how the Church thought about education remained rooted in a strict neo-Thomism/neo-scholasticism sponsored by the Vatican in spite of the intense pluralism within neo-Thomism and a return to patristics.[40] Educational content was to be guided by Pius XI's encyclical on Christian education (*Divini Illius Magistri*), distinguished by its anti-modernist tones, its rejection of naturalism, and its focus on the close connection between family, Church, and state. Article 30 reads: "In the first place the Church's mission of education is in wonderful agreement with that of the family, for both proceed from God, and in a remarkably similar manner. God directly communicates to the family, in the natural order, fecundity, which is the principle of life, and hence also the principle of education to life, together with authority, the principle of order."[41]

Before Vatican II, the sisters attended lectures and courses to analyse the encyclical of Pius XI, but, as mentioned before, they were also exposed to pedagogical ideas and conceptions of education coming from the normal schools, as well as curricular changes influenced in the late 1920s and 1930s by the principles of progressive education. The normal school in Winnipeg, Manitoba, through its director, William McIntyre, embodied these influences. The private parish schools followed the provincial curriculum, as did the separate schools and, of course, the public schools, albeit in a mediated fashion; however, we do not know the extent of the mediation. The textbooks for religious education at the high school level were in line with strict neo-Thomism as interpreted by the Magisterium – such was the case with *Bible Studies*, originally published in 1881, and *Our Quest for Happiness: The Story of Divine Love*, published in 1951.[42]

What made the Franco-Manitoban communities unique was the French issue and its close connection with the Catholic Church, which worked to influence the pedagogical dimension of the schools. In all the French-area schools in which the RNDM taught, the students participated in the provincial French "concours" (exam competitions).[43] The teaching of French was conducted through various means, one of which was drama, with pieces of classic theatre directed by a sister (in the case of Letellier, it was Sister Marie Ste Reine). Among the works the sisters mentioned in journals was *Marcia or the Conversion of a Vestal*; the selected pieces were Christian, and the students were motivated to take on the soul and spirit of their respective roles. There were also literary clubs. The ultimate goal for the sisters was that the children learn to love the "Bon Dieu."

In general, regarding life in the schools in which the sisters were involved, there were intersections of regulations and directives that came from the central administration of the congregation, the Vatican, and the congregation's General Council, along with actual demands emerging from the communities, the local and regional Church, and the provincial curriculum – all amid the political changes affecting education.

Thus, on 18 February 1937, Archbishop Sinnot of Winnipeg circulated a letter to the clergy:

> In accordance with the wishes of the Holy See, as expressed in Canon 711 of the Code of Canon Law, I am very anxious that the Confraternity of Christian Doctrine should be established in every parish in this Archdiocese. The general purpose is to bring to all the faithful, adults as well as children, a better knowledge of Catholic doctrine and to that end to group together those in every parish who are interested in the spread of Christ's Kingdom upon earth.
>
> There is, no one can deny, a deplorable lack of knowledge of Christian truth among our Catholic people.
>
> ...
>
> In almost all the annual reports reference is made by the different Pastors to this subject. The universal cry is that our people do not know their religion and it is on this account that they are lax and negligent in attendance at Mass and in the reception of the Sacraments.[44]

Indeed, the sisters taught the Catholic truths without questioning or even thinking of enquiring about them. An editorial of *Stella Oriens*, the 1942 yearbook of Sacred Heart College, reads: "Especially are we shown the Catholic viewpoint on all matters, the rightness of the Church's mind, thus enabling us to uphold and defend our Christian Faith. The story of the ages has been unfolded to us, in which we see the Church as the greatest civilizing and uplifting force in history."[45] The college, as said before, offered liberal arts courses towards a bachelor of arts degree for young women and was recognized by the University of Ottawa. The college also embodied the tensions that existed between the necessary adaptation to socio-economic pressures, the Church's conservative teachings, the charism of the congregation, and the workings of internal theological movements within and at the margins of the Church. The documents available suggest that, in the 1940s and 1950s, the RNDM's vision of education was in line with the Magisterium, but also explored pedagogical possibilities in terms of teaching and learning the subjects required by the Department of Education. In the case of schools, sisters interviewed in 2012 could not articulate what would be unique to an RNDM understanding of education. The responses were similar and pointed to methods they learned in teacher preparation coursework and in workshops and observations of other sisters' classes.[46] One of the sisters who started teaching in 1959, Hilda Lang, said: "[T]he values we wanted to instil in the children were God's unconditional love and the model of Jesus in their lives."[47] Sister Cécile

Granger said: "I understand it [education] as seeing a personality. It's not hammering stuff in their heads; being kind, no scolding as much as possible. It's our behaviour in the classroom. Being a model, calm."[48] One sister who taught from 1952 in Saskatchewan referred to the importance of values: "Values that an effort was made to instil: love of God ... It is difficult to describe how spirituality permeated life in the classroom because goodness, virtue, prayer, connection to the Church are caught more than taught. It was probably more a process of osmosis than anything."[49] Religious education remained very indoctrinating, as the sisters did not have theological formation at the time. Reflecting on the past in light of Vatican II, Sister Cécile Granger said: "I loved it [Vatican II]. I was hoping things would come out. I was not at ease with the Church. I had not theology, nothing like that. But I knew that they were doing something beautiful."[50]

In November 1954, the RNDM houses in Ste Rose, St Eustache, and Elie received a canonic visit as part of a review, organized by the Archdiocese of Winnipeg, of women religious of the French language. The writers of the report observed that the austerity observed in each of the communities made them greenhouses that kept the sisters in strict observance, even to the smallest detail, to the point that it impeded a just exteriorization of their personality; that their semi-cloistered environment imposed more than what the Canon Law demanded for the same kind of congregations located elsewhere; and that the practice made of each convent a closed garden, where the sisters' communications with the outside world, even with the alumnae, were reduced to a minimum. The conclusion drawn was that the semi-cloistered life the foundress had established was a part of her time and did not allow the sisters to fulfil the original aims of the congregation. In particular, an observation was placed in the conclusion that the semi-cloister did not facilitate an encounter with a young woman that could be grounded in a mutual understanding in a way that could lead to a vocation. The report also questioned the prescribed number of little prayers that the sisters had to recite at various times, including when they dressed, with no or doubtful value, and questioned the time spent in the Office of the Holy Virgin in contemplation and saying prayers. In the authors' view, the congregation had to adapt better to the times. Pius XII was moving towards a level of adaptation; however, there was a cautionary word included in the introductory component of the document: that in the effort to adapt to progress in contemporary mores, the congregations should not lend themselves in some way to the exigencies of the world, to its mad seductions and appeals, in order to have vocations.[51]

Chapter Seven

The Church and the Classroom before Vatican II: Spirituality in the Schools and Recruitment

Examining material culture is significant to understanding the process of enculturation, whereby young women were assimilated into the life of the convent, in which the building itself was used to adopt appropriate behaviours and attitudes. The grille played a central role in leading the sisters to a semi-cloistered life when the conditions were there; quite often, however, the living situation was not conducive to this life of contemplation and work. The tabernacle dwelling of the King of Kings had a special significance. Having "our dear Lord under [our] roof, where, henceforth [we] would be able to come each day to open our hearts and lay the offering of our acts of fidelity, self-sacrifice, and generous devotedness"[1] was important, as Jesus was their divine spouse.

As soon as the sisters were able to build a "real convent," its spatial ordering (the grille, the parlour, the chapel as a sacred space), the need to respect the space, the behaviours in relation to different spaces, such as walking without running, and the small rituals and silences were part of the enculturation. The building of a "real convent" was therefore fundamental to the leaders of the congregation in order to keep uniformity through complex rules that could not be enacted in the early years of the foundations in the prairies. Everything converged towards reinforcing norms and the passing on of norms, ranks, appropriate ways of behaving, and the virtues of humility and obedience, which were all reinforced by the discourse the sisters weaved into every aspect of their lives.

The language of sacrifice is threaded all through the writings of the first decades. The narrations of the first years of the Sacred Heart Convent in Regina share the language of narrations from other foundations: references to "flowers of destitution" and privations. The sisters' house was uncomfortable, the constant care of the stove was inconvenient, and there was no central heating; space was tight, as the chapel, separated by a curtain, was also used as a parlour and music room.[2] Young people in the community were sometimes amused by the sound of the bell ringing for community exercises and would scream "Auction sale" or "Dinner is ready" upon hearing the bell.[3] These experiences were construed in the sisters' written memories as crosses to bear of privation, hard work, and even painful opposition, and, yes, they also write about those days being the good old days. We may wonder, however, how these were considered to be the good old days.

The sisters and the clergy greatly emphasized the notion of the sisters as spouses of Jesus. We can still find references to the spouses of Jesus in the publication celebrating the Golden Jubilee of the congregation in Canada in 1949. This concept appears in all the narrations, but starts to fade in the 1950s. There are no theological references in the writings of the sisters. There is, however, emphasis placed on the understanding of the relationship between sacrifices and good grounding of their missionary work. In general, the crosses to bear, painful separations from family, and serious sicknesses were considered to have been granted by Divine Providence to His humble servants; these were all gifts and no less beneficial than the positive aspects of life. This thinking was based on the notion that the Divine Master inseparably united the cross as the instrument of both grace and redemption.[4]

Veronica Dunne, who in more recent times served as provincial superior, said that "as both a student of the RNDMs and later as a teacher [she started teaching in 1968] the ethos of faith permeated our classrooms and our teaching. I remember pictures on the walls, the sodalities and confraternities of Christian doctrine that were part of everyday life. We also studied and taught about our faith."[5] It is difficult to trace the spirituality intrinsic to the congregation in the sisters' school life beyond particular devotions and religious feasts. The spiritual core was provided through the values of the Church and its understanding of true Christian education, as set by the official Catholic literature and popes such as Pius XI, as well as its ongoing resistance to modernity. The schools celebrated religious feasts related to the congregation; in the case of the RNDM, the first patronal feast is Pentecost and the second is the Visitation of the Blessed Virgin Mary, in line with the inspiration of the congregation. There were many religious celebrations, with a major emphasis on those related to the characteristics of the communities: in Franco-Canadian settings in the prairies, the feast of Saint John the Baptist (or Saint-Jean-Baptiste) was very important; in Irish communities, or where there was an Irish sister in the house, St Patrick's Day became a major feast. However, the missionary work and its intersection with the politics of life in the communities often laid the foundation for complex spiritual, political, and educational configurations, and the festivities themselves embodied efforts to keep cultural values that were not part of the dominant ethos.

The parish priests had an influence on the schools' religious observances and festivities, in particular in relation to special devotions. At St Edward's in Winnipeg, for example, there were many devotions, especially in the 1950s. One of the sisters recalled that Monsignor Rheaume had a special devotion to Ste Therese and that, for the twenty years that he was parish priest, there were novenas or triduums in her honour. There was also the crowning of Our Lady at the end of May. As in other parish schools, there were the Children of Mary and special clubs; in the 1930s, many girls were in the Society of the Holy Angels, while the boys were in the Society of St Alphonsus, and children in grade one were in the Society of the Holy Infancy. In the 1940s, there were the Crusaders. High school girls were in the Agnesian Club and the boys in the Altar Society. The Knights of Columbus gave prizes to students in the various schools.[6]

The sisters' language of happiness and joy in their first twenty-five years in Canada appears to be related to their authorization to have "the presence of the most Blessed Sacrament" in their new houses and their joy in attending Holy Mass. There is also a language of pain and sacrifice, as mentioned before, happily offered to God.[7] For example, the sisters construed the parishioners' scorn and indifference to their presence in Portage la Prairie as a sign of predilection from Divine Providence, who desired to be their only resource.[8] This approach was reflected in a form of traditionalism in the schools, where all the answers to religious questions were already given, thus providing a sense of direction.

The silences, rules, special rooms, statues of saints, internal celebrations, visits of statues, like the replica of Our Lady of the Cape being brought to Regina in 1950 and the enthronement of the Sacred Heart, among other special celebrations, were powerful enculturating elements. On the occasion of the visit of the statue of Our Lady of the Cape, the "Children of Mary formed a living rosary in her honour and sixty students of Sacred Heart Academy, wearing their uniform, veils and blue mantles, represented either the beads of the Mysteries, or the prerogatives of Our Lady; the Prefect of the Sodality placed a crown of white, red, and yellow roses at the feet of the statue."[9]

As late as 1958, *The Message* registered the enthronement of the Sacred Heart in the RNDM community and the Sacred Heart Academy – the blessing and placement in various rooms of statues related to the Sacred Heart devotion. The ceremony was quite elaborate. Weeks

7.1 Statues related to the Sacred Heart devotion. Source: Author's collection.

before the ceremony, the students learned that with the enthronement would come rich graces and blessings for the faculty and students. On the day of the ceremony, the priest spoke to the students about the Sacred Heart devotion. The record reads:

At three o'clock the solemn hour had arrived, and the girls entered the Chapel for the enthronement ceremony. The altar and sanctuary had been decorated with great care. The statues which were to be enthroned in the various classrooms were in a place of honour ready to be blessed. Rev. W. Wadey officiated at the ceremony and was assisted by Rev. J. Deutscher and Rev. J.C. Frey. After the official enthronement hymn was sung, the solemn blessing took place. The Apostles' Creed was recited by all as an act of faith and reparation for all schools that exclude the truths of our faith. The short address which followed impressed on all the meaning of the enthronement and our obligations to the Sacred Heart prayers, sacrifices, and love for the Eucharist. Finally, there was voiced a plea to all students to be true, undaunted apostles of the enthronement. An Act of

7.2 Enthronement of the Sacred Heart ceremony. Source: Author's collection.

Consecration was read followed by prayers for absent students, living and dead, former students, for the sick, and for all their families. As the twelve promises of the Sacred Heart were read, a girl from each class walked forward and placed a fresh rose before the newly blessed statues. While the students sang a hymn in the Chapel, the Sisters formed a procession.[10]

The students moved in a close Catholic milieu; from that positioning, one can understand their submersion in the Catholic ethos. In French communities, Catholic Action was particularly strong in the 1950s, adding a different layer with its social vision. However, the intense processes of secularization, rapid social changes in a pluralized and open world, and the social movements of the long 1960s would challenge the meaning-making process.

Recruitment during the Depression and Post-War Years

The schools were sites for recruitment, spaces that cultivated ways of being Catholic and the subjectivity of the Catholic girl. A 7 January 1932 journal entry for the Virgo Fidelis Convent in Letellier provides one of many examples. In the afternoon, the reverend mother provincial accompanied the reverend mother superior of the congregation, who was visiting Canada, to the classes, particularly those of the higher grades.

The rooms had been decorated in preparation. The children welcomed the visitors with enthusiasm and expressed their best wishes to the visitors in English and French. The reverend mother superior responded with maternal words and fervent zeal for the salvation of souls. The narrative says that she asked the students how many of them felt the call to religious life and "encouraged those who had that desire; then she showed the beauty of the Catholic religion and the privilege of a truly Catholic education."[11]

But the schools, in particular in French-Canadian settings, were exposed to new movements such as the Jeunesse étudiante chrétienne (JEC, a Christian youth association) that grew in Montreal first, starting in 1934. This movement involving the classic colleges, related to Catholic Action, would be influenced by French Catholic philosophers such as Emmanuel Mounier and Jacques Maritain, who were opening new avenues in theology that would engage the laypeople and the world. The movement grew in the 1930s and early 1940s. An entry from 8 November 1942 in the Letellier journal informs us that, towards the end of October, the school had received distinguished visitors representing the "Croisé-Jéciste" (JEC) in Canada. The group included well-known JEC promoter Father Lalande and Ms Benoit from Montreal, and Abbé Couture and Ms Laporte from St Boniface. The visitors talked to different groups of children and encouraged them to be involved in apostolic work in their milieu.[12] There were follow-up visits as well, and thus Father Blais, director of the Crusaders and Jécistes in the Diocese of St Boniface, visited the Crusaders and the Jécistes, spending part of the day with them in prayer and conferences.[13] The congregation held meetings with Father Blais to be informed of the movements.[14] It is important to note that, from the mid-1930s, Catholic Action – as groups involved in charity and social organizations – had a central role in the life of the parishes and the schools in French-Canadian communities and was a site of recruitment. During the Depression years, a number of young girls from the various places where the RNDMs had houses entered the novitiate. Many of them had high school or college education.[15]

After the war, recruitment methods became more sophisticated. The brochures that circulated starting in 1946 aimed at motivating girls to enter the congregation. One of these brochures had a front page showing the image of the Virgin Mary with the title "With Mary: In the Conquest of Souls" written in French.

The information inside the brochure was written in French as an imaginative dialogue in which a young girl asks questions of two nuns during a trip by train. The girl approaches the sisters with questions

7.3 *Avec Marie: À la Conquête des Âmes* (With Mary: In the Conquest of Souls), recruiting pamphlet. Source: RNDM-UK A/2E/7/3/12.

about the congregation, while her friend at first remains in her seat. When, during the conversation, the second girl, who has joined her friend to be introduced to the sisters, indicates that she loves nursing, the sisters point out that the congregation welcomes nurses who want to work in India, Australia, and other places. The young girls are also informed that to enter the congregation (to become a postulant) they need to be fifteen years of age or older. As illustrated by this example, the imagery of foreign missions became central to the congregation's recruitment strategy in the post-war period. The sisters tried to engage readers in the history of the congregation and its work through a professionally written and easily readable dialogue. A great deal of space in this particular brochure was occupied by pictures that conveyed the message that sisters were working in many different countries; there was even a picture of two Canadian sisters going on a mission to India in 1950, although the Canadian sisters did not travel very much. The emphasis was on the active life of the sisters, even as they were semi-cloistered. There were also pictures of the Chapel of the Novitiate in Ville Jacques-Cartier, Quebec, the congregation's novitiate for French-speaking aspirants, and of Canadian Church authorities, students in Ville Jacques-Cartier, various buildings in Canada, and the sisters' work in India and France. In reality, however, the opportunity to go on missions was very limited up to the late 1960s, when the Canadian sisters opened a mission in Peru.

The Generalate of the congregation also published a shorter professional pamphlet in English in 1946. This one was written in formal language and explained the aims of the congregation, its major goal of the salvation of souls, and the meaning of personal holiness. It was fashioned in the shape of a sister in her habit. On the first page, the stages of religious life were described, while a picture of the congregation's motherhouse in Hastings, England, conveyed the power of the institution, and a picture of a chapel communicated the presence of the Church. The pamphlet also made clear that, although applicants had to be at least sixteen years of age and no older than thirty, interested girls could begin earlier, at thirteen, in the Juniorate, where they would continue their schooling and have the opportunity to see the life of the sisters first hand. The written part was very formal, conveying the seriousness of the institution. This short pamphlet had an interesting feature: one drawing of the habit in black and one in white – depending on the place of mission. Upon turning the page, on the back of the shape were the words, "I am a Sister of Our Lady of the Missions ... My dress is very different, isn't it? I am different, too, for I belong to God in a special way." At the end, it said: "God loves me specially because I have given myself to Him, and He is preparing a special reward for me in heaven."[16] This pamphlet placed the sisters beyond the level of ordinary people, since they were said to be entering a life that would lead them to a very special eternal place, a life of perfection.

The Canadian province also produced a very elaborate booklet that explained who the sisters were, when the congregation was founded, where, and why. This publication was addressed to high school graduates, and "After graduation what?" was the leading question. However, many hands were needed in the convent, and girls who had not finished high school were also welcomed. The booklet suggested the convent would provide novices with the joy of work, in companionship

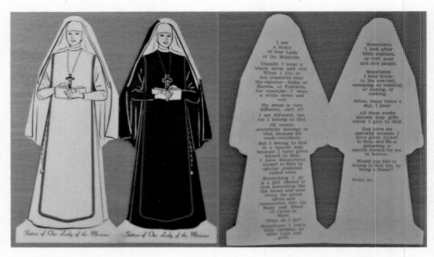

7.4 Recruiting pamphlet, 1946. Source: Congregation of Our Lady of the Missions pamphlet, 1946, RNDM-UK A/2E/7/3/12.

with others, and the joy of soul and of eternity. The steps from postulancy to the end of the novitiate were detailed. The pictures showed almost celestial-looking scenes of postulants receiving the habit. The novitiate was introduced to the prospective candidate as a challenge to undertake, but pictures that conveyed a joyful life in which there was room for recreation occupied most of the space. There was also information about the vows, and the vow of obedience was described as one in which the postulant renounced her own will: "Hence-forth she will do nothing but the will of God as manifested by her Superiors and the Rules and Constitutions." The sisters were also shown working in the schools through photographs of various activities, including helping the priest prepare his vestments for the Mass. The application form was part of the booklet. The prospective candidate was advised that if she made the decision to become a sister, she must act on it resolutely. The booklet concluded with the words: "In the meantime doubts and temptations against your vocation are sure to arise. Why? Because the devil will do all in his power to keep you from doing Christ's work. For a religious is one of his worst enemies."[17]

The sisters always talked of the call, of how they were touched by God. However, the congregation, like all others, was always active in attracting recruits in various ways, including active recruitment through

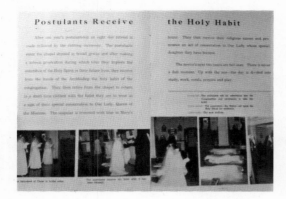

7.5 RNDM recruiting booklet. Source: The Congregation of Our Lady of the Missions, RNDM-UK A/2E/7/3/13.

retreats, presentations by priests, religious classes, and even agents.[18] I did not find any evidence in the archives of the involvement of professional agents, at least in the Canadian province. Sister Hilda Lang recalled that "on occasion we had visiting sisters from abroad speak to our students according to age levels to give children the notion of missionary activity at the international level of our congregation."[19]

The recollections from some of the sisters, who recreated their experiences in light of the changes coming with Vatican II, acknowledged the limitations in their formative years as novices. Aileen Gleason, who became a postulant in 1943 when she was nineteen, recalled the following:

So I went to the novitiate [Sacred Heart College]. But my novitiate was, like I often consider my formation, was deformation. And I have said that, but I was never told why it was so [the deformation]. We didn't know the Scriptures, we said the Psalms in Latin. We didn't know anything. The catechism of the vows, I suppose. And I can remember the evening conference after supper and recreation and before night prayer, and they would read us an article from out of *Sponsa Regis* or *Review for Religious*. And we weren't allowed to read books. We needed permission to read a book. So yes, you see, I've taken part in the formation of young sisters in Kenya, and I was involved in their formation.[20]

Another sister, Sheila Madden, when asked what struck her most from the novitiate (she entered in 1956, in Regina), gave this account:

Sheila: In the novitiate, the penances, we had not been raised on penances and, kind of, the shame around the body. This was new to me. We were four girls and two boys at home, and we didn't – like, if we were in our underwear and we had to go and get something, we'd go in our underwear and [we] got it.

Dora (Interviewer): So, your notion of the body was good.

Sheila: So that there was something of Jansenism in the convent. Not from our novice mistress but from the readings, and taking the discipline and all of that.

Dora (Interviewer): Did you have that?

Sheila: Yes, we did, and I took part in this. But I stood by the leg of the table and I was heavy on the upswing and very gentle on the downswing [we chuckled]. You know what? My saving grace was that I never believed in those things. But those who bought into it, as soon as the rule was lifted, they were gone. I did it because I had to. Life was much deeper than that and more beautiful.[21]

Chapter Eight

The 1960s: Changing Context and New Experiences

In the "long 1960s," an expression coined by Marwick that denotes the time span from 1958 to 1974,[1] an era of cultural revolutions, teaching congregations encountered the new world that emerged and took new shapes in the aftermath of World War II. Canada took on a renewed "modern" and global identity, maintaining residual ties to its British colonial past while aligning – in an often uneasy alliance – with the United States in the midst of the Cold War. The period of the Cold War took the shape of an ideological battle that would penetrate the language of education and the language of the Church. Canada, the United States, Britain, and Europe went through political, military, and technological changes that had an impact on education, the centre of the RNDM's missionary effort. The mainstreaming of Keynesian economics, the implementation of the welfare state, and unprecedented economic growth generated optimism in the West. Technological changes continued after the war: the jet engine, the transistor, and the digital computer set the stage for globalization; new media technology such as television transformed subjectivities, opening up new worlds and experiences, while forms of massive manipulation developed.[2] Being an international organization, the congregation was uneasily positioned in this new world, while also being an integral part of an emerging configuration that had as its core the Church's engagement with the world, as would be articulated in Vatican II (1962–65).

Thus, the Canadian province had to deal with a changing educational landscape and its political context. In the post-war era, as in the United States, money did flow into education. The theory of human capital gained ground, and, with the launch of the Soviet Sputnik, education became a primary Cold War battleground. The 1960s proper was a time when approaches that had previously been considered radical were

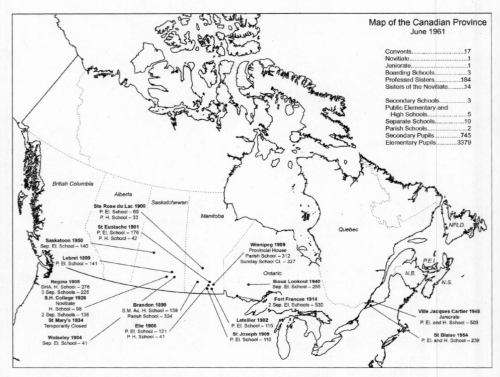

8.1 Map of the Canadian province, from June 1961. Source: Author's collection.

mainstreamed, as revealed in the new ways of approaching pedagogy.[3] Cole and McKay described it this way:

> Underlying all these developments was an assumption – shared by leftist activists, technocratic liberals, politicians, and the business community – that society could only progress if the individual was made free and democratic through an enhanced liberal education in tune with profound changes in the lives of individuals and the society they share. That is, what was achieved for a short period of time was a form of radical democracy, in which liberals and socialists alike worked toward a new way of thinking about society, one that dialectically went beyond existing ideological positions.[4]

Many Canadian sisters have recalled how this wave of change reached their own classes. In particular, they remember the open classroom designs of the late 1960s and 1970s, and how happy they were when schools returned to using the walls and doors of more traditional models. At the same time, a process of "scientification" of education was taking place, which reflected a profound belief in science and technology, and then, in the late 1970s and 1980s, came the dominant positioning of cognitive psychology with its focus on research on mental activity.[5]

No less important at the time, given its influence on Canada, were the dramatic changes taking place in the field of US history – mostly because of ongoing revisions concerning the place of race in the nation's history and the changing meanings of freedom and justice – which inspired new questions regarding the origins of racial inequality and the rights movements.[6] In Canada, in a move towards decoloniality, Indigenous political organizations entered a new phase during the 1960s; particularly important was the creation of the National Indian Council that would split into the National Indian Brotherhood (representing those with formal Indian status) and the Canadian Métis Society (representing mixed-blood groups and non-status Indians). The government of Canada's 1969 statement on Indian policy, known as the White Paper, which attempted to eliminate the Indian Act and treaties and fully assimilate all "Indian" people under the liberal construct of a just society, generated a backlash and the counter-document "Citizens Plus," also known as the Red Paper.[7] The Indigenous people's right to control their own education was at the forefront of their demands. The salvation of souls and the religious rationality behind the racialization of subjectivities and the building of Catholic subjects were shaken by this organized awareness in a new context that was changing rapidly on many fronts.

Education and the school system were going through important transformations. In Saskatchewan, school districts had been consolidated in 1944, but the sisters had their private schools and their place in the separate schools, the number of which increased after World War II. In 1964, the legislation was changed to allow tax support for separate Catholic high schools.[8] In early 1963, a new building was attached to the Sacred Heart College, and the secondary school there, a private one, was renamed Marian High School. This decision was made within the context of the need for schooling and its intersection with the notion of preparing human capital, which was embodied in the production of knowledgeable workers for an increasingly technological economy.[9] However, in 1965, the separate school system would absorb Marian High School and the Sacred Heart Academy, both private schools.

The changes affecting the Canadian province and their school work came on many fronts. Already, in 1960, the RNDM sisters had sold part of their land at 25th Avenue in Regina to the Sister Adorers of the Precious Blood for their monastery and, sometime later, a second piece to the Regina Catholic high school system; on the latter piece of land, the district built a co-educational high school called Le Boldus. The remainder of the sisters' property on Albert Street was sold to the separate schools in 1975.[10]

In 1965, the Separate High School Board took over the Sacred Heart Academy. The list of teachers at the academy in 1966 shows that the sister-teachers had degrees, mainly from the University of Ottawa and the University of Saskatchewan, but also that eleven out of sixteen teachers were lay teachers, three of whom were male teachers who taught mathematics, physics, and physical education.[11] It was no longer a private school, and, by the end of June 1969, the school had closed due to low enrolment. Academic enrolment had steadily decreased from 279 in 1965, to 175 in 1966, 167 in 1967, and 148 in 1968.[12] The year before the school's closure, the board had taken over the academy, sending out a letter that read: "In light of this decrease in demand for services which the Academy can provide and in light of the limited academic program such small enrolments allow, the Sisters of Our Lady of the Missions and the Separate High School Board have come to the unavoidable and difficult decision of bringing to a close the operations of the Academy effective the end of June 1969."[13] Sacred Heart Academy served its student community from 1910 to 1969.[14]

In Manitoba, the Brandon Public School Division incorporated the Brandon Catholic schools within the framework of an agreement between Father Maurice Cooney and Superintendent Jack Hill, so that the school could retain its identity. As Sister Sheila Madden recalled: "[T]hen we were paid some salaries, and then we could become members of the Manitoba Teachers Federation. And St Edward's parish school was much later. I can't remember when it became part of the system and members of the MTS."[15] The sisters thus became teachers in the public system.

The RNDMs, along with other congregations, had a relevant role through their teaching in building the identity of what Marcel Martel called the French-Canadian nation, which included Quebec and communities outside Quebec.[16] However, the understanding of Quebec as the "basic polity" of French Canada in the 1960s and the movement away from the pursuit of a common identity for all French Canadians created a new political and educational scenario. The quiet revolution took shape along with an intense process of secularization.

In Manitoba, as Taillefer demonstrated, after 1964, although religious teaching had its place, French education had actually become public, separated from the influence and despoil of sentimental and patriotic inspirations.[17] This separation was clearly revealed in the lack of religious content in the examinations. In 1964, the transfer of responsibility for French instruction from l'Association d'education to the province's Ministry of Education precipitated the changes in curriculum. The consolidations of school districts that took place in 1959 and again in 1967 moved the institutional power from religious congregations and parishes to lay teachers and school administrators serving larger pluralistic communities.[18] Finally, in 1970, the official recognition of French as a teaching language under the control of the Ministry of Education lessened the influence of the Catholic Church on education.[19] The consolidation of school districts in Manitoba in the 1960s resulted in the elimination of hundreds of school districts and brought to an end the relative autonomy that had favoured the sisters' educational work in various ethnic communities. In Manitoba, where consolidation had been a contentious issue for decades, following the recommendations of the MacFarlane Royal Commission on Education, published in 1959, the Public School Act was changed to create new secondary school boards that would cover larger areas; in 1964, unitary boards were established across the province for all levels.[20] The sisters participated in the consultation meetings sponsored by the government.[21]

The sisters left the schools located in the Franco-Manitoban communities. In September 1960, the sisters who taught in Letellier's public school wrote in their journals that they had stopped teaching the high school grades; the following year, in 1961, they closed the convent.[22] In Ste Rose du Lac, the sisters continued their work in public schools into the 1960s.[23] In 1971, the convent in Ste Rose, Manitoba, dedicated to Our Lady of Fourvière of France, was sold to the village. Two sisters remained in Ste Rose and continued doing work with young people in the town and helping out in the parish: "In September 1972, the two sisters, both retired teachers, continued being busy doing the Lord's work. Sister Laroque looked after the business of the house and continued to work with youth, while Sister Houde became the homemaker, sacristan for the Ste Rose de Lima parish and the Leisure Apts, visitor and companion to the sick and to family and friends. Hospitality to others at our home was also their special care."[24]

By the early 1970s, the RNDM's presence in the educational landscape in Canada had changed. The congregation's process of re-accommodation was not easy; the Second Vatican Council would be a watershed that would move the congregation to new directions in the midst of an unexamined internal crisis and a diminishing number of postulants. The characteristics of the liberal educational state were changing drastically: education started to be conceived as playing a fundamental role in fostering the human capital required for an increasingly technological knowledge-based economy, while the cognitive turn placed an emphasis on mental activities and a scientific renewal of education. The school systems were becoming more complex and centralized. The RNDMs, like other sisters in Canada, walked into the 1960s with an anachronistic language and remnants of the stiffened anti-modernism evident in the Vatican's teachings on the education of youth that were nourished by neo-scholasticism and interwoven with Cold War–era anti-communist rhetoric. The Magisterium in Rome enforced a neo-scholasticism that reached the schools through classes on religion and the ethos of the schools until the end of Vatican II.[25] Consequently, experiential, affective, or intuitive modes of thought were rejected, and the notion of divine truth led to proper answers. The texts used in the religion classes reflected that position. Priests and teachers took an anti-modernist oath that remained in effect until 1967.[26]

In 1964, the sisters' intended force behind their narrative of Catholic education, their intentionality, was still grounded in the 1929 encyclical of Pope Pius XI on Christian education, *Divini Illius Magistri.*[27] This document contained anti-modernist tones and a vision of education that did not fit with the 1960s, not even with new theological developments. An interesting example is the argument that the congregation put forward in 1964, in the midst of financial problems, for a special agreement with the separate school board in Regina, Saskatchewan, regarding Marian High School and Sacred Heart Academy, both private schools. The agreement would allow the sisters to receive a per capita fee or the payment of teachers' salaries and operational costs by the board, while keeping control of the schools. This agreement was previous to their integration into the separate system in 1965. The sisters made the point that all sisters and lay teachers were certified and argued that, inherent to the philosophy of the schools, and in conformity with the encyclical on education by Pope Pius XI, was the belief that Catholic education is better realized when the high school level is provided in separate institutions for boys and girls. The sisters stated in the proposal for an agreement: "Following this belief the Sisters over a period of sixty years have striven to establish girls' schools providing students with the means of enabling them to procure an academic training second to none and a spiritual formation in accordance to the philosophy and ideals of Holy Mother Church."[28]

The wording just quoted would soon be questioned. The Canadian RNDM sisters' symbolic universe did not function as a level of legitimation integrating various and new layers of meanings.[29] The sisters lived the contradictions between the congregation's subculture and the world around them. In addition, they were becoming familiar with the work of theologians such as Yves Congar and Karl Rahner, precursors of Vatican II, who tuned the Church to the world. Vatican II, in particular *Perfectae Caritatis*, would become an enabling means for the congregation to deal with a changing pluralized world in which contingency and choice were taking a central place in the formation of subjectivities. The sisters would work on the resignification of their mission and vision, and start to move towards a broader notion of ministry and education.

SPIRIT WIND

Divine Maestro, your flute is ready
Blow, breathe, bestow
Your breath in me;
Blow surely and strong
Freeing me of those fetters which
Tie me still
I want to sing, harmonize, make music;
Birth in me anew, your rhythm and tune
Breath of God, recreate me and convert me
At every moment into that disposition of
Surrendering myself into your hands;
To render a melody that is new
And full of You!

Christina Cathro

PART THREE

The Reception of Vatican II:
Epistemic Shifts and Visionary Changes

Chapter Nine

The Setting That Framed the Reception of Vatican II

The RNDMs cultivated a Trinitarian spirituality, as explained earlier; however, the missions were not guided freely by the Spirit, but by the Church and its political intentionality. The missions were situated within an ecclesial missionary framework. After the first pioneering years in the Canadian missions, the General Council of the Congregation progressively enforced the strictures of a semi-cloistered life, and the convents made accommodations for the design of the space in order to follow the foundress's vision of contemplative life as a major foundation of apostolic work. There were two major forces at play that would become visible during the process of renewal. One was the Generalate and its General Council, with its structurally and bureaucratically centralized organization and its inability to respond to the desires, needs, and historical circumstances of the provinces, in this case the Canadian province. The connection between disparate sites was accomplished through the General Council, which tried to deal with cultural disjunctures by creating an appearance of uniformity through rules and regulations. The other force, described in previous chapters, was the lived experience of the Canadian sisters, including the intense process of enculturation in the specific missionary milieu at the intersection of local Catholic communities and the dynamics of education in those communities. The Canadian province, which was by and large constituted by Canadian sisters and sisters who had been in Canada for decades, had developed a way of being Canadian in line with the sisters' experience in the prairies and their more informal ways of responding to needs, along with their views that questioned the official stand of the congregation. During the renewal process, as I will discuss in this chapter, the sisters of the Canadian province developed a strong sense of being Canadian and a desire to assert their identity. The renewal process gave the sisters an avenue to claim recognition and to move towards an encounter with the world on new terms – not perceiving it as evil, but as a changing world in which modern feminists struggled for new freedoms and spaces for action and desire.[1]

The Second Vatican Council deliberations and documents have been construed as a paradigmatic shift because they became an enabling legitimizing force through which to pursue or open new directions. John O'Malley, in his powerful analysis of the council, clearly concluded that the council kept "not only with the central tenets of Christian faith and the practices of the Catholic tradition but also with movements and aspirations of more recent vintage."[2] The Second Vatican Council deliberations took place in a context of developments that started to take shape in the 1950s: a new awareness of the role of lay groups such as Catholic Action; the coordinated action of women and men religious, such as with the Canadian Religious Conference (CRC); a previously repressed inclination to self-questioning that emerged in the congregations; the progressive decline in religious vocations; and theological currents that redefined the Church's relationship with the world and were at odds with the Magisterium, for example, the works of Yves Congar, Henri de Lubac, Karl Rahner, and Pierre Teilhard de Chardin, among the better known, and to which many sisters had access. Gregory Baum summarized the outcome of the council: the Church redefines its relationship to outsiders – dissident Christians, Jews, members of other religions – in terms of dialogue and cooperation; the Church assumes social justice as an imperative of the Gospel and as an integral part of spiritual life; and the Church understands the need to reinterpret its teaching in response to the present.[3]

In the background, the 1960s brought social movements, such as the civil rights and feminist movements, and new views on religion and spirituality in a pluralistic world. These opened doors for the sisters to explore the self – the religious self, but also the dimensions of the self as a component of the wider construction of the sisters as individuals. Seigel's identification of three dimensions of selfhood is useful here. These three are the bodily or material dimension, involving the physical or corporeal and ways of seeing and treating our body; the relational dimension, which develops from social and cultural interactions, connections that generate collective identity, shared orientations, and specific language; and the dimension of reflectivity, which refers to the capacity to make the world and our existence objects of our observation, attend to our consciousness, and create distance from our own existential conditions.[4]

In spite of the sisters' experience of living in misalignment with the world, which they later recalled as a feeling of being trapped within inadequate language and structures, the RNDM Generalate remained too attached to old rules and to the Vatican, as did other women's congregations. This attachment, however, made sense in light of the ultramontanism of the time of the congregation's foundation, the Canon Law of 1917, the history of the papacy supporting women's congregations who tried to ensure a certain level of autonomy from male congregations and/or bishops, and a general fear of the implications of change. RNDM foundress Euphrasie Barbier had the support of the papacy in her struggle with the Society of Mary in building her own congregation.[5] Thus, the sisters remained loyal to Rome "until Vatican II's emerging theology of local church began to encourage a more discerning appraisal of the role of the papacy," as Susan Smith, RNDM, wrote.[6] The loyalty to the papacy became an issue during the renewal process and when interrogating the past to imagine the future. This process was further complicated by conservative reactions and contradictions emerging from the Vatican and the persistence of old structures that signalled the desire to avoid radical transformations.

Three of the documents produced by the Second Vatican Council had direct implications on the congregation's mission and on the sisters' collective identity: (1) *Lumen Gentium: Dogmatic Constitution of the Church*, placing religious life within the larger mission of the Church and extending the notion of the fullness of Christian life to all faithful;[7] (2) *Perfectae Caritatis*, focusing on renewal in light of the original spirit of the congregation;[8] and (3) *Gaudium et Spes*, addressing the presence and activity of the Church in the world today.[9] *Ecclesiae Sanctae*, Pope Paul VI's apostolic letter, provided directives for the renewal process.[10]

Tensions between the Canadian Province and the Generalate, 1966

The preparatory documents of the 1966 Regular General Chapter display a conflict in the discursive interactions between the members of the Canadian province, who were eager to engage in the process of change, and the central administration of the congregation. The 1966 Chapter opened the early phase of the process of institutional and individual renewal that lasted from 1965 to 1970. The relationship and interactions among the Vatican, the central governance of the congregation, and the Canadian province can be characterized as forming fields, to borrow a construct from Bourdieu – that is, conceptual spaces containing a history, an internal logic, and a symbolic capital, each exhibiting a configuration of interwoven conflicting views.[11] In such fields, the old patterns and dispositions – particularly those enclosed in languages, that is, their *habitus*, as Bourdieu conceived it – would be resilient.[12]

The exchanges between the Canadian province and the Generalate during the preparation process of the 1966 Chapter point to two major issues defining the province and its positioning: the interiorization of locality, in other words, the affirmation of local consciousness, of being Canadians requesting to keep their own uniqueness and space; and the reconstruction of the individual and collective self as community. The latter was an integral part of the discussion about the religious habit.

A letter dated 1 May 1966, sent to the Canadian province and signed by outgoing Superior General Mary Dominic Savio, reveals that some sisters communicated with the Generalate denouncing widespread discontent in the Canadian province. The letter stated that some sisters were wavering in their vocation and "that unless the decisions of the forthcoming General Chapter end in accordance with their views they will leave the Institute, and that in fact, some are seeking a dispensation from their Vows now, because their views about renewal have been rejected."[13] The superior did not read the letters she had received from some sisters as an expression of their fear of change within the province's context of a strong drive for renewal, or even with a sense of urgency. Instead, Dominic Savio made the case to the provincial superior and the sisters in the Canadian province – particularly those who were not happy with the paucity of changes – that they had false ideas. She went on to detail the changes that had taken place in the movement towards "renewal and adaptation." The superior enumerated in the form of questions the following points: (1) the sisters in Canada had the opportunity to express their views; (2) the results of the sisters' discussions were presented to their Provincial Chapter, and its recommendations in turn would be submitted to the General Chapter; (3) the congregation had obtained permission from Rome to change from the Little Office of Our Lady in Latin to three hours of the Divine Office in the vernacular; (4) the method of elections had been changed, giving the sisters more freedom and representation at the Chapters; (5) the sisters were allowed to attend education meetings, conventions, and courses to better perform their apostolate. Superior General Dominic Savio's point was that the congregation was complying with the directives of the Holy Church and that the sisters were consulted in accordance with the decree on renewal and adaptation in religious life.

The superior general appealed to the Holy Father and the rule – to the patriarchal structure of the Church – when she asked: "Is it not stated in the decree and by the Holy Father himself that the decisions in this matter must be made by the competent authority, namely, the General Chapter? ... If, therefore, Superiors insist on observance of the rule and constitutions they are only following the directives given by the Church, and it cannot be claimed that they are unwilling to change once the proper authority has spoken."[14]

The Generalate formed a field – a space – in which old patterns of power were part of a contradictory configuration, where they coexisted with the renewal process as dictated by the Vatican and with the push from the Canadian province to which the Vatican had to respond. In maintaining the hierarchical structures, the superior general tried to move the congregation to a controlled process of change. Thus, the superior made clear in her letter that "the congregation will do all that Holy Church requires her Religious to do. It will not lag behind, but neither should it go ahead of the Church. It must move with the Church."[15] Notably, the superior called for the sisters to be careful and be influenced by the rightful authority, and not by writers in newspapers and periodicals who had no knowledge of religious life. She went on to say that it was not helpful to listen to other congregation members who were making unfavourable comments about their own family. Her point was that the sisters could only see other congregations from the outside and could draw conclusions from appearances only. Fear permeates the letter's contents: "Discussions with Religious of other Orders are indeed very helpful if they are objective, but if they bring about loss of love for one's own religious family, they fail in their purpose."[16]

The Canadian province very early on read the foundress in light of the Vatican II documents. But Superior General Savio argued in the letter under discussion that the goal expressed by the Canadians of "going to the missions and working with the poor" was grounded in a misquotation of the foundress. Savio went on to say: "[S]he [the foundress] herself also established – what were then called – "select" schools, not that the Sisters should educate only children of the better class families, but that they might be able to work for every type of people."[17] This statement, however, neglected to consider the early work of the foundress and her commitment to working with poor girls in northern France in Armentières, which started in 1876, and in Houplines, begun in 1889 – work that ended in 1901.

The letter made reference to a recurrent concern among the sisters of the Canadian province that the central administration in Europe did not understand the needs of the province. The superior did not, however, capture the roots of the Canadian preoccupation. Instead, she explained that only one member of the General Council represented Europe and that the others were representatives of the other provinces, expressing only her interest in improving representation.[18]

In order to understand the response to the situation from the superior of the Canadian province, Mother Marie Jean d'Ávila, it is important to bring to the discussion the circular letter of 12 May 1966 (prior to the General Chapter of July of the same year) signed by Superior General Mary Dominic Savio; the circular had attached to it a copy of an excerpt from a 1965 speech delivered by Cardinal Antoniutti, cardinal prefect of the Congregation of Religious, to "mothers general" (superior generals) assembled in Rome at the beginning of December 1965.[19]

Antoniutti did not consider the modification of the habit that had begun to take place to some extent in the 1950s under Pius XII, who tried to make it more convenient for the apostolate, an essential point in the "aggiornamento" and rejected the idea of a radical change of habit.[20] The Conciliar Decree, he reminded the sisters, said that the habit had to be simple, modest, poor, becoming, hygienic, and suited to the place where they lived. Antoniutti stated that it was necessary to preserve the gravity and dignity of the religious habit as a sign of consecration to God. His language in speaking of the body of women religious shows a binary view in organizing the identities of masculine and feminine religious, with the latter in a relation of subordination. Thus, the dress had to safeguard the sisters' modesty, it was necessary to keep the veil when the constitutions prescribed it, and, he clarified, it should not be reduced to a decoration. On the dress safeguarding modesty, he said, "let your habit be long, simple, sober, so as always to be able 'to present a chaste virgin to Christ.'" Antoniutti wanted the sister to be distinguishable from others even in her dress, and asserted that the people required the sister to appear in the habit as a symbol of poverty, charity, and dedication to the service of the neighbour.[21] In Antoniutti's speech, the language of the body was in line with the gendered structures of the Church and its hierarchical ways, and the habit was an expression of multiple forms of domination through discipline and control. It is notable that externally and in their lived experience, however, the habit signalled authority, a form of capital for the sisters.

The superior's letter requested that the sisters give full consideration to Cardinal Antoniutti's observations on the habit. She wrote: "One wonders how much truth there is in the notion that the world today is put off by a religious habit and thinks us to be a queer lot of people, so that we might miss making contacts which we might make if we were not wearing any special garb. It would also be interesting to know what the results would be if a census were taken among laypeople on this question."[22] There were, on one side, contradictory tendencies inside the Vatican, including a conservative reaction to Vatican II; on the other side, the Generalate had difficulties leaving aside the habit, a visible representation of their authority, and paid attention to reactionary forces that tried to deal with possible threats to patriarchy. The circular and the attachment reveal the main force at play in the Generalate, a field in which change was to be controlled, as mentioned earlier, having the Vatican and its contradictions as a point of reference.

In the letter, the superior general made clear the congregation's duty to seek out and to know the Holy Church's expectations of the religious in the matter of renewal and adaptation, and stated that this knowledge should guide the sisters in their deliberations. Having this in mind, the superior indicated that she had invited Father O'Riordan, a lecturer at Regina Mundi College in Rome and a former member of the Conciliar Commission, who was, in her view, qualified to inform the sisters of the mind of the Church on many questions. The superior also quoted a Father Plé: "The more the spirit of the Gospel, the more the Holy Spirit, the more the spirit of your Foundress lives in you, the better you will be adapted." Father Plé's quotation was followed by the superior's definition of "adapting" as being "the act of finding the perfect balance and harmony between the letter and the spirit of the Rule and Constitutions. It is to seek the more effective use of the means of self-sanctification and of the apostolate within the congregation."[23] The attachment to the past, the habitus conveyed in the language used, and the affirmation of a collective identity that was in crisis set the framework for the superior's approach to change. Her difficulties with change and fear of uncontrolled change can be found in her reading of the foundress, Euphrasie Barbier. She reminded the sisters that one of the distinctive features established by the foundress was that of an unostentatious zeal, described in chapter four of the constitutions, which would help the congregation to adapt to the conditions of the day. She quoted a Father Gallen as saying, "Adaptation seeks to retain but to revivify the discipline that is good, to remove the idle and useless, to substitute the better for the less efficacious, and to effect the realization that an oppressive, merely annoying, and too minute religious discipline is self-destructive."[24]

She then called for a detachment from affection towards temporal things in order that the soul may freely tend to God. In her words, "[a]daptation cannot and does not deny or enfeeble the complete detachment, mortification and abnegation demanded by this purpose of the religious life. I strive to find, intensify, and promote the most suitable and efficacious means for this purpose."[25] She did not hesitate to reiterate that "renovation is not worldliness but greater sanctity; adaptation is not self-indulgence but more intelligent and appropriate mortification."[26] The religious language dealing with the relational and reflective self of the pre–Vatican II era is fully displayed in the letter, but is decontextualized from the various social and linguistic spaces emerging in the provinces, in this case in Canada.

The provincial superior, Mother Marie Jean d'Ávila (Jeanne Roche), responded to the superior general on 29 May 1966, to both the letter of 1 May and the subsequent circular containing Antoniutti's excerpts.[27] It is clear she did not consider the mood in Canada to be one of "discontent," although she acknowledged that there had been much unrest caused by the feeling that adaptations were taking too long. In part, the unrest was nourished by the news that three highly influential high school teachers were leaving the congregation, even though the decision was not necessarily tied to the General Chapter. Although in her response the provincial superior acknowledged that there had been progress, she made the point that some of the sisters had found the twelve years since the 1954 Chapter had asked for a change in the habit to be very long. The 1960 Chapter, she said, had come and gone with still no change. She construed the change in the habit as a symbol of adaptation or lack of it. The letter conveys to the reader a sense of frustration; the Canadian sisters were positioned to question the old ways (habitus) and even the structures that underlined those ways and kept conditioning their lives as women religious. The provincial superior wrote of the situation:

> When we hear that the big sleeves were retained because chapels in Europe are chilly, the reasoning does not seem valid. When we hear that the rule of companionship was retained because English bishops "wouldn't hear of Sisters going on the streets alone," we wonder why Canadian bishops couldn't have been consulted about what would be appropriate for Canadian Sisters. We are almost frightened when an address by Cardinal Antoniutti is circulated among the delegates as the "official" word on religious habits. Is he one of the Cardinals whom the Pope himself had to tactfully circumvent in some of the deliberations of the Council?[28]

The tension between the centralized and bureaucratic governance of the congregation and the assertion of locality and experience is explicit in the letter. The sisters appreciated the broader scope for voting to select delegates, the provincial superior remarked; however, many of them had found that when it came to who was chosen, they knew very few sisters in the province – so that all but two of the delegates were people who had at some time helped in some position that made them a little better known. The questionnaires to explore the sisters' views in light of changes were an excellent idea, she wrote, but some of the questions were ambiguous or obscure. Then she posed the question, "Why are we required [to obtain] permission to discuss matters which are so obviously the concern of every member of the Congregation?"

In her view, community meetings were better places for discussion than clandestine meetings, the latter of which ended up strengthening everyone's ignorance instead of being a venue for confronting differing views. The sisters had been impatient waiting for the General Chapter, a feeling that was "spurred sometimes by clergy who fail to understand the rather complex hierarchical structure of our Congregation's government."[29] Notably, the report on the canonical visitation to the RNDM convents in Regina, requested by Archbishop O'Neill in 1960 in relation to the process of adaptation recommended by Pius XII, had recommended greater autonomy for the provincial and regional superiors. The sisters were far from the Generalate, and conditions in Canada were quite different from those in England, Ireland, and France. The report said: "Your superior[s] here should be the ones to adapt the application of central rules to the local needs."[30] The report was grounded in testimonies from the sisters.

In her letter, the provincial superior went on to say that the sisters were delighted with the resolutions from the Provincial Chapter – held before the General Chapter – and were full of hope. But, of course, the sisters were aware that the Provincial Chapter was not the governing body, and, on this matter, the superior said, "Perhaps this is the source of much Canadian uneasiness. We increasingly feel that we should be able to make decisions for ourselves. It is more and more difficult to understand why our government is so exceedingly centralized."[31] She further made her case by saying that every person in a position of authority had to submit most of her decisions – she clarified that this submission was actually asking for permissions – to someone higher up the scale. In her view, this practice was the crux of the matter. It was for this reason that the Provincial Chapter had suggested that provincial superiors meet annually to discuss congregation business. Overall, the letter spelled out what the writer qualified as constructive suggestions to improve governance. The letter conveys the sense that the Canadian representative on the council was out of touch with the reality of the Canadian province: she had been away from Canada for a long time; furthermore, the superior mentioned her perceived favouritism of sisters who were directly in touch with the central governance (Generalate) of the congregation.[32]

The letter contains a record of how some of the sisters felt at the time. But the interesting point here is how the provincial superior developed her argument and how she positioned herself and the congregation. She wrote: "Please do not consider us either rude or rebellious. We are merely Canadian. I have been teaching the history of our nation for 13 or 14 years and I think I appreciate our nationhood most intensely.

A study of the history of the Commonwealth reveals that Canada, in her progress from colony to nation, has been the pace-setter from the beginning."[33] The superior thus set the grounds for a claim for more autonomy, a new way of relating to the Generalate, by appealing to Canadian history. She then explained that Canada was the first, after Britain, of those who remained in the Empire, to achieve representative government; the first to bring government to responsibility; the first to confederate; the first to negotiate its own treaties; the first to send foreign ambassadors; and that the Canadians were the first Dominion troops. She went on to say:

> Ours has been 200 years and more of maintaining our own national identity against the imperialistic British and the expansionist Americans. We have clung to the British ties to keep us from the U.S.A., and we react almost violently against suggestions that we are an American satellite. Tory J.A. Macdonald sidestepped the suggestion of a federal government for the Empire in 1893 and Laurier parried to move for a joint foreign policy with an offer of preferential tariff in 1897. And so has been our story.[34]

The provincial superior then introduced her interpretation of another historical dimension to her argument, this time to question central control:

> The English-speaking and the French-speaking elements have been united in these common efforts, and now, since the First World War, we have in our population what sociologists call the "third element." These are the people of non-English, non-French origin who form one third of our nation. These are the children in our schools who see no useful purpose in a monarch resident in Britain. These are the people who cheer the lowering of the Union Jack, yet demand that the French "talk white." And these are the Sisters who, along with the French-speaking, motivated by anti-clericalism in Quebec, and the English-speaking, treasuring a long tradition of "struggle for self-government," are seeking greater autonomy for our Canadian Superiors.[35]

Notably, the Indigenous peoples, the First Nations of Canada, do not have a place in the narration.

The argument for autonomy and the critique of a centralized governance structure could be interpreted as a violation of the vows of obedience. Hence, the provincial superior also took pains to clarify that she did not intend to shake off the idea of religious obedience with her points. They were instead, she wrote, made out of a desire for a smaller,

more compact family group, for reasoned obedience freely given to superiors who were in that role and knew the situation. In her words, her
letter did not signify "a desire to break away from the Generalate, this
would not be in keeping with our national traditions, but we Canadians have shown a certain genius for going our own way while keeping
the bonds of affection and tradition."[36]

The letter concludes with the disclaimer that it was not meant to be-
speak disloyalty or a lack of affection towards the congregation. The
thoughts came from someone who was most anxious that the congregation survive; one who was frightened at the small numbers of novices;
and one who wanted to see her sisters going joyfully about their works,
unimpeded by the fear of misunderstanding or misrepresentation.[37]

General Chapter of 1966

The Acts of the General Chapter of 1966 show that the resolutions were
far from the vision of the Canadian superior and the sisters who shared
that vision.[38] The structure of monastic life started to be weakened;
there were small changes made, such as a new openness to ecumenism as per the Decree on Ecumenism of Vatican II,[39] some flexibility
with permissions to visit with family, and a degree of personal responsibility in the life of prayer. However, basic regulating practices and
rules regarding spirituality persisted within an authoritarian model,
and the tired language of obedience and a strong liaison to the Church
as an institution were reinforced. The micro-policies shaping the soul
and the body in the form of penances were prominent. The expectation was that a religious should humbly submit to her superior, who
was there in place of God, and in this way become closely linked to
the Church. The foundress is quoted as saying that holy obedience is
the main virtue of a religious.[40] The ecclesiastic notion of mission, in
other words, a mission that responded to the institutional needs of the
institutional Church, remained unchanged. The sisters were urged to
become more conscious of the greatness of their holy vocation that gave
them the privilege of participating in the extension of the kingdom
of God to the world, in particular to "infidel" or non-Catholic countries. An ethnocentric colonial view of mission remained. However,
there was a resolution that would have great impact on the Canadian
province and on the congregation as a whole. In an early attempt to
go back to the original mission, one of the resolutions states that each
province will help, within their possibilities, any existing missions or
will begin a mission in a territory within the geographical context of
their country or in an underdeveloped region. This mission would be a

provincial foundation. The Canadian province decided to begin a mission in Peru.

In spite of signals of radical changes in the educational scene and the diminishing number of recruits, the Chapter referred to chapter one of the constitutions to reiterate that the principal apostolate was Christian education in service to God and the Church. In this early movement towards renewal, the congregation seemed to go back to their origins in a way in which resistance to change and a degree of disorientation became dominant forces in the direction of the congregation. The Second Vatican Council had produced, in 1965, the Declaration on Christian Education (*Gravissimum Educationis*),[41] a document that is ambiguous in relation to the modern world, but to some point open to it, while keeping a traditional Catholic social order wherein the Church determines the nature of the common good.[42] The sisters did not discuss the document in the Chapter, but stated:

> It is essential, therefore, that all the Sisters be thoroughly imbued with the spirit of the Church and well informed on papal documents concerning it, such as Pope Pius XI's encyclical letter "Christian Education of Youth" and Vatican II's "Declaration on Christian Education" and the "Decree on the Church's Missionary Activity." The most distinctive feature of these documents is their insistence upon the integration of Christian education into the whole pattern of human life in all its aspects.[43]

The reference to the "Declaration on Christian Education" in relation to Pius XI's encyclical letter is not surprising, since the letter is often quoted in the declaration, as is customary in these kinds of documents. Not even at the 1969 Chapter of Aggiornamento, however, would the question of the habit and the veil be solved in a manner satisfactory to the Canadian province. On 5 July 1966, when the superior had already left to join the Chapter, Archbishop of Winnipeg G.B. Flahiff, SSB, responded in a letter to a question posed by the provincial superior about the bishop's right to authorize changes in "garments and style of living for nuns and religious orders in their area." The superior was motivated by a statement in a local newspaper. The archbishop had not received instructions from the Holy See, and he took the opportunity to say: "For too long, men have been attempting to settle such things [garb; lifestyle]; to a limited extent, they are doing so still; but, more and more, you must decide for yourselves. Even if the first attempts at modifying and up-dating do not meet with full approval, you should continue to ask for whatever you decide is best for you. The changes

9.1 General Chapter, 1966, Hastings, England. Source: Sister delegates Box 9, pictures general chapters, 2744CPSHSB.

already introduced by certain Communities in Western Canada are proof that modifications can be made. I find that all of them still preserve the notion of indicating a person who is consecrated to God."[44] The provincial superior was actually seeking an avenue for the change of habit, a cause so substantial, in her view, to the rebuilding of identity.

Writing the New Constitutions within the Context of the Renewal Process

After the 1966 Chapter, the congregation as a whole was engaged in the process of writing the new constitutions following guidelines from *Ecclesiae Sanctae* and the principles of *Perfectae Caritatis*, but in the process becoming familiar with all the documents of the Second Vatican Council. The superior general, in a letter addressed to all reverend mothers and sisters, pointed out the "factors" that should influence the work: (1) the desires of the Church expressed in the council; (2) the present needs both of the world in which we have to work and of religious today; (3) the genuine spirit of "our Venerated Mother and the Congregation."[45]

The tensions coming out of the desire to control the renewal process and from a fear of going beyond the given parameters were clear in the superior's stress of loyalty and love to the Church in another letter to all reverend mothers and sisters, dated 30 October 1966. She was eager to cultivate the ties with the institution without questioning the structures, and quoted Paul VI, who said, when speaking to religious in May 1966:

> The Church loves you for all that you are and all that you do in her, for all that you say, for your prayer, for your renunciation, for the gift of yourselves. Have you ever doubted this love of the Church for you? No, indeed: there are the words of our predecessors which bear witness to the sentiments of the See of St. Peter with regard to you; there are the documents of the Council which, in very beautiful passages devoted to holiness and to religious perfection, show you how much the Church of today loves with a love of predilection and how much she expects from you.[46]

After affirming the love of the Church to her religious, the superior asked the sisters, "Do you love the Church?" The Church and her council attended to the problems of present life, not through a need for novelty, but in order to present to the world the Gospel in its missionary impulse and its apostolic opening up so that souls could be saved. The invitation to renewal was also an invitation to welcome the Church's directions and motherly authority. It was a call for loyalty.[47]

It is clear that the "adaptation to the times" took the shape of an uneven process; the Canadian province was ahead of its own international congregation. The Vatican and statements made by the pope reveal a field where the positioning of the pope was defined by the power structures the Vatican wanted to preserve. Obviously, there was concern over making drastic changes, which was made clear in the recording of a rather minor change relevant to the Canadian province: the habit. The *Sacra Congregation per I Religiosi e Gli Instituti Secolari* distributed a statement in April 1968 referring to a complaint that "the Sacred Congregation is blocking aggiornamento and is therefore against Vatican II," lodged on behalf of the Immaculate Heart of Mary. The statement made clear that the decree *"Perfectae Caritatis* (no 4) and the Motu Proprio *Ecclesiae Sanctae* (no 6) entrust to the religious institutes the responsibility of carrying on the desired adaptation, but do not exempt the Holy See from the obligation of supervising so everything is accomplished in accordance with the Conciliar prescriptions."[48] The document made the case that the congregation had encouraged – not blocked – adaptation, but rather had provided guidance; however, it also needed to make sure

that the norms laid out by the council were respected. With reference
to the habit, the statement said that when the habit was determined by
approved constitutions, it could not be eliminated completely, but that
prescriptions from *Perfectae Caritatis* had to be faithfully observed. In
other words, *Perfectae* permitted changes and adaptations to the habit,
but did not allow the "outright suppression of the habit."[49] The document stated that the "local Ordinary [local bishop of the Church] has
the authority to forbid priests and religious, even though they be exempt, to wear secular garb";[50] that community life must be observed in
principle since it pertains to religious life; that the religious life is not to
be subordinated to the apostolate in general, nor to any apostolate in
particular; and that the first contribution to apostolic works is through
prayer, works of penance, and personal example.[51]

At the 1966 General Chapter, Reverend Mother Mary Gertrude had
been elected superior general; in one of her letters to the sisters' superiors of the various provinces and their houses and in preparation for
the Special Chapter of Aggiornamento, she tried to articulate a balance
in her approach to governance. The Church, she wrote, was no longer
in isolation, but in union with the whole human race, and Catholicism
was no longer segregated from other Christians; there was now unity.
She applied this principle to the congregation, explaining that the superior was the leader of the community and must govern through dialogue with her sisters in the spirit of humility, with the understanding
that a close relationship with her sisters does not destroy the authority
of the head but rather strengthens it. This unit would be strengthened
even further when superiors (house superiors) stood by the decisions
resulting from their dialogue under the direction of the mother provincial. In her view, "the mark of wise government is the good judgment
of the Superior to blend her orders with an allowance of freedom for
her subjects. A discerning Superior finds the balance between imposing
her own will on another person and letting her formulate a responsible decision. The perfection of active and responsible obedience cannot be reached in a day, and an understanding Superior will know that
the persons entrusted to her will learn it by trial and error."[52] The letter
contained old habitus, or ways of expressing, a language that tried
to convey the desire to generate a new model of governance without
breaking with central concepts of the past such as obedience. The key
for her was balance.

The emerging lived history of the sisters in the Canadian province
and the acknowledgment of difference in their lives that had been suppressed challenged the statements of the 1966 Chapter. *Perfectae Caritatis*[53] opened an unexpected door to the discovery of the self in its rather

modernist sense. In an interview in 2011, Sister Cécile Granger, who had entered the congregation in 1942 and at the time of the interview was ninety years old, when asked about her reaction to *Perfectae Caritatis*, put it this way:

> *Cécile*: I remember. To me it wasn't enough. It didn't go far enough. You know, throw the veil out, get another suit, you know. They did not say all those things but it wasn't *Perfectae* [*Caritatis*] enough. I wanted something in the heart, to change the heart. The best change there was when we had these sessions on religious life. A certain priest came from France and taught us this and that: how to relive our life. I got more from him. He set me in the right direction. It was in Villa Maria, all nuns, full house and we were listening to this Father. You might know his name.
>
> *Dora (Interviewer)*: Father André Rochais?
>
> *Cécile*: Yes. And there were all kinds of people there, sisters. When the sisters heard him talk about things they were crying away.
>
> *Dora (Interviewer)*: Crying about what?
>
> *Cécile*: Sad things about the past. This priest had so many things to tell us about ourselves, living with yourself. And when I got home, I was trying to tell them what I heard. Some of the older sisters said: "Oh no, don't tell us about that." But I kept on going all the same.[54]

The priest mentioned was Father André Rochais (1921–90), and the "many things" were introduced in courses and taught by Rochais and his teams. Rochais focused on human development and on a reconstituted relationship with God, under the title "Personality and Human Relations." Rochais was a French educator who had been influenced by Carl Rogers's work, in particular Rogers's 1961 book *On Becoming a Person*, and who had developed his own guidelines for personal analysis. The congregations were attracted to the notion of a person's growth to their full potential, the search of the subjective, and the concept of existential freedom. The sisters learned through these courses to discover meanings within themselves and to listen to their own self-experience and find direction from within through being aware of their own sensations. An important goal was to live in personal harmony and to be true to one's conscience.[55] All of this was a revelation for many sisters. Sister Cécile Campeau, provincial superior between 1968 and 1971, recalled that there was a desire for greater freedom in every sense of the word, a trend towards further education beyond teaching certification and even an interest in various spiritualities and healing practices.[56]

As examined by Heidi MacDonald, "between 1965 and 1975, the number of women religious in Canada fell 32 per cent from approximately 66,000 to 44,127."[57] Sister Claire Himbeault, provincial superior between 1971 and 1977, recalled that, after Vatican II

> a great number of sisters were leaving for various reasons. Perhaps, it was that they for the first time saw that there was something else for them, that this was not really their place. So I found myself accompanying many of the sisters as they made their discernment and lived it with sadness and pain. At the same time, it was really the right thing for many people, but I nevertheless felt it, felt the separation.[58]

The sisters had started to have an idea of the function of difference in their lives and no longer wanted to ignore difference. The process of renewal became a recreation of basic tenets of modernity in a peculiar version that had followed a long process. The implications were both personal and collective, as we will see when examining the attempts at rebuilding the identity of the community as a collective. The sisters were conscious that there was indeed a religious crisis affecting Christianity in the Western world in the 1960s; the question under debate, as Callum Brown put it, has been, "What was the religious crisis of the 1960s?"[59] Brown's conclusion (grounded in A. Hasting)[60] that it was a crisis of the total culture makes sense in the Western context. It was a challenge to Christian hegemony as well.[61] Certainly Peter Berger's emphasis on pluralism is useful here. He wrote that "the co-existence [of] different worldviews and value systems in the same society is *the* major change brought about by modernity for the place of religion both in the minds of individuals and in the institutional order. This may or may not be associated with secularization."[62] The Second Vatican Council had led the sisters and Catholics in general to relativize their understanding of faith, to move away from the assumption that it was the only possible truth. Thus, the door was opened for an inevitable dialogue with the secular, as well as with other religious discourses, and also regarding "contamination."[63]

The Canadian province affirmed their local consciousness and wanted to keep their own way of doing things, to keep their own space. They took a clear position in favour of changing the habit and removing the veil, which they linked to their reconstruction of their social self. They had realized that rescuing the genealogy of the congregation would first require cleaning their original vision of the accumulated directives from the authorities of the Church and from Canon Law, all of which were embedded in a patriarchal vision.[64] The habit and the veil were contentious issues.

Chapter of Aggiornamento

The General Council had decided that the Special General Chapter of Aggiornamento required by the Vatican would be held in July 1969 in Hastings, England. In her letter to the congregation, the superior general quoted Pope Paul VI: "Your Chapter is above all the concern of your Congregation, but it also affects the life of the Church which draws from the flourishing conditions of religious life much of its vigour, its apostolic zeal, and its keenness in the quest of sanctity."[65] The superior general went on to say that, in the spirit of their Venerated Mother (the foundress), so loyal to the Holy Church, they might at all times remain faithful to the directives given to them.[66] She had a concern around the disregard for authority and with deviations from the faith. Thus, in another circular letter, the superior general once again mentioned the Holy Father to remark on the necessity to speak frequently of faith. The quotation from the pope read: "However, even today, faith is the object of many a denial ('Faith is not given to all' says St Paul, 2 Thess. III), and it gives rise to much controversy even among believers. You may have heard the echo of erroneous opinions which dare to uphold arbitrary interpretations, casting a slur upon sacrosanct truths of the Catholic faith."[67]

The Canadian province was ahead of the overall congregation in their search for a renewed identity. In 1967, the province, ready to open a conversation, started a quarterly publication entitled *The Small Candle*. Two sentences in an anonymous article called attention: "The present crisis that is hitting religious life in general is making itself felt in our own Congregation, and specifically in our province"; and "We can love only what we know, and we are at last getting to know our Sisters."[68] In another article, entitled "We, as Religious, Have Renounced the World," the sister author made the case that they actually don't renounce the world because to do so would constitute "the renunciation of the one place which God, through his son, chose as the place where he could help us find our salvation." The sisters began *The Small Candle* as a sounding board to share their ideas and ideals.[69] This publication thus reflects the vision in gestation and how the forces of change delineated in the field formed by the province. Sister M. Bernard Gropp, who was also the editor, made a suggestion that, in her view, was as old as the primitive Christian community itself. Her idea was to increase the number of councillors from one or two to as many as the number of sisters in a community. In other words, that "we all accept our responsibility, under the superior, for running our house. After all – IT IS OURS – it is not only, nor even primarily the superior general's, the provincial's, the local superior's, the councillors', rather is it *ours*, yours and mine!"[70] For the community to grow, the same article said, "community problems" had to be known and handled "by the only people who have the right and duty to work at their solution, the community – that unit composed of US."[71] Even as the superior was the official representative of God, and as such was ultimately responsible as bearer of the charismatic gift of authority-service, the sister made the point that they should not forget that "the group no less (perhaps more so) has God in its midst and as such shares in the charismatic gift of the Church – the active presence of the SPIRIT. Let's start to make full use of our GIFT."[72]

The RNDM provincial sisters were freely in touch now with other congregations, which was a significant development. Sister M. Zita Bolingbroke was studying at Regina Mundis (pontifical college for women founded by a Jesuit, Father Dezza, in 1954) when she got in touch with the Sisters of the (Holy; by then this part of their name had been deleted) Humility of Mary, a French congregation with the motherhouse in Pennsylvania. She wrote that this congregation had been wrapped in tradition as were the RNDMs, but that they had decided to offer a choice of dressing in any of three dark blue modern suits and any of five styles of white blouses. Other than their uniform colour, the sisters in the Humility of Mary congregation were identified only by a silver chain and a medal – no veil, as it was considered superfluous.[73] Sister Zita advocated a homier community living environment. Why, she wondered, must sisters wear a veil even in the cloister? The veil was a big issue. Sister Zita paid particular attention to the Sisters of Our Lady of the Cenacle, who had provided a renewal program that extended over the entire year in Rome. They brought in theologians, psychologists, Scripture scholars, and qualified writers – "all liberal men with a Vatican II outlook on Religious life." Among these invitees were Father Bernard Haring, CSSR; Father Sean O'Riordon, CSSR; and Father Bernard Mullahy, CSC. The highlight of the renewal program was, in Sister Zita's view, a three-day forum on the vows in light of Vatican II, directed by Fathers Sean O'Riordon and Paul Molinari, SJ. Molinari was a peritus at Vatican II, a member of the Theological Commission, and secretary to the subcommission that composed chapter seven of the Constitution on the Church and provided guidance in the deliberations that produced the decree *Perfectae Caritatis*.[74]

On one side, there was a clear movement towards change; on the other, a degree of confusion. Thus, when Sister Zita referred to the conservative Cardinal Antoniutti, whose views on the religious habit had disturbed the provincial superior, she was not able to assess whether the cardinal was conservative. Sister Zita found his concerns with radical things that were, in his view, happening in some religious congregations quite legitimate. The cardinal had expressed his preoccupation that some congregations had only concerns with external things, rather than internal renewal. However, Sister Zita's reading proved to be quite shortsighted.[75]

In line with the sense of locality and the uniqueness of the Canadian experience, Sister Zita, in the lengthy article, mentioned that when she was at the RNDM motherhouse in England, she was struck by the desire of the English province and the governing body to understand the Canadian province better. "Of us, they invariably say: 'You Canadians are different – we like you – you're open – you're above the board.'"[76]

The Small Candle opens a window to understand the RNDM sisters' process of renewal and their search for personal and community "growth." In her article, Sister Mary Gerald talked of courage, emergence from timid silence, growth towards openness without fear – a disposition that had not been easy to develop – and the difficulties of learning to speak out at meetings without fear, frankly, and with love.[77]

The context conveyed in *The Small Candle* helps us understand the positionings within the Canadian field during the renewal. Thus, if we think of the way the Vatican was maintaining the parameters that defined its own field, and how the Generalate (the governance of the congregation) was concerned with drastic change, one can follow the interactions of these three fields and the conflict situations. As introduced earlier, one of those situations was in relation to the change of habit and removal of the veil, which the sisters in the Canadian province linked to their social and individual self.

On 19 February 1969 – before the General Chapter of Aggiornamento that took place in July of the same year, Provincial Superior Cécile Campeau (Marie Emilia) conveyed to the sisters the response from Rome to the motion that had been approved at the provincial level, which had said: "Moved by Sister M. André and seconded by Sister M. Ignativa, we request permission to leave off the habit and replace it by appropriate casual wear when the situation calls for more suitable attire, for example, 1. Sports and field trips; 2. For occasions when the apostolate is positively hindered by a conspicuous religious habit. Carried unanimously. May four different Sisters experiment with the use of casual wear?"[78] The central administration (Generalate) had consulted with the Sacred Congregation. The reply was, of course, that this permission was beyond the General Council of the Congregation's authority and that the sisters had to wait for the Special Chapter of Aggiornamento that would take place in December. The provincial superior wrote, "Rome has spoken. Naturally we'll obey. Please think twice before asking to wear slacks etc., for bowling or skating. Of course, this seems the only feasible thing to wear. But yet, we can wait – can we not? Mother General and her council do have a special charism, which must be respected if we are to be true RNDMs."[79] In April, Sister M. Stephen, who had designed a habit that in its variations seemed to be in line with changes of other habits in Canada, was asked to model this habit to the other houses. The sisters were invited to send remarks on the habit to the president of the General Chapter at the motherhouse in Hastings, England.[80] In May, the provincial superior mentioned that the sisters might have gone beyond the bounds of experimentation regarding the habit and that she would appreciate it if some of the sisters would return to the ordinary habit. Those wearing the blue habit identical to the black one were in order because the change of colour had been approved.[81]

The question of the habit and, in particular, the veil was not resolved at the 1969 Chapter of Aggiornamento, which made the veil obligatory. On 10 February 1970, Provincial Superior Cécile Campeau informed the sisters that the General Council of the Congregation had requested that the Provincial Council delete statutes (articles) 19 and 20 of the 29 December 1969 Provincial Chapter Statutes that had been sent for approval.[82] Those statutes had to do with the habit. The 1969 Provincial Chapter had decided that they would continue to wear the Canadian habit, which was the religious habit of the congregation, but that sisters could also wear on an experimental basis the variations presented by the province at the 1969 General Chapter, in blue, beige, or black. Furthermore, in the detailed procès-verbal, statute 19 read: "A ready-made dress or suit may be bought if a similar style without decoration can be found. Vote 15 for; 10 against";[83] statute 20 read: "The following clothing for special occasions is approved: a) We wear suitable clothing for sports (picnics, camp) or conducting physical education classes."[84] The letter included the decision of the General Council of the Congregation regarding the veil, which reiterated the 1969 Chapter's decision to make the veil obligatory, a great disappointment for the Canadian province. Following the Chapter of Aggiornamento, the Provincial Chapter of December 1969 had decided, after studying the condition of the Canadian province, that the sisters were convinced that the veil had to be optional in Canada and asked the provincial superior to apply for the right to approve this change.

The General Council embraced a controlled notion of change emerging from the Vatican. The habit signified, for the sisters in the General Council, the authority of the religious and of the Church among laypeople, a form of symbolic capital that was actually losing ground in the new social secularizing context. For the conservative forces in the Church hierarchy, the habit embodied humility and restraint, in line with the Vatican policies controlling the body within the patriarchal order of the Church. The letter from the General Council censuring the provincial decision – fully transcribed in the letter of Provincial Superior Cécile Campeau to the sisters – contained a puzzling paragraph:

> I am confident that you will accept all without reserve. Some of us have been told by priests "to laugh in the face of authority, then do as we wish." Is this not destructive? I realize the pressures from without are strong. We will be told many a time that we are among the last religious to dress in secular [attire]. Many of us are adamant in saying that the dress does not make the Nun. We have daily occasions to prove this.[85]

The letter from the General Council included quotations from the pope supporting the council's resolution. It reads: "He [Pope Paul VI] said: 'The nun, as for that matter the priest and the Religious from other points of view, is faced with a terrible dilemma: either to be saints totally and without compromise, to reach their full dimension, or to be reduced to jokes, to caricatures, to failures and – let us say it – abortive beings.'"[86]

The letter from the General Council also said that, at an international gathering of 550 religious superiors in the Vatican's Clementine Hall, Pope Paul VI acknowledged the need for "interior renewal" and "exterior updating," but warned against the wiles of the world that could lessen the value of a life of poverty and obedience. Furthermore, it stated that the pope asked religious women "to give themselves to the Church because [the Church] needs them."[87] The council went on to say that he (the pope) encouraged the superiors to welcome renewal, but to be on guard lest there be a giving in "to the modern mentality," in other words to "transient and changeable attitudes and fashions to merge with the world."[88] The pope was quoted as talking about the danger of secularization and the perils of "economic independence" and individualism, warning the communities against individualism and small fraternities. The letter quoted him as saying: "It [the Church] relies on you not to disappoint the hopes of the Church but to respond beyond its very hopes."[89]

Provincial Superior Cécile Campeau, after quoting the entire letter from the council, closed by saying that the letter would bring relief to some and bitter disappointment to others. She closed with the words: "Let us live our calling, and in joy and sorrow let us remain united."[90]

The Vatican, as a field, was a gendered and hierarchical structured space, where many positions were taken that were linked to an old habitus or way of talking and behaving. As I write elsewhere, "the changes squeezed through that pattern, opened their way with the support of those who believed in the need for a major redirection."[91]

The opening address to the Special General Chapter of Aggiornamento, by Reverend Mother Mary Gertrude, superior general, reflected the persistence of residual elements, the habitus aligning the direction of the congregation. The speech represents an effort to deal with various positionings that would emerge in the Chapter, where the Canadian province appeared to be set in clear contrast to the direction of the congregation.

Reverend Mother Mary Gertrude opened the General Chapter of Aggiornamento by asking the delegates "to be conscious in all your deliberations and discussions of the need of a united effort. While this Chapter primarily has relevance to our own Congregation, we need to recall that its results will influence the Church."[92]

After setting the framework, the superior addressed change – a key concept in the process of renewal – in counterbalance with possible abuse, sustaining a notion of controlled change. She said:

> For the required and much desired renewal in our religious life, an attitude and disposition to accept change is imperative. Change is a necessary element of human life, a necessary condition of existence and growth. On the other hand, exaggerated craving for change merely for the sake of change, novelty and sensation, without valid reason and positive need, is an abuse which creates prejudice and aversion, a powerful and enduring obstacle to the acceptance of any further changes, even reasonable ones.[93]

The superior stated that the understanding of decentralization and the movement towards a loosening of structures, demanding more responsibility and initiative at the local level, should be counterbalanced by the principle of unity as a guiding principle. The superior expected a diversity of opinions with reference to the adaptation process, but made a call for charity and respect. In her opinion, an important task of the Chapter was to build the spiritual and apostolic life of the congregation, and she thus tried to find the correlation between prayer and charity, response to the voice of God, and the encounter with God. She acknowledged that these goals were not always reached, given the emphasis on formal prayers and external spirituality. These, she went on, were errors of the past, but now the danger was in going to the other extreme.

The same tone permeated the superior's leading statement on the vows of chastity, obedience, and poverty. In the past, the sisters had emphasized the negative side of chastity, the notion of sacrifice; now the superior was calling attention to the positive side, to chastity as giving a greater capacity for love. She quoted a Jesuit, Father William Bier: "A woman has greater emotional needs and greater yearning, because of her womanly sensibility, to love and to be loved. She also needs support in her strivings, even when these consist in life-long dedication to Christ."[94] The superior acknowledged that the congregation had been too fearful of particular friendships, moving the religious to experience lonely lives.

There is a reference in the speech to *Perfectae Caritatis* that addresses the nature of obedience: "Through the profession of Obedience, religious offer to God a total dedication of their own wills as a sacrifice of themselves; they thereby unite themselves with greater steadfastness and security to the saving will of God. In this way they follow the pattern of Jesus Christ, who came to do the Father's will."[95] The superior took care to remind the sisters that obedience could only be achieved through human intermediaries – in this case, the superior – who should understand authority as being in the spirit of loving service. She then quoted Karl Rahner, saying: "In religious life, on final analysis, there can be no real democratization of obedience. But there can be objective and clearly defined methods of procedure for achieving the counsel and information needed for the decision."[96] She appealed to the essence of the vow of poverty, that is, of sharing in the poverty of Christ through the detachment from all that is not God.

This opening address issued a call to reassess the missions, which were at the core of the life of the congregation, with the goal being "to ascertain whether we are serving to the best advantage, the needs of the Church, today." In fact, the Chapter stressed the ecclesial nature of missions in line with the foundress's close relationship with the Vatican. Meanwhile, the Canadian province had begun a mission in Peru in 1968 – a late response to John XXIII's call for missions in Latin America – and had also moved to a conscious option for the poor, while being exposed in time to the spirituality of liberation theology. Liberation theology starts from the praxis, from people's reality, and asserts that there is no salvation history apart from world history; the incarnation of Christ dissolved this duality.[97] In Canada, the sisters had also expanded their ministry to children with disabilities and intellectual challenges in what was called the Marian special class in 1969, which would evolve over the years into a school.[98]

The Chapter did not resolve many of the issues – such as the habit and the veil, autonomy, and a more horizontal structure – that preoccupied the Canadian province, but continued moving ahead in terms of working on the draft of the constitution ad experimentum – already begun before the Chapter; it also began experimentation with a personal budget, understood as the authorization to personally use a sum of money on a monthly or an annual basis (or over any other period of time) for specified purposes and subject to the approval of a competent authority.[99] It was clear that the use of the allowance was not considered a freedom to spend indiscriminately, but rather the privilege to practice a personal poverty that had been willingly and voluntarily asked for.[100]

The Chapter had invited four priests to lecture to its members. Father Michael O'Reilly, Oblate of Mary Immaculate, was attached to the RNDM's Generalate and worked on constitutions. Father Sean Fagan, a member of the Society of Mary and director of studies at the Marist International House of Studies in Rome, was a specialist in drafting constitutions. Father Gilbert Volery, who was Swiss, was a member of the Society of St Francis de Sales and secretary general to the Union of Major Superiors of England and Wales, as well as an expert on the religious life and aggiornamento and an advisor to various congregations, including the RNDM. As mentioned earlier, Father Paul Molinari, Jesuit priest, postulator general of the society and a peritus at Vatican II, was a member of the Theological Commission and secretary to the special subcommission that composed chapter seven of the Constitution of the Church. Father Molinari was part of the commission responsible for drafting *Perfectae Caritatis*.[101]

The exchanges in the Chapter of Aggiornamento regarding the ceremony (liturgy) of consecration show the Canadian delegates went with proposals for, in their words, changes leading to authenticity, including the use of spontaneous prayers during the ritual for religious profession; instead of fixed forms, the words, they said, should harmonize with the thinking of the candidates. The Canadians embraced the simplicity advocated by Vatican II for the initiation into religious life. The Canadian province had been active in preparing for the Chapter and the constitutions, as well as for changes to their own government and community life. In a document written in preparation for the Chapter, the Canadian province discussed key concepts of governance, such as co-responsibility (in opposition to authoritarianism), decentralization, subsidiarity, decisions (decision-making power being given to assemblies), and liaison (continual contact for the sharing of ideas towards the development of policy). The notes reveal a preoccupation with

areas of responsibility: the Generalate expected to formulate and implement general policy; the Provincialate expected to adapt policy to the
requirements of the province and ensure its implementation; and local
communities expected to implement provincial guidelines according to
the particular circumstances of each community.[102]

The Experimentation Commission in the Canadian province was active from 1969, and its documents reveal imaginative proposals showing
that the innovative forces in the community had a dominant positioning. The commission, which used a secret ballot, decided in relation to
community living, for example, to establish a fraternity wherein the
sisters, in freely choosing to live together, would share more intensely
and build a more vital community and prayerful life; the community
would be linked to a parish and share its life in some way.[103] It is interesting that the province decided that the new community in Peru
would be organized as a fraternity; this approach was not mentioned to
the Generalate until the mother provincial went to Rome in September.
The general administration, not happy about the development, made
this observation in writing. The administration was disappointed that
the province had appointed a local superior in Peru instead of making
a suggestion to the General Council, which in turn would have considered the suggestion and actually made the appointment.[104]

Mixed Blessings of Renewal: Emerging Issues

Vatican II gave room to new experiences of religious life for the sisters,
with a new network of bonds and engagement with the self-constitution
of their individual lives, something new in their thinking. Consequently, the sisters revised their understanding of mission and vision
to one that they needed to articulate as a collective, at a time when they
were discovering their own self and their desires and when many were
moving away from teaching. There was a focus on personal development and, along with the renewal, came a deep questioning, even of
the vows.[105] Patricia Wittberg wrote that the religious language moved
from theological constructs to psychological paradigms – the latter not
being adequate to explain what was desirable in their life as religious.
Wittberg, who studies US religious congregations, pointed out that religious congregations went through an alarming loss of identity and
reacted in a defensive way, thus generating a self-defeating pattern. The
statements of mission or charism became vague enough to encompass
various interests – different apostolates – which made any planning
difficult. The interpretation of community was done in terms of the
needs of the members, instead of sustaining collective commitments.

Wittberg thus made the case for a coherent and lived ideological frame as necessary for the survival of a religious movement.[106]

The Canadian Provincial Chapter of 1969 reflected the resignification of their original primary mission as teachers in school settings. As we examined before, the congregation began to leave the schools. The Chapter addressed the transition in the following way:

> In the time of Mother Foundress, instruction was the great need of the people; in our time, a broader educational apostolate may be the greater need. In our Canadian province we are being progressively freed from commitments in schools and so are able to widen our field of apostolic endeavour. Now is the time to determine the greatest need in the Church for us to fill and to begin to train sisters for this work.[107]

The first mixed blessings of renewal became evident. The understanding of members of a community as individuals is the trademark of modernity, something that, as Bauman wrote, is re-enacted daily.[108] The delegates at the Chapter were concerned by the decline in attendance at community recreation activities and by sisters being excluded from the small groups that formed naturally for recreation, as the needs of those sisters were never met. Planned recreation occasionally helped make attendance more attractive. The "daily reshaping and re-negotiating of the network of mutual entanglements" – in this case called community – worked in a different context without the rules of past history, making the inherent individualization of the process of renewal unpredictable. This situation recreated the irruption of modernity on a small scale.[109] The ambiguity of daily life was also part of the process that moved the sisters towards autonomy and self-assertion. Thus, the Chapter was led to acknowledge that there was no moral wrong in drinking alcohol or dancing; still, it called for sisters to keep in mind the basic principles and ideals of their commitment to Christ. The Chapter decided that sisters should be careful at social functions to maintain the ideal of religious life. Smoking had become a serious problem in many religious communities, and the RNDM Provincial Chapter decided against it, as a form of asceticism. There were also health and wellness activities that the sisters now wanted to pursue, for example, swimming, that might require public places, and there was assent on that. The issue of poverty generated a complicated discussion – one perhaps somewhat unusual for the secular reader – that included outlining the advantages of renting and owning buildings and the necessity of owning one or more cars (while the kind of car and its price would serve to witness poverty – a peculiar thought). With individualization, the enactment of vows, including the vow of poverty, was more difficult. For some sisters, to ask permission to dispose of, or use, material goods was something negative and, even more importantly, would retain the superior–inferior concept. There was also the major issue of the financial situation of the houses, which needed to be known by all the sisters. The point here is that, to this point, the sisters' identity had been a given identity, and in the process of building and rebuilding their self, they assumed responsibilities they had not known before. The stiff frame of religious life was no longer there to direct their lives.

Moving into the 1970s

Experimentation in terms of organization, governance, and personal budget, among other items, took place in the various provinces of the congregation, with authorization from norm seven of *Ecclesiae Sanctae*, powers conferred on the General Council by the Chapter of 1969, and a meeting organized in Rome in April 1970 by the International Union of Major Superiors with the approval of the Sacred Congregation.[110] Experimentation was a central component of the process of building a personal and collective identity.

Each province approached this experimentation in specific ways in line with their own history. In the case of the Canadian province, the process was embedded in a modernist frame, while also intersecting with the liquidity of post-modernity.[111] What was the meaning of experimentation for the sisters? In their words, it would generate an increase in apostolic effectiveness, move them towards a search for truth, and be a means for reviewing existing religious values, which, they thought, would be beneficial to all. Experimentation, they said, would be possible only if every sister accepted the views of every other. It would require encouragement and support, especially in failure or disappointment, as well as patience; it would be important to recognize the need for creativity and initiative as a part of co-responsibility; it would require positive acceptance of the courage and service of those who were willing to search for truth and new modes of life and to face the possibility of disappointment in order to find a means of survival for all in the community. It did not mean a search for emancipation, it was stated, or a means of escape from community responsibilities, but rather a recognition of each sister's role as a mature member of the community. Finally, it was expected that experimenters would have a certain openness to the possibility of failure and a willingness to recognize that their plans might be imperfect.[112]

In 1971, evaluations of experiments completed or in progress in the Canadian province, completed by 75 per cent of the sisters involved, showed that the management of a budget was generally accepted and that the sisters' sense of responsibility increased. Some sisters reported a sense of freedom and personal dignity. For some sisters, the experiment with the budget had little spiritual significance. Regarding clothing, many sisters reported that they felt better accepted by the public, closer to them, and less set apart as objects of reverential awe or escape. Several sisters commented that the habit motivated negativity or indifference rather than positive reactions in people at the time. Only two or three sisters wrote favourably of the desire for anonymity, and expressed the idea that leaving the habit indicated shame and a lack of pride in one's religious commitment. Many indicated advantages that had to do with hygiene, a new view of their body and their sense of personhood, and an opportunity to exercise responsibility and express their personality. At first, there was an excessive preoccupation with clothing. There were expressions used such as "freedom" and feeling "more human." These sisters did not see the habit as social capital; on the contrary, they saw it as socially costly.[113]

The community living experiment in Peru worked well. The sisters in Peru reported that, as far as personal witness or community witness was concerned, they found very little difference whether they lived separated or not. They were already understanding mission as witnessing, ahead of the congregation as a whole. Their report on obedience was simple; the feeling was that, whether the superior resided with the group or not, the same spirit of responsibility to the group existed.[114] The experiment with the habit in the Canadian province that began in January 1971 led to the following conclusion:

After more than a year of wearing contemporary clothing, sometimes exclusively and sometimes alternately with variations of the "Canadian" habit, many sisters have grown to look on this as the normal way for them to dress. Emphasis is on the person as the witness, rather than on what she wears, and most sisters consider a cross or ring to be a sufficient external sign of our dedication. Convenience and suitability are major factors in choice of clothing and the sisters are increasingly aware of the possibilities for witnessing such virtues as modesty and simplicity.

The Recommendation to the General Chapter of 1972: Since secular dress is generally acceptable for religious in Canada, and yet a substantial number of sisters prefer to wear a habit, we recommend that the Provincial Chapter establish a habit for those who wish it, but that choice of clothing be left to the discretion of each individual sister in Canada.[115]

This recommendation was accepted.

There were difficulties emerging from the international/transnational character of the congregation and the need to articulate in some way the aspiration and visions of the different provinces. The constitutions, even in their final version, reflected changes within certain parameters. The language of the oral narrations and even the various positions at the Chapters – especially the Canadian one – went beyond the language of the constitutions. On this matter, Provincial Superior Sister Cécile Campeau said: "The congregation soon discovered that the constitutions at which we had worked so hard reflected very little of the spirit and the spirituality of our congregation. So the constitutions were soon replaced – I think in 1972."[116] In fact, the constitutions' "ad experimentum" of 1969 were amended in 1972 and 1975. In August 1977, at a session of the General Council with members of the Constitutions Commission, observations were made by Father Jean Beyer, who was quoted as saying that the 1972 constitutions were a beautiful compendium of the Vatican Council, but they did not contain anything particular to the congregation, for example, the spirit and charism of the foundress did not come through. He pointed out that "Recreated in Hope" (Acts of the 20th General Chapter of the Congregation in 1972) contained more spirituality of the Mother Foundress. He also asked to revisit the congregation's rule, which was the Rule of St Augustine. Interestingly, he observed that there was not enough with regard to subsidiarity, or decentralization. The constitutions were amended again, and the rule and constitutions were approved by the 8 December 1978 decree of the *Sacra Congregatio Pro Religiosis et Institutis Saecularibus*, as a text defining the congregation's identity.[117] A cursory reading shows that the original core of the mission as established in article 2 of the first constitutions – which stated that sisters would devote themselves to the instruction and Christian education of children and women, above all in "infidel" and non-Catholic countries[118] – was re-proposed in article 58 of the new constitutions. It then read: "We share in the missionary task of the church principally through the works of Christian education. Other works in keeping with the mission and spirit of the congregation are also undertaken."[119]

Resignifying Mission

The understanding of mission and vision began to change earlier in the Canadian province, inspired by contextual changes and the sisters' face-to-face encounter with social injustice in Peru, where they had begun their own mission in 1969, as we will see in chapter eleven. This encounter resignified that mission from the bottom up. In Peru, the province came into contact with liberation theology and the impact of the 1968 Document of Medellín. The document was the outcome of the Conference of Latin American Bishops in Medellín, Colombia, in 1968 and brought a fresh liberating utopia grounded in liberation theology, which aimed at a new model of society. At the international level, the congregation lived through the processes of decolonization; however, there is no self-critique of the congregation's role in the colonial projects. Superior General M. Bénédicte, in her opening address to the General Chapter of 1972, "Recreated in Hope," projected a new vision for the congregation. She said:

> What is the meaning of our "mission" in the church and in the contemporary world? We know that we cannot live it as we did in the past. We must review our missionary vocation in the light of new conditions of life and environment. New worlds are springing up everywhere and the Church is not present in them. Modern society begets hidden misery; imbalance between affluent and poor countries is growing. Are we going to respond to the cry of the poor? For us it is no longer a question of looking upon charity as a "help to be given to the neighbour," but of resolutely entering into "combat on the side of justice, peace and liberty for others" (J.B. Metz).[120]

The language of justice was coming into the congregation as well as the notion of the "new man" – a notion quite dominant in Latin America and one which the superior took from deeply committed ecumenist Dominican father and theologian Jean-Marie Tillard from Ottawa, Canada. There is no discussion of the role of the congregation in processes of colonization in the minutes of the Chapters. At the international level, the apostolate in the 1970s had an older tone: the primary service was stated as being education, especially in non-Christian and de-Christianized countries; however, as members of a "pilgrim church," they saw the obligation to move forward, to be sensitive to the needs of the time, and to be open to the Spirit in their vision of the future. They talked of a renewed missionary thrust and followed what they called "the trend towards interpreting our primary work of education in its widest sense."[121] The General Chapter of 1972, "Recreated in Hope," changed the concept of education – one central to the spirit (charism) of the congregation – making it very broad, partly because there were problems in identifying a common vision.

There was ambiguity in the transition to a renewed apostolate. In a report of April/May 1973, the superior general who visited Canada wrote with reference to the sisters' apostolic and missionary activity:

We must not forget that *education* remains our primary service in the Church. There exists today a disaffection for so called teaching properly. However, I believe it still has an apostolic value and it continues to be an excellent means of reaching the young.[122]

She questioned "why so many years of study [are needed] to obtain necessary qualifications [to serve as teachers in the system] if afterwards the sisters turn to other activities." The superior general, however, was aware of the inevitability of change and the need to broaden the scope of the congregation's educational trust: "To be sure, I do not envisage education in the restricted sense of the term. I am convinced that religious have roles to fulfil in pastoral catechetics and in works of a social nature such as Jean Vanier School, etc., and I fully approve them."[123]

In the 1970s, and particularly at the Enlarged General Council of May 1975, there was a drive to study the "charism" of the congregation, a term that became dominant with Vatican II to refer to the original inspiration of the congregation. The sisters did not often use charism; for them, the term embodied a desire to have a more "profound understanding of Mother Foundress" and of her vision of the congregation within the Church.[124] The sisters tried to clarify key concepts such as Trinity, Mission, Contemplation and Action, and Spirit of Mary. The studies were conducted in all the provinces, and Claire Himbeault delivered numerous workshops in the Canadian province.

A provincial document from 1978 portrays well the situation of the congregation at the end of the 1970s. The key problem was identified as follows: "We do not share, understand and accept the various expressions (apostolates, attitudes, lifestyles, etc.) [of] our common vision, and so we lack a sense of belonging and of mutual commitment."[125] The sisters concluded that they shared a genuine RNDM vision, although they did not articulate it at this point, but that it was expressed in widely different ways in their daily lives. They were not used to communicating with each other. They said that the "deep probing and intense communication in[to] which we were forced" by the renewal process made them aware that along their lives they had communicated little and poorly.[126] Consequently, there were misunderstandings, tensions, and fear in their relations with one another and with God. One example given was, "It is hard to be committed to someone I do not understand, and harder still to believe that she is committed to me."[127] The sisters went back to their context and the conjuncture in which they were inserted to understand their situation.

The sisters presented a multipronged explanation that shows the conjuncture in which they were going through "adaptation." The intersections in this "conjuncture" were various. The Catholic Church in Canada had its own problems. The progressive attitude of the Canadian bishops had precipitated a conservative backlash and resulting polarization; the emerging role of the laity had changed the role and status of clergy and religious, generating a certain holding back on the part of the clergy as it was unsure of its own role; and there was a severe decline in the number of vocations for religious life and for priesthood. The sisters thought that their own alienation and insecurity had to do with transformations in society at large, which had taken place in the long 1960s and beyond. The features selected in the report actually show various transitions, including the changes of the 1960s, the movement towards neoliberalism, the difficulties that came with having to deal with their own sense of authority, and the unevenness of the process of change. They mentioned mobility, loneliness, the breakdown of the family unit and of nuclear families, the loss of extended family, and changes in education, writing that "young people are taught to think rather than to learn facts, to question rather than to have answers" and asserting that "this questioning attitude affects older members of the community as well as new recruits."[128] Another intersection in the conjuncture was the situation in the Canadian province. It was pointed out that educational and diocesan developments in the provinces of Manitoba, Saskatchewan, and Quebec, and in Peru, had led to differing pastoral and educational needs, and consequently to varying apostolates. These experiences were seen as major factors influencing different lifestyles in different communities. The experience in Peru, examined in chapter eleven, brought an even newer theological understanding, since the sisters there were exposed to liberation theology, to Medellín, to Paulo Freire's notions of education (including his early notion of conscientization, of education for either liberation or domestication), and, of course, to the various approaches taken by the Church on social justice. The report also made reference to the repercussions on the community of the English–French situation in Canada due to difficulties in communication, emotional reactions, and different world views. Finally, the other issue in the Canadian province was, in the sisters' view, the various theological and spiritual schools of thought received by the sisters depending on their place of formation. The report concluded with the view that the apostolic and cultural diversity to which the province was exposed was divisive rather than enriching.

There were problems with common understandings of the concepts of subsidiarity, obedience, authority, accountability, and fraternal correction.[129] To an important extent, the Canadian province was a field with polarization, in which the transformative leaders experienced difficulties in creating commonalities with some sisters because, despite the aforementioned perception of possessing a common vision, not everyone agreed with the points of reference that had become dominant. Some members of the community had difficulties adapting to a diverse, pluralistic world in which, in a natural process, they were exposed to and contaminated with ideas and values foreign to old Catholic ways.

The original inspiration of the congregation's foundress was an issue explored in the 1970s and early 1980s. It was an important step in rethinking the congregation's vision and mission. Jesuit fathers were either cited or invited in person to discuss spirituality and the concept of spiritual leadership. Superior General M. Bénédicte started with Father P. Molinari's view that there was no explanation for the inspiration of the foundress because it was something that the Holy Spirit put into their hearts in order to discover behind her expression – grounded in the language of the time – the real depth of her original inspiration, her notion of "divine missions," and her understanding of the missionary nature of God.[130] Jesuit Father J. Beyer worked with the sisters on the notion of charism and defined it as "a gift given by God, entrusted to his Church, not only to the Institute – it is a gift to the Church – and preserved by his grace."[131]

The ecclesiological sense of mission (missionary work defined by the needs of the Church) was persistent in the life of the congregation until the mid-1980s, when the congregation became fully engaged with social justice. A letter from the provincial superior, attending the Enlarged General Council of 1982 in India, talked of two Jesuits, Fathers J. Neuner, an Austrian and professor of theology in India who had attended the Second Vatican Council, and J.A. Coelho, tertian master of the Jesuits at Varanasi, India. The latter Jesuit challenged the sisters to be strong within themselves and, above all, to be women of God. This father directed them in practicing yoga.[132] Very early in the conference, a diocesan priest, Father Barreto, who worked at the Indian Social Institute in Bangalore, talked about the situation of the current world, of social inequality in India, and of the monstrous gap between rich and poor; he traced the history of capitalism, the logic of which is profit, that has brought us to our world of gross injustice. He talked also of the need to openly profess solidarity with the poor.[133]

The Enlarged Council of 1982 set the stage for the General Chapter of 1984. The letter of convocation to the Chapter made clear three points: the sisters had to evangelize themselves and conform their lives to Jesus Christ in truth; engage themselves in their mission of evangelization wherever the Church was calling them by making internationality and mobility more effective; and live the preferential option for the poor and promote justice and peace for the sake of the kingdom. The letter placed emphasis on opting for the poor in choosing radical conversion and referred to Vatican II, Medellín, and Puebla. The radical conversion had to be practical, spiritual, and theological. That meant a movement from charity to justice, a movement that would aim at development and liberation. The practical aspect of conversion implied a movement from a spiritual theology, which stressed prayer and rites, to a theology of incarnation with a presence in the world.[134]

The missionary experience of the Canadian province in Peru, which started in 1969 and was situated in the midst of the "Peruvian revolution," the presence of liberation theology, and the sisters' work with the people, had challenged the notion of mission as Church mission and its redeeming character and led to an original approach that framed the Latin American reception of Vatican II as expounded in the Medellín document. Not everyone understood the experience, but it had a great impact on the life of the province and its delegates to the general chapters and enlarged councils. The Canadian province fully embraced the resolutions of the General Chapter of 1984, "Witnessing to the Gospel: Beyond All Frontiers," which made social justice central to the life of the congregation and challenged the sisters "to develop a world vision and to be ready to move out in response to the great needs of today's world, e.g., in Latin America, the Far East ... to respond ... to the changing needs of those around us."[135] Enculturation in every milieu was central in an apostolic plan that committed the sisters to "on-going programmes for education and conscientization in the areas of social justice,"[136] as well as to "education and conscientization of the non-poor and non-oppressed to realize that structures that protect their interests are very often the cause of misery for the poor."[137] The Chapter included a call to develop justice and peace programs in the congregation's schools in order to conscientize students and expose them to injustices in their own and other societies. The Canadian province naturally embraced the Chapter's resolutions and further developed a program with Indigenous peoples and refugees; at the same time, the Peruvian mission was about to gain autonomy, and it did so in 1986.[138] The Canadian province, however, had been moved away, by and large, from school teaching for some time. Instead, the province was active in inserting itself into local social configurations – but still contended with the parameters of the Church's gendered, hierarchical organization.

The reflections of Superior General Claire Himbeault's visitation in 1989, herself a Canadian, conveyed a clear shift. She wrote: "We believe there has been a significant movement in the Province towards the ideal of mission put forth in the 1984 General Chapter and emphasized in your own Provincial Documents resulting from your Chapter and Assemblies, 1984–1989."[139] The notion of Christian education had been considerably widened within the Canadian province: there was a movement to reach out to the poor, the marginalized, and those suffering injustice; there was a concern with the plight of refugees; there was evidence of greater awareness regarding the Indigenous and Métis peoples; and, overall, social justice issues were receiving more attention. The apostolic work had also been extended to ministry with the sick and the grieving. The quality of the work was there, even as the congregation was aging and there were few new vocations.[140]

The superior wanted to examine the possibilities of enacting a new way of being missionary and a new way of living communion, following the new model discussed at the Provincial Assembly of the Canadian province in October of 1989. This new model of mission was defined as incarnational, liberating, and contemplative, and as involving ministering in another culture, social class, or country.[141] Mission in this model was to be a way of life in which the people would see the missionary as one of them, as one who shares in their lives and their experiences. The province made substantial changes, moving away from larger structured communities to smaller communities; some of the latter functioned through the concept of "shared responsibility," where each sister was responsible for and accountable to the small group as a whole.[142]

The 1980s closed with a re-articulation of the congregation's vision and mission led by Superior General Claire Himbeault. The 1990 General Chapter produced *RNDM for Mission*, two documents conveying statements of what the sisters believed and wanted to accomplish. They said:

> It is time to be who we are: Sisters of Our Lady of the Missions, women for mission as was Euphrasie Barbier. We are women committed to accept[ing] daily the call of God to be sent ... It is time to live the fullness of who we are: women committed to prayer and community based on the radical living of the Gospel's values to further the Reign of God. The rediscovery of the centrality of Mission in our Charism is giving unity to our lives. Contemplation, Communion, Obedience, Poverty, Chastity are for Mission. It is the integration of the different aspects of our Charism and of our lives that we are being called to live.[143]

In living out the option for the poor, the marginalized, and the oppressed, the sisters chose women, youth, tribal and Indigenous peoples, and refugees as the priority for their apostolate; they believed that it was important to address racism, inter-religious dialogue, and language and communication across cultures.[144] The way of living a mission, in their view, should be incarnational, contemplative, prophetic, and collaborative: "Let us be with the poor as they seek to empower themselves and to transform unjust structures ... Let us live together our RNDM call to communion/community for mission, a communion that called for mutual appreciation, reconciliation, [and] a sense of wonder."[145] The sisters decided to foster a style of leadership that would be collegial, participative, and collaborative.[146] The influence of early feminist thea/o/*logians, such as Rosemary Radford Ruether, who examined religion and sexism and put forward ideas for a feminist thea/o/*logy by the mid-1980s, Mary Daly, who wrote about women's liberation, Elisabeth Schüssler Fiorenza, who addressed the invisibility of women, and Elizabeth Johnson and Sandra Schneiders, was present not only in the critique of structures and power but also in the new ways of doing things. The engagement with feminist thea/o/*logy became prominent in the 1990s and 2000s.[147]

There was awareness that serious demographic changes had occurred in the congregation. There were 1,240 sisters in 1972; in 1990, there were 975. The provinces of Vietnam, Myanmar (Burma), India, and Bangladesh had remained stable, whereas those of the British Isles, France, Aotearoa New Zealand, Australia, and Canada had experienced a noticeable diminution that was largely due to deaths, departures, and fewer entries. The geographical and cultural map of the congregation was changing.[148] The sisters embraced – as Vatican II did – the involvement of the laity. Since the fundamental inspiration of Euphrasie Barbier was the missionary nature of God, recognizing that all missions had their source in the Trinity, the sisters concluded that this conception was an understanding of mission that could and must be shared with the laity.[149]

Chapter Ten

Resignifying Vision and Mission: The 1990s and 2000s, and the Movement towards Eco-Spirituality

As mentioned in previous chapters, the need for changes such as a new style of leadership and the recreation of the congregation's vision and mission were vigorously pursued in the 1990s and 2000s. At the same time, the RNDM sisters expanded on the related themes of their mission, moving into an approach based on eco-spirituality and a celebration of womanness and love for each other.

In the 1980s, the congregation had begun to move towards a reignocentric mission approach (directed by the needs identified by the congregation), rather than an ecclesiocentric approach (directed by the needs identified by the Church). The provincial and international chapters were called, in some cases and particularly in the 1990s, gatherings, in a manner breaking with the formality of the notion of a General Chapter; the General Council, in turn, was called the leadership team. The new terminology was inconsistent and was not officially recorded in the booklet containing amendments to the constitutions.

With the reignocentric mission approach now firmly in place, it was at the General Gathering of 1996 in Rome that mission – which addresses injustices and oppression – was conceived as universal, as being in relation to everything, while also recognizing God's presence in ourselves, in others, in society, and in the whole of creation.

The 1996 General Gathering resulted in many decisions regarding the new focus of the congregation. Internationality, an integral part of the charism (the now recreated vision and mission of the congregation), would be enacted by holding one another in prayer worldwide; by sharing time, talents, spirituality, and culture; and by continuing to form international communities in the administrative units. There would be a strong focus on women who were voiceless, which would take into consideration the strategic actions delineated at the 1995 Beijing Conference on Women. Justice, peace, and the integrity of creation would continue to be integral parts of the congregation's individual and communal life; it was proposed that each administrative unit make affiliations with existing non-governmental organizations (NGOs). It was also recommended that international missioning be done after clear discernment. Finally, the congregation determined that entering into dialogue – interfaith dialogue – with peoples of other faiths and traditions would be an integral part of their mission.[1]

Communion was one of the interesting concepts that would fully affect the life of the congregation going forward. The sisters decided that it would include formation, leadership (a participative, collaborative style, with flexibility), resources (to be shared), and opening up to lay associates. The related statement said: "By respecting the lands, cultures and individuality of our Sisters and the peoples among whom we live and work, we can draw closer in community and unity."[2]

Contemplation, another important concept driving the congregation and its focus, was understood as being part of reaching the right relationship with God, the self, the other, the earth, and the cosmos. Collaboration was another principle that the sisters would newly apply to their work with the Church; they considered the congregation as being part of an inclusive Church at the parish, diocesan, and national levels, where all take an active role in the life of the Church. A powerful statement set up their new and very different approach to the Church hierarchy: "We recognize the struggle and hold the pain of those oppressed by the institutional church, and as sisters of Euphrasie we know that we too may find ourselves in situations of tension with the hierarchy. We celebrate the various ways of being Church and [of] living inculturation. We continue to be attentive to opportunities to respond to the hunger for spirituality in our world today."[3] The principle of collaboration also referred to walking with people on the margins of Church and society. Two other principles were included in the new approach: reconciliation (living positively and recreating one another in love, together, through naming, holding, reconciling, and healing one another's pain) and inclusivity (there was a call for full inclusiveness in the community of sisters through empowering and giving voice to all).[4] The congregation as a whole was moving beyond fractures and towards mutual understanding across difference and a renewed vision.

The Canadian province examined the direction of the 1996 General Gathering in terms of the various challenges the province was facing. For one thing, the province defined itself as an aging congregation and, as such, had identified the need for care provisions. This issue was one of the major challenges to the rebirth of the congregation's vision and mission, but there were also others. The province determined that its community did not hold a common vision/understanding/image of the "associates" (lay members), and thus it would try to explore creative ways of being "in association." Furthermore, the province had often found that improving communication in the community required the professional presence of a facilitator, and thus it identified the need to grow in terms of communication skills. The province also affirmed the need to continue working with and searching for ways to be with, present to, and sensitive to Indigenous communities and issues, and identified the need for a commitment to a growth process on both individual and community levels. There was a search for inner freedom. Notably, the province struggled with the way the Eucharist was celebrated, especially with the lack of inclusivity given women's place in the Church.[5]

The 1999 Provincial Gathering, "Women at the Door 2000," celebrated womanness and an awareness of the need to challenge patriarchy and to love one another, and of the sisters' prophetic role. The question of who the RNDM sisters were as individual women and as community leaders was at the forefront, and they fully repositioned their sense of self as religious women, stressing the relational dimension of the self. Solidarity had become a coordinating force behind the meaning of the resolutions.[6] Songs, prayers, reflections, narratives, and the construction of fairy tales during this celebration helped the sisters to open a figurative door – one that would bring hope for the new millennium – look through it, and move together through the door. Central ideas that were considered by all as gifts that came out of this gathering were the notion of experiencing aging as something to celebrate; the natural wholeness of body, mind, and soul, the three of which cannot be separated, as in dualistic theology; and the importance of cultivating a nurturing mindset to restore wholeness in the sisters.

The provincial sisters showed at the gathering a strong critical view of the patriarchy and a sense of the otherness generated by the official Magisterium. Solidarity was at the core of these women's thinking of themselves as a community of women standing at and going through the door of a new millennium. A comment collected from one sister's speech at the celebration summarized well their embracement of solidarity:

> Who am I standing with at this time? What is our sisterhood that will help us go through the door as a community? It is important that we hold the experience of the other, their truth, their language and at the same time trusting the integrity of my truth, loving in a non-interpretative manner. Your story is my story – my story is your story. There is a profound sense of connectedness established when we receive and hold the story of the other.[7]

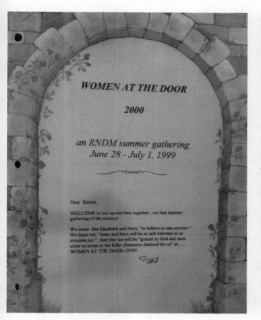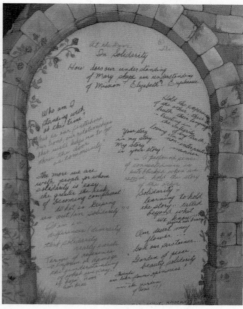

10.1 Signed poster for "Women at the Door 2000," the RNDM summer gathering held from 28 June to 1 July 1999. Materials provided by then provincial superior Veronica Dunne.

Together with the "Women at the Door 2000" posters and documents, there were also printed copies of two emails dated in May 2000.[8] They refer to the notification from the Congregation for the Doctrine of the Faith in Rome that prohibited a Society of the Divine Savior father and a School Sisters of Notre Dame sister from pastoral ministry to lesbian and gay people. The email from Father Robert Nugent, SDS, talks about the notification his superiors received from the Congregation for the Doctrine of the Faith prohibiting him permanently from pastoral initiatives with homosexual persons and their families.[9] The other email is a statement from New Ways Ministry condemning the silencing of these religious through forbidding them to talk to members of this particular community group. In the email, the ministry responded to the notification by inviting gay and lesbian Catholics, "particularly those who work in Church structures to use this event as an opportunity to speak the truth of their lives to their brothers and sisters in Christ."[10] The email also contained strong words against the repressive and exclusive policies of the Vatican and considered the case to be one of freedom of conscience. The sisters kept these emails with the documents related to their gathering at a point in which they were rejecting the otherness created by the official Magisterium. The congregation was opened to embrace difference.

Feminist thea/o/*logy, which continued to develop in the 1990s, had, by and large, an inter-spiritual character, and contextual feminist the*logy, in particular, included many women scholars who started to reflect from their experience (loci theologici), not only in a discursive form.[11] This focus easily led to an eco-theology that was in dialogue with a variety of political, cultural, and environmental theories, as well as various disciplines within an ecumenical context, and that led to an engaging praxis.

The Canadian Province: Nurturing an Ecological Spirituality

The 2000s signalled a major shift in the vision and mission of the congregation, one that had been already hinted at in the 1990s: the cultivation of an ecological spirituality. This shift had profound roots in the Canadian province, and it would define the 2008 Congregational Chapter when it took place in Thailand.

At the 25th General Gathering in Pattaya, Thailand, in 2002, the congregation stated that the RNDMs connected with the deepest yearnings of peoples across the world for peace, justice, and the integrity of creation.[12] There was a call for each province to work personally and as a group with issues of racism, ethnocentrism, and classism – a goal that, the sisters acknowledged, was within them all to accomplish, individually, communally, and as a congregation. Still, in 2002, the sisters were committed to clearing away the colonial residual elements of their original missionary work, now that they were entering into another phase of their process of recreation.

The provincial retreat of June 2003, entitled "Earth Story, Sacred Story, Nurturing an Ecological Spirituality," embodies a powerful landmark. It was a call to cultivate awe and wonder and compassion and healing. Eco-spirituality, in the sisters' view, challenged them "to see all life forms as part of the same sacred body, earth, recognizing the sacredness of all." It was "a commitment to the entire web of life."[13] In their recreation of their vision and mission, the sisters attempted to grow in sensitivity in relation to the natural world in the same way in which they attempted to grow their sensitivity towards God and towards an openness to all humans, justice and care being a sacred responsibility.[14] The program of the 2003 retreat, under the section titled "The Call to Awe and Wonder," contained the following topics for discussion: "The value of Story, Genesis, the new understanding of our Sacred Universe and our place in it"; "exploring the three values/principles of our Sacred Universe that are in effect since its origin, and how we are invited to be part of it as a society, and as an earth community"; "identifying the present cosmology that has shaped our worldview and its impact in our lives and institutions"; and "discovering a holistic Cosmology that reveals our place within the Earth community. What signs do we see of it now?" The rituals conducted at the end of each day show an open approach to spirituality marked by new syncretic practices. The sessions on "The Call to Awe and Wonder" included the following "Ritual/ sharing of wisdom" activities: "Summer Solstice – Celebrate Cosmic Wedding of Earth and Sun"; "Mirror Walk"; and looking at slides of the astronauts and reading their journal entries.[15] The program's focus illustrates the sisters' goal of trying to find their place within the earth community and noticing the signs they could see of that place.

The program for the next day's sessions, under "The Call to Compassion and Healing," included the following topics: "Our ecological footprint"; "Our role in the urgency of making wise choices for the well being of the planet"; the question, "What are the local concerns?"; "Council of all Beings – A process to heighten our place within the Earth Community"; and the question, "How do we nurture an Ecological Spirituality?" There was also a focus on St Francis, the mystics, and current authors who fostered ecological spirituality. The final day's program was on the topic "Challenge to Religious." Each of these daily sessions also closed with a special ritual: "Truth Mandala, or Two Circles, or Dance"; "Debriefing/Dance"; and "Experiencing the Cosmic Walk as Our Story." The closing ritual on the final day of the seven-day retreat was not described further in the program.

For guidance, the sisters went to several authors (there are no citations of the particular works in most cases, just the names of the authors), such as Jay B. McDaniel, Gerard Manley Hopkins, Sallie McFague, Jane Blewett, and Thomas Berry. Former provincial superior, Sister Veronica Dunne, mentioned that the RNDMs recognized the parallels between the scientific insights of the new cosmology, the wisdom traditions of Indigenous cultures, and the insights of major world religions. She further mentioned Brian Swimme, Mary Evelyn Tucker, Elizabeth Johnson, Rosemary Radford Ruether, Ilia Delio, and Matthew Fox – among others – influential eco-theological thinkers who had impacted numerous Canadian RNDMs. Through their studies, the sisters construed the characteristics of an ecological spirituality as including the following: "the interconnectedness of all things, the intrinsic value of all of life, the continuity of all life and the compassion of God for all of life (human and non human)." They viewed this new spirituality as being "tolerant and open to all religions"; as seeing neither God nor the world as "changeless objects on which we cling"; as "a faith without absolutes"; and as a panentheistic (finding God in everything) "way of imaging divine Mystery as the mind or heart of the Universe and the Universe as the body of God." Eco-spirituality, they wrote, also incorporates the notion that "things happen in the world that even God cannot prevent," and thus "it does not trust God to prevent crosses, but rather to heal and to resurrect." Eco-spirituality is, they believed, open to the earth as being a living organism that has "value in its own right" – referring to the "sacredness of physical matter," the land as evolutionary and as a donated gift, and the "value of all living beings." It is "sensitive to the aliveness of the earth" and the fact that we, humans, are also "made of earth." It is a spirituality that is "able to find God in the joy of dance, the pleasure of food, the quietness of breathing." And it sees the sky as a "perpetual reminder that life on earth is itself part of a larger cosmic story and ultimately a larger Divine Story." This spirituality "seeks to be open to [both domesticated and wild] animals, to recognize our bondedness." Moreover, "it seeks to be open to all humans to whom we have the deepest connections, while justice and care are our sacred responsibilities. Listening, speaking, identifying with the human poor and oppressed [being] a social agenda of the Christian ethic." Finally, ecological spirituality, they wrote, acknowledges "growth, revision, [and] criticism, and sees itself [as being] in a process of becoming." In other words, it is a spirituality that does not "absolutize itself." There is no dualism, and there is a deep respect for diversity.[16]

Michael Dowd's *Earthspirit: A Handbook for Nurturing an Ecological Christianity* was also used at length in the retreat, acting as a point of reference to explain the interrelation and interdependency of all things; to present the universe as having a spiritual dimension as well as a material one; and to examine us, as humans, as *being* the earth. The concepts discussed also included the awareness that humans are, indeed, totally dependent upon the health of the wider community of life for our own health – that what we do to the earth, we do to ourselves. Consequently, it follows that humans are an integral part of the earth, not superior to it, and "in our relationship to God is the entire community of life, rather than humans in isolation."[17] An interesting quotation closed the notes taken by the sisters: "We are deceived if we think that we can love God and honor God's holiness without loving others (humans and non-humans) and honoring the holiness of nature."

The retreat was rich in activities, readings, songs (earth songs, songs by Jan Novotka), and special prayers, including the Earth Litany from the United Nations Environment Programme's Environmental Sabbath/Earth Rest Day. There were suggestions in the handouts regarding what to do during and how to experience one's walking time (taking a walk) and "inner spirit times," including a short list of Reflection Questions to consider during these moments; they were written by Sister Constance Kozel, Sister of Mercy of the Americas, a freelance writer on environmental issues and one of the "founding mothers" of the Mercy Earth Harmony Network. Sister Kozel's focus was on leading retreat participants to a sense of awareness of what surrounds us as humans, as well as to a mindfulness of the body and of the feelings, the mind, and the soul. There was also a "Prayer for Global Restoration," led by Sister Michelle Balek, OSF (Order of St Francis), from Iowa, the leading lines of which are suggestive of the sisters' focus:

Good and Gracious God
                    Source of all Life,
                        All creation is charged with your Divine Energy.
Ignite your spark within us,
That we may know ourselves as truly human and holy,
                                Irrevocably part of the Web of Life.
All creation
                    – each star and every flower,
                    – each drop of water and every person,
                    – each and every atom, down to its very electrons,
                        Explodes with the revelation of your Sacred
                                Mystery.

The critique of Western cosmology discussed at the retreat showed how it is closely intertwined with Western economics, law, and ethics. Thus, Western morality has been solely concerned with human behaviour towards God and other human beings; the way humanity treats the earth has not been considered a moral issue. Corporations are able to "legally poison air, water and soil, and forests and species can be obliterated because our morality and laws are human-centered rather than life-centered." Moreover, the handout read, creation in the Western world was conceived as patriarchal and hierarchical: God was the Father; men were considered superior to women; male children were thought to be more important than female children; animals were considered above plants, and plants above insects, worms, and bacteria; and the inanimate rocks and elements of earth were placed at the bottom of the pyramid. It was believed that this hierarchical structure was the way God set up the world at the beginning, and the way it was intended to remain. Institutions including schools embodied this perspective.[18]

The working groups tried to clarify principles such as differentiation, interiority, and communion, and to solve problems, for example, how one could better respect and reverence the interiority and differences of others. The right of animals to live in their environment without humans encroaching on that right was an important issue. As well, there was a preoccupation in the group discussions regarding how to explain the principles and how to integrate them into daily life and spirituality. It was decided that, for their purposes, differentiation referred to the uniqueness of each element of the universe, be it a flower or a human being. Interiority referred to the concept that "everything that comes into existence *is a voice* that reveals an aspect of the deeper inner mystery that no other voice can reveal" (emphasis added); in other words, everything that exists is alive, even a rock. Communion, the sisters agreed, referred to the notion that the "universe is one communion experience"[19] and that "relationship is the essence of existence."[20]

There was also a discussion of a text, "The Scriptures of Earth," written by Jane Blewett, which saw the newborn infant, who emerges from the womb with human form, as "already linked to a common mammalian form that the Earth invented and adapted over some 500 million years." When the child takes the first gulp of fresh air, "that air has already passed through the lungs of all the great men and women, the great black bear and the tiny chipmunk, all creatures that have breathed throughout history." The child is "welcomed into the community of spirit-air, into the breath community of Sarah and Abraham, of Miriam and Moses, of Mary and Joseph, Jesus, Dorothy Day, Einstein, Mahatma Gandhi, and the women martyrs of El Salvador." And, Blewett wrote, this new life will bring its own never before, and never to be repeated, "breath of life for all future generations." The author wrote that she often asked herself: "What have I breathed into the community of life in this day? What has emerged from within me that will give life to future generations?"[21] The text led to the exploration of the deepest connections among all living creatures and the continuity of life, and to the complex attempt to bind all differentiated interiorities into one cosmic whole. The sisters were in the process of critiquing the dominant Western cosmology and embracing an emerging cosmology, relational in character and inclusive of the entire planetary system. This new cosmology, grounded in interconnectedness and an egalitarian ethos, would nourish awe and imagination, and hence cultivate a creative engagement with the world well beyond the human world.

Earlier Cosmology	Emerging Cosmology
Mechanistic model	relational model
Earth as object	living planet system
Supply and demand	
Alienation of the body	self generating, self organizing,
	Self governing/nourishing
Punch in punch/ out at work	self educating/healing
We are a machine, determined	
by the clock.	
Objective, value free facts	Subjective, mystery, revelatory
Competition- law of economics	interdependence, belonging,
Survival of fittest (richest)	cooperation, communion,
Compulsive, greedy	egalitarian, participative,
	Equality.
Dualism- subject/object	
Spirit/ matter	one, unity, interconnectedness,
Economic world is ladder like	unfolding, birth/life/death cycle

Circle image
All history is sacred for God was at
work in creation, we need to listen to
the evolving Story

Reason, rational thought	Imagination, intuition, awareness,
	creativity

Future steps of evolution-
To awaken an inner capacity for awe, wonder, reverence,
nonviolence, mutuality, compassion and community of life:
one single living community

10.2 Cosmology handout from RNDM retreat, 2003. Sourced from handout materials from the RNDM retreat for the sisters of the Canadian province, "Earth Story, Sacred Story, Nurturing an Ecological Spirituality," held at Villa Maria Retreat house in Winnipeg and led by Sister Judy Schachtel, SMS, 20–27 June 2003; provided by then provincial superior Veronica Dunne, August 2014.

The Canadian province displayed a powerful sense of their time. In spite of being an aging group, as they well recognized, the sisters explored and celebrated recreation – the purpose of recreation being to create again and to move forward together in this recreation, to create the Sabbath of the soul. Recreation was the theme of the RNDM Provincial Assembly, held in 2006 and called "Visitation to Pentecost." The sisters continued their search in light of the Pentecost because "in Pentecost we celebrate all that is and we get out there and 'do it' – with NO FEAR. We are re-created for a purpose/a mission."[22] The emphasis was on a deeper understanding of Church and mission (with no fear). However, it was more oriented to practical aspects of the life of the congregation and familiarity with processes and procedures.

In 2008, the congregation asserted its international identity at the 26th Congregational Chapter in Pattaya, Thailand. The congregation called itself the "RNDM Earth Community"and had recreated its mission through the lens of an earth community. The work of Thomas Berry, CSP, had inspired the sisters with his notion of the earth as a developing community of beings. The theme of the Chapter was "We are One, We are Love." The report reads: "We joyfully nurture relationships that are life-giving and based on a spirit of trust, cultural sensitivity, mutual respect, appreciation and encouragement. We participate actively and responsibly in the Mystery of the Universe and in the unfolding story of the Congregation."[23] It was at the 2008 Chapter that the congregation committed itself to valuing the importance of interfaith/inter-religious dialogue and to cooperating with interfaith partners-in-action towards global peace, justice, and the integrity of creation.[24] The congregation also committed to developing new structures to reflect their growing consciousness of the new cosmology and to further developing partnerships as well as facilitating provincial and regional networking and cooperation. At this time, the Chapter also mandated that a new constitution be written.

As I have shown in this chapter, the RNDM congregation recreated its own spirituality, placing it in a new dimension that moved beyond patriarchy and hierarchy, in a new cosmology that still harmonized and unified the members' life of contemplation and apostolic mission. A new configuration emerged that was far from the ecclesiocentric notion of mission and was indeed inspired by the Spirit. *Perfectae Caritatis*, in other words, opened a door full of light for the congregation. The resulting journey went well beyond a new reading of the original vision and mission with the "infidel," which had been conceived within the framework of an ultramontane theology, although with some original commitment in France to social Catholicism. The search led to a new

and unforeseen place, to a positioning that not only questioned patriarchy but also worked on alternatives and articulated new theological
stands. The Canadian province and the congregation as a whole were
nourished by their experience in Peru and their close contact with liberation theologians and activists in the early years of that mission; by
the large body of work on feminist thea/o/*logy (although it is not often mentioned in the records); and by the literature on eco-spirituality
developed by Catholics as well as non-Catholic secular authors. For
the layperson, it is difficult to relate all of these new developments to
developments that built on the origins of the congregation. However,
the records of the 2008 Chapter clearly connect for us the link to the
past:

> We long to make real in our time,
>
>   The cry echoed by Euphrasie,
>   THAT ALL IS One, all is Love –
>   That we are One and we are Love[25]

The congregation found a way to read their past in light of their present
and future.

The Canadian province played a pioneering role in the congregation's
renewal process. However, the demographic changes in the congregation, particularly in the Canadian province, brought to the forefront
the understanding that sisters in the province were part of an aging
congregation. In 2015, there were only 42 sisters (with no novices or
temporary professed) in the Canadian province. Their numbers had decreased from 192 sisters in 1965, including 6 novices and 21 temporary
professed. However, they remain part of an international congregation
of 886 sisters (although, notably, there were 1,307 sisters in the period
from 1959 to 1964) – who also reflect the new geographical map of the
Catholic Church, having vocations mainly from Asia – that has been
able to articulate a renewed mission and vision that has eco-spirituality
and social justice at the core.

TRUE FREEDOM

To wish like a child- to be open and free -
To rejoice and embrace the freedom of God's open space!
To soar like a bird, unburdened by cares
To fly up and beyond, to pass by a cloud,
To dip and to dive, then mount up, up to the sky!
Oh what freedom - to be free of all fears!
Where are you going - oh bird up on high?
I scarcely can see you, now again you appear!
Are you enroute to your nest or looking for food?
Where do you go? Do you know or care?
      North - South - East - West?
Do you know your directions - which way to go?
No sign posts, no roads, nor stops for a breath,
No worries, no cares seem to hinder your flight.
While on you go, and on, in sheer delight!
It is instinct, we say - God's gift to His creatures.
But is it not true, O bird up on high
'Tis God's power in you that fits you to fly -
That guides your way and gives you direction
Then what about me, made to His image and likeness?
Does He not guide and direct my daily "flight",
Teaching me to rejoice, to be glad, to delight
In the faith that in me He abides -
Deep in my heart, Creator and Lover?
What more could one ask?

Isabel Rabnett

PART FOUR

The Province Engages in a Foreign Mission

Chapter Eleven

The Mission in Peru

Twenty-nine years ago I set off to Peru as a missionary, with the enthusiasm of youth in spite of my 30+ years. The initial period of adjustment was difficult. I became as a little child not only unable to speak the language but unable to take advantage of all my previous experience ... At a deeper level, I came into contact with a culture with a somewhat different set of values than those I had absorbed in my youth. This was challenging and I discovered a need to question all values, both theirs and mine, to rediscover Christ's values in my new life. This process became an opportunity to [experience] deep spiritual rebirth. It was one of the greatest graces with which the Lord has gifted me.

– Sister Marilyn LeBlanc, RNDM.[1]

The mission in Peru was the only foreign mission of the RNDM's Canadian province. Given the richness of the experience, particularly in the 1970s, as well as its impact on the congregation, the mission will be fully discussed here on its own. It coincides with the events that occurred in the wake of Vatican II, in particular the Document of Medellín.

Following the regular General Chapter of 1966, the leadership of the Canadian province began to discern where the province was being called to open a new mission territory. On this matter, the Acts of the General Chapter 1966 reads:

> Clause a) That the Sisters be sent to countries on Missions, and that before starting the work, they must study the language, the customs, the culture, during at least six months, and if possible, they will take a course in missiology.

[This was in line with the directives of the Second Vatican Council as per Ad Gentes, No. 26.]

> Clause b) The Sisters will prepare Sisters of the country in educational work and in social development. Each province will provide help, as much as possible, to one or another of the existent missions, or it will found a house in a missionary territory depending on the geographical place of their own country, or in an under-developed region of that country. This foundation will be part of the province.[2]

The congregation's resolution was an early reaction to *Perfectae Caritatis*, an attempt to return to the roots of the congregation and its original spirit that had motivated their foundress, Euphrasie Barbier. In 1969, in her opening address at the Chapter of Aggiornamento, the superior general had called for a reassessment of their apostolate, especially of the missions, to ascertain whether they were serving the needs of the Church to the best advantage in the current day.[3] This ecclesial nature of missions, which responded to the agenda, or needs, identified by the Church, did not change until the 1980s, when missionary work was defined as a reignocentric activity. By the 1990s, the sisters had construed the "Mother Church" as an oppressive structure.[4] The experience in Peru offers a look at an interesting historical situation in which the sisters' ideas and practices were transformed by the needs of progressive sectors of the Church, causing them to develop their own contextualized notion of mission.

Provincial Superior Sister Marie Jean d'Ávila and her councillor, Sister Marie Genevieve Belliveau, sought counsel on the choice of missions from the members of the Canadian Bishops Committee on Missions and from the Canadian Conference of Religious. The sisters were first advised to respond to the call by Pope John XXIII on August 1961, asking religious congregations and lay Catholics for a renewed mission in Latin America.[5] Sister Marilyn LeBlanc, one of the missionaries who went to Peru, recalled the appeal as "a response to the needs of the Church in Latin America as the faithful there were inundated by sects and were being drawn away from the traditional Catholic faith."[6] The second recommendation offered to the sisters was to take their mission to a place where they might know missionaries who would be able to provide them with some initial orientation as the sisters became inserted among the people.[7] As a result, Sister Marie Jean d'Ávila and Sister Marie Genevieve Belliveau set up a meeting with Father Carlos Sebastian, OFM, provincial superior of the Franciscan province of Christ the King (Western Canadian Province). He and his friars were well known to the sisters in the Regina area. Father Carlos was looking for sisters who could help his friars in the work of evangelization in Moquegua, Peru.[8] The congregation decided to go to Peru, its contact with the Franciscans facilitating the decision. As of this writing, the sisters are still there, although the mission ceased to depend on the Canadian province after 1986. My analysis of the mission will be limited to the period between 1968 and 1986, with occasional forays into later history.

Context

Beginning in the 1940s, Peru received a large number of foreign missionaries. From 1940 to 1984, forty-two new groups arrived, twenty-five of which arrived after 1960.[9] The Western Canadian Franciscans arrived in 1947. Foreign missioners conducted work in the new slums (*pueblos jóvenes*) and in rural areas, particularly in the Andean south. By the 1950s, Maryknoll missions were playing a central role in Peru in remote rural communities in Puno, in urban centres in Puno and Lima, and in the poor neighbourhoods of Lima and Arequipa. The Maryknolls provided guidance to John Kennedy's Peace Corps and to the Papal Volunteers, the pet project of Maryknoll Father John Considine, director of the Latin American Bureau of the National Catholic Welfare Council. Between 1960 and 1968, Considine made sure to maintain close ties with the US government. The catechetical system provided a medium for anti-communist activities in southern Peru well into the 1960s.[10]

There was a large number of foreign clergy and congregations in Peru that provided food aid, literacy classes, and health and hygiene programs to the poor, a population that was mostly unreached by the government at a time of economic changes, including the movement of large numbers of people from rural areas to the cities. Fitzpatrick-Behrens has argued that the Catholic missionaries acted as an indirect arm of the Peruvian state by reaching remote communities, the urban middle class, and the new urban *barriadas* (slums). This connection, she points out, provided a structured network, and the Church and government reinforced each other through the contributions of the foreign clergy and the US governmental aid delivered by Catholic Relief Services, as well as through Inter-American Development Bank loans for Catholic housing and cooperatives. There were also development initiatives through the Alliance for Progress and the Peace Corps, both of which were supported by the Vatican. As Fitzpatrick-Behrens correctly states, foreign aid, resented by Peruvians, appeared as Church aid.[11] This observation is an interesting point. The Church–government

11.1 Sister Marilyn LeBlanc with Luis, one of the children of Hogar Belén, on an outing to the park in Moquegua, 1995. Representing the sisters' renewed conception of mission, this photograph does not appear to "other" the child, as the sister, in plain clothing, places herself at the child's level and openly expresses affection towards him. The photograph depicts integration into the child's environment as opposed to the differentiation between the sisters and the children shown in the 1935 illustration in figure 1.3. Source: This information was originally published in Rosa Bruno-Jofré and Ana Jofré, "Reading the Lived Experience of Vatican II – Words and Images: The Canadian Province of the Sisters of Our Lady of Missions in Peru," *CCHA Historical Studies* 81 (2015): 31–51; material from page 46.

11.2 Sister Marilyn LeBlanc leading a prayer service on the sacredness of all life in Moquegua, 1997. For Palm Sunday, the participants were given a tree seedling and asked to commit to caring for the tree. Photo provided by Sister Marilyn LeBlanc.

network would acquire a new political meaning with the Peruvian revolution, as I will soon explain.

When it came to the RNDM's mission to Peru, three sisters were initially selected from the many who had volunteered. Sister Loretta Bonokoski would work in catechetics and in the parish's programs of evangelization. A second sister, Sister Irene Oliver, would be in charge of the parish. Their missionary efforts were initially concentrated on catechetics, education in small elementary parish schools, and social work directed at the poor. The third sister was Sister Marie Jean d'Ávila Roche, who had completed her term as provincial superior. She would become known as Madre Juana and would work with the sick, the poor, women's groups, and so on.[12] After making her final profession of vows, Sister Margaret Dawson joined the fledging community in August 1969 to assist in the catechetical and pastoral work.

The program followed by these first sisters to learn Spanish in Puerto Rico was considered deficient;[13] the sisters who followed them received better preparation at the St James Society in Lima. Later on, before going to Peru, the RNDM sisters studied Spanish in Cochabamba, Bolivia, in an institute run by the Maryknoll society. In her testimony on the

11.3 Moquegua Valley, Peru, 1973. Photo provided by Sister Marilyn LeBlanc, RNDM.

mission, Sister Marilyn LeBlanc said: "We were missioned without any prior preparation other than that received through a study of the Vatican II documents. However, we were aware that we were there not to impose our own culture but to learn from the people among whom we lived and served." She went on to say, "Our formation within the country was excellent, ongoing and deeply rooted in the principles of education propounded by Paulo Freire. Our missionary efforts became directed towards empowering people through education for a growth of critical consciousness."[14]

The first sisters arrived in Peru in December 1968, after studying Spanish in Puerto Rico. They started their mission in the field early in 1969. By that time, neither the aforementioned call made by Pope John XXIII on 17 August 1961 nor the Alliance for Progress, launched in Punta del Este, Uruguay, the same day as an expression of the Kennedy administration's modernizing vision for Latin America after the Cuban revolution, had given the expected results.[15] The close involvement of the Church (the Holy See and the North American hierarchy) with US policies for Latin America had been under extensive criticism in Latin America. In 1967, Monsignor Ivan Illich, who directed a network of centres in Cuernavaca, Mexico, including the well-known Centre of Intercultural Documentation, and who had trained missioners going to Latin America, published "The Seamy Side of Charity." It was a scathing critique of the US mission to Latin America and shows the strong anti-imperialist discourse dominant in Latin American leftist circles and among early liberation theologian advocates at the time. Illich, while critiquing the notion of progress embraced by the Church and distrusting modernity, wrote that "Church policy makers in the United States ... must review their vocation as Christian theologians and their actions as Western politicians."[16]

The sisters had decided to go to Peru with no knowledge of its history or of the Church's history in the country; they also knew nothing of the complex paths taken by the Church's strands within Latin America. They were not aware of the political history of the relationship between the North American (United States and Canada) Church hierarchies and the Latin American bishops. Nor were they aware of the Holy See's attempts in the 1950s to build a Catholic Inter-American Cooperation Program from the top down and on its own terms.[17] In 1955, the Episcopal Latin American Conference (*Consejo Episcopal Latinoamericano*, or CELAM) was born as a result of a meeting convocated by the Holy See in Rio de Janeiro, Brazil. CELAM's mandate was to study problems of interest to the Church in Latin America, promote and support Catholic works, and prepare the Episcopal Latin American Conference when it was called by the Holy See. Interestingly, at the 1968 conference in Medellín, Colombia, CELAM produced the Medellín document, a reading of Vatican II through the eyes of a suffering Latin America.[18] In other words, these documents contained an attempt to Latinamericanize conclusions from the Second Vatican Council with a radicalized new line, while keeping continuity with the council.[19] Meanwhile, liberation theology, already in the making for some years, took shape in the late 1960s in both historical Protestant and Catholic circles, and provided a defined language of change.

Medellín was fresh as a liberating utopia, although it also contained the signs of its own constraints. In fact, Medellín kept continuity with the Second Vatican Council, which had been an expression of liberal progressive thought, adapting the Church to developments in the Western world and within the capitalist system, while also rooting its statements in liberation theology. However, the contradictions that were set by Medellín and, later in the 1970s, the stepping back of the Vatican and even CELAM gave room in the end to a reformist post-conciliar position, while Christian groups nourished by liberation theology took more radical positions, and conservative sectors remained attached to a traditional pastoral ideology and allied themselves with the upper classes.[20] In Peru, however, a unique convergence of the Peruvian revolution, after the coup d'état led by General Velasco Alvarado in 1968, and progressive sectors of the Catholic Church that embraced liberation theology and Medellín took place. This framed the work of the sisters, who became engaged in a process of political awareness. As Fitzpatrick-Behrens has argued, the Velasco regime's reforms were made possible by "a mutually reinforcing alliance between the Catholic Church and the military."[21] The coup was introduced by Velasco Alvarado[22] as a liberating revolution that would lead to social justice, to the second emancipation of Peru. He defined it as the beginning of a "Nationalist Revolution." He described Latin American dependency as being a consequence of the nature of the economic, financial, and commercial relations between "our countries" and the developed nations of the world – relations that he saw as prejudicial to Latin American countries.[23] The important thing to notice is how the progressive Peruvian hierarchy and the Velasco regime converged in a top-down program of reform. Fitzpatrick-Behrens has also argued that the network among the rural and urban poor, established by mostly foreign missionaries, provided the government with access to the communities and to the barriadas and infrastructures that it could initially rely upon to implement the reforms.[24] According to this view, foreign clergy, in line with liberation theology, started to distance themselves from their countries of origin and from their aid. As such, a number of congregations such as the Maryknolls refocused their work, eliminated the provision of food aid, and also distanced themselves from projects that favoured an emergent middle class.[25]

The contradictions that emerged from the reforms coming out of authoritarian institutions led to a conflict between the Velasco government, engaged in promoting reform in the name of the poor, who had little autonomy for political organization, and the progressive Catholic clergy, which opted to support the poor, who then suffered repression in the process. This conflict was, of course, accentuated when General Francisco Morales Bermúdez ended the revolution in 1975.

The RNDM sisters lived through this process and experienced divided positions within the Church itself – an outcome of the contradictions of Medellín within a Church that had changed very little. These processes provide the context fundamental for comprehending the sisters' work in Peru, as well as their narrations and feelings that other members of the congregation did not understand their experience. As happened with other congregations, the process of insertion of the mission moved the work in a direction of its own.

It is important to notice here that, in 1972, the Velasco government introduced an educational reform viewed as an integral part of the revolution. The architect of the reform was the Marxist philosopher and educator Augusto Salazar Bondy, who adopted and adapted Paulo Freire's methods and theories, including his early notion of conscientization. This concept referred to an education that leads to liberation and self-actualization, that is fully dependent on the liberation of society, and that is an authentic education in that it is based in communities and the particular realities of the participants and is related to the community and directed by the community as a whole. Therefore, the reform included a national literacy program that, at least on paper, used Paulo Freire's methodology. The aim of the reform was ambitious: the creation of "a new Peruvian man," one who was "creative, critical, cooperative, and committed."[26] Núcleos, school community centres, with a director appointed by the ministry and an elected council, were expected to serve as the administrative units of education. In practice, the operationalization of núcleos did not work, as the communities had other urgent priorities. There was also a major contradiction between the rhetoric of participation, the transfer of power to the people and central control through official unions, curriculum, and teacher training programs, and the authoritarian tradition. The Ministry of Education represented a highly bureaucratized and centralized power house. The class structure of society thus revealed itself one more time in the schools. Given its apparent embrace by Salazar Bondy, it is not surprising that the sisters became familiar with Paulo Freire's work. They also became familiar with the contradictions plaguing the system.

Political Configuration

The mission was inserted in a particular space, Peru, and in a particular conjuncture; as indicated previously, there was an early convergence of progressive clergy involved with liberation theology and the nationalist reformist Peruvian revolution – which did not last long after the

11.4 The first three sisters who went to Peru. From left to right, Sister Loretta Bonokoski, Sister Irene Oliver, and Sister Juana Roche (Marie Jean d'Ávila) in Moquegua, Peru, in 1969. Photograph provided by Sister Marilyn LeBlanc, RNDM.

repressive element of the regime became evident. The nationalist discourse brought the *"campesino"* (peasant farmer; rural poor) and the Indigenous population to the discursive arena. Quéchua (an Indigenous language) became an official language, Indigenous Inkarri festivals were promoted, and Indigenous historical figures such as Túpac Amaru became highly valued. The sisters, inspired by liberation theology and a renewed understanding of mission, developed a horizontal integrative relationship with the Indigenous communities, the barriadas, and the rural poor that was rooted in a commitment to the poor and their suffering.

11.5 Sister Loretta Bonokoski in Moquegua, Peru. This collection of photographs shows that the sisters' mission was no longer about "bringing civilization" to the people, but instead about becoming a part of their community. These photographs, archived and preserved in a binder, record Sister Loretta Bonokoski participating in the Fiesta of the Cross in Moquegua, Peru. The top photo features her in the centre, and the sister's documentation noted that the people honoured her for her work with the children in the Hogar. This documentation is indicative of a shift in perspective and values. Indigenous people are no longer portrayed as part of a landscape to be tamed, or as needy children, but as autonomous people whose approval is desired and valued. These photographs memorialize and respect the cultural rituals of Indigenous people and try to promote the idea that the sisters are "one of them" in this celebration. Source: This information was originally published in Rosa Bruno-Jofré and Ana Jofré, "Reading the Lived Experience of Vatican II – Words and Images: The Canadian Province of the Sisters of Our Lady of Missions in Peru," *CCHA Historical Studies* 81 (2015): 31–51; material from pages 48 and 49. Photographs provided by Sister Marilyn LeBlanc, RNDM.

11.6 Sister Loretta Bonokoski with children in Moquegua, Peru, 1975. The
sister is shown here surrounded by a group of little ones of the Hogar.
She does not place herself above them, but among them. Photograph provided
by Sister Marilyn LeBlanc, RNDM.

The sisters, who had arrived in Peru with little or no knowledge of
Latin America, took an active role in attending seminars and workshops, where they became familiar with the development of the Church
in Latin America and the documents from the Conference of Latin
American Bishops, such as those produced in Medellín in 1968 and,
later, in Puebla in 1979. They also took part in the yearly conferences
for religious of the country and the region, including the Conference
of Religious of Peru and the Conference of Latin American Religious
(CLAR). The context moved them into the sphere of liberation theology. One of the testimonies reads: "The concepts of liberation theology
were the daily bread as well as the spirituality of liberation theology."[27]
This thinking was to be expected given the context of their insertion
in Peru at the beginning of the Peruvian revolution, which was itself
initially related to liberation theology, and the embracing of liberation
theology by foreign missionaries. During the 1970s, and even in the
1980s, the sisters attended regular workshops held for teachers of religion and pastoral workers in the city of Arequipa. Among the speakers were Peruvian Father Gustavo Gutiérrez, the main exponent of

liberation theology, and Peruvian Father Jose Marins, who talked of the Indigenous culture, history, political structure, religious beliefs, and so on.[28] Some of the sisters were familiar with the writings of Ivan Illich, which were circulating at the time, and with the reports that came from the Center for Intercultural Formation (CIF), as well as publications from the Centro de Investigaciones Culturales (CIC; Centre of Cultural Research) and later from the Centro Intercultural de Documentación (CIDOC; Centre for Intercultural Documentation).

The 1975 coup led by General Morales Bermúdez meant the end of the Peruvian revolution as proclaimed by Velasco Alvarado and a shift to the right in an effort to gain investors' confidence and to satisfy demands from creditors amid a "degenerating economic situation after 1974."[29] Gilbert argues that Velasco Alvarado's revolution perhaps favoured "already privileged urban classes over urban and rural masses by promoting a pattern of industrialization which was import intensive and oriented toward middle class consumers."[30] The policies regarding foreign capital and the processes of nationalization generated hostility in international capitalist centres, while the foreign debt continued to increase. The corrective measures to deal with the country's debt (by 1978, Peru was at the brink of default), designed by the International Monetary Fund and a consortium of major international banks, led to processes of denationalization, a cleansing of leftist opposition, control of the press, and the dissolution of the Confederación Nacional Agraria (CNA; National Agrarian Confederation), which, having been created by Velasco's government, had become a political body representing the peasantry of the Sierra. There was a rise in food prices as well as in prices for fuel and public transportation, and the government resisted workers' demands. People were seriously impoverished and repressed. The overcompensation paid to the US-owned Marcona Mining Company, which had been nationalized previously, generated further cuts in the funding for social programs and caused popular reaction.[31]

During the second half of the 1970s, social unrest in Peru was profound. A major national strike took place in 1977, followed by teacher strikes and others. During the general strike of 1977, a large number of teachers from Ilo were arrested and taken away to Lima.[32] One of the sisters travelled there to visit the prisoners in jail and acted as a liaison between them and their families by passing on messages. The sisters remained faithful to their option for the poor and committed to the progressive Church and continued supporting the people and their problems.

The approach taken by the sisters generated a horizontal integrative relationship with the communities where they worked. This relationship is evident in the photographs they kept to memorialize their apostolate at the time, which are provided throughout this chapter. The mobilization of communities took the shape of popular education grassroots projects of various sorts (under the premise of adult education as a technology for change); at the core, these projects were related to alternative visions of society with different levels of radicality and utopia, some nourished by Catholic pedagogue Paulo Freire's vision and others going beyond his approach.[33] By the mid-1970s, popular education practices had become a movement with continental dimensions. The sisters used the principles of popular education to analyse Catholic documents and texts.

At the core of the sisters' apostolate were the human person, her inherent dignity, and a social Catholic understanding that saw people in relation to one another. In this quest to affirm human dignity, the sisters collaborated on projects in which they tried to convey the vision of a Church committed to the poor, projects that were geared towards a transformation of society. Not all of the clergy shared this commitment. Important sectors were allied with the dominant classes. Nevertheless, and in spite of the tortuous path followed by Peru in the decades since they had arrived, the missionary sisters' fire did not die. When, in the 2000s, Sister Loretta Bonokoski, who had at that point spent a great part of her life in Peru, expressed criticism of the Catholic ways encouraged by many Peruvian bishops, in particular conservative ones, she wrote:

> Peru for years has been called a Catholic country: it is Catholic in name only. There are many very active sects who certainly know how to attract a starving people looking for something more than just the traditional Catholic faith based on processions, devotion to the saints and reception of the sacraments without a real commitment. Most of the people coming from the mountains hold Christ Crucified in high esteem, but their roots are in nature, quack or witch doctors. The popular or traditional religion is highly approved by the Peruvian Bishops, especially by those in "Opus Dei." Some bishops, including our own, are encouraging the formation of Christian communities based on scripture. We have given a name to our new method of evangelization: "The New Image of Our Parish and the Diocese." This new life is especially well accepted by people in the "pueblos jóvenes" [shanty town slums], where the poor live.

She then continued:

> We feel the focus of the future is in the lines of evangelization and solidarity with the poor. Therefore it is necessary to have people who are fulltime workers in the pastoral work of our mission, in communication with our

11.7 A youth group outing to the olive grove in Ilo, Peru, 1985. This photograph portrays a trip taken by a youth group from Moquegua. The sister here is represented as being in camaraderie, sharing a laugh with the girls. Photograph provided by Sister Marilyn LeBlanc, RNDM.

pastors. To succeed in such an effort we need to prepare our youth to be "messengers": people who visit families, encouraging them to form Bible and prayer groups. In time they will become our "Nueva imagen de la Parroquia" the New Parish Image.[34]

The sisters' approach to their mission in Peru had shifted from one based on authority – as illustrated on the 1935 cover of *The Message* (see figure 1.3 in chapter one), in which the sisters bring the word of God from above – to a more people-centred and horizontal approach. This shift in philosophy is clearly documented in their photographs, especially the ones showing their affectionate relationship with the youth.

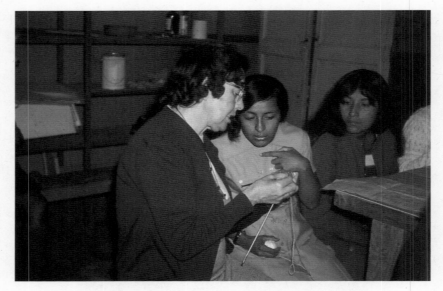

11.8 Sister Juana Roche teaching young ladies to knit in Moquegua, Peru, 1971. Similar to the situation shown in figure 11.7, this photograph reveals the sister's attitude of affection towards the people, rather than an attitude of authority. Photograph provided by Sister Marilyn LeBlanc, RNDM.

A Profile of the Apostolate

The Beginnings in Moquegua

In December 1968, the sisters went to Moquegua, Peru, to join efforts with the mission of the Franciscan province of Christ the King from Western Canada. Moquegua, known as the city of the eternal sun, is located in the coastal valley of Moquegua, a strip of green surrounded by desert mountains. The Moquegua River gets its life from the mountain ranges during the rainy season (December, January, and February). The fields need to be irrigated by channels that bring water from the mountains when it is available. When the sisters arrived, agriculture was underdeveloped and the mining industry was central to the area's economic power. Social problems abounded, along with racism against Indigenous people who were migrating to the city and a marked classism that the sisters quickly discovered.

The apostolate in Moquegua involved social work, which at various times included visiting the homes of the sick and the poor, helping the poor to get jobs, finding and building homes, getting medical help for the sick, teaching adult education literacy classes, teaching sewing and knitting, and distributing food, medicine, and clothing. Catechesis was, from the start, a major endeavour on various fronts such as in state schools, where the sisters also coordinated the religion program, assisted teachers in class preparation, and provided audiovisual materials. The sisters trained staff for the catechetical office and coordinated youth groups and helped lead them in prayer. They also helped plan retreats and pastoral activities.[35] Some of these activities took the form of popular education initiatives that had become a set of complex grassroots expressions conveying a desire to deal with inequality, discrimination, and assertion of identity.

The RNDM sisters responded to the socio-economic crisis in their commitment to the poor and the grassroots communities by situating themselves beyond the politics of sectors of the Catholic Church that positioned themselves on the right. One of the major expressions of their profound commitment to the community in Moquegua was their establishment of a group home, called Hogar Belén (Bethlehem Home), which was a home for abandoned and abused children, abused mothers, and others in dire circumstances because of health problems.[36] It was co-founded by Sister Loretta Bonokoski, whose criticism of some bishops in Peru was quoted earlier, with the help of the Franciscans.[37] The home was not planned, and was originally the sisters' residence; however, it began to come into existence in 1974 when Sister Bonokoski found a nine-year-old girl on the street who had been abandoned by her family. The judge for minors placed the girl in the custody of the sisters, and she lived with them for a number of years.[38] Over time, the sisters began to accept others in need of assistance, taking care of the young and the aged in what also became their home. The home received abandoned children left at the door as well as mothers whose children were sick and who had no money for medicine or food for them and no means of obtaining these necessities on their own. Gradually, other children were received as their situation warranted. For the first few years, there were only a few children, until around 1980 when the economic crisis became more acute. Previous to the crisis, the larger family unit had been able to help out nieces and nephews upon the death of a parent or in other emergency situations.[39] By 1982, the sisters were providing a home for approximately twelve people (the mission document stated that the number was flexible), ranging from an eighty-year-old woman, to several young mothers, to teenage girls and young children,

11.9 Harvesting potatoes on the farm in Peru. Photograph provided by Sister Marilyn LeBlanc, RNDM.

all of whom for one reason or another needed a home. It was reported that all were educated in Christian living and they shared in the household responsibilities; they learned to cook, to keep house, and to take care of the younger children. Another eight or nine children from the community received a noonday meal and stayed for supervised study before returning to their homes in the late afternoon.[40] By 1985, the number of children living in the home had grown to more than fifty. By 1989, the sisters' new extended family numbered 133, and the old adobe house – also the home of the sisters – could not accommodate one more person; with only three washrooms, it was even unsanitary.[41] At this point, the sisters approached the mayor of Moquegua, asking for some land on which to build. A piece of land located on a hill on the periphery of town was donated to the sisters, and the Southern Peru Copper Corporation offered to construct a new building, which was later expanded to two floors with the financial help of the Canadian embassy and support from parishes and friends. In the 2000s, the home accommodated 150 people, from babies to adults, and during the day around 150 more would arrive to help in the house and receive meals.[42]

With the assistance of the Canadian embassy, the sisters next purchased a three-hectare farm and built a bakery. The farm produced bread, milk, eggs, vegetables, and some meat. Everyone helped to produce for their own needs in the house and for the soup kitchen. The Dutch embassy helped to build a workshop, and the tools were provided by the Good Women's League, while The National Food Assistance Program (Peru) provided staples such as rice, noodles, and flour. The Franciscans contributed staples as well, though the Province of Christ the King also did not hesitate to provide financial support.

The Mission in Ilo

The initial foundation in Moquegua was followed in 1971 by the foundation in Ilo. A neighbouring town only an hour's drive from Moquegua and, at the time, a growing port on the Pacific Ocean, Ilo is located in the southern coastal desert, three hours driving distance from the border with Chile. At the time of the sisters' arrival, the town was the site of a large fishing fleet recently denationalized under Morales Bermúdez with the consequent loss of benefits and job security; at the same time, those subsisting through craft fishing were encountering great difficulties in placing their catch. In 1977, the sisters reported that the denationalization had resulted in many being unemployed, leaving families desperately poor. They wrote: "Donations received from home and abroad have been shared with many needy families in an effort to provide school uniforms and textbooks for children."[43]

On the outskirts of Ilo, although also economically integrated with the town, is Ciudad Nueva (New City), the company town of the Southern Peru Copper Corporation. Ilo is the terminus of the railway that brings ore from the copper mine at Toquepala, and is the site of the copper smelter. The mining company built a large seawater desalination plant to produce water for the mining complex. The area also has olive trees and grasslands available for grazing by cattle and goats. The point of note here is that, at the time the RNDM mission began in Ilo, hundreds of Peruvians who barely made an existence on the mountain slopes were moving to the city looking for work. The sisters recorded that the newcomers were easily recognizable as they arrived in town dressed in their native costumes and carrying their few earthly possessions. The sisters expected to help "these Peruvians attain their potential as Christians in the new Peru."[44]

Within their apostolate, the sisters became part of the communities in which they were inserted. They were respectful of the ways of the

11.10 At the shoreline with a youth group, near Ilo, Peru, 1979. Photograph provided by Sister Marilyn Leblanc, RNDM.

people in the villages, many of whom were Indigenous, and of how they lived their faith. Thus, one of the sisters wrote:

> In Peru, May is dedicated to the Cross. The customs surrounding these celebrations take place in almost every small village, and various sections of the cities, where the traditional faith of the mountain people is maintained. In the parish of Miramar, Sister Ines and Brother John helped the people celebrate the religious significance of the feast with a Triduum of three evenings. The preparation concluded with the Sunday Mass in the chapel on May 1, followed by a procession which terminated on the hill overlooking that section of the city. Men, women and children accompanying the lilting music of the "zampanas" (flutes) made their way along. The Crosses remain there during the year as a reminder of God's protection for His people.[45]

The sisters' work was always linked to the local Church. The sisters did not have their own schools, but a sister was asked by the clergy to serve as director of the local parish school in two of the missions – in Moquegua in 1969 and in Ilo in 1971. These were schools serving middle-class families and their children, although there were always children from poor families who were offered the opportunity

11.11 Procession of the Lord of the Miracles in Ilo, Peru, 1992. This event was a popular devotion of the coastal area. Photograph provided by Sister Marilyn LeBlanc, RNDM.

to attend. However, the sisters withdrew from this work within the first seven years because, according to their testimony, of the resistance of the parents and some teachers to accept the principles of liberation theology. A record of events reads: "I overheard a teacher explaining to her students that poor children should not cry because they are poor, 'they are poor because God wanted them to be poor. If God wanted them to be rich they would have been born in a rich family. So they should do nothing to try and change that.'"[46]

It is worth noting, as one example, that the San Luis School in Ilo was a private school, and the majority of the students paid fees to attend, although "a group of promising youngsters from poorer families attended on scholarships."[47] Students in this school were taught English in an intensive English program that occupied one third of the teaching day.[48] This school was one of the schools that the sisters decided to abandon, as the work there could not coexist with their commitment to spread the principles of liberation theology. Thus, some of the sisters in Moquegua and Ilo worked with teachers of religion in the public schools, helping in the preparation of lesson plans and lending didactical materials that incorporated the concepts of liberation theology.[49]

The documents and conversations with the sisters provide glimpses of their apostolate as being in the midst of a difficult political and economic situation that had resulted in tremendous basic needs not being met in the community. In a letter from Ilo dated 13 April 1984, Sister Kathleen related that she and three other sisters from Ilo had had the opportunity of attending a two-week course in Huacho (two hours away from Lima). The course was given in a centre of rural education that worked with mostly mountain farming people who had not had the opportunity to further their education. People stayed at the centre for two months. There, they were taught how to build, using materials produced in their own areas, as an alternative to buying imported goods or expensive materials. Emphasis was placed on the development of people as whole persons, and on how one lives in a community. The course was given at the centre, but taught by instructors from the Coady International Institute of Antigonish, Nova Scotia, Canada, which was created in 1959 by St Francis Xavier University and considered to be a centre of excellence in community-based development. The course was intended to develop community working groups and to form cooperatives that would unite people and help them to become independent and self-supporting. The sister attending the course wrote that the course was giving her a sense of where to start. She said: "Coady [Reverend Dr Moses Coady, a leader of the Antigonish movement] says, 'education is our only weapon.' They [people from the Coady Institute] set out to change poverty – not by violence but through justice by using education."[50]

It is commonly said that missions aim at changing deep spiritual commitments and beliefs by means of conversion and the introduction of different ways of life. In this case, it was the missioners themselves who were transformed. The RNDM sisters went through a dramatic process of personal transformation that affected their collective identity as members of the congregation. The general chapters had moved towards a new language of mission and an option for the poor that was rooted in authenticity, as the sisters in Peru themselves were living through the same poverty with their people. This process took place before the congregation questioned the understanding of mission as an ecclesiastic one.

Their personal transformation did not prevent the sisters from actively defending Church positions on matters like birth control, although their approach from their liberation theology perspective generates an interpretative conundrum, an understanding of which requires some background. On 30 July 1968, the Vatican announced the encyclical *Humanae Vitae*, considered a victory of the regressive forces – those questioning the changes brought by Vatican II – within the Church and of Cardinal Alfredo Ottaviani, although they were in a minority position.[51] The pope, who was concerned with the emerging desire to share the values of the modern world, sided with the conservative position and opposed birth control and any other artificial form of avoiding procreation.[52] There were international and national repercussions. Robert S. McNamara, president of the World Bank, reiterated the need to control population growth on 29 September 1969 at a joint meeting of the International Monetary Fund (IMF) and the World Bank before two thousand delegates. Latin American governments were caught between the two directives.[53] The revolutionary military government of Juan Velasco Alvarado did not support contraception and sexual education.

The RNDM sisters took a strong position against the pill, linking their opposition to health concerns and a critique of the capitalist system. One of the sisters wrote that contraception was being imposed on women, even without them being told of the risks of side effects, including cancer of the uterus and changes of character (moods) for women who used the pill. One of them quoted a priest as saying: "The Western World is afraid that they will have to share too much of their wealth with this Southern part of the world, so best they control its growth."[54] The sisters had to contend somehow with the fact that many of the poor women with whom they worked were victims of poverty and chauvinism, unable to control what happened to their own body. The issue could not be conflated with a critique of the capitalist system. It was an unresolved conundrum, and the sisters did not have the tools to solve it, but they were developing a critical understanding of the politics of the Church in relation to their positioning supporting liberation theology.

Over time, the experience of the RNDM missionaries led to a critical view of the Church and of the place of women in the Church. One of the sisters wrote:

> It would seem that the new archbishop of Arequipa appointed in 1980, Fernando Vargas Ruiz de Somocurcio, a Jesuit, was not open to liberation theology. I have a strong memory of his first Ad Lumina visit to Rome. Before leaving he announced to the media that theology of liberation would be condemned at that time. However, when he returned he had to admit that it was not condemned but that the bishops were warned to avoid the extremes. Nevertheless, he continued his opposition to this theology in his own archdiocese. The Maryknoll Fathers had to leave the archdiocese. Nothing was said to the women religious and they continued to work quietly. Amongst ourselves we commented that as women we were not even considered.[55]

Candarave

In 1977, the Canadian province approved a new foundation in Candarave, a town situated in the Andes Mountains with an altitude of over 9,842 feet (over 3,000 metres), located halfway between the coast and Puno on the *altiplano* in the province of Tacna. The sisters were put in charge of the parish, which consisted of Candarave and seventeen villages with a total population of about 20,000 inhabitants. Recalling their first years, the sisters said that their initial responsibility was to provide religious services, teach the faith, and prepare for the reception of the sacraments; however, that plan had to be redesigned when they discovered the lack of any meaningful healthcare services in the area and the haphazard system of education, with the latter caused by teachers who were taking more time off to go to the coast than they were spending in their classrooms. The schools were poorly equipped, and the sisters recorded that many teachers did not have certificates. *La Voz del Pueblo, Boletin Parroquial S. Juan Bautista, Candarave* (The Voice of the People, Bulletin of the Parish Saint John Baptist, Candarave), first published in 1982, interviewed parents from Candarave and surrounding villages to ask about the education of their children. The voices conveyed a sad picture of public education and a portrait of the class bias that existed even among the poor.

One father told of his worries around his children's education:

> I am poor. The fees for matriculation give me lots of problems. I have four children, and they are not accepted until I pay the *cuotas* [dues] for each

11.12 Lay leaders arriving for the monthly session of formation in Candarave, 1979. Some of them walked for as long as four hours, leaving in the dark at 4 a.m., in order to arrive on time for their training, which was held from 8 a.m. to 4 p.m. Photograph provided by Sister Marilyn LeBlanc, RNDM.

one. Also, they demand that they [the children] wear a uniform, shoes, and runners and *buzos* [a sort of jogging suit] for physical education. Those who have economic means send their children to Puno and Tacna. I am afraid that they will soon close the *secundaria* [high school]. I don't know what to do.[56]

One mother said of the teachers:

The education of our children is backwards here in Candarave. There is no professional preoccupation on the part of a number of teachers. For example, at the end of the month several teachers go to Tacna to get their cheque and miss one or two weeks of classes. There are also teachers who [have] stopped in the pub (cantina), leaving our children abandoned.[57]

Still another father said: "If we complain to the teachers thinking [of] the well-being [of our children], they take revenge with our children.

11.13 *La Voz del Pueblo*. Source: Boletin Parroquial S. Jan Bautista, Candarave, año 1, no 8 (April 1983), mimeo 8A3125. RNDM, General Administration, Rome, Peru, Provincial Administration, Bulletins, Provincial News, orange box, section G, shelf 9.

They also try to humiliate us using the education they have. For these reasons we keep quiet."[58]

The sisters recalled that the battle for a good education for the children took a long time, as parents had to deal with the bureaucracy as well as with teachers who wanted a job, but also wanted a fair amount of time off. They said: "It was more of a struggle as often the teacher made the children of parents who spoke up and demanded a better education suffer the consequences of their parents' criticism."[59]

The population was described by the sisters as consisting of people of Aymara descent "with little Spanish mixture," and although the languages were Spanish and Aymara, Aymara customs prevailed. People from some of the villages were actively involved in the parish, but because of distance, they had less contact with the parish and were less inclined to take part in religious practices, other than the Patronal feast.[60] Some of those who had been working in the fields migrated to Tacna, when they had the means, in search of a better future for their children, but many worked their fields and cared for animals and just survived.

11.14 Catechists studying the document of Puebla, Mexico, in Candarave, 1979. This photograph shows the participants in the program of formation of lay leaders. Sister Marilyn LeBlanc can be seen in the background. Photograph provided by Sister Marilyn LeBlanc, RNDM.

Still others were *"peones,"* working for others with very minimal pay and living in misery. Despite these many hardships, the sisters found a well-developed community spirit in the villages where farmers worked together on communal projects, although these villages were isolated and marginal to the interests of the government, particularly in the 1980s.[61]

One of the sisters wrote that they worked with lay leaders from the various villages in the parish. She went on to say: "Our monthly workshops dealt with not only the basics of the catechism, but with the social teaching of the Church as outlined in the outcomes of the bishops' meetings in Medellín, Colombia, and later Puebla, Mexico, which dealt specifically with the social issues and systemic injustices facing the people of Latin America."[62]

The sisters obtained a grant from Misereor, a Catholic aid organization in Germany, to pay the salary of a dedicated nurse for a year. In their view, having the services of a nurse would enable the people to realize

11.15 Family seeking to have a child baptized. Outside the parish house in Candarave, Peru, 1985. Photograph provided by Sister Marilyn LeBlanc, RNDM.

what they were entitled to and had not been receiving. The sisters and the people were then prepared to fight the bureaucracy on the coast to obtain all the health services they needed. They recorded: "It took more than a year, but the people finally received health services as adequate as could be expected."[63] The process represents a clear example of the practices of popular education in the late 1970s and early 1980s in Peru. A sister (I assume Marilyn LeBlanc) wrote: "We knew we were having an impact when the local police challenged us to refrain from anything other than leading prayers in the Church. Social issues were not ours or the Church's responsibility."[64] The tasks did not end there.

The sisters reached the most distant villages in the parish on a regular basis, crossing the canyon on foot or by horseback. Once a month, three of them would cross the canyon by jeep to celebrate liturgies in three of the villages, and, on several evenings, they packed up the jeep to go off to other nearby villages for the weekly prayer.[65] A narration from 1983 reads:

> This past week, Srs Veronica and Patricia made a pastoral visit to the farthest villages, Calientes. The seven hour climb to the other side of the volcano, Yucamani, started across the Canyon. Their guides were two catechists from the village. The journey began with a splash as Sr Patricia slipped and fell into one of the irrigation canals! All else went well that day. The following day house visits were made. The farthest was a three hour walk. However, the hospitality of the people and the natural beauty of the area made it a memorable birthday for Veronica. On Sunday nearly every family was represented at the day of reflection and dialogue which concluded with a Communion service.[66]

After Vatican II, the RNDM congregation as a whole moved to a recreation of the understanding of mission, which is fully reflected in the work in Peru, even as it takes its own meanings from the context. At the annual General Chapter of 1984, called "Witnessing to the Gospel: Beyond All Frontiers," the sisters sought to be in tune with the world: "We too are called to listen to our world, especially to the poor, and to be attentive to the continually new movements of the Spirit. To listen well we need hearts that are free and ears that are trained."[67] In this way, the congregation exhibited an effort to resignify mission that appears to be related to the preferential option for the poor, to the incarnation of the poverty of Christ, and to striving to become enculturated in every milieu. The latter would be achieved by studying the culture with its religions, ideologies, and philosophies; such work entails discerning the Gospel's values inherent in the culture and discovering, along with the people, the values in their heritage that authentically express the presence of God in their lives. This work also requires dialogue with the people, the promotion of the local Church, and, very importantly, helping to find suitable expressions of doctrine and liturgical prayer.[68] In 1984, solidarity with the poor was at the core of the missionary work in Peru, which was the illocutionary force that gave meaning to their statements and documents. This solidarity was not always in tune with positions assumed by the Catholic Church at various levels, such as in the case, mentioned earlier, of the archbishop of Arequipa, who was appointed in 1980.

The RNDM's experience in Peru exposed contradictions in the process of changing its mission and vision, along with attachments to the past that the congregation as a whole was not ready to relinquish. The intended force behind the practice in Peru did not coincide with the congregation's notion of ecclesial mission. To be sure, as I have stressed several times before, the congregation held from its beginnings a strong loyalty to the institutional Church, in particular to the Holy See. The RNDM's foundress had made this clear in the first constitutions: "They [the sisters] accept likewise, but with the consent of the General Council, other works of charity such as work-rooms, orphanages, refuges, etc., under the direction of their Lordships the Bishops or Vicars-Apostolic in order to assist them in their apostleship."[69] Interestingly, the dissention of foundress Euphrasie Barbier with bishops and priests is part of the congregation's own "myth of foundation," according to which Barbier was accused of aspiring to autonomy and independence for herself and her sisters in the government of the community.[70] In those conflicts, she had received favourable support from the Holy See. The ecclesial character of mission was also emphasized in the 1979 Constitution, which stated: "By approving the Congregation and its Constitutions, the Church confirmed the charism of our Foundress and conferred on the Congregation an ecclesial existence as a religious missionary congregation with its own identity within the community of the Church."[71]

The process of resignification of the missionary work at the congregational level kept residual elements from the past, while the experience of the Canadian province in Peru had, in practice, led the sisters to move away from an ecclesial notion of mission. Thus, the General Chapter of 1984, in spite of the strong commitment to the poor and attention placed on the people and their needs, still affirmed the ecclesial nature of missions, even as the notion of mission was resignified in relation to the Gospel. It said: "The Spirit of God urges us to look with realism and courage at the world in which we live, to re-examine our present missions and apostolic works, being attentive to the signs of our times and the appeals of the local and universal Church." The contradictions would emerge largely in the field, from the quiet resistance to the archbishop in Arequipa to the full embracement of *Humanae Vitae*.

The sisters in Peru embodied the resignification of mission. This resignification arose from their own lived experience and in relation to the Peruvian context, long before they articulated their reinterpretation of mission in various councils and chapter assemblies. Furthermore, by the time of the Second Vatican Council and its aftermath, the Canadian province had already anticipated the signs of the times and, as discussed in a previous chapter, had expressed both the desire to move to a less hierarchical administration and a commitment to the poor. From the mid-1980s onward, as Susan Smith wrote, the congregation began to move away from the ecclesial nature of missionary activity along with the new theologies of mission and the involvement of sisters in extra-ecclesial activities. By the late 1980s, the congregation had moved to a reignocentric language – the sisters would follow the needs of the kingdom and not necessarily the Church's agenda.[72] By the 1990s, many sisters in the congregation had become aware and had named the Mother Church as an oppressive structure.[73] The document from the General Gathering of 1996 reads:

> We desire open dialogue, to foster and be part of an inclusive church at parish, diocesan and national levels where all take an active role in the life of the Church. We recognize the struggle and hold the pin of those oppressed by the institutional church, and as sisters of Euphrasie we know that we too may find ourselves in situations of tension with hierarchies. We celebrate the various ways of being Church and living inculturation. We continue to be attentive to opportunities to respond to the hunger for spirituality in our world today.[74]

The missionaries in Peru were in touch with missionaries from all over the world. The international congregations working in Peru fully participated in conferences and workshops together, and the sisters from various communities generated lasting bonds among themselves. On the other hand, the diocesan Peruvian congregations were more constrained and did not participate.

The character of the mission in Peru went beyond the institutional boundaries of the congregation. The mission had been founded by the Canadian province. The missioners in the various foundations in Peru behaved as a group and worked as a community, while the provincial in Canada continued to make all the decisions about who would be missioned to Peru; therefore, the requests for approvals – including appointments, decisions on budget issues, and responses to them – had to travel from Peru to Canada (where they had been founded), then from Canada to Rome (where the motherhouse had been moved in the mid-1960s), and back again. The appointment of a regional coordinator somewhat mitigated this difficulty, but the frustration with these processes finally led to the creation of a new entity, the Peruvian Region, directly responsible to Rome. In July 1986, the Enlarged General Council stated that the regional superior and her council would report directly to the General Council, not to the Canadian Provincial Council,

11.16 The parish house in Candarave, Peru, 1985. Pictured are Sisters Margaret Dawson, Irene Oliver, and Loretta Bonokoski. Photograph provided by Sister Marilyn LeBlanc, RNDM.

although the latter would still provide financial support to the new mission. The Peruvian mission continued to grow. On 30 March 1987, Elsie Valenzuela, a secondary teacher, became the first Peruvian RNDM sister to make first profession in the congregation in Moquegua. The Peruvian mission has since become international, with sisters not only from Canada but also from Australia, New Zealand, the British Isles, and India, in addition to the local vocations from Peru.

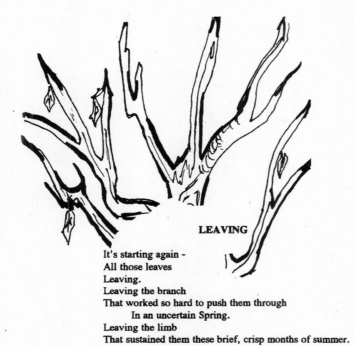

LEAVING

It's starting again -
All those leaves
Leaving.
Leaving the branch
That worked so hard to push them through
     In an uncertain Spring.
Leaving the limb
That sustained them these brief, crisp months of summer.

I can feel the rip and tear as they part.
I can hear them scream as they plummet to the ground,
Their yellow-orange-crimson coloring
Leaving a trail of blood.
Leaving a bunch of leafless trees.
And treeless leaves.

I'm not making this up,
am I?
It couldn't be me who resists so much
The change in a life or a season?

Veronica Dunne

Coming Full Circle

This book provides a particular historical case showing the complexity of the Catholic Church, its historical shifts, and even ruptures over the longue durée – exemplified by the ultramontane Vatican Council I (1869–70) and the profound paradigmatic change generated by Vatican II (1962–65) – and the intersection of the Church and its plurality of cultural formations with state-led education systems, socio-economic demands, and modernity at large. Euphrasie Barbier founded the RNDMs in 1861 in what O'Malley describes as the long nineteenth century – from the French revolution to 1958 when Pius XII died.[1] This long period was characterized by its anti-modernism. Neo-scholasticism, a form of neo-Thomism mediated by the Magisterium – the exclusive Church's intellectual framework that served as both the weapon against and remedy for modernism – influenced Catholic education. There was, indeed, resistance by theologians who were at the centre of the modernist crisis at the beginning of the twentieth century; furthermore, from the mid-1930s, "nouvelle théologie" would develop outside the Vatican walls and influence the Second Vatican Council.[2]

The mid-nineteenth century witnessed an explosion of religious congregations, old and new, with missions in education and health that were bolstered by confessionalization as a driving force in the midst of intense processes of colonization. Still, Catholic schooling took different forms and institutional expressions due in part to the process of differentiation of Church and state, the particular vision of the congregations (charism), and the ways of carving a space for the Church in particular educational states. The Canadian province of the RNDMs played a variety of political and social roles not envisioned by their foundress, whether in Franco-Manitoban communities, in the Catholic separate school system in Saskatchewan, or in English-speaking areas with immigrants from eastern European countries, among others.

The book opened with the vision the foundress had for the congregation, and a description of her early life and her particular religious call as it was gathered by the sisters and priests involved with the young congregation in what is known as the "myth of foundation," which was cultivated as an internal memory of the RNDM. This story includes both her struggle with the clergy to establish her foreign mission and the spirituality that she embraced as a sustaining basis for the new congregation. The language of the congregation is somewhat foreign and mysterious to secular people – even to me as a historian of all things Catholic. Barbier embraced a Trinitarian spirituality – not common in the nineteenth century – and the notion of divine missions; the mission was not something that people did – it was what the Trinity did *through* people. The foundress placed the congregation under the patronage of Mary as a way of honouring the divine missions to which Mary had the most profound fidelity. She had received the divine mission. The Holy See did not accept the concept of divine missions; it was removed from the constitutions, and the congregation kept the oral tradition until the sisters discovered documentation during the renewal process after Vatican II. The Trinitarian spirituality could have had radical implications; however, the vision in the Church was that God sent the Son, and the Son and the Father sent the Holy Spirit to sanctify the people through the Church (the institution). In a current rereading explicit in the conversation among former provincials that separates the action of the Holy Spirit from the institution, Veronica Dunne saw in the notion of participating in divine missions a theological avenue to expand the debate on women's ordination and support it (see Appendix A, pp. 288–9). It is an interesting perspective.

The first missions in the Canadian prairies in rural schools became a challenge to the congregation's strict rules regulating life and its semi-cloistered character and core devotional duties, considered essential to produce the desired identity. The negation of the self, emphasis on obedience, and limited contact with the world set clear parameters to the relational and reflective dimensions of the self, and were in line with a highly centralized, hierarchical, and bureaucratic organization; the regulations were later emphasized by the 1917 Canon Law governing congregations. This kind of hierarchical organization would become, at various points, the object of misalignment with the Canadian province of the congregation, an issue that became full blown after the Second Vatican Council. The early work with Catholic communities, particularly in rural areas and in Franco-Manitoban communities and Saskatchewan, did not offer the conditions to comply with the regulations.

Women teaching congregations have an important place in the history of education in the prairies and in Canada. They served the Catholic population, while intersecting with its social fabric and imaginary and promoting the Vatican's agenda/intentionality, which was to carve a Catholic social order and keep control over the education of the Catholic flock. The RNDMs were invited to come to Manitoba at a time when public funding for confessional schools had been eliminated in the province. Once in Canada, the RNDM soon expanded their educational work to Saskatchewan (1905) and later, on a small scale, to Ontario and, in the 1950s, to Quebec. They taught the official curriculum, opening spaces to inculcate Catholic ways in public schools, parish schools, private schools, and in the Catholic separate school system.

Whom did the schools serve? The RNDM opened foundations in Franco-Manitoban communities and taught in public schools favoured by the existence of hundreds of school districts in rather homogeneous communities. They became part of a provincial and national institutional network asserting French-Canadian rights, an ideological and religious configuration. The schools were nested in the socio-economic characteristics of the places, amid demographic changes and political struggles. Parish schools attracted Catholic immigrants who were eager to gain social recognition and a place in society, as well as to preserve their cultural values. In the case of St Augustine parish school in Brandon, priests were able to conduct religious teaching in the language of the communities. Private schools would, by and large, attend to the needs of Catholic girls – many of them children of immigrants – belonging to emergent and established middle classes: such was the case of St Michael's Academy in Brandon, a private boarding secondary school, and of private schools in Regina, Saskatchewan, such as the Sacred Heart College, which in 1926 had been awarded the status of Junior College by the University of Ottawa. Locality and the "social imaginary" of the communities played a major role in the life of the schools and the relationship with the sisters. The sisters' apostolate also had a Westernizing agenda clearly observed in schools with large numbers of Métis students.

The sisters adapted their educational work to the Catholic neo-scholastic philosophy of the Magisterium, which was pedagogically and, in terms of objectives, mediated by the official curricula and also by the formation the sisters obtained in normal schools and universities – with the latter happening more often from the 1950s onward. The schools, through enculturating religious practices and the very materiality of the school and its design and religious content, were also sites for recruitment of future members of the congregation.

The congregation entered the post-war years after a long haul that had opened with the dusty years of the Depression. The post-war period brought a new socio-economic and political reality, and the work of the sisters flourished for some time. Pius XI's encyclical "On Christian Education," with its outdated gendered approach and its anti-modernism, provided the framework for Catholic education until the mid-1960s, even if the sisters mixed in other educational conceptions.[3] By the mid-1960s, the sisters' role in building the French-Canadian nation, which included communities outside Quebec, through their teaching was over. The quiet revolution was taking shape along with a process of secularization. Very early in the 1960s, the sisters left the schools located in the Franco-Manitoban communities and, within a decade, had left most schools, although some sisters were hired as regular teachers in some of them.

The RNDM private schools did not survive the changes of the "long 1960s": deterioration of the buildings, lack of necessary facilities, decline in the number of women religious as teachers, a new market, and processes of consolidation were contributing causes to their demise. The public school boards took control of a number of schools. The emergence of new social and ideological configurations, including a process of secularization of consciousness, the feminist movement, social movements, the decolonization process, and intense pluralism, along with new views on spirituality, opened ways to a new concept of the self among the sisters.

The RNDM, like other sisters in Canada, had entered the 1960s with an anachronistic language and lived the contradictions between the subculture of the congregation and the world around them. The Second Vatican Council began its deliberations in 1962 in the context of developments in theology that had started long before outside of the Vatican walls, a strong presence of lay groups in the Church such as Catholic Action, and the active work of organizations of women and men religious, such as the Canadian Religious Conference. At the time, the congregations had begun to experience decline in religious vocations, while a number of women's congregations had become familiar with the work of theologians who looked for a fruitful encounter with modernity at the doorstep of post-modernism.

Vatican II brought a profound paradigmatic change by opening up to other religions in terms of dialogue and cooperation, reinterpreting the teaching of the Church in light of the present, and declaring social justice an imperative of the Gospel.[4] Of course, the outcome of the council also brought resistance and reactions in the Vatican itself and by the leadership of some congregations.

The habit became a symbol of change in the Canadian province from 1966. All the dimensions of the self, mentioned in the analysis, were at play in this reimagining of the habit and the challenging of its meaning and actuality. The material dimension of the self can be seen as linked to the critique of the hierarchical, centralist, and bureaucratic character of the central administration and to patriarchal interference from the Vatican. In a general way, the encounter of the Canadian sisters with a pluralistic world in which different world views and value systems coexisted, from a relativized standpoint – the sisters were not holders of absolute truth any longer – along with the general openness generated by Vatican II, clashed with the extremely bureaucratized and hierarchical organization to which the sisters found themselves subordinated.[5] It is not surprising that it was not until 1971 that the international congregation actually gave all its members freedom regarding the habit.

The interactions in the 1960s between the Generalate (the central administration of the congregation), the Vatican (Holy See), and the Canadian province are conceptualized in the book as constituting fields following Bourdieu – conceptual spaces containing a history, an internal logic, and symbolic capital, with each containing a configuration of interwoven conflicting views.[6] These interactions show the resilience of old patterns and dispositions as conveyed in the leadership of the international congregation, who for a while pursued controlled change, and in the Vatican's attempts to preserve power structures. The process of change in the congregation shows a liberating, intended force.

A commitment to social justice and a preferential option for the poor took roots in the Canadian province in the early 1970s, inspired not only by Vatican II but also by the missionary experience of the province in Peru, where it started a mission in 1969. This experience exposed the sisters to liberation theology (they even attended meetings with leading liberation theologian Gustavo Gutiérrez) and to the 1968 Medellín document (which interpreted Vatican II through liberation theology). In Peru, these RNDM missionaries refounded the basis of their missionary work and its intentionality, reframed notions of social justice, worked with grassroots communities, and generated a new missionary language, but not without internal divisions. Nevertheless, the international congregation fully embraced social justice in 1984. Notions of social justice and "living mission" resulted in the abandoning of ecclesiocentricism and the embracing of a reignocentric approach that also addressed racism, inter-religious dialogue, and language and communication across cultures. In other words, the congregation did not follow the institutional agenda, but rather acted in accordance with the needs the sisters identified in the world (the kingdom of God). At that point, the Canadian province had already moved away from school teaching into work with Indigenous peoples, refugees, women, and the disabled.

From the 1980s, and particularly in the 1990s, the sisters further cultivated their initial familiarity with Teilhard de Chardin and Catholic priest Thomas Berry, eco-theologian and cosmologist, among others. The influence of feminist thea/o/*logy, especially of contextual feminist the*logy that reflected from experience – in particular the work of Rosemary Radford Ruether, Mary Daly, and Elizabeth Schüssler – and Indigenous wisdom led not only to institutional critique and the sisters' recognition of their own oppression, but to an eco-spirituality. The adoption of eco-spirituality represented the most powerful break – one most apparent in the pioneering activities of the Canadian province in the late 1990s and early 2000s. Fully discussed by the General Gathering of 1996, the international congregation as a whole formalized the concept of the RNDM Earth Community in 2008, with the phrase "We are One, We are Love."

The province had developed an elaborated understanding of themselves as individuals and as a community in relation to the earth, the universe, and the non-human world. This understanding was grounded in a critique of Western cosmology and the exploration of principles such as differentiation, interiority, communion, and ways to respect and revere the interiority and differences of the other. The congregation as a whole made a serious attempt to relate the new cosmology to social justice and advocate for an inclusive Church in their eco projects and community work.

The history of the RNDMs in Canada illustrates a congregation whose foundress was nourished by ultramontanism (papocentric view of the Church) and influenced by Jansenism, in particular its moral rigorism that even led to forms of suffering to reach spiritual perfection. In the field, the sisters lived the unique experience of their missionary venture in the Canadian prairies, developed a Canadian identity, went through the crisis and renewal process of the long 1960s, and underwent a transformative experience in Peru. The sisters in the Canadian province emerged with a vision of the self and their community that had a pioneering tone and reflected intense interaction with the international congregation, which was searching for its own identity. The renewed vision moved the congregation as a whole beyond modernism, while remaining constrained by the power structure of the Vatican.

The Canadian province recognized itself as an aging community – but experiencing aging, it said, was something to celebrate through paying attention to the wholeness of the body, mind, and soul (not separable as in dualistic theology) and by cultivating nurturing sensibilities to restore wholeness in its sisters. The sisters henceforth aimed at a full reconstruction of the various dimensions of the self within an emerging cosmology grounded in interconnectedness, perceiving the earth as part of a living planetary system. The matter of the habit became part of their history. The important spiritual aspiration was to become witnesses. New vocations currently coming to the congregation as a whole are from Asian countries, and the Canadian province is receiving some of them to share its experiences and vision.

Making Sense of Memories: Conversation among Former Provincials – A Literal Transcription

This appendix consists of the transcription of an open, reflective, and sincere sharing of memories among former provincial superiors of the Canadian province of the RNDM, which took place in Winnipeg on 23 March 2012. The former leaders shared their inner voices emerging from their understanding of the process of living a religious life at a time of profound transformations. They tried to make sense of their own lived past and their "space of experience," grounded in their expectations for the future ("horizon of expectations") at the time.[1] These memories and reflections are tainted by the lenses of the present in their search for existential meanings.

The meeting was organized by then provincial superior Veronica Dunne, who provided the sisters with two texts as inspiring tools for reflection and a list of questions. The first text was from Reinhold Niebuhr's *The Irony of American History* (no bibliographical data attached) and said:

> Nothing that is worth doing can be achieved in our lifetime; therefore we must be saved by hope. Nothing which is true or beautiful or good makes complete sense in any immediate context of history; therefore we must be saved by faith. Nothing we do, however virtuous, can be accomplished alone; therefore we are saved by love. No virtuous act is quite as virtuous from the standpoint of our friend or foe as it is from our standpoint. Therefore we must be saved by the final form of love which is forgiveness.[2]

The provincial superior added: "Faith, hope, and love are the theological gifts that sustain us on life's journey in the present, creating the future that eventually becomes the past."[3]

The second reading was a poem by Ruben Alves, Presbyterian theologian, poet, writer, and educator, one of the major voices of liberation theology, originally from Brazil.[4]

What is hope?
It is the pre-sentiment that imagination
is more real and reality is less real than it looks.
It is the hunch that the overwhelming brutality
of facts that oppress and repress us
is not the last word.
It is the suspicion that reality is more complex
than the realists want us to believe.
That the frontiers of the possible are not
determined by the limits of the actual;
And in a miraculous and unexplained way
life is opening up creative events
which will open the way to freedom and resurrection –
but the two – suffering and hope
must live from each other.
Suffering without hope produces resentment and despair.
But, hope without suffering creates illusions, naïveté
and drunkenness.
So let us plant dates
even though we who plant them will never eat them.
We must live by the love of what we will never see.
That is the secret discipline.
It is the refusal to let our creative act
be dissolved away by our need for immediate sense experience
and is a struggled commitment to the future of our grandchildren.
Such disciplined hope
is what has given prophets, revolutionaries and saints
the courage to die for the future they envisage.
They make their own bodies the seed of their highest hope.

Sister Veronica Dunne gave the sisters a long list of questions, the answers to which were to be prepared by the sisters for the meeting. In the first part of the meeting, the sisters responded to the first five questions, and then Sister Veronica invited the sisters to express their feelings and views, and to generate an exchange.

Cécile Campeau, provincial superior between 1968 and 1971

What stands out for you over the years you served as provincial?
I served as provincial from 1968 to 1971, when the great Vatican Council was over but all doors and windows were wide open. It was a time of great rejoicing, also a time of grieving and letting go. What stands

A.1 A conversation among former provincials, March 2012. Facing the photographer, from left to right: Denise Kuyp, Imelda Grimes, Winifred Brown, and Claire Himbeault. Source: Author's collection.

out for me is definitely the great renewal in the Church and in religious life. Our Canadian RNDM sisters had sent their first three missionaries to study Spanish in Puerto Rico in view of beginning the first mission in Moquegua, Peru, and in Ilo [Peru] to follow soon after. More Canadians, of course, embarked later on foreign mission work, and its possibilities became a reality. Hope for real mission fields were renewed, and many volunteered. Canadians experimented with new models of the religious habit, we returned to our baptismal names, and many more sisters were sent to further their studies at home and abroad. We also made visits to our families. Especially for our pioneers who went back overseas for the first time, these visits were very much encouraged. Of course, we also accepted the liturgical changes in the Mass and in the Divine Office. Consultative votes for provincial elections were a new experience in those years for us, and the RNDMs from the east and the west met as a body for the first time when we held our first Provincial Assembly in St Norbert at Villa Maria. New and deep friendships were formed. I have a feeling that we did not know each other from east to west, and it was the beginning of getting to know our Canadian province better. We also had an international meeting of the provincials at Via dei Laghi in Rome in 1968 in order to prepare for the extraordinary Chapter that was to be held in '69, and we were to rewrite the constitutions at that time of the post–Vatican II era. So we were inspired by the new documents of Vatican II, by contemporary theology, and I can remember putting much emphasis on co-responsibility and subsidiarity. The congregation soon discovered that the constitutions at which we had worked so hard reflected very little of the spirit and the spirituality of our congregation. So the constitutions were soon replaced – I think in 1972.

What was a great joy for you? I think from there, a great joy was my acceptance as provincial superior by the sisters because I was very young. I was taken out of the classroom and was not knowledgeable as far as provincial administration was concerned. I was very touched by the courage and obedience of the older sisters and the vitality of the young ones, too, in particular. There was *life* and it was interesting.

What was a great sadness for you? One of our great sadnesses was that we closed several of our houses and also that quite a few of our members left.

Of what are you most proud? So, when my term ended, I felt that everything was unfinished. I have no regrets because I think I had done pretty well to the best of my ability, even if it hadn't always been my way. I was also quite conscious that Claire would be our next provincial leader, so it was easy letting go without any sorrow. As far as legacy is concerned, I don't believe I have left any legacy, but I certainly made long and lasting friendships.

Claire Himbeault, provincial superior between 1971 and 1977, and superior general of the congregation between 1984 and 1996

What stands out for me over the years that I served as provincial? Well, Vatican II was being implemented and that meant that there was a great deal of enthusiasm but also a certain amount of fear. In the province, the polarization became more evident. Those who feared what was going on and then those who were way up there wanting with great enthusiasm to implement change, and so that stands out. And it was like trying to hold the two ends together and keep that unity. I felt that really was the mission of my six years.

The joy that stands out, the great joy for me, of course, was the enthusiasm at what Vatican had brought. Vatican II actually changed my life, and I was different even in my relationships to the sisters because of it.

The great sadness for me was, of course, what was happening in the province. A great number of sisters were leaving for various reasons, different people had different reasons. Perhaps it was that they for the first time saw that there was something else for them, that this was not really their place. So I found myself accompanying many of the sisters as they made their discernment and lived it with sadness and pain. At the same time, it was really the right thing for many of them, but I nevertheless felt it, felt the separation.

What I am most proud of, I suppose, is the fact that the sisters had a great deal of confidence in me, and I was able to communicate with those who were having difficulty accepting what was happening and to be with them, while at the same time being with those who were introducing new things such as "fraternities" and also the new way of living community, a number of the things that Cécile just mentioned. The religious habit during my terms of office went from the interim habit to wearing ordinary secular clothes, and then there were some that were still very much afraid of that.

What did you feel unfinished when your term ended? I think that, even though there was a great deal of change, external change, we were just beginning to deepen the meaning of Vatican II and deepen the meaning of our religious life. We were looking into our charism, so I would say the whole spiritual renewal was in process and very much unfinished.

Winifred Brown, provincial superior between 1977 and 1983

My approach of course was much more personal than yours, sisters, so my answers are brief.

What stands out for me over the years that I served as provincial? Two things: My participation at general chapters and the Enlarged General Council, those were very important. The other thing was a personal one: how hard it was to make decisions, partly because it is hard for me to make decisions anyway and partly because I had a lot of different kinds of advice coming at me. An example of that was the renovations at St Edward's. I felt they were needed, and yet I often felt that they were unnecessary. So that kind of thing was hard for me.

What was a great joy to me? Again, that was a personal thing. The one joy that really stands out for me was how Sister Mary Aselle Martin recovered when she went to Brandon. The whole idea of having a convent in Brandon was very important to me – having that place for an infirmary and knowing that we were looking at the future and seeing that we needed to look after our older sisters and that hospitals were not necessarily the right place. And I remember specifically Sister Aselle, because she was living in a dark room with the blinds pulled down, and when she went to Brandon and stopped at McDonald's for the first time in her life and had hot chocolate. Then one day she said, "I could be going to Mass." That really stands out for me.

What was the great sadness for you? The other thing that stands out for me was my failure in not going to Sister Mary St Fortunat's death-bed [cries] when Sheila phoned me and said that she was dying and asked if I wanted to come, and I said, "No." I haven't done anything like that since.

Of what are you most proud? I don't have anything I am proud of.

What was unfinished? I don't remember.

Marie Baker, provincial superior between 1983 and 1989

I had to do some searching of memories because I live in a different milieu.

What stands out for me is our closing of several houses: Longueil, St Eustache, Saskatoon, Elie. And Brandon was just in the process, and I probably forgot some others. Yes, Sacred Heart College. It was sold during Claire's time. My other memory was the growth in the Peruvian missions and visiting there – just seeing their vitality and work with the poor, that stood out for me. They were on their way to having an independent government, although not becoming a province yet. At that time in Canada, Sandy Bay, Kramer House, and Pinewood were opened. So there were some new areas for us there.

What was a great joy for you? One of the events that were significant for me, and I think for several of the sisters, was Doctor Margaret Anne Schlintz's healing retreat. That seemed to be a growth point or a healing for some of the sisters. The Cathedral Courts project, I think, was just beginning, and I found it exciting that it was a joint project and not just a new way of using a building, and so on. Sandy and Tara's profession of vows were special to me at that time. Also the fact that Pablo was being accepted as a Canadian citizen, I found it very encouraging just to know that at St Edward's we were able to find a place for him and then to keep fighting in the courts for him.[5]

What was the great sadness for you? Vocations were very few. I pushed for and started the RNDM Associates project, which has gone defunct since, and I am okay with that. There were some laypeople who were quite enthusiastic at that time. Somewhere along that time, there was a court case over our Brandon property – I can't remember what it was about, taxation or whatever – but I know we went to a courtroom and we had to present our case. I also remember that Denise and I were involved with the separate school board in Regina over the Marian High School closing. It was not very pleasant to deal with them over that issue. That was a difficult time for me.

What I felt was unfinished, well, I guess the changes at Brandon and Cathedral Courts – also our Sacred Heart College community – a couple of sisters really put up quite a resistance to moving out of the college and that was a painful time, but then a house was found at 2710 22nd Avenue. I realized that, when I finished as provincial, there were a couple of sisters that were hurt because I suggested that they needed counselling and so on, and it has happened since – but at that time they were angry with me. I guess two or three out of whatever [laughter] wasn't too bad. On the other hand, several other sisters started asking for and finding places like Southdown for counselling, healing, and growth, and were making use of those programs, which were becoming acceptable and helpful for many of the sisters.

Sheila Madden, provincial superior between 1992 and 1998

When I came to the question, **What stands out for you over the years you served as provincial?**, it struck me that it was a rather foreign territory for me because I never considered myself as provincial. And I tried valiantly to convert the thinking and the perception of others, for better or for worse. I was provincial canonically only, and in reality I was one among equals and that came out of our discernment, and the discernment followed a month of living the "Gospel Way."[6] So those were two very significant experiences for me. For me, the grace of that was the gift of the circle that we were – the demolishment or dismantling of the pyramid and the formation of the circle. I think it was a particular gift. I mean, I saw it very clearly: I was one of three when it was the team; I was one of nine when we met with the support group; and I was one of ninety when we met as a province. That was very clear for me, and I am grateful for that to this day. It was six years of much transition. We were three on the team, but two full-time and one at a distance, and then Denise was away for a year, so it was one and one and one – so the configuration of the team of three had many shifts. In that time, too, Elaine's mother died, so there was much upheaval in terms of Elaine's life over that, and Denise and I walking with her. It was an era of people finding themselves, and I think overtly for the first time in terms of a sexual orientation. So we had lots of innuendos, it seems to me, about things like that, I remember. I think the first time we talked about it as a group was when we were in assembly. So those are the kinds of things that stand out for me on that.

What was a great joy for me? The great joy was in terms of the sisters, many of the sisters making very clear declarations of their support and their loyalty. One of my memories is meeting with many of them in terms of their will. We had to do something about a will, and many of the older sisters said, "What I wrote there, I wrote." Like "Amen, I don't want to redo it, don't need to." So that sticks out as a memory for me, and so a kind of special relationship with many of the sisters and very humbling actually.

What was a great sadness for me, as I understood it, relating to the thrust of those six years that had come out of our discernment before, was trying to help people to come to an understanding of their own personal authority, that they couldn't be obedient to anyone else until they were obedient to that inner self and that was a struggle for many people. So it wasn't a sadness really. I remember, however, when we were trying to plan some retreat and I thought that if I could just get some sisters to indicate what was their great desire, what desire lived in them, but so many had no answer. That still rests as a sadness there, that something had happened that they couldn't name a desire.

Of what am I most proud? I am most proud of God's fidelity to me and to us and that life unfolded as it needed to.

One of my regrets is a very simple one. I often wish, especially in these last couple of years, I wish that I had pushed harder to buy the Marianists' house at the corner of St-Jean-Baptiste and Avenue Cathédrale in St Boniface. The Marianists built it and then they were selling it, and I was saying that we ought to buy that, especially for the French-Canadian sisters so they would have a place to live, but I never got anywhere. In hindsight, I have often regretted that I didn't push harder for that.

What did I feel was unfinished when my term ended? Well, I had a sense that the reality of "team" might be over, so I wished that we had done more to deepen our discernment of "team," a sense of being a team of equals, and that we would have deepened our sense of discernment. I think we are asking sisters to take on personal authority without maybe giving them as much help as we could have.

Imelda Grimes, provincial superior between 1998 and 2004

What stands out for me over the years I served as provincial? The team concept is great ideally, but it is especially difficult when personalities are so different. Our sisters are very understanding and accepting – that's something that stood out for me, and I think particularly from the older sisters who do have a sense of authority and respect, and that was nice. Also what stood out for me was the fact that sisters coming from other countries to work here need much orientation, and I think that was something that was really lacking at the time. I think we welcomed them well enough, but we failed to really help them to adapt and prepare for their new mission in Canada. So that stands out for me as a regret.

What was a great joy for you? My joys circle around our times of celebration like the Lebret Jubilee, the Brandon Jubilee, and also the sale of places – now some of you have mentioned here your sadness over the closing of houses and so on. That was not a sorrow for me because I felt it was time for us to leave these places – and I was glad when we had the Lebret sale and the Elie sale, as strange as that may sound. Another joy for me was Claire's safe return from Senegal – we all thought she was a goner – and also learning the importance of medical travel insurance. The successful purchase of the condo for Betty Iris and Jacky: Jacky remembers to this day what she calls my standing up to the realtor and asking for a lower price. I don't think Jacky thought I could possibly do that – but I did! So that was a joy. The sisters' desire to improve themselves personally, spiritually, that was always, always good.

What was the great sadness for you? The sadness for me was the many difficulties within our team. We were not a model of unity, and I am sad to this day about that. The situation around the Early Learning Centre – I really wanted to just give them the building, and I felt kind of ambushed about the whole thing. But then I was happy when we finally got a price for it. Audrey's death was so sudden [she was only sixty-four] and the removal of Aggie from Garrity, these were two great sadnesses for me.

Of what are [you most proud?] I don't know that I am particularly proud of anything.

For what is unfinished, well, I guess everything is unfinished. All of us, each of us is a work of art in progress. So how can anything be totally unfinished? I don't know.

Denise Kuyp, provincial superior between 2004 and 2010

Well, I guess the thing that stands out for me is closing more houses, big ones, St Michael's and St Edward's for sure, and many others of various sizes.

What was a great joy for you? I don't know that there is any great joy. I enjoyed the work. I think it was a joy for me that, in thinking about it, there are close to twenty sisters that either came to Canada or went from Canada to other countries for short-term missionary service in that period of time. I was amazed actually that there was that much exchange. So I am glad about that, because for me it speaks of who we are.

I think that **what was always a sad point for me**, when working with sisters, is how to balance individual and common good. When it comes to discernment and decision-making in the case of individual sisters, discerning the next step, in my sense, is quite individual – and so it's yes, taking into consideration the individual and the community and even the congregation, if you will. For the community, I found there was no common ground where we could meet and decide with certitude in terms of a direction or priorities for the province. I don't know how to explain it other than it was a more isolated process rather than communal discernment. That was always a point of struggle for me, even of sadness.

Of what am I most proud? I can't think other than mostly I hung in there.

What was unfinished for me? Well, certainly the eco-project was an unfinished thing, and some sense of direction for the next twenty-five years. I have a sense that that was unfinished, and it is my desire that as a group, as a body, we articulate what is our hope for the future direction.

General Discussion

Veronica Dunne: Wow! That was like a quick review of some forty to forty-five years of our history. We each had a chance to speak. So now we will just open it up and if you want to respond to what others have said or add whatever you wish to say.

Claire Himbeault: About the international sisters coming from other provinces and how to prepare them that Imelda mentioned, I think there is the other side of it too. We as a province have to learn to be much more welcoming – and, of course, you were saying that too. But that whole attitude, which shifted somewhere back, instead of seeing ourselves as Canadian belonging to a province and so forth, the whole attitude of we belong to a congregation and, of course, you mentioned that. We belong to a congregation, and so the provincial aspect is in administration, an administrative reality, and so we are open to whatever and open to whomever because they are all ours.

Cécile Campeau: I'd like to question Denise on this sort of "individual" rather than "community" – I am not too sure I understand what you are saying with this – could you clarify?

Denise Kuyp: I am not sure I can explain it very well – I guess it is my sense that, as a province, sometimes we did not have a clear direction, or I guess you might say, a province plan where as a province we were going in this direction and that all of us were working together in the same direction you know ... to implement or to give flesh to something, rather than as isolated individuals – "Well I will find this ministry or I will find something to do or ..." Do you know what I mean? It wasn't part of a larger picture often, and how to help sisters or be with them in a helpful way.

Cécile Campeau: The reason I asked this is that definitely one of the things in your administration – and I'm not saying it wasn't done anywhere else – is that I felt myself taking part in the decision-making. Especially like at these summer assemblies or special meetings we had, and this is a very great feeling and a great thing to be doing. It is not only the members of the council that are making the decisions but we also had our say in everything. So I sort of questioned that, but you would see it in a different light. In many of the decisions that were made we *were* consulted.

Denise Kuyp: I think I am trying to get at something else, like when an individual sister was trying to discern her path in terms of where to live or what to do or that kind of thing.

Cécile Campeau: I feel almost guilty of this in a sense. I want to give you an example: I had mentioned to you when you first started that I was interested in Berkley, and you told me to apply, that it takes about a year – which I did, and it was a wonderful experience for me. Then I came back and was able to step into parish administration. It really had nothing to do, in a sense, with the rest of the community, but it was a great thing to be able to reach so many people. I think maybe it is more of a modelling thing that had been happening – as Imelda knows what I am talking about – so I was wondering. For me, it was a great mission because I felt that I, and we as RMDMs, had reached so many people that were very open. It was a different mission in a sense. So I was wondering if this was what you were trying to say that, definitely, first of all, it was a private matter but at the same time a sense of calling and a spirit-calling. I don't think I had that kind of problem when I was provincial because everything was so controlled. One thing I would like to add here was that, when I became provincial, as I say I was just in and out of the classroom and had not much training. But I asked Sister Mary Genevieve if she would be my secretary and my bursar. She was a woman of great experience, great spirituality, fidelity, and a very big support to my ignorance [laughter], but I never mentioned it to Genevieve. I think we do have people in our province – and in the world over – who are not only right there, but are they ever accomplishing much! Genevieve took on the finances. I mean, what would I have done? And then she also did the secretarial work. At one time, I had to make a decision that was contrary to the advice of the Provincial Council – all the members of the council were against it. And so I went to Genevieve, and she said, "Cécile, you have to remember that as provincial, there are times when you have to act on your own." And I did. It was a big decision about whether to keep a sister or not, and so she stayed and became a very great missionary. So I think the Spirit has been at work all the time in our various administrations for sure.

Winifred Brown: I think too that what Sheila said and what you said are just about the direct opposite – that here I am a leader of a team and the team would like to be the whole province, but if you are making that kind of decision you have to do it on your own. There are times when there has to be one person to make the decision, and I don't know precisely what Denise is talking about because (I don't mean you're not clear), I mean there are personal things involved that cannot be said – but I think that conflict continues among us partly because our constitutions are hierarchical and partly because there is a difference between the people at one end of the age spectrum and those at the other. Some of us have lived with people who cannot make a decision for themselves. They don't know how, they have never been allowed, and it just can't happen for them. So it is an ongoing problem of how do you deal with that, how do you put together Sheila's team notion, and what has been and appears to be from the top right now – a very authoritarian sort of government. I think it is a problem we have in the whole congregation, not just in our province. It is like the elephant in the room – we don't name it but it's there, and I don't have any solutions. But I can see that as an ongoing thing.

Sheila Madden: And I think we use the word "discernment" without really having delved into how to do discernment ongoingly. When Renée comes and leads us, that's one experience, and those have been good. But for helping people individually along the way, I remember Claire and Kathleen coming and doing that once at Brandon on a weekend and presenting the elements of discernment – which was good – and I have often felt badly that we didn't follow up more with that, to have in-depth discernment with the local communities. I think when I was talking about deepening the sense of team, it is much the same as what I think you are saying, that, as an individual,

I am discerning but I am doing it in light of the whole somehow, not just me alone, and I think that's like what you are saying too, Denise.

Denise Kuyp: Yes, basically, when you ask people, or they propose something for themselves and you suggest other things, or "would you take some more time with this, talk to your spiritual director," and the person comes back and says "no" – this is what it is, this is what it is regardless.

Sheila Madden: We would sometimes say "go back and talk to your community," and they would look at us as if we had ten heads.

Winifred Brown: It's a very big problem. I was just talking with an Oblate friend. She had lived alone for twenty years in Assiniboia doing parish and youth ministry, and now she is here, head of a community group of eight people, four of whom are deaf, etc.... How do you combine personal discernment with community needs? It's just not that easy. That is a very profound statement, I recognize that. Talking too about the challenges when sisters come from Asia or from Samoa, I think we shouldn't forget the aspect of racial prejudice. It is different from when they came to Canada from New Zealand in 1905, for instance. These sisters were educated, and they came to take charge of schools. But when we went to India, the population was "a little less" than us, and when they come here, we also have to face that unnamed and much detested attitude that we may find in ourselves. Even to saying, "well, I had a taxi driver the other day, and he was clearly Muslim from the way he treated me." Is that prejudice on my part or is it a simple statement of truth? He also has a prejudice against women who are telling him what to do. So I think it is just really complicated, and I agree with Imelda that people who come are not always accepted for what they are, for their innate abilities. Nobody ever said it was easy. I mean, even Jesus had trouble with his apostles. "'Cast your nets on the other side.' How dare you say that to a professional fisherman? This guy is a carpenter!" [laughs].

Veronica Dunne: I was struck by what you said when you were talking, Marie. When others mentioned people leaving and houses closing, you also mentioned houses opening. I don't know if that was unique to that era. And there were also a couple of profession of vows during the time you were provincial. So it's interesting just to think back on it. What that was like – like a blip or rhythm in history or what else?

Marie Baker: Well, I mean this was twenty-five years ago, so there were still sisters going to Peru – and Sandy Bay opened, but I mean it wasn't the best situation either actually. I think there was good work done in those four years. Pinewood, I don't know how long – but

I mean there was a need – and then, of course, Kramer Home still continued. But I also mentioned there were five places that closed. I also thought afterwards it was the time when Marcelle Granger and the two other sisters came back [from Quebec], that was the end of living in Quebec. And then they got the house on St Jean-Baptiste Street – which was no different situation than it was over there. It was the end of an era of living in Quebec. One of the things I felt when I was provincial – and it was still the provincial and the council – but I guess we were blessed with good councillors. I felt we worked as a team. You were there, Denise, and I think, Imelda, you were for one term also. After the meetings, I realized that we really worked as a team, and I was very grateful for that. I guess how the council functions depends on the persons a great deal.

Sheila Madden: My biggest contribution on Winifred's council was telling her: "Winifred, you *are* our provincial." I remember that somebody was always trying to promote someone else.

Winifred Brown: When I think back about my being provincial, I came from being a school principal. Our staff meetings at the academy from 1955 to 1969 were not very frequent, and for a time there were only sisters at those occasional staff meetings that we had. Then when I went to Marian High School, it was a whole different ball of wax. For instance, I had Joe Duffy, who had been principal until I came home from the General Chapter. We were good friends; otherwise, he would never have put up with the situation that he was just demoted and I was made principal. But at the same time, he challenged me lots at staff meetings. What I am really getting around to saying is that I never had any training in leadership. So when I became provincial later, I followed the model of provincials before me. I remember once Sheila saying to me, "I would like to be asked my opinion." I thought that the role of councillors was to *give* their opinion. And I guess I was not even saying, "What do you think?" because I expected them to give it. I didn't have any training in leadership, and people before me and probably people after me had no training in leadership either, so how do you run a meeting when, in the end, you are the one who has to do it [implement the decisions]? For instance, if it's "this sister should not be accepted for vows," that's discussed, but you're the one that has to bell the cat. I don't say that in self-defence; it's just an admission of part of the reason I'm not very proud of having been a provincial. I didn't think I did a particularly good job, and maybe people think I did, but that doesn't matter, it's past. We live in community with people with such different backgrounds, and you can go into a community and never be accepted by some of the people who are there. What do you do about that? You just struggle along, and you try to face it, or you ignore it, or you avoid it, or whatever you do. The whole question of leadership is very different today from what it was fifty years ago in our religious congregations. It was the same in the past generations. I was brought up by my parents and by sisters. Really, what my parents said went most of the time. And when it didn't go, I would get a strong reproof, so I grew up obedient. So you expect that when you are in leadership, it will be the same. I don't mean that as an excuse, it is just admitting a simple fact that it is different with an eighty-year-old and a sixty-year-old and especially with a fifty- or forty-year-old.

[COFFEE BREAK]

Veronica Dunne: [Now we'll be] addressing the question, **What do you think are the significant challenges today?**

Cécile Campeau: Well, I have mentioned some of the challenges, and I think that these are still ongoing. I think we do, or have to do, quite a bit more studies in spirituality, the various spiritualities. I feel stronger than ever having just followed CND [Congregation of Notre Dame] Lorraine Caza's retreat. It sort of brought back to me this whole spirituality of listening, and that's really what *Verbum Domini* is all about really, listening to the Word. This is one thing I felt, I would definitely have to deepen, and I felt it would be such a renewal in the Church also, if even priests went back to this whole idea of listening well. Lorraine used the whole Gospel, but highlighted just a few passages of Scripture and made a lot of comparison of different texts. It is a different study of Scripture [exegesis], but, at the same time, it is a deepening. Of course, another challenge is the cosmic spirituality. More than ever, I keep hearing great people doing great things, great people among ourselves, and I think that women have to become more and more involved in the Church with a feminist spirituality, which is extremely important – well, it is based on Mary. And I think there should be quite an emphasis on that, because a woman brings so much depth and you are not always "up there," especially on a retreat, you are not up there trying to figure out everything about the Trinity. We are able because we are women, because we are very sensitive, to get deeper into what the whole Scripture is saying there, and we need to have more of that. I don't think there is anything wrong in what Lorraine was doing: she was giving the homily on the readings of the day; it was very short but very apropos. I dare any priest or bishop, I won't say the pope, because she really brought out the spirituality of Pope Francis through the *Verbum Domini* document.

I had never heard any homilies so beautifully presented and yet so simple and in just a few words. So maybe we do have something to offer the churches, the homilists. I think we have missed the boat, I did anyway, and I don't think I am the only one. So this is what I said to Lorraine, that we need women in the Church – and "yes," she said, "we do." I said I mean in the liturgies, and I think that is something we could do, we have to think about it. Maybe we are an aging community, but that doesn't change anything. It just adds to what we can give. Don't be afraid to speak to your clergy or to your bishop; I am going to talk to the bishop too about Lorraine, like they get these great big theologians to give a retreat to the priests but if they had somebody that was down to earth, I tell you things would change, and maybe they would give something more substantial to the people. But maybe we are the ones who have to lead the way because we have definitely received a lot: we have doctorates, a lot of studies, and we have to get those out.

Claire Himbeault: I would repeat, the challenge of today is the eco-spirituality and deepening that, and feminism, as Cécile said, and then the reality of who we are as a province – like France and Australia, how to live in hope. This would be a challenge, to live in hope as we bring the province as we know it to closure – whatever that means, I am not sure.

Winifred Brown: I looked at that from the point of view of the differing ideas that exist in the province about what is an appropriate apostolate and about how is the right way to live community. I don't have any ideas for that, but I think those are challenges that we are now facing.

Marie Baker: I don't know if this is a question or what's happening elsewhere today, but I would think some of those challenges are the same as ours in the sense of having just fewer people being able to do apostolic work or thrust, and the challenge of new membership, and then of looking after the elderly and infirm and having time to do other ministries. Those challenges are what I see.

Sheila Madden: With all of the above, I agree. I think the particular challenge is the quest to live well into our future, whatever it is, so I think the challenge is living in a right balance: facing what the reality is, the diminishment and the unravelling, and also living in hope and faith and balance so that we don't go too far one way or the other. I think that is a great challenge. I read an article not too long ago in terms of what you were talking about, women in the Church and the need to be there, which is a challenge to me because sometimes I say it is better to be on the fringe and not get caught in the middle. But to effect some change, I need to be where I can do that. On the weekend, I looked up some information on the LCWR [Leadership Conference of Women Religious, United States], and the challenge they've had from the Vatican. So I was trying to find out what I could about that, and one of the headings I saw was something from Tony Blair about these women of faith that are his heroes, and it was about women religious. It is a beautiful article, and I found it very encouraging that somebody is out there saying this about these women who are working in the field of trafficking of women. In his understanding of what they are doing, they have left the sanctuary, the safety of the sanctuary, and are out there on the streets working with people, empowering, helping those women to find their own power and their own dignity, helping those for whom dignity would be a strange word. So I see that as the whole call to balance to which we have always been challenged in our lives. But I think each time, each era, has its own components of that balance that we seek. So for me, that is significant for today.

Imelda Grimes: Well, my comment is just mostly agreeing with what you have said. I think about the whole question of housing and the care of the elderly – because now it is really the elderly ministering to the elderly – and the amount of energy, or lack thereof, is problematic for sure. I think the whole thrust of our 2008 Chapter and its documents was that stress on eco-spirituality and unity – we can't go wrong on either of those – but really entering into that is a big, big challenge. My question here is, How do you live in hope and faith in Church leadership?

Winifred Brown: What a shocker!

Denise Kuyp: I agree with everything that has already been said. In terms of challenges for the congregation or the province, I would say the challenge that faces us is, How can we continue to be part of the larger congregation and they part of us? For that relationship is rather on the edge; we're out here, we are not in France or in Europe where people are coming for courses, or for deepening our charism, or to visit Mother Foundress's tomb, following Euphrasie's footsteps, etc.... For we are out on the edge here. So I think there is the challenge of deciding what kind of future our province has. I think that discernment has to be done with the larger congregation somehow. And then we need to put the necessary structures in place for whichever way we are going. I also think the real question certainly for us is, How can we continue to companion one another no matter in whatever stage of life we are? That, to me, will be a challenge for us. In terms of the larger world? Well, of course, the planet is in peril and what, as RNDMs, are we able to offer in that regard?

Veronica Dunne: We will now move on [to] the questions, **How were your interactions with the congregational leadership? Were there particular challenges? Were there particular experiences of collaboration?**

Cécile Campeau: It was a very, very difficult interaction with the congregational leadership [in Rome] for the Canadian province there in 1968, and I think the reason for that is maybe that they over there had not been hit by Vatican II the way we were. So in the province we had a very enthusiastic group, and it was good because it did bring about the changes that we thought should happen. But what happened down there was very different somehow. I just felt that I did not have to take the responsibility for that, but I certainly had to take the blame in a sense, for what? I am not too sure. So I will leave this blank for what had happened in the province. There was a lot of pressure on the part of the Generalate [congregational leadership] to keep the sisters the way they were as though they didn't seem to have been influenced by what we thought the changes were about: the important things such as much more freedom for the sisters and the change of habit or religious garb. And this freedom, I think that, I certainly felt anyway, that it started in Canada, and so I was called by the Generalate, and I had to answer – a little bit about the veil, a little bit more about the smoking, and it was almost as if it was all my fault. Winifred had told me that once, that I take the responsibility for things that really are not mine. Everything that I was hearing about the Canadian province, I felt it was my fault, and, in that sense, it was very difficult to go to these meetings and so much so that, at one point, mother general said, "Sister I think you will have to give up as provincial." And I said, "Oh well, what will I do then?" And she said, "Well, you can go and study in France, and we will put somebody else there." Now that was a very hard thing to hear, and I don't think it was the work of the Spirit, but it was extremely difficult. And as the Chapter went on, there was a lot of talking, and I think the delegates that year brought a lot of knowledge. And somehow, towards the end of the Chapter, things had sort of subsided a bit, and I kept my place, I kept my position. The reason for all that I would say is that we are in the Americas. I think that we have a lot of exuberance here in the Americas. Definitely within Canada and probably in the States, we were freer, we just went straight ahead with things that we thought we had to do and that was because of this freedom, I think. I felt very badly because I had listened to all the sisters, especially the younger ones. I got very close to the younger sisters, and I could sense that it was not ill on their part, but it was something that you had to dig deeper into and to really understand people more. But that was a very hard message to carry over there as we were trying to revise our constitutions. I can remember one person saying, "Well, maybe we could make these regulations for Canada and other countries in Europe, but I don't think we should bring any changes to the sisters of India, and the sisters in Bangladesh." – Well, I lost it! Because I said, "How can we act as a Generalate then?" So there was an awful lot of reaction. Gradually, we came to an understanding, but it was a terribly difficult three years for me. There was no way I could have taken another term. It was extremely difficult for myself because I was taking a lot of blame personally. No, the interaction was not good. The best thing that I heard was from one of the team members from the Generalate who said to me, "You know Sister, I am sure glad I am not the provincial of Canada." That was the most consoling thing I heard there [laughter].

Claire Himbeault: I think that the congregational leadership and the sisters generally throughout the congregation saw the Canadian province as out there sort of pushing the frontiers, and I think that's true. I have a theory that we are all children of pioneers, and our parents and grandparents pushed the frontiers physically right here in the prairies.

Cécile Campeau: This applies to French Canadians too. We have that in our blood because we helped to keep the faith, and had to fight to keep the language if we wanted to keep the faith.

Claire Himbeault: So you had to push the frontiers, and I have been told that the Canadian sisters are seen as aggressive, and I said, "No, we are not aggressive, but we're pushing for change." We were at that particular time anyway. That was the situation we were in – so yes, I was at that Chapter that Cécile was referring to, to the point where I do remember that my companions from Canada had all given up, and I was standing in the middle of the floor and still trying to give the position about the veil and feeling like the last one to be knocked down – but anyway that was the feeling. As far as my personal relationship with the congregational leadership, it was okay, but I have to confess I did a lot of things that I didn't report [laughter]. As provincial, I was really trying to do what is right, and I authorized what I felt in discernment was the right thing in some cases. A sister, for instance, just wanted to go home and take care of her father because there was nobody else to do it. Now, at the time, she would have had to apply for a leave of absence from the community, and

I said, "I'm giving you an obedience to go, but come back on the weekends, and when you have somebody else coming over and helping, come back to your community, but this is your work." I did that three times until we had a visitation, and I was told, "You should have asked [us permission]." It was that kind of thing, you know. I felt the personal freedom to be able to say that "this is right for this sister and let's not complicate her life any more by this" – because sisters felt terrible about it, being known that they had a leave of absence. So, it might have been dishonest, I don't know what it was, but I felt that I was doing what was right for the sister at that particular time. When I reflect on it now, I suppose it was like knowing how to find the cracks. I am sorry, but I have to confess that's how it was then [laughter].

Winifred Brown: I don't remember my interactions with the congregational leadership. I really don't have any memory of that. I went to India for an Enlarged General Council meeting, and I went to England to prepare for that. Marie Bénédicte was the general when I was provincial. I don't remember any particularly bad things. I am a little bit like Claire: I don't tell everything that I am doing, and I can forget things that people have told me, so I really don't know that I dodged around the bullet at all. I really don't. I would have more recollections of dealing with teachers on my staff.

Marie Baker: I want to say I just learned something new about that. I mean, I knew it was difficult for you, Cécile. I want to say how both of you have come out of it with such a healthy forgiveness and a healthy outlook on the congregation – I mean, going through something like that and feeling you're just standing alone for the Canadian province. So thanks.

Sheila Madden: Well, some of those that were on the congregational leadership team for four of the six years while I was provincial are right here, sitting around this table with me. There were some rough spots in there, but I have nothing but good memories of it because I think we were able to work through, we were able to collaborate. Certainly you, Claire, were particularly supportive, as well as Kathleen, Louise, and Margaret. We would get letters quite often, little notes on this and that. Much like Eleanor O'Brien's notes, they said a lot in a few words. I have a couple of Louise's just encouraging us. She would send articles every once in a while relating to the web or the team, or on different topics of interest to help keep us going. So I think you were always there for us, and we were maybe causing more problems, but that was all in good faith.

Claire Himbeault: It was pushing the frontiers there too.

Sheila Madden: With the next administration, for me it is less clear what our relationship was. That was when Louise got sick, so for me that is a big part of those last two years, Louise being sick, and I not being clear on our relationship. So I would apologize for the pain I caused – to both.

Claire Himbeault: That was pushing the frontiers too.

Imelda Grimes: I don't have anything to say in that regard. It must have been okay because I don't remember any great upheaval or anything.

Denise Kuyp: Yes, my experiences there didn't really leave too much of an impression, you know, sending in the monthly minutes and you didn't get a reply. I mean, in terms of interaction, there hasn't been a great deal that comes to my mind anyway. I have written some hard letters myself – and mostly that had to do with finance, because often there was a request out of the blue, "Would you send this to so and so." And just the whole direction things were going, what was happening, and there would be no feedback. I felt the financial dealing couldn't continue that way. So I think that was probably the most difficult, but apart from that, it is kind of vague; we live our lives, and there isn't too much interaction, really, to my knowledge or in my experience anyway. Then Maureen came, and that was good, and the forum of the five was a good experience as well, in terms of the larger congregation and the leadership there – but I can't say if it's been very helpful or not.

Veronica Dunne: Claire, you have been on both sides of it, people living in Canada just going along and just living our own lives here, and not having a lot of contact with the congregational leadership. Could the same be true of the congregational leadership? Like what I am thinking is, would it have been helpful if, in your memory of being in congregational leadership, to have received more feedback, more interaction with the various provinces?

Claire Himbeault: I really don't know. I have to say that I think that lack of interest on the part of the congregational leadership is more recent.

Denise Kuyp: I don't want to give the impression that they are not interested, but there is certainly not a great sense of interest.

Claire Himbeault: Because I think the concentration is on the young and therefore on Vietnam, because their visits to Vietnam are frequent or to Davao [Philippines], that's another story. So visits to where there are more young sisters – in Vietnam, because there are hundreds of young sisters there, and in India. But now, because vocations are fewer in India – mind you they are getting vocations in great numbers there too – it's going to be another story. Then in Bangladesh and Burma, so we have many young people, and the congregational leadership is looking at Asia much more than, I would say, Canada and Australia. Now both Canada and Australia are saying, "Well, we are fine! Sisters can come and learn English here," and that's good. But we don't have situations where it would be good for a community or a group from Vietnam to come and live and work here. At least we haven't seen it, and we cannot in our imagination see it happening anytime soon. Something different is happening in France, because France, being the cradle of the congregation and the motherhouse now in Rome, several Asian sisters go and live there. But the number always seems to stay about twenty-five or so, because as these sisters die there are more coming in. I don't know what the sisters in Peru and Kenya are experiencing, I have no idea, because they are at the fringe too.

Sheila Madden: In my experience, with your team, Claire, we were more like friends, like of Augustine would say, "friends in search of God." That would be my memory of the relationship with your team there, Claire, Kathleen, and Louise. We had frequent communication. Kathleen was the contact person, but we would hear from Claire and from Louise as well, and from Margaret sometimes in terms of money. Margaret was working on the common purse, and we would get communication from her on that specific topic. But particularly with Kathleen and Louise, we were friends.

Claire Himbeault: Particularly because Louise was coordinator of social justice and peace, so she would be communicating about these. Whatever you were doing, she would encourage and would make you aware of other things. So I don't know if that answers the question.

Veronica Dunne: It gives another perspective of it.

The next question that we will look at is **some of the major trends in the evolution of the Canadian province as you see it**.

Cécile Campeau: I would think that there was certainly a great desire or a desire for greater freedom in every sense of the word. Going to the missions: we had quite a few people asking to go to the missions, and quite a few went. And also there was a trend in furthering our education beyond just the teacher's certificate. I think we also developed a trend in or an interest in the various spiritualities, individually especially. Many of us have attended healing workshops and wellness centres and so forth, and this is something that I appreciated very much, not only because of the Generalate being open, but the growing up and everything else. We were encouraged, I was encouraged – that was by Marie – to go to Ladysmith, and it was a wonderful time of healing. So I think these were definitely trends that were beneficial for all – as well for me especially.

A.2 Former provincials continue the conversation. From left to right: Sisters Claire Himbeault, Sheila Madden, Marie Baker, and Cécile Campeau. Picture provided by Veronica Dunne. Source: Author's collection.

Claire Himbeault: To everything that Cécile said I would like to add the psychological aspect of it. The sisters were anxious to have knowledge about themselves, and we had that workshop with Bruce that went over probably a year in different periods, and then finally at the camp, which of course different people might look at this and say, "Well, it wasn't such a great success." But I think that everybody did profit one way or another. It is connected with personal freedom I think, and knowing oneself and being able to function from the inner self rather than just waiting for the signals from outside. So sisters became more confident women.

Winifred Brown: Looking at the whole picture, it seemed to me that the Canadian province expanded pretty much from 1899 until into the 1940s or perhaps the 50s. Then it seemed there was a period of stagnation; everything was there. We had expanded our apostolate, we were teaching throughout the whole school year, but, aside from that, teaching music and catechism during the summer, that's all part of what we were doing. Then, while I was still a student in the

1940s, there was the expansion of St Andrew's, which as a student I found very exciting, that these sisters were opening a new place. And then, after I made my vows, there was Saskatoon, and Sacred Heart College was adapted into Marian High School. Then later, we had Jean Vanier and other events going on, so there was a burst of activity at that time. We had heavy involvement in schools, and then we began to go into parish work. When I came back from Rome, people were moving out of education and into parish work. We were also beginning to be more involved not only with the handicapped but also with the refugees, so we were going into other areas of work. And then, of course, we are now into a period of dying if we are not careful, because everybody is getting older and nobody is doing much new. So that is how I see the trends and the evolution of the province. I would like to use this opportunity to say that it is not impossible that some of our sisters could come from somewhere in Asia if our bishop would accept them [in the diocese]. The sisters that are coming now are taking work with the Aboriginal people or working with the Vietnamese community, and they have to learn English. Somebody said something to me the other day that shocked me, but I can see its truth, that the priests that are coming here from Asia are coming, as far as they are concerned, to a pagan country. They consider our Church is in a really bad shape. On the other hand, you hear people complaining not just about the fact that it is hard to understand them the way they speak but that they really don't think that we go to the sacraments often enough, we don't pay enough respect to the priest, all these things that are happening. And our bishop has just come back from a long stay in Vietnam where he visited the families of all the Vietnamese priests who are in the diocese. He also tried to negotiate with some others. Maybe some of our Vietnamese sisters could learn enough English that they could come and work with their own people as both Euphrasie [Nguyen] and Hong Doan have done. I don't think that we need to die as a province. One difficulty that we experience, of course, is that our government is so keen on accepting mainly immigrants in who already know the language. It's a great blessing both in Australia and New Zealand to have the young Vietnamese sisters come to study there because it gives them life. I hear about it all the time when the sisters write about how nice it is to have those sisters from Vietnam, and it is just really hard for us to get them in. I think we don't have to die if we have courage enough to try to do something else.

Sheila Madden: The first evolution that came to my mind was our one province divided into two, then coming back to one, and when it was one province it was very vast – from Quebec, Ontario, Manitoba, and Saskatchewan. And then the diversification in our understanding of education – education was beyond schools. And one of the evolutions in terms of leaving teaching to work in parishes. Then there was the move to ministries beyond the Church, like the Addictions Foundation of Manitoba, and working with different groups that were non–church-related you might say.

Imelda Grimes: What strikes me is the broadening, the expansion to other apostolates, and you called it diversification, Sheila. I think in most of that, we weren't really moving away from education because, for example, there is a lot of educating going on in parish work and when you prepare people for the sacraments. I agree very much with the different notions of community that have evolved, but I am not sure that it is totally healthy. Sometimes I think I need more [community], and I am feeling that maybe I don't have courage enough to challenge that we should be doing this, or you always think you are laying heavies on other people. But community life is different for sure.

Veronica Dunne: I was thinking that we have had a lot of that diversification just happen. I mean, looking at it now, it was like a drift. It wasn't as if people said, "Okay, let's just live alone or in groups of two; and even if we live together, let's not pray regularly together," and things like that. But over the years that has happened, so now what?

Winifred Brown: I suppose we try to do something about that by getting together, like at Christmas time and at Thanksgiving when we all get together for a meal. For us, there is no better social event than a funeral. So we do try to keep together, and you do here too, you have your clusters and then the clusters get together with one another, but it is different, it is a different way of living community.

Veronica Dunne: We certainly are moving along well with our questions. Are you up to one more round before we go in for lunch? All right, that would take us to [the questions], **What impact did Vatican II have on you, on the congregation, on the Canadian province? What did it mean in terms of your leadership?**

Imelda Grimes: I loved Vatican II. I was in Wolseley at the time, and these changes in the liturgy I just thought were great, the vernacular and the priest facing the people and all of this. I was pretty young at the time, but I just couldn't believe it was happening, I couldn't believe it. Anyway, the priest was not home at the time when I got back. I don't know if I had been on retreat or what, but anyway, I decided that I would move the altar out and Father would just absolutely have to go behind, so Hazel and I moved the altar. Father was fine; he didn't say anything though he was a bit surprised – this was Father Marcotte. I loved being involved when we were allowed to do the readings and various other things. So it had a big impact on me and I think on the congregation, but I really don't know how it affected other sisters. I think, even for our province in some respects, it was quite a bit slower and had less of an impact than it had on me personally. I remember also that we were supposed to get notice when we could go into the new habit, and I think every day when the mail came in, I was looking for that letter and it never came until I don't know how long. So that is how much I was struggling to get out of that habit. And I think maybe at first it was more the external changes I was looking for. I think it took a while longer for the spiritual renewal and inner transformation to take place. For instance, in the early 70s when we began to make the thirty-day retreats, I welcomed that too, but it took longer for me to really appreciate this simply because I was all caught up in those external changes and the new freedom that was so different.

Sheila Madden: Well, Vatican II was wonderful. For me, it was a sense of freedom and a sense of expansion, a call and a chance to be out with the people, rubbing shoulders with laypeople. I wrote down that it was a call to be real, you were who you were. My primary remembered experiences would be around the Canadian catechism and parent meetings, and we had lots of them. I remember meeting with a different grade nearly every week, so there was like that whole rapport, taking off the scales somehow, not the weight scales, the eyes. One of my happy memories would be Marge Denis and Mary Veilhaber, primarily, and sometimes Fathers Ken Bernard and Ken McDonald would come and stay at St Michael's and do a teach-in. They always brought new life, new vigour, which I am happy to remember. There was Father Hanley presenting Teilhard de Chardin, and I remember driving into Winnipeg to go to those classes and drive back home to Brandon and be up and ready to start the next day with a full load of teaching. Then there was the whole idea out of this, in my memory, that tertianship[7] began and we started going. Sisters would go and come back with new ideas and enthusiasm, and we began to meet and share more often. Prior to that, sisters who had gone to general chapters would know RNDMs from other provinces, but with tertianship that whole base expanded. This, I think, has been a very positive thing. Changes to the habit, I have very strong memories of that. For us, it depended on when you got the alterations made. Well, I was a seamstress, so I made most of the habits for the others. So I was one of the last, and the kids would say to me, "Sister, when are you going to get your new dress?" So I had told them it would be after the long weekend in May, and I had it all done except the hem, so I went to school on that Tuesday with the old habit and they were all lined up against the fence waiting for me to come. Somebody picked me up that day, that didn't happen too often either, and I got out of the car and the kids all in a chorus said, "Chicken!" [laughs]. I had told them that if they were good and went home right away after school, I would go home and hem it and I would wear it that night. And they were all there, and as I walked into the arena in Brandon, they all whistled, that's my memory of hanging our habit. It was exactly what I wanted for sure. My sorrow today is that so much of that [impact of Vatican II] has been lost. I remember somebody saying that Vatican II was like a wave coming in. It comes in and, unless you do something about it, it goes back out again. So the idea was to capture the essence [the essentials of Vatican II] and hang on to it, but somehow we haven't done that so well.

Marie Baker: I was in formation at Sacred Heart College in Regina during Vatican II, and I remember the first Easter vigil with Campion College SJ priests coming over to celebrate in the vernacular, which was so much more meaningful. It was also in the aftermath of Vatican II that we started praying our office in English. I also remember Sister Mary Martin at one of our meetings saying, "You know, we are just rattling through this now that we are saying it in English, it's not meaningful." So we got Father Andrew Britz, OSB, come and help us to pray it the right way. As far as leadership goes [by then Vatican II was over], there wasn't any particular impact when I was in leadership, I don't think, or else I missed it.

Winifred Brown: I was very excited about Vatican II. I remember Father Wadey celebrating Mass at the cathedral in Regina for the students from Sacred Heart Academy following the new ritual in English and facing the people. It was so more meaningful. This was an exciting time for everybody. I remember that our Generalate in Rome had asked us to study the Vatican II document on religious life and the document on the Church. Every night at five o'clock when we went to chapel, I would read those documents, and I marked what was important to me. I really got to know them well. Then when I attended the General Chapter and many of the sisters hardly knew what they were about, I was quite happy to be familiar with them. That was also where we first began to try various models of habits, and the Canadians had brought one. The new general superior tried it on and paraded it at the Chapter, so this was really quite the thing. But it was going to take a long time before the Indian sisters would change. The other thing that I remember from that Chapter – there are many things that I remember – for instance, when we were talking about government and general superiors, Mother St Denis, the former general superior, was holding up some document and Sister Mary St Floride, of Vietnamese origin, stood up and said, "I would like to remind the reverend mothers that the General Chapter is a collegial occasion and every voice is of equal value."

Sheila Madden: And you wanted her there in '78?

Winifred Brown: I sure did. I think that didn't just come out of her, coming from Vietnam. I think it came out of Vatican II, and that, as you spoke, people became freer. So those are the things that stand out in my mind of the immediate time after Vatican II. I mean, changing the habit was a big thing, and I remember when the picture of our dress was sent to Rome and the approval came back. It was okay, you could have a short veil, you could have the skirt half way down your legs, but "the sisters should be wearing black stockings!" We all said, "What priest in Rome is going to tell us what colour of stockings to wear?" So that line we ignored [laughter]. Once at a Serra meeting in Regina, one of the sisters who was there – I don't know whether from the Philippines or where – came up to me after and said, "We have been told that too, that we were supposed to wear black stockings," and she was as indignant as I was. Anyway, it was just a really exciting time. I think that Canada was more aware of it because our priests were more aware of it too.

Sheila Madden: I remember you referring to the 1966 Chapter as the second Battle of Hastings.

Winifred Brown: Roberta and I were both there, so they had a strong opposition from Canada, and Gwen Mary was precious too. The mentality of other sisters was different. They were afraid to say what was on their mind. There were two blood sisters who lived in the same community. One of them was at the Chapter. She would come to me and say, "Say this, say that," and I would say, "Say it yourself." She would reply, "But I have to live with them afterwards."

Sheila Madden: When I was in England last year on retreat, many of the sisters told me over and over again that they looked forward to Canadians coming to the chapters because we brought a breath of fresh air. Numerous people said they really looked forward to see us, and some wondered what we would be wearing this year. They were happy when we came pushing the boundaries [laughter].

Veronica Dunne: What was the nature of the resistance?

Winifred Brown: Well, some said, "Why would we ever want to change the habit when it was so beautiful and Mother Foundress designed it," or "I don't know, why use the vernacular because everybody can understand Latin," [laughs] or "We have a translation in our missal." I truly don't remember, but I think the resistance was about questioning authority coming from up above. I can remember when Mother St Denis came to Sacred Heart College to visit, and I was up washing windows in the novitiate house when I was a novice, and she walked by and she said to the novice mistress, "Sister Winifred's petticoat is too short." I mean, I think I had my tunic under there [great deal of laughter].

Sheila Madden: She probably saw your knobby knees [much laughing]. The sisters in England would refer to the fact that they had "little freedom" and were scolded if they stepped out of line. They also had little experience of being a province because the congregational leadership was there and was their local leadership as well at the time.

Claire Himbeault: Well, they only became a separate province when Sister Thomas Good became their provincial.

Sheila Madden: So there was a lot of pain around that. They were also treated as one province, but they were really international – with England, Scotland, Wales, Ireland, and Northern Ireland. It was like five countries in one province. So, I mean, there was a fair amount of confusion, and still to this day, a lot of pain and struggle over all of that.

Winifred Brown: Fortunately we have nothing like that in Canada.

Claire Himbeault: The impact of Vatican II on me? It changed my life, it really did. The impact was very, very strong. And on the congregation, well, you have given a lot of examples and on the Canadian province too. What did it mean in terms of my leadership? I truly believe that, because of the new freedom I found within myself and my ability to be real with the sisters, it really helped me in my leadership as provincial, and it would have been because of the space that Vatican II gave us.

Cécile Campeau: In my case, I think it awakened every fibre of my being, it was a breath of fresh air, after breaking a few statues and everything else [laughing], and then over the years I think – I look at the present, I guess – and I was very struck when we met at Calling Lakes to see the different sisters from the various countries all looking like beautiful ladies, "les belles femmes," and this was a result, I would say, of Vatican II. It gave us something definitely more personal perhaps, and much more feminine. Down East [in Quebec] they have a term for women who have gone through the stages of growth with their studies and everything else, and they call them "des femmes formées" and that is beautiful. This is what Vatican II did for us definitely. I think for all of us religious women, we are much richer in every sense of the word. Yes, we took our place among the women of the world.

Sheila Madden: Talking about that, I just want to add that when Claire and I were both in Davao [Philippines], we had to do our life history, and each of us spoke with the young sisters in terms of the influence of Vatican II. Some of them hadn't even a clue what we were talking about.

Claire Himbeault: Then someone said, "This is the first time I meet somebody that was alive during Vatican II" [laughs].

Winifred Brown: It's like talking about World War I when I was teaching, it was so long ago. And now if you talk about World War II, nobody knows what you are talking about. They have heard about the Holocaust, but like for these kids that are going back to visit Vimy Ridge, it's a whole new experience for them, but because I had an uncle in World War I, I had some concept of it. I don't know if I have ever told you this, but when I was in Lebret teaching, we had Luke Schille and Bobby Marasik in grade twelve, and they were studying in June and getting ready for their exams. And Bobby said to Luke, "Do you know about the Second World War?" And Luke said, "I never heard anything about it except that Sister Winifred's brother won it." And my uncle won World War I, so you see – [laughter].

[LUNCH BREAK]

Veronica Dunne: Okay, now we are starting with [the next] question, **What reforms did you try to implement as a provincial, and what resistance and/or support did you experience with our Sisters of Our Lady of the Missions?**

Denise Kuyp: I am not aware of trying to implement any reform. No, really, I don't have a sense of that. The only one reform – and if this is a reform, I don't know, I don't think it is – perhaps it was changing how we would define community as the sisters moved out into other various locations from St Edward's [the provincial headquarters in Winnipeg that was being closed]. Clearly, what is community and what is mission? So what would community be? What would it mean to be a community, what would mission mean? In terms of reform, I don't necessarily call that reform.

Veronica Dunne: So I suppose, like with any innovations, it needs redefining.

Winifred Brown: What about the whole eco-project?

Denise Kuyp: I wouldn't think of it as a reform either, but more as an evolution of many trends.

Veronica Dunne: Would you think of it as an innovation?

Denise Kuyp: No, those words don't fit.

Imelda Grimes: I too, I am not aware of any reforms as such, or even of anything very innovative.

Sheila Madden: When I read the question, I thought it was following on from [the earlier question] of Vatican II. I think what reforms Vatican II did, we tried to implement. So I said, in my time, we were well past any of that. For me personally, the reform was around the veil and a few other things. Anyway, for my term of leadership, it would certainly be the whole idea of "enfleshing" the concept of circle that I was certainly very conscious of, as part of my deliberate consciousness. And resistance? Certainly, the ultimate in support and probably the ultimate in resistance was there, so you kind of get it as a case of "and also." I think anytime when you try to implement anything that's new and different, you get both reactions. So that's what I had.

Marie Baker: I don't think this would be considered a reform, but the sisters in Peru were wanting more self-government, and I don't think we resisted it here in Canada. I don't think the Generalate did either. It is not exactly reform as much as growth. That's all I can think of.

Sheila Madden: That came out of the 1984 Chapter, when we gave more self-government out to all the regions.

Winifred Brown: I don't know it as a reform, but I think that one of the things that I tried to do was get our young sisters to learn French. I sent both Denise and Veronica to study and live there [France] and learn it [the language/culture]. Also, Veronica and Sandra went on foreign mission. Prior to that, other people had gone to Peru, and now they were going to Senegal, and that was all part of my thinking why we needed to be more bilingual. Everybody would be in favour of bilingualism as long as it didn't have to be them that had to learn the language. That's all that I can think of in regard to that.

Claire Himbeault: The one thing I think of is that the sisters really wanted much more participation, and the Provincial Chapter at the time was done by sending delegates, and so we introduced that any sisters who wanted to come could come as observers. There were pros and cons to that, but anyway, it was like a step towards greater participation.

They could participate but not vote, and we did it in parts. I know we had one part in St Eustace and another part at St Michael's College in Brandon, so different people didn't have to always travel great distances in order to attend. So this was towards greater participation by everyone.

Cécile Campeau: I don't think I needed to implement any reform, they were mushrooming. I can recall chatting with the older sisters, to listen to them, and they knew that there was no rush, they did not have to do any of the changes as far as the habit was concerned. I think they definitely were happy with the changes in our prayer lives, the Mass and the Office [the official prayer of the Church]. There were criticisms, of course, like we were maybe going a little too fast – or way too fast. I would just like to say that I was really impressed by many of the old sisters that, when we left the habit and they did not really have to, but felt that they should leave the habit that they had treasured all their religious life – or at least pretended to treasure – I am not too sure. They sort of went along with whatever was changing. I think it was done gradually; it didn't come out all at once like a sudden shower. I don't recall any very negative reactions as far as that was concerned. I just admired them, especially the older people. Sometimes, we had a few outbreaks there with the younger ones – I won't look at anyone here – as Mary Marceline used to say, "You know who you are!" [laughter]. So, altogether, it was a good time, a time of growth.

Sheila Madden: My memory of the '70 assembly at Villa Maria was that every day after lunch somebody would say to me, "Will you cut my hair?" because I was cutting hair in those days. And I would cut their hair, and they wouldn't wear the veil that afternoon. So every day, it was some of the older sisters' turn, so they did come to it generally.I thought of two other things too, and I think it was in your era, Claire, I am not sure when, that the October yearly meetings were established and an assembly every three years. For me, I would call that a reform. It has been a significant one for me because we were getting accustomed to meeting and talking about what was significant.

Claire Himbeault: Another new project that I just thought of, which was not actually initiated by myself but I supported it, was the opening of a house for the poor. It was Bernice Hergott, Evadne, Marjorie Beaucage, and Veronica – different people at different times who were involved. It was just very much an open community where people would come in and just be there with the sisters. So that was quite innovative. Like I say, I am not one to get the ideas, but I can support people, I can recognize the possibilities of things, and that was one of them. Other innovations might come to mind later.

Veronica Dunne: Yes, Betty Gropp and the House of Prayer in Winnipeg.

Claire Himbeault: That's right – the House of Prayer – yes, I was responsible for endorsing that.

Sheila Madden: St Michael's converted into an infirmary was in your time too.

Claire Himbeault: That's right.

Denise Kuyp: One of the things that was coming to my mind, whether it is a reform or an innovation, when I was local superior in Brandon, asking Pat O'Sullivan [a layperson] to do the books and other things for us. It was getting this out of our hand as there was no one [among us] to do this bookkeeping. And now, going a step further with moving more of the administration and the finance and all that into the hands of laypeople.

Claire Himbeault: June and Gertie went up north there at Oxford House, that was being faithful to the missionary thrust. Again, it was more supportive than an initiative on my part.

Denise Kuyp: Well, I don't know. It came out of the '84 Chapter with its focus on refugees and Indigenous peoples and youth.

Sheila Madden: It was after the 1990 Chapter that those sisters were named to Oxford House.

Denise Kuyp: Was it? Because, in my mind, I can still see it in "Beyond All Frontiers" – anyway. So in terms of Hospitality House – things, I think, evolved. People had a call or took the initiative to make it move. It is not so much because we said we would do that as a group, I think that was part of the struggle too. Like it was a person who felt the call to that, and yes, the congregation supports that, but then has to plan for others to continue the work, and so on. Certainly, the presence of sisters and other people on the board, so the group homes for the handicapped are now well assured. I mean that they are still going on.

Veronica Dunne: Just for your information, those next questions on that page are more about Peru or have to do with Peru. And Marilyn LeBlanc wasn't able to come to this meeting, but she spent quite a bit of time just trying to respond to those questions specifically from her perspective of the time she was in leadership in Peru. So that would be part of the documentation that comes out of this conversation as well. I was saying to her that would be very helpful. And, at some point, it would probably be helpful to have another conversation with people whose primary context is Canada, if they could speak, and if people whose primary context is Peru could also speak, because it [our work there] impacted both Canada and Peru. So that might be another step to take down the road. Right now the linkages with Peru seem to be more in terms of relationships of persons, as Marilyn is still in touch with folks in Peru. But as a province, ever since they have become a region, they are rather on their own.

Claire Himbeault: Other than the fact that we still have Canadians that are out there, people from the Canadian province.

Veronica Dunne: Yes, we have four Canadians who are there. There is static in the relationship with Canada with some of them as well, so it's just something that I think is unfinished in terms of our relationship with the province of Peru.

Marie Baker: How many Peruvian sisters are there?

Claire Himbeault: There must be at least fourteen or so – I am saying fourteen out of the hat, but that feels right.

Marie Baker: I think probably Elsie would have been the first one.

Claire Himbeault: Elsie is the eldest one, yes. She is celebrating a jubilee – it must be her twenty-fifth.

Marie Baker: I was at her profession because I spoke Spanish.

Winifred Brown: And we have one Bolivian sister now. One thing that is new too, that you may not know about, is that Margaret and Beth have a house, a retreat house, now in Cochabamba or somewhere near there. This, I think, is a promising development for them.

Veronica Dunne: Okay, we can move now to the next question, which would be the following: **Vatican II precipitated profound changes for RNDMs worldwide. What do you see as being the most significant changes for RNDMs in Canada, what did we gain, what did we lose?** As someone mentioned before, this is very similar to the question on the impact of Vatican II, so it would be good if there was anything further that comes to mind.

Cécile Campeau: I am trying to read what I have written here, and it is sort of a duplication of what has been said before so – except maybe the fact that definitely we have become much more universal. Our RNDM universality, I think, has developed in comparison to our little world [before Vatican II].

Claire Himbeault: I think that one of the significant changes that followed was a more open community rather than ... because we were semi-cloistered before; we were – yes, well, we were cloistered [laughter]. So what did we gain? I think that we gained probably an ability to widen our vision and, as we associated more and got more and more involved with co-workers and friends, we probably were able to communicate better as well. They questioned us, they would challenge us. So we became wider in our perspective and in our vision. What did we lose? That, I am not sure. I can't think of anything we would have lost. For me, it is more of a gain and that includes, of course, the different apostolates with other congregations and apostolates with laypeople, whether it was a catechetical program or other areas. I suppose, in all that, we have lost a common community apostolate, teaching – that at one time was a very strong unifying and identifying factor – yes, a community apostolate.

Winifred Brown: The response that immediately came into my mind was that I think we experienced a certain freedom in our attitude towards the Church – that I could disagree with my pastor, with my bishop, even with the pope and still be a good Catholic. I think about the fallibility of the Church, even all the scandals of sex abuse and so on that have driven some people out of the Church – and for others, they can feel stronger towards the Church because it is wounded, and how is it going to get healed if everybody turns against it? You know, it is like your brother commits murder, you still visit him in prison. So I think that, somehow, in our mentality and our approach to the Church, there has been a fundamental change. Maybe it is a kind of ownership that it is my Church too. I also think we could say that we RNDMs lost a certain amount of the community aspect that we used to have as a congregation that came partly from living together but also from dressing the same. Everybody who looked at us knew that we were Sisters of Our Lady of the Missions. Then, since it gives us a little more freedom, that is kind of contradictory but ... I think that, in a way, we have lost that sense of cohesiveness and yet, in another sense, it is a freedom because I don't have to teach at Sacred Heart Academy to be a teacher. I don't have to be a teacher to be a Sister of Our Lady of the Missions – I can go out and do something else. Even our great growth in educating our members is partly a result of Vatican II. We have a right to become theologians. And when you look at our sisters from Vietnam, they all seem to be going for PhDs, for goodness' sake! There were no PhDs among RNDMs of my age; there were three of us, I think, with MAs in the whole congregation. I don't know how much of that came just because of the fact that the twentieth century has passed.

Sheila Madden: I think some of it has been said before, but one of the things was that we responded to the needs of the time plus our whole initiation into social analysis. I think that was good. I am following up on what Claire and Winifred were saying. I think one of the things we gained was that we learned to stand on our own two feet. We rubbed shoulders with laypeople, and we needed to be who we were. What we lost was that we were no longer one of the good sisters – we were just Sister Claire or Sister Imelda. So I think we were called to claim our own personal identity and to be more responsible.

Denise Kuyp: I think we gained a lot in terms of participating in our own lives, both individually and as a group. What did we lose? I think that whole sense of a communal identity based on common apostolate or through dress. We had it through all those external things before that.

Sheila Madden: I think we had to search for our identity. Rather than just assume we were one of the sisters, we had to struggle to know who we were. This is a never-ending quest.

Denise Kuyp: I entered just after Vatican II in 1965, and I remember I was at St Michael's, I must have been there for my graduation because that year it had been at the beginning of October. And just before I was leaving, Betty Iris said to me, "Now don't worry because there are going to be lots of changes coming in our lives because of Vatican II, just so you know – a little heads up" [laughter].

Winifred Brown: So you weren't just joining the old gang.

Denise Kuyp: Well again, what I knew of religious life from St Michael's as a student.

Sheila Madden: There was really a ferment in the Church though – we had changes but the laypeople were going through changes too, like claiming the Church, it was the Church of the laity too – well that was new for them too: "We all are the Church!"

Imelda Grimes: There were wonderful theologians that mushroomed, yet some of them were silenced, you know. What a struggle!

Denise Kuyp: I would say too, the Sister Formation Conference was a big thing in Canada – well probably in other parts of the world too – that was so life-giving. All these formators from different congregations and the people that they would bring in as speakers, it was really quite exciting. And the CRC, the Canadian Religious Conference, too. I don't know when it came on the scene in terms of Canada and us.

Winifred Brown: That really began in the 1950s, before Vatican II.

Marie Baker: That was also, I think, during Roberta and Geraldine's terms of office.

Sheila Madden: It started nationally first, I think. And then they had this publication, *Donum Dei*, and we used to look forward to that coming out. One of the things we used to do in those days was spiritual reading together, which I am sorry we didn't continue to do.

Marie Baker: When I entered, it was a period of many vocations – we were thirteen, one of the large groups. It is kind of contradictory that, with the CRC and the Formation Conference and Vatican II, when all of these developments that should invigorate the religious call were happening, and it has been the opposite. There has been a decline.

Certainly the laity has grown; the laypeople are really involved; some very much so, but as far as religious vocations?

Sheila Madden: According to the way we understand it.

Veronica Dunne: Sean Sammon [who spoke at the 2012 Formation Conference] says that he thinks that this is just like a "time of waiting" in terms of the historical rhythms of religious life, and that there will be a comeback.

Imelda Grimes: Who thinks this?

Veronica Dunne: Sean Sammon, the Marist brother who presented at the Formation Conference that Chris and I attended, so "when all the evidence seems to be pointing to the contrary, to hold on to our faith ..."

Marie Baker: Well, there are other religious groups forming too, and they are not all Catholic. Plus there is this whole new monasticism in the States and in parts of Canada too.

Sheila Madden: It's quite strong in Ireland, and it is Catholic.

Marie Baker: Well, the ones I am aware of are not. They might be both for all I know.

Sheila Madden: I don't know if the official Church of Ireland recognizes them, but the people are Catholic, and they maintain that they find a new depth in that new movement.

Marie Baker: I mean, for them the Gospel is important and working with the poor, from what I have gathered.

Veronica Dunne: It is part of what we have been looking at ... and it leads into [the next question], which is looking at **changes in the core concepts of the congregation that took place during the time that you were provincial**. For example: mission and postcolonial critiques, what we knew of those, the spirit of the congregation, understanding of charism, development of spirituality, understandings of women and spirituality, understandings of the vows, etc. So we are looking at the changes in those concepts.

Denise Kuyp: I don't know what changes in core concepts took place during my time. I think this has been ongoing for a while, and those would be the whole understanding of community, of mission. I think of the vows somewhat too in terms of how we understand obedience. Poverty has been a struggle for sure. Well, ever since I entered really, all of it has been in evolution. I don't know that we have come to a place yet that we can say, "Yes, this is it for the RNDMs."

Imelda Grimes: Well, in addition to what has been said here, and I agree with what Denise says in terms of it evolving and that we are continuing to work at it. But I think something rather new has been the whole notion of how finances work in our provinces and the help that we have had, like this new project that we started last year with that company and the work that they did and are trying now to implement. I think that's quite new for us.

Veronica Dunne: The HBC [*Handbook for the Congregation*] review?

Imelda Grimes: Yes, the project with that company to give non-perishable food to the poor in Peru, that's what I am talking about. Then the whole notion of common purse, that's something that we have heard about for quite a long time, and I am not sure that we – that all of us – understand it completely.

Sheila Madden: Well, when I did this reflection on my own, one of the things that struck me was the Beijing Woman's Conference during the 90s. I remember being there and what that meant. That was the first time that the congregation made a commitment to be present for a women's conference. It was also during that time that we began our geographic meetings, which was a new development, where RNDM provinces that had areas of some similarity would hold meetings together. I remember being at the one in Australia. That's when a solidarity fund was established where sisters in different countries would build up a fund that would have finances available for projects sponsored or supported by the sisters in various other countries. That was new in the 90s, and I think a positive evolution. Also the decision that came out of the 1990 Chapter of discernment for leadership, that rather than each person writing out her own comments and sending in names as potential candidates, a country would first be involved locally in some form of discernment for leadership. What seems like a very minor thing, but was very significant for me and for us. Another development was that, in preparation for the '96 Chapter, we launched a preparation phase, so we had small local meetings with our sisters. I remember we were invited to wash each other's feet. That is probably insignificant in one way, but somehow I think it affirmed the principle of inclusivity, you know, it wasn't just the people who were going to the Chapter that had to prepare, it was everyone – all were involved, invited to participate in the unfolding. I also think again of that understanding of obedience and of personal authority. Those are the memories that came to me.

Marie Baker: I think that the "tertianship," not that it was started during my time but it was one of the things that I think helped a greater understanding of spirituality and of commitment to the congregation. What were the big words for people at the one General Chapter that I attended in 1984? Instead of mission, it was "internationality" and "mobility" – everyone answers, is involved in one way or other. That certainly was a new congregational concept or thrust. We had

Fullenbach and Dr Margaret Ann and another retreat that was on women and spirituality and the vows, if I remember correctly. Those are part of what helped bring about the changes in the core concepts.

Winifred Brown: Well, I was provincial at the 1978 Chapter when the new constitutions were written, and I personally liked those constitutions. I know lots of people didn't, but I liked them very much, and I felt that there was an effort there to develop some of these notions in our constitutions. Maybe not very much about understanding of women and spirituality, but understanding of the vows, development of spirituality, understanding the charism. I don't think that there was so much change in the core concepts, but maybe an attempt to deepen our understanding of what these concepts were.

Veronica Dunne: These constitutions you are referring to, Winifred, were they the interim constitutions?

Winifred Brown: No, the '78 constitutions were the ones that were approved by Rome. They are the ones that we are now revising again in 2016.

Claire Himbeault: I'll say, like Denise, I think when I was provincial these things were budding, and there were papers coming from the congregation about St Augustine and the Rule, and things that were found in the archives about our first constitutions. Like nobody knew before then that it was in the preliminary chapter of the first constitutions approved in 1877 that "the divine missions" were mentioned and explained in a footnote, even though we had this expression "divine missions" in our directory. Even that was wrapped around the divine mission of Jesus and not really talking about the divine missions of the Trinity as Euphrasie understood them in 1877. So that post–Vatican II period of 1971 to 1977 was a time of awakening, a time of discovery in the congregation, particularly at the Generalate level, a lot of discovery of elements that eventually were included in the new constitutions of 1978. The discovery of that preliminary chapter and then of other related letters was communicated to us, but, I think for myself and for most people in the province at the time, it seemed that was just more papers from our Generalate and we weren't taking time to question or absorb their content. There was probably too much already with the Vatican II documents, and now there was all this new material coming out. I remember hearing, "Oh, not another paper to study!" During the 1971–1977 period, the place of women wasn't predominant [in our concerns]; it was more the spirit of the congregation and going back to try to understand – everybody was trying to understand what the charism was about. So, in a sense, there was a lot happening at the centre of the congregation, which was communicated to us in Canada and all the other places, that maybe we weren't somehow paying enough attention to. And it just occurs to me now, being in leadership, I just had too many other things to do. I didn't really take any leadership role in trying to deepen those papers because of what was going on then. It happened later, but not as this information was coming in.

Cécile Campeau: Well you were surely struggling, Claire, but I was struggling even more than you [laughter]. I can recall here that we were happy because we grasped our own personal mission better, taking that we understood a bit more the divine missions and the RNDM mission. I will go back to the 1968–69 General Chapter. Definitely, we struggled a lot with the words, "charism" for instance, "qu'est-ce que c'est?" and we had Marie Bénédicte, with "le mot juste." And then we had this famous concept of "co-responsibility and subsidiarity," "qu'est qu'on fait?" So we learned new words, but, as far as the meaning, definitely it was not clear. I did quite a bit of arguing and everything else, "consultation." As far as understandings of "women and spirituality," I don't even know if that crossed our minds at the time because we were definitely so still much under the masculine influence. I don't remember the words "feminist" or "feminism" being spoken then. Being there, yes, but not spoken. So, I mean, we knew something about those concepts, but not much.

Sheila Madden: Yet, at the 1970 Assembly, you had Susan McCarthy from Toronto come in and speak on women – so there had to be some awareness.

Cécile Campeau: Well, you know, I was told I was always a feminist, but without knowing the word.

Sheila Madden: Also, "women and sexuality," which was quite new, quite innovative.

Cécile Campeau: It was new for a lot of people, yes, that is very true, but it was a big blur really because of not knowing the terms we were working with. Don't forget, we were writing the new constitutions with a penchant for what came out of Vatican II rather than our own spirituality – I mean, it was quite a mix-up there.

Imelda Grimes: Can I ask a question please? What is our charism? What is it? We don't really talk about it anymore. I don't know what it is.

Cécile Campeau: Isn't it the reason why we are what we are, isn't that charism?

Claire Himbeault: In that letter that Euphrasie wrote to Father Bruno, she used the expression "that's our raison d'être" – and she develops the idea of divine missions, "honouring the divine missions." In our 1977 constitutions that we still have, we often use the words "participating, sharing in the divine missions," and so forth. Euphrasie never used that, she said "honouring." She said "we honour the divine missions" – which is a little different. Then she said, "By that I mean the mission of the Son and the mission of the Holy Spirit – and that of Mary." Mary who is our model is the one that opened herself to the divine missions. Well, she participated in it, I guess we can use the word "participate" and share if we are following our model, Mary. Then Euphrasie said, "This is our reason for being." But, at the time that we were working on our constitutions, everybody had some trouble with "how do you actually understand that?" With our new constitutions, we had more or less the elements of our charism – communion, contemplation, and mission. I think, to simplify it, we can state what our charism is this way: We are a missionary congregation and honouring the divine missions is our spirituality. But definitely Marie Bénédicte is the authority on this subject. She doesn't use the word "charism," she uses the word "initial intuition," and she said the fundamental intuition is that we honour the divine missions. The Trinitarian relationship is the Trinitarian aspect of mission. The more I think of it, isn't the Holy Spirit [Love] how the Father and the Son relate to each other?

Imelda Grimes: But wouldn't other religious be called to that too?

Sheila Madden: Yes. I have often heard that charism pretty well was CCM – contemplation, communion, and mission.

Claire Himbeault: Which other congregations also have.

Winifred Brown: I think we claim that our foundress had a special insight into that, like St Theresa, the Little Flower, had a special intuition of the fact that God loves us unconditionally, and "I am his little flower, I am his rose, and no matter how bad I am, he is still going to love me," that seemed to be her intuition. Our foundress's intuition was that God sent the Son and the Son sent the Spirit and so we are sent. I don't have that much penetration of that mystery, but I think that was her intuition, that somehow she could see that. And it is all tied up with the mystery of the Trinity because, in fact, those three persons are one, so it becomes a very deep mystery, which I can't begin to wrap my mind around. Therefore, this gives us an impetus to be a missionary no matter what we do. And you come and visit Sister Agnes and sit with her for half an hour because you have been sent there by the Father and the Son. It deepens our awareness of this reality, and, if we think about it, it also deepens our whole life.

Claire Himbeault: And even at this very moment we are on mission, because we have been called to come and do this together. It is that whole idea of being obedient – to God – in the moment.

Cécile Campeau: Lorraine put it very simply: "You listen to the Word in your heart."

Marie Baker: That is very "Benedictine." [laughter].

Cécile Campeau: That's what Mary did and Paul on the road to Damascus. So yes, I am not too good with words, and all these expressions are beautiful in poetry. But when it comes to the really greater thing that God is telling you – and I think this is why we have the *Lectio Divina*, to learn to listen to the Word of God – we are all called to this type of prayer.

Winifred Brown: In a sense, we are all "Verbum Dei" – we are all a Word of God in one way or other.

Marie Baker: You know what has come to mind – and this is not from the question, but talking about our charism – in my time some of the sisters were quite strong in this kind of contemplative life, like Mary Paula and Teresa McCutcheon. Well, Teresa didn't stay with the Carmelites, but Paula still is. And then, of course, I heard in talking to sisters that Imelda Taylor always wanted to go to the foreign missions and never did for whatever reason. When she was younger, there wasn't the thrust, and how individual sisters had a leaning, and I guess for myself too, in a way. I agree with Winifred. I think the RNDM's specific charism is that Trinitarian idea of mission: the Father sending the Son, and they send the Holy Spirit, and we are sent the same way. That is our foundress Euphrasie Barbier's intuition and notion of divine missions.

Imelda Grimes: This is all enlightening.

Sheila Madden: I think another core concept that came to me while we were talking would be something around the value we have for our heritage. I think the fact that Aileen was the first general archivist named, I think that was a significant move for the whole notion of treasuring our heritage and giving it prominence. I think that was in your time, Winifred.

Winifred Brown: That was long before I was provincial, so I don't know. I guess she must have been called before that, because I didn't send her. I don't remember when she went. Roberta would have been the one that actually suggested her, but it was in Marie Bénédicte's time as general. I know she was there in Rome before me. I only went in 1984.

Sheila Madden: She went there after studying in Ottawa, I think.

Veronica Dunne: One of the things that was going through my mind, as you were saying that Euphrasie's words were "honouring the divine missions" but "participating in the divine missions," I was thinking that, in the endless debate about women's ordination, it's that kind of narrow theology, where Jesus ordained twelve men, that's all there was, and then that's the end of it. But, if we were to say that we participate in the divine missions, and to have an experience of that and what it really means, that is huge and quite radical. It just strikes me this afternoon.

Winifred Brown: It gives everything that you do a whole new importance. If you really see yourself sent to do what you are doing, then everything that you do is worthwhile, and everything you do is for the greater glory of God.

Veronica Dunne: And somehow I'm caught up in God in that mission. I mean, it is part of prayer.

Winifred Brown: And every Christian is called to the same thing. Our foundress had an insight into that. That in a sense is a gift to us.

Veronica Dunne: And a gift to the Church. I remember when Denise and I co-presided the Our Lady's Missionaries' General Chapter, they were quite taken up when we spoke about mission in those terms because it was new to them. They had never thought of it that way: sharing the life and mission of the Trinity. They were a missionary congregation too, but this wasn't part of how they saw themselves. Now, if we have been given this charism, then it's not just for us either, it's for the Church, so what we are saying is that all people are incredibly important. Our mission, every person's mission, is incredibly important. I am just beginning to have this new grasp of it. I fade in and out of grasping it just now too.

Winifred Brown: We got a card from the staff at Santa Maria in memory of Mary Haggarty, and they said she was everybody's mother from the first day she came and she was the one person who never complained [tears – "I'm sorry, I always do this"]. She knew that everybody was important, and I don't think, in the four years that I taught with her, I ever heard her put anybody down. She could certainly put you in your place, but it wasn't "down" you know, and I think that somehow our "old mothers" all knew that, and so do we. I don't know if it is any different for us than it is for the Benedictines or the Our Lady's Missionaries and others. We all have that calling, but some people live it better than others.

Cécile Campeau: I would like to say on this, Winifred, we had a question here with regards to our foundresses here in Canada ... and I did not spend too much time on it because I hadn't read much about them. I had answered that they were fine, they did what they had to do, and they were wonderful. But what about the sisters in our own time? Maybe what has brought that to my mind are the two last biographies that you have written, Winifred. They were powerful. I was just overwhelmed by those.

Winifred Brown: They were all extraordinary women when you really think of it that way – they were extraordinary women.

Cécile Campeau: So I think we have a wonderful way of doing things, spreading the biographies all over, and some of our sisters that are now dying or ill are saints really. They most probably did more than our foundresses here in Canada. I don't know what it is, but I was extremely struck by this question and also by the biographies – they were so well written and so true. There are so many things that we don't know. I worked one year with Mary Haggarty, and I did not know one fiftieth about her. I think that the fact that we have a really good writer is important too.

Sheila Madden: There you are, Winifred! [General agreement – many voices].

Marie Baker: When a sister dies, we also have a practice of sharing our memories the day before the actual vigil. Marion, our last sister that died, had written in her form that she didn't want that and had said that if we had something good to say about her to say it while she was living. But we don't do it then, or we don't think of all the wonderful things that some of our sisters have done until they're gone.

Winifred Brown: Forty-five years with not one year off. I hated her when she was my principal because she never missed a day of school. And I would get a cold and I would go to school, killing myself because I didn't want to miss, and I finally got pneumonia, and Marion said I could have a few days off. One day during her last illness, I was talking to her, and she moved in her bed and kind of winced, and I said, "Your knee is hurting you, isn't it?" And she said, "How do you know that?" And I said, "Because you winced when you moved it." She said, "I shouldn't have let you see that." "I am not supposed to make you suffer with my pain" is what she was saying. Now maybe she wasn't always like that at home when her knee first hurt, I don't know, but that was what she said then. And about two days before she died, the last full sentence Marion said when somebody asked her, "How are you, Sister?" she said, "I am just fine." She was dying and couldn't swallow any more, she was hardly opening her eyes. She knew she was on her way, of course. Really, some of these women are extraordinary. The truth is that everybody is extraordinary.

[BREAK]

Veronica Dunne: We still have other questions to address. Winifred does not want to do one of the questions. Okay, so we will start with [the next questions], **How did you (the province) redefine leadership over the time of your tenure? What did that mean for you? For the province?**

Denise Kuyp: I really didn't redefine leadership that I know of. If I did, it certainly wasn't intentional.

Veronica Dunne: I think another way of saying that is, what was expected of leadership, what did you see that was expected of leadership – by the sisters, by you? How were you trying to respond? I mean different times, and different people too, call for different styles of leadership, while some people try to hold on to the past ways, I think.

Imelda Grimes: Well, I didn't redefine leadership either. I did try to carry on what had been started in '92 with this whole idea of "the circle and the team," and I think probably we were all trying to do that from that time on, because I too had the conviction that the team approach was good. But even in our efforts, I also know that it doesn't always work so well, for some personalities do not lend themselves to that, and so that's all that I would be able to say, that I just tried to carry it through, but I don't think I did very well at that.

Sheila Madden: I have said this a few times already: it certainly would be the concept of a team, a concept of embracing a circular model of leadership – in a sense we are all called to exercise leadership. In the post–Vatican II era, co-dependency having been rampant in the past, the ability to work as a team became a criterion in the discernment we had to make before elections to leadership. This would have been in response to that, trying to call everyone to take on their personal responsibility, to claim their own authority. It is also the idea that the stronger the individual is, the stronger the group is.

Marie Baker: During my time, I think I still followed the old model, so I don't think I redefined leadership. I think twenty-five wonderful years ago, we still had a lot of apostolic work and houses and that kind of ministry going on as well as elderly sisters in places like the college and academy and St Michael's. I followed the old model too, I guess. And, as I said before, I was blessed both terms with wonderful council members.

Veronica Dunne: When you say you followed the old model, what was that old model?

Marie Baker: Well, "the provincial and her council," but I think we also worked as a team, even though we didn't use that term. I don't know if the people who were on council at that time felt the same way, but I think we tried to work that way.

Denise Kuyp: I was just going to say, I mean, I am still not sure myself what makes a team a team, or not a team, because you could well have a hierarchy that functions as a team, that's just the way it is. So, I wonder if it isn't rather how decisions are made, who makes them, and which ones, and based on what in the end. I don't know. I am aware that in other parts of the congregation, they call them teams yet some are anything but that, so it's not the label that makes the reality.

Winifred Brown: Well, I think as provincial I probably acted more like a misplaced principal than a well-placed provincial. There wasn't any redefinition of leadership in those days. You led as best you could, and you took advice as well as you could, and you tried to consult with sisters and give them some freedom in their choices. For example, most often it was sisters themselves that said they really wanted to get out of this house, so you took her out of that house. If somebody said we needed to get that sister out of the school, you said to the superintendent: "You fire her, and I will look after her." There were things that had to be done, and I did them, but we weren't working as a team. I didn't know how to lead, for one thing, except that whatever I did, I did as a principal. Not to say that I think I was a bad provincial, I just didn't know how to do it as well as other people.

Sheila Madden: Even so, you were very well organized.

Winifred Brown: That's not necessarily good either.

Sheila Madden: I was on both your councils, so I can speak to the fact that you always knew what was on the meeting agenda and you had lots of detail ahead of time. So, I mean, you were well prepared for what you did, and your job was not easy either. That translates our appreciation.

Winifred Brown: Thank you.

Claire Himbeault: I think that when I was provincial that I really did everything I could to work as a team with the councillors as I understood it at that time. As time moved on, there was more enlightenment. I think too that, at the personal level, I did more listening and walking with the sisters than anything else. Again, that was more by intuition. I think I did it because of the situation we were in. There was impatience for more change from one part of the province, and fear and anger from another. And I thought both needed to be heard, and I listened. What did that mean for me and for the province? I think that the province appreciated it, and, for myself, I think it was a bit of my natural way there too. That's what I am by nature – more than anything else, I am the one that listens.

Cécile Campeau: Well, in the good old days when I was provincial councillor, we didn't call it "leadership," we called it "the government." I guess we didn't lead as a team either. There was no initiation. We had to attend and learn. That was how I was initiated. One of the first meetings I attended was about whether or not we accepted certain candidates that were being received as novices or making their vows. So, there we were sitting around the table, and we each had two beads, a black one and a white one. The name of the postulant was brought up, and we read the report from the novice mistress, but we discussed very little because it was all written in the report. After that, we would kneel down and pray a Hail Mary and I am not sure what else. Then we voted: the white bead was for "yes, I accept the candidate," and if we put the black bead down, it was "no." This was the type of discernment that somehow I can remember doing. And so when I was named provincial in 1968, someone said to Mary Geraldine about me: "Gosh, she's just a kid!" And she replied: "She's just a kid? – Well, I will help her." I just felt like that sometimes. I think we just continued doing whatever Juana had been doing before. I don't know what it brought though. There was a meeting, and we did some thinking and came up with decisions. I don't know that the word "discernment" existed for us then. It is just so interesting to hear you people talk about "your team and our team" and the whole notion of discernment and of leadership. When we wrote that first draft of our new interim constitutions in 1969, I was with Marie Bénédicte working on the government section. We did come up with the words "collegiality" and "co-responsibility." Bénédicte was strong on that, and she was really very methodical too. As for myself, I would say that, as provincial, I think my greatest asset for the province was the listening that I was able to do. I thought that was important, and, as I was doing that, I was learning an awful lot. That was at the very beginning – post–Vatican II barely. I am sure that I did listen to the councillors when it came to making decisions. I guess I had to be listening to what was going on, but it's pretty vague in my memory. I feel really humbled listening to all of you and all your more modern, more human ways of dealing with leadership. You know, we have made a lot of progress.

Marie Baker: That was the model in those days, but I think a lot of leadership depended on how you related with the sisters outside of meetings.

Sheila Madden: You were very human, Cécile, you were very human in your leadership.

Cécile Campeau: Yes, I knew that I was a listener from the start.

Sheila Madden: And you did put me to bed with a sleeping pill one time. It was very kind of you.

Veronica Dunne: Two things that strike me: We were very much influenced by the times in which we lived, plus the situations we inherited. So these problems we are talking about, we were not all creating them in the congregation. I think what's happening in the world and society impacts us too. Also, when one of you raises a question or points out a problem, and then each other person brings her own particular gifts and abilities to the task of finding an answer, that shapes our leaderships too. So that, if you are a good listener and I am a good organizer, this gives a different flavour to the solution. Each of us helps us move beyond the times and what we inherited, beyond what's going on in the congregation and what's going on in the world, and beyond our own selves.

[Now we'll move on to the next question], **What new theological approaches did the congregation develop after Vatican II, and how conversant with the work of feminist thea/o/*logians were you or the sisters?** The other question [is], **What were the main documents produced by the congregation on each of those topics and the main elements of those documents, and what impact did they have on the province?**

Cécile Campeau: I really feel I've talked quite a bit about the interim constitutions that were written in 1969. I don't really have much memory of what were the main elements of these documents, which were not complete. I don't think they had much impact on the province either. I can't even remember how they were presented to us – they were not in a finished document in '69. There again, we had good people. As a matter of fact, I think Anna Fidelis, one of the sisters who was a theologian, may have been there at the motherhouse when those constitution were revised in '78.

Winifred Brown: Betty Iris Bartush, Claire Himbeault, Marilyn LeBlanc, Frances Bonokoski, and Louise Oberhoffner were on the committee.

Veronica Dunne: For those interim constitutions, were you the committee for Canada or for the whole congregation?

Claire Himbeault: For Canada only. That was in preparation for the Chapter in '69 – and actually that's when we started having local community meetings and the first assembly in Brandon for the two parts of the province (east and west) together. We must have met about four or five times during that year. What we did was to send to the local communities an outline, and they would discuss this constitution outline. We had never met together to discuss anything like that before, so it was quite an experience. And then each group would send us back anything that they wanted to tell our committee about their vision on the various topics. So we had probably five of those meetings in community and met in St Eustache for the whole month of July because the General Chapter was in September. In April, we had the Provincial Chapter, even though what we had put together was still incomplete. There Frances Bonokoski, Louise, and myself were elected to the Special General Chapter of 1969 with Cécile, who was our provincial. As delegates, we met together and wrote a document with the criticism about the interim constitutions not really being RNDM. It was more of what the Vatican Council had said about religious life, and that was true. When you look at it, there are bits and pieces that are really RNDM, but the total format was more Vatican II Council. We presented this document to the General Chapter assembly. Much of our document formed the basis, chapter by chapter, of the new draft for the revised constitutions. What we had written could be put side by side with this new text, and we could say: "Yes, this has been changed, and no, that has not been changed." So those new constitutions had a history. It was at that same Chapter that we asked not to have to wear the veil. And the Australian delegates were saying: "Well, what will you do when you go to Mass?" Because we still had to cover our head in church at the time. That was really a shock for us ... and just too soon for them! So, when we came home with this absolute no, no question of the veil, what happened in the province was that the constitutions were not accepted very well. There were too many other issues that were questioned. So, sometime later, I think you were still provincial, when Gertrude who was the general and Marguerite Dewan came to the province and interviewed everybody, and, before leaving the province, they told us it was all right for the Canadians not to wear the veil.

Cécile Campeau: I would like to say that every province did the same thing as we did in preparation for the General Chapter of 1969, working in groups on the constitutions. And then at the Chapter, parts of these provincial drafts were also collated and included.

Claire Himbeault: Then in 1972, Sister Marie Bénédicte was elected general and by that time there also had been quite a bit of research done into our beginnings – and she felt that those interim constitutions did not reflect who the RNDMs were truly. So the General Council began working again. Initially, they had a committee, but, eventually, it was Anna Fidelis, one of our sisters who was a theologian, that did all the script and then brought it back to the General Council, and they would study and criticize it. Then there was Father Breyer, a Jesuit in Rome, who was a consultant and came very frequently to advise them, telling them, "You haven't got enough of this" or "You can't put that in," and so forth. Those were the constitutions that were prepared for the 1978 Chapter, at which time we voted for, article by article. Then, once that was done, we went to the Sacred Roman Congregation for Religious with our new draft, and they held it for a long time, but eventually sent it back with the amendments and comments they had to make. After we made the corrections and sent back the amended text, we received the approval from Rome. As soon as that happened, which by then was in 1979, Marie Bénédicte and Anna Fidelis went from province to province to introduce the new constitutions to the whole RNDM congregation. I was elected to the General Council in '78, but I didn't get there before '79 because I was in charge of formation here until Imelda replaced me. In the meantime, I was doing my "white and black bead" over the phone. Actually, I'm joking, because during that year if something came up on which the General Council wanted my opinion, they would telephone me. Then I left for Rome, right after Kathy Derringer's profession in 1979. So this is that part of the story of our constitutions. As a matter of fact, to answer your two questions more fully, I think there were some documents that were very badly received in the provinces. When I was provincial, we had an assembly of provincials, what they now call the Enlarged General Council, and different members of the assembly gave papers on different topics. One of the papers contained a whole lot of remarks about slacks and that kind of thing. So, when I brought the summary report back to the province, I talked about everything else, but I didn't say too much about that part. I don't remember exactly what the title of the paper was, but I know it had "Return to Our Sources" in it. This may have been the title. I still have a copy at home. So, I guess when I was provincial there were two things – the constitutions and that particular paper – that were not well received because we were on different wave lengths and putting emphasis on different things. Then, after that I was in Rome, so I really don't know what was happening in the province for the next eighteen years or so. But I would say that, as far as a congregational assembly is concerned, we had this meeting in Bangalore where Sister Marie Bénédicte had talked a lot about where we were going and all this. And I remember being there when Marie Bénédicte and Marie Laurent were talking, and Marie Laurent said: "I just wouldn't be able to invite anyone [a new recruit] to come into the French province." And I said: "But somebody coming in is not entering the French province, she is entering the congregation." That was said during a little meeting we had. And just a few days later, Sister Marie Bénédicte had developed the whole idea into a diagram of a tree showing the development of the congregation and so forth. She was emphasizing that anyone entering the congregation, enters the congregation and not an RNDM province only. Anyway, it was a turning point, and again, I don't take credit for it because of what

I had said. I don't know why I said it – but I know I said it – and it was truly a turning point. Then Marie Bénédicte said other things about mission and so forth. What she said was ordinary enough, but somehow, you know how Marie Bénédicte always read her papers, but this time she talked, just talked in her more or less broken English. But what she said was so powerful that everybody went from there as from a Pentecost. The sisters were really impressed by what had happened there. Then afterwards, before the 1984 General Chapter, she wrote a letter entitled: "RNDM, What is your Mission?" It was a question that gave the new thrust for the '84 Chapter, which seemed to be a new turning point marking a real change – but it had already started in Bangalore. The meeting in Bangalore would have been in preparation for the '84 Chapter when I was elected general superior. So, that was my mission from there on: to promote what had happened at that Chapter. The emphasis was very much on international mobility at that time and also on enculturation. So that is my answer to our questions here. It was one of the turning points. There have been many others since, but this '84 turning point put a greater emphasis on the reality that we are a missionary congregation.

Marie Baker: I cannot remember the document, but I certainly can remember those words "enculturation and internationality." We must have done some study at an assembly or in our different convents.

Denise Kuyp: "Witnessing Beyond All Frontiers" is the name – you would have brought that document back home from the 1984 Chapter.

Sheila Madden: And I think, for Canada, something happened then. This is my memory, in terms of that document, that for some Canadians, the idea was that you were a second-class citizen if you weren't on foreign mission with all the things happening there, and if you don't go, then somehow you are not as good as those who do go. I feel sorry about it, but I think there is a remnant of that still alive among us and it started from there. I can remember some of the comments at the time. So whatever happened? Either those of us who were addressing the subject didn't present it right or people weren't open to hear what was said. For me, that had been a powerful document, and I never heard any of those ideas in it, but it is unfortunate that happened. Am I the only one that thinks that way?

Denise Kuyp: I've heard people say that too.

Sheila Madden: But I can remember it starting there.

Denise Kuyp: Yes, well, that's where we would have first talked about internationality and the papers coming out from Marie Bénédicte. There was quite a ream of them coming out in preparation for that Chapter, and then the event itself and the follow-up. I remember that and, you know, why was it us? Was it the way people hear things? I think this is the downside, but it is true, this idea about foreign missions has carried on till now for some.

Sheila Madden: The '84 Chapter was a difficult one for a variety of reasons, but it was a powerful one as well, I thought. I can remember Marie Bénédicte, the general leaving office, and you, Claire, the one coming in, both standing under the Samoan fibre mat as a symbol of reconciliation. I can still see that. So that General Chapter was powerful in its own way, and I think the document was powerful too. I remember Michael Crosby picking up on it and saying, "Probably the next frontier for most of you will be the interior frontier that you are going to cross," you know, the whole reality of attitudes and mindsets and world visions. We can go beyond what is common. It is one of the griefs of my life that it didn't really happen for everyone. One of the other things that we did at the '84 Chapter was the Better World Movement with the plan of action. We worked hard at that, and I remember one provincial saying, "Well, I guess if we give up all other apostolates for six years, if we take care of this six-year plan of action and learn our new constitutions, that will be our life!" So I think that was forward planning and deliberate, and it was very helpful. Then the 1990 Chapter, the one with the web, where we were naming our priorities. And the other part that stands out for me is the discernment for leadership, with a kind of new focus, a new way of being. In the 2000s, we had the *Handbook on Leadership* and the one on the congregational mission plan, and now we have the HBC [*Handbook for the Congregation*] and then the 2008 Chapter document. What impact did these have on the province? I think the impact depends on each person. To a great extent, it depends on how much you get involved in it or how committed to it you become. For me personally, I was down alone in Union Island when the 1990 Chapter document came out, and I know that document very well because I treasured it and because I was there alone. I remember your letter, and writing to one another and sharing our experiences of Jesus. I remember writing to many people about that. So it depends on what you do about it and with it.

Veronica Dunne: Do you remember what that document was called, the 1990 one?

Sheila Madden: There were two, one had a peach cover and there was the web. I don't remember what the names were. One was more like of a "how to" paper and one was like the principles, but I don't know what they were called. I could look it up though.

Claire Himbeault: I have a little book where I have listed all the documents going right back to '84, with Marie Bénédicte's letter at the beginning.

Veronica Dunne: It would be interesting to have all that information in one place – what all the documents are about and what they are called.

Sheila Madden: The other documents were the three that Maureen McBride [the next superior general from New Zealand] later wrote for meetings according to geographic areas that took place between '96 and 2002. And for the older provinces, the meetings were to be about what we were experiencing during that same period. But I can't remember what the thrust was. Maureen had prepared papers for what the focus would be in each of those geographic regions. The other document she prepared was on Catholic schools. There was a meeting of educators in India, and there was quite a large document in preparation for that meeting, as I can recall.

Veronica Dunne: I find it interesting, Claire, to hear you say there were documents that were not well received in the province.

Claire Himbeault: Yes, there were. At least not received well enough in my estimation [laughter].

Sheila Madden: At the Bruce and Elsie session, you had given us warning – you were asking us to prepare ourselves that there would be parts in it we wouldn't like. Do you remember that?

Claire Himbeault: No. I don't remember everything.

Sheila Madden: I listened well, you see.

Claire Himbeault: I know, I know the Holy Spirit works in people, I guess, and sometimes works through you too, and other people say, "Remember the time you said this?" [laughs].

Imelda Grimes: I cannot get over the amount that is remembered here. You two [Sheila and Claire] must have a photographic memory.

Sheila Madden: But I also forget to mail a letter.

Claire Himbeault: I shared about what I was very involved in and with a great deal of emotion, so it sticks in my memory quite well [laughter]. Whereas, there are other things that I have forgotten completely.

Denise Kuyp: And that CMP document, the "Congregational Mission Plan" came out of the evaluation of ministries, with a whole other bag of goodies.

Sheila Madden: It came out of Nairobi, the EGC [Extraordinary General Council] at Nairobi is where it was.

Denise Kuyp: In reading it, I didn't read it as a plan but more as a reflection of where we are at. I didn't see it as a congregational mission plan, as I understand a plan.

Sheila Madden: Well, there was a great emphasis on the point that sisters from those countries would be educated and invited to First World countries – off the top of my head, I don't remember what else. The other important thing was that sisters won't be asked to do a job without having sufficient preparation or at least some preparation. That is one of the decisions that came out of the geographic meeting in Nairobi.

Veronica Dunne: It was about more recent subject matter, not about back in the olden days.

Denise Kuyp: No, and all I am saying is that when I see "congregation mission plan," I don't have a sense of it impacting Canada at all.

Sheila Madden: And we didn't do much with it unfortunately.

Claire Himbeault: I suppose maybe there is something to be learned from that. As when you talk about Nairobi, I hardly remember that an important meeting was held in Nairobi. I read everything but that's it, you read it and then ... So if we want something to have an impact, there has to be some kind of a study, a commitment, and action, one, two, three. Otherwise it is going to go in our heads and out again, and maybe that's happened too often with different extremely valuable material that came out – because when you reread it later, you say, "Were we saying that then?" You know, the document comes, and it goes on the shelf and, "We'll take care of it later." Maybe that's something we can learn from that experience.

Sheila Madden: I know we did very little with that plan of action on mission.

Claire Himbeault: And there were other things at that time that we missed. Maybe we missed something essential.

Winifred Brown: My experience would be that if it's going to be done, it needs to be done in a larger group or it is not going to happen in the local communities.

Claire Himbeault: And that's why it is good to have the assemblies. I know that the state we are in now, assemblies can't be too long and need to be paced because we can't take too much more than that at our age. Half the sisters in the province are older than me, older than eighty-one.

Sheila Madden: Well, we know Melvina and June are the dividing point. So you are in the old kids group.

Winifred Brown: I think too that we need to watch the language that is going to be used, partly for us who aren't up to the modern language in theology, and partly for the people who use English as a second or a fourth or a fifth language. I know an effort has been made in that regard. But I try faithfully to read all the newsletters that we get from all the provinces – not to mention the Easter and Christmas and Pentecost cards. Some of their English is quite weak, and it must be difficult for them to get reading material that comes over to them in modern theological terms.

Veronica Dunne: I know, for myself, I remember the "Return to Our Sources" document when you say that. I remember that was the title, and I remember "Witnessing Beyond All Frontiers," but I really don't remember other things. And it speaks to your point of finding a way somehow [conversation].

Claire Himbeault: And the new formation documents, there is excellent stuff in there.

Winifred Brown: Then all the information that comes to us about the missions, I have to print everything because people can't read off the screen. So I print everything and try to do it in two pages, on one sheet, but an awful lot of good news comes in. It is wonderful, but to get it all read and then, in our house, you have to read it to Jean. Well, she and Francis have finally figured out a way to get that done, and I try to leave it to Jean to make sure it gets read to Frances. But it is really time consuming, and for a person that watches four hours of television a day, that sounds like a very weak excuse, but by after seven o'clock at night, I am not up to reading material from foreign missions and from learned general superiors.

Veronica Dunne: Is there anybody else who has anything further to say? I have kind of lost track of where we are.

Claire Himbeault: Certainly, we didn't hear everyone on [some of] those questions ... There are other people that might have something to say but didn't get a chance.

Denise Kuyp: I really don't have anything to add.

Imelda Grimes: Nor do I.

Winifred Brown: Nor do I.

Veronica Dunne: Okay, Sisters, are you at a place where we can round off this part of our conversation? Have you said everything that you wanted to say about some of these questions? Or is there something burning in you that you wanted to say that you haven't said yet?

Winifred Brown: No ma'am.

[Other people say "no".]

Veronica Dunne: So, we can end this part of our sharing and thanks for your reflections and your time.

A.3 Crucifix sculpture by Peruvian artist Edilberto Mérida. Photograph provided by Sister Marilyn LeBlanc, RNDM.

Reflecting on the Conversation

The conversation among former provincial superiors of the Canadian province gives us a glimpse, not exempt from candour, of a process in which the congregation gave their past a new meaning in order to understand their present and reimagine their future. The conversation shows the difficult transition from a hierarchical, patriarchal, and restrictive way of life, in which obedience and uniformity, punctuated by moments of resistance and common-sense transgressions, were central to the notion of community, to the acknowledgment of a dynamic reality in which discernment, freedom, development of the self, and participation had a privileged place. The superiors did not glorify their past; instead, they carefully navigated the difficult relationship between memory and a critical understanding of their past.

The conversation is an interesting example of how the congregations broke with the regimen for controlling their emotions, rebuilt the relational component of the self, and cultivated their reflective self-questioning of their existential conditions in which they had been enculturated before Vatican II. The presence of feelings in the sisters' language is very central to the various arguments they expounded. For example, they talked about fear of change among some sisters, the fear of being free, of making decisions, of being themselves. The sisters shared the need to heal wounds of various sorts. The process of accompanying sisters who had decided to leave the congregation was described with full understanding and pain. They had to walk through the past to enter into the future.

The existential uncertainty after a life of obedience is fully reflected in the difficulties they faced in figuring out a desire; when asked what their great desire was, what desire lived in them, many, said Sheila Madden, could not respond. This condition persisted and defined many moments of the process of change in which the desire and enthusiasm of many to move forward encountered the fear of those unable to break with the past.

The sisters discussed discernment again and again, most particularly in relation to decision-making and the difficulties in building a common ground and determining how to combine personal discernment with community needs. The Jesuit spirituality and language reached many congregations, particularly through spiritual exercises and in the process of writing the new constitutions. The emergence of the private in their lives and its intersection with community, and with spirit-calling, created a conundrum. Difficulties had also to do with the circulation of concepts across contrasting cultural spaces. Leadership and teamwork are examples of dominant concepts that the sisters translated to their own circumstances and history, and tried, as revealed in the conversation, to understand through their own practice imaginary and experiences. As one of the participants, Denise Kuyp, said, "I am still not sure myself what makes a team a team, or not a team, because you could well have a hierarchy that functions as a team, that's just the way it is. So, I wonder if it isn't rather how decisions are made, who makes them, and which ones, and based on what in the end. I don't know." For Sheila Madden, the concept of a team was related to a circular model of leadership and to discernment. A language of collegiality and co-responsibility came up, often imposed, to define their new experiences. The sisters actually contextualized these concepts, creating their own understandings of leadership and sisterhood.

The changing socio-economic, cultural, and political contexts, as explained in chapter nine, and the theological changes that were brought to the forefront by Vatican II forced a profound process of rebuilding the personal and collective self in the midst of a post-modern woven web. The sisters encountered pluralism with an awareness, after Vatican II, of the relative positioning of their faith; it was no longer the only true faith. Postcolonial thinking made the sisters aware of the unexpected dimensions of their mission, while new demographic dynamics in the congregation led to the movement of sisters from the east to the west, where vocations dried up, creating a new scenario, a new notion of internationality in the congregation.

There are indeed big themes in the conversation that point to current challenges, the most prominent being women in the Church and the need to be there, because, as Sheila Madden said: "[It] is a challenge to me because sometimes I say it is better to be on the fringe and not get caught in the middle. But to effect some change, I need to be where I can do that."

When talking of the relevance of their heritage, an "Aha" comment came into being. Winifred Brown made the point that the foundress's (Euphrasie Barbier's) intuition for the congregation was "that God sent the Son and the Son sent the Spirit and so we are sent," a point discussed in chapter one of this book. Veronica Dunne took this intuition of "participating in the divine missions" in relation to women's ordination. It is of value to quote her reflection here: "I was thinking that, in the endless debate about women's ordination, it's that kind of narrow theology, where Jesus ordained twelve men, that's all there was, and then that's the end of it. But, if we were to say that we participate in the divine missions, and to have an experience of that and what it really means, that is huge and quite radical."

The journey of the congregation and of the province and its commitment to eco-spirituality, explained at the end of chapter ten, is not complete, as the congregation, smaller and with a new demographic base, enters a transformative process once more.

Religieuses de Notre Dame des Missions (RNDM) Sisters' Houses in Canada

Dates	Name	Location	Functions
1898–1923	Our Lady of the Snows Convent The sisters left after fire destroyed the convent in 1923.	Grande Clairière, Manitoba Diocese: St Boniface, Winnipeg (1916)	Public (bilingual) day school, grades 1–8. Population French Métis.
1898–1900	Holy Heart of Mary Convent The sisters left because of too much control by the Oblate fathers.	Lac Croche (Crooked Lake) Cree Indian Reserve in Saskatchewan Diocese: St Boniface	Teaching elementary grades. Residential school for First Nations children and parish work with the Oblate fathers.
1899–2005	St Michael's Convent for sisters and student boarders The RNDMs replaced the FCJ sisters.	Brandon, Manitoba Diocese: St Boniface, Winnipeg (1916)	St Augustine's Parish School, grades 1–6. In 1968 joined the Brandon School Division but kept its Catholic identity. St Michael's High School, grades 9–12 until 1968.
1899–1998	St Gabriel's Convent for sisters and student boarders	Lebret, Saskatchewan Diocese: St Boniface, Regina (1910)	Public day school, grades 1–8. From 1924, grades 9–12 were added. The last sister to leave teaching at Lebret was Hilda Lang, approx. 1978. Hilda moved her class to Fort Qu'Appelle and retired there in 1980.

Dates	Name	Location	Functions
			(Louise Oberhoffner and Regina Anne Boechler taught at Fort Qu'Appelle earlier and retired before 1980.)
1901–72	Our Lady of Fourvière Convent for sisters and student boarders Two sisters commuted to Crooked River rural school weekly (1901–10). Novitiate house for RNDM candidates.	Ste Rose du Lac, Manitoba Diocese: St Boniface, Winnipeg (1916)	Public (bilingual) school for First Nations, Métis, French, Belgian, English, and Irish population, grades 1–12.
1901–84	Ste Madeleine Convent for sisters and student boarders Novitiate (1922–26).	St Eustache, Manitoba Diocese: Winnipeg (1916)	Public bilingual school, grades 1–8 (1901–47); grades 1–12 (1948–84).
1901	Couvent St-François It was closed because parishioners had not been consulted and sisters did not feel welcome.	Fannystelle, Manitoba Diocese: St Boniface	Public bilingual elementary school.
1902–61	Virgo Fidelis Convent for sisters and student boarders From 1903–05, two sisters commuted weekly to St Joseph.	Letellier, Manitoba Diocese: St Boniface	Public school, teaching in English and French, grades 1–8; gave private lessons in music, typing, and accounting.
1904–83	St Raphael Convent for sisters and student boarders	Wolseley, Saskatchewan Diocese: St Boniface, Regina (1910)	Bilingual parish school, grades 1–8. Became a Catholic separate school in 1910, and a public school in 1917.
1905–69	Sacred Heart Convent for sisters and student boarders Sacred Heart Academy 1910–69 Holy Rosary Parish School, started in 1910 (in 1915 was transferred to the Catholic Separate School Board; grades 1–8; three sisters on the staff)	Regina, Saskatchewan Diocese: Regina	Private day school, grades 1–12. Sacred Heart Academy was transferred to the Catholic Separate School Board in 1965.

Dates	Name	Location	Functions
1905–2001	St Martha's Convent for sisters and student boarders St Martha's House of Prayer (1990–98)	Elie, Manitoba Diocese: St Boniface, Winnipeg (1916)	Public bilingual school, teaching in English and the Association d'éducation French program, grades 1–12. Officially bilingual until 1916. Sisters left the school in the 1960s.
1909–79	St Martin's Convent with student boarders	St Joseph, Manitoba Diocese: St Boniface	Public bilingual school, grades 1–8 with French program. Bilingual until 1916. After that, the school also followed the program of the Association d'éducation.
1909–2007	St Edward's Convent, Adele Street Provincial House (1956–2005) Home base for several ministries in Winnipeg.	Winnipeg, Manitoba Diocese: St Boniface, Winnipeg (1916)	St Edward's Parish School, grades 1–8 with music department; pastoral work at parish and diocesan level. Now partially funded by government (80 per cent funded). There are presently no sisters on staff. The last sister was Jacky Bartush (who was also principal). Sister Bartush retired in June 1997.
1914–39	St John the Baptist Convent It was closed because students went to the public school during the Great Depression of the 1930s.	Portage la Prairie, Manitoba Diocese: Winnipeg (1916)	Teaching in private elementary day school.
1914–98	St Jude's Convent for sisters and student boarders	Fort Frances, Ontario Diocese: St Boniface, Thunder Bay (1952)	Teaching in three Catholic separate schools: St Michael's & St Francis (K–8); St Mary's (K–12).

Dates	Name	Location	Functions
			Fort Frances: Hilda L. was the last to leave teaching in Fort Frances in 1986. The sisters officially left Fort Frances in May 1998. Hilda stayed on in Fort Frances to support Sister Betty Kennedy from 1998–2001.
1926–92	Sacred Heart Convent and College (both convent and school were named Sacred Heart College) Transfer of Novitiate from St Eustache to Regina.	Regina, Saskatchewan Diocese: Regina	Sacred Heart College acquires status of junior college awarded by the University of Ottawa. It closed in 1949. High school with the same name opened in 1955. It was followed by Marian High School, opened in 1963 beside the convent and transferred to the Catholic Separate School Board in 1965.
1925–60	St Mary's Convent and Catholic separate school for sisters and student boarders	Regina, Saskatchewan Diocese: Regina	On Saturdays, sisters taught German classes at St Joseph School and taught disabled children weekly at the Red Cross Centre.
1940–74	Our Lady of Perpetual Help Convent for sisters and student boarders	Sioux Lookout, Ontario Diocese: St Boniface, Thunder Bay (1952)	Teaching in Catholic separate school, grades 1–8, replacing the Loretto sisters.
1942–48	St Andrew's Convent (in a small rural Catholic Scottish community) Closed due to lack of students.	Wapella, Saskatchewan Diocese: Regina	Teaching in private day (elementary and high) school. Church and community involvement.

Dates	Name	Location	Functions
1948–82	Convent St Joseph for sisters and Formation House for francophone candidates	Ville Jacques-Cartier, Quebec Diocese: St-Jean-Longueuil	Teaching by sisters and lay staff among the poor at Hélène-de-Champlain, public elementary school for girls.
1950–86	St Joseph's Convent	Saskatoon, Saskatchewan Diocese: Saskatoon	Teaching in the Catholic separate school system, grades 1–8 with three RNDMs on staff, with lay teachers. The sisters taught primarily in St Joseph's School. They also taught in St Francis school (1970–79), St Michael's (1988–92), and St Thomas. They left in 1992.
1952–57	Notre-Dame-de-Fatima Convent	Ville Jacques-Cartier, Quebec Diocese: St-Jean-Longueuil	Teaching by sisters at public elementary school, grades 1–8.
1954–66	Saint-Blaise Convent	Saint-Blaise, Quebec Diocese: St-Jean-Longueuil	Public elementary school, grades 1–8.
1962–68	RNDM Juniorate for young sisters at building of the Sacred Heart College	Regina, Saskatchewan	Temporary Vows Formation.
1968– arrived in December 1968	Opening of first mission in Peru by the Canadian RNDM province	Moquegua, Peru Diocese: Tacna-Moquegua	Began by teaching English in the schools. Then moved into pastoral work, catechism. Solidarity with the poor.
1968–82	RNDM residence on University Crescent becomes Provincial House in 1969	Winnipeg, Manitoba Diocese: Winnipeg	For a short time: Juniorate House of Studies for temporary professed; provincial administration.
1969–70	RNDM residence on Bétournay Street in Windsor Park, St Boniface; moved to Langevin Street in 1970	Winnipeg, Manitoba Diocese: St Boniface	Pastoral work in St Boniface Cathedral Parish. Teaching at St Boniface College Secondary School (2 years).

Dates	Name	Location	Functions
1970–72	RNDM residence on Davidson Crescent	Regina, Saskatchewan Diocese: Regina	Satellite to Sacred Heart College (institution was closed). Sacred Heart College was still operative at this time – as a residence for the sisters. The school part had become Marian High School.
1970–82	Brault St Longueuil, Quebec	Diocese of St-Jean-Longueuil	One sister teaching in the public system.
1971–	Opening of second mission in Peru by the Canadian RNDM province	Ilo, Peru Diocese: Tacna-Moquegua	Pastoral work, catechism. Humanitarian work with the poor.
1971–75	RNDM Fraternity on Agassiz Drive; moved to Glengarry Drive (1971–73) and then to Belair Road (1973–75)	Winnipeg, Manitoba Diocese: Winnipeg	House operating by consensus.
1972–77	RNDM residence on Austin/Elgin Street	Winnipeg, Manitoba Diocese: Winnipeg	Pastoral work among the poor.
1972–77	RNDM Fraternity House	Ottawa, Ontario Diocese: Ottawa	House of Studies.
1972–97	RNDM residence, satellite to St Edward's Convent	Oxford House, Manitoba Diocese: The Pas-Keewatin	Teaching at First Nations elementary day school, pastoral work, and religious education.
1975–88	Lavallée, Longueuil, Quebec	Diocese: St-Jean-Longueuil	One sister teaching in the public school.
1972–	RNDM residence on 22nd Avenue	Regina, Saskatchewan Diocese: Regina	Pastoral work at Blessed Sacrament Parish. Two sisters also tutored students at Miller High. Later, sisters participated in various volunteer ministries. This house is still open.
1973–77	RNDM residence	Dauphin, Manitoba Diocese: Winnipeg	Pastoral work in Dauphin deanery.
1973–2006	RNDM residence on Halifax Street Becomes Garrity Home, an RNDM foundation.	Regina, Saskatchewan Diocese: Regina	Satellite to Sacred Heart College; becomes a residence for adolescents and adults with Down syndrome.

Dates	Name	Location	Functions
1975–88	RNDM residence on Lavallée Street	Longueuil, Quebec Diocese: St-Jean-Longueuil	Grades 1–8, pastoral care ministries in local school and parish.
1975–80	RNDM apartment	Altona, Manitoba Diocese: Winnipeg	Nursing in local hospital.
1976–90	Opening of third RNDM mission in Peru, satellite to Ilo	Candarave, Peru Diocese: Tacna-Moquegua	Pastoral and humanitarian work; training of lay catechists.
1983–88	Sisters lived in a trailer (mobile home)	Sandy Bay, Saskatchewan Diocese: Regina	Teaching in public school. Radio station: weekly broadcast. Two sisters.
1984–	RNDM Novitiate House for Latin American region	Arequipa, Peru Diocese: Arequipa	Formation of RNDM candidates.
1986–94	RNDM residence Sisters lived in the church rectory at Pinewood and later moved to the rectory in Rainy River.	Pinewood-Rainy River, Ontario Diocese: Thunder Bay	Pastoral work in two parishes. One sister taught in the school at Rainy River.
1987–97	RNDM residence on Oxford Street	Moose Jaw, Saskatchewan Diocese: Regina	Pastoral work.
1988–2006	Kramer Home RNDM foundation on Queen Street; continued to operate under a board of directors after the sisters left in 2006.	Regina, Saskatchewan Diocese: Regina, Saskatchewan	Teaching adolescents with disabilities and homemaking for adults with Down syndrome.
1990–96	Resident in Catholic church rectory	Raymore, Saskatchewan	Pastoral ministry – church administrator.
1990–	RNDM House for Latin American Region	Callao, Peru Diocese: Callao	Regional administration, orphanage, pastoral work, RNDM associates, and ministry to alcoholics.
1990–	Lima and Tarata RNDM residences Tarata closed in 1991. The sisters did not live in Tarata.	Lima and Tarata, Peru Diocese: Lima	Pastoral and humanitarian work.

Dates	Name	Location	Functions
1990–2004	Broadway House, RNDM Novitiate House	Winnipeg, Manitoba Diocese: Winnipeg	Formation of candidates.
1992–	Cathedral Courts, residence for seniors: laypeople and sisters (13th Avenue)	Regina, Saskatchewan Diocese: Regina	Former Sacred Heart Academy, sold in 1992 to a seniors' complex firm.
1992–	Hospitality House, at 60 Mortimer Place Two RNDMs worked and resided there until 2002.	Winnipeg, Manitoba Diocese: Winnipeg	Joint Anglican-Catholic refugee sponsorship ministries spearheaded by RNDM sister.
1992–2003	Turco RNDM residence	Turco, Bolivia and Cochabamba, Bolivia Diocese: Cochabamba	Pastoral and humanitarian work, training of catechists.
1992–	Cochabamba RNDM residence	Diocese: Cochabamba	
1994–2001	Smithfield – rental house	Winnipeg, Manitoba	Two sisters – one teaching at St Edward's, second as Canon lawyer in diocesan marriage tribunal.
1995–2001	RNDM apartment	Norway House, Manitoba. Diocese: The Pas-Keewatin	Pastoral work with First Nation.
1995–2003	RNDM apartment	Estevan, Saskatchewan Diocese: Regina	Pastoral care director.
1996–98	Resident in Catholic church rectory	Whitewood, Saskatchewan	Pastoral ministry – church administrator.
1999–2014	RNDM apartment	St Anne, Manitoba Diocese: St Boniface	Pastoral work, helping elderly sick parents, leadership team member.
1998–2008	RNDM residence – in church rectory	Ile-à-la-Crosse, Saskatchewan Diocese: The Pas	Pastoral work with First Nation and Métis.
1999–2016	RNDM apartment on Preston Avenue	Winnipeg, Manitoba Diocese: Winnipeg	Volunteer work and reflexology.
2003–09	RNDM apartment	Edmonton, Alberta Diocese: Edmonton	RNDM director of Doctor of Ministry program, St Stephen's College at University of Alberta.
2005–15	RNDM residence, Westwood Drive for two sisters working with the Diocese of Winnipeg Chancery Office	Winnipeg, Manitoba Diocese: Winnipeg	Winnipeg Catholic Marriage Tribunal work as Canon lawyer and as intake interviewer.

Dates	Name	Location	Functions
2001–14	RNDM residence for two sisters in St Germain South	St Adolphe, Manitoba Diocese: St Boniface	RNDM provincial team member/treasurer and coordinator of elderly sisters living in retirement and nursing homes.
2005–15	RNDM residence (apartment)	Brandon, Manitoba Diocese: Winnipeg	One sister teaching at Brandon University Music Department.
2005–	RNDM residence on Scotia Street (apartment)	Melville, Saskatchewan Diocese: Regina	Pastoral administrator in Catholic Parish of Melville.
2005–	RNDM residence on Chestnut Street (apartment)	Winnipeg, Manitoba Diocese: Winnipeg	Spiritual direction and retreat ministry in Winnipeg and Brandon. Leadership team.
2005–15	RNDM centre at 310 Provencher Boulevard (St Boniface)	Winnipeg, Manitoba Diocese: St Boniface	Canadian RNDM provincial administration headquarters.
2010–14	RNDM residence at 442 Langevin Street (apartment)	Winnipeg, Manitoba Diocese: St Boniface	Spiritual direction, group facilitation. Leadership team.
2010–	RNDM apartment at Hampton House, Plainsview Drive	Regina, Saskatchewan Diocese: Regina	Provincial RNDM team member, coordinator of retired sisters in Saskatchewan. Retreat director/ facilitator.
2015	Provincial House, 382 and 393 Gaboury Place	Winnipeg, Manitoba Diocese: St Boniface	Provincial House; offices; residence, hospitality for visitors. Administration and pastoral work.
2016–	RNDM apartment at Hampton House, Plainsview Drive	Regina, Saskatchewan Diocese: Regina	Volunteer work and reflexology.
2017–	Apartment on Thomas Berry Street	Winnipeg, Manitoba Archdiocese of St Boniface	House for sisters involved in new mission project. Working at Kateri parish in Archdiocese of Winnipeg.

Notes

Introduction

1 This research was done with the help of an Insight Grant from the Social Sciences and Humanities Research Council of Canada (SSHRC 435-2013-0538 award as per DSS#31637).

2 Jerrold Seigel, *The Idea of the Self: Thought and Experience in Western Europe since the Seventeenth Century* (Cambridge: Cambridge University Press, 2005), chap. 1.

3 Elisabeth Schüssler Fiorenza uses thea/o*logy in an open form to avoid the gendering of G*d, while other authors have suggested theology; see Elizabeth Schüssler Fiorenza, *Congress of Wo/men. Religion, Gender, and Kyriarchal Power* (Cambridge, MA: Feminist Studies in Religion Books, 2016), 2n5.

4 Susan Smith, RNDM, *Call to Mission: The Story of the Mission Sisters of the Aotearoa New Zealand and Samoa* (Auckland, NZ: David Ling Publishing, 2010).

5 Susan Smith, RNDM, ed., *Zeal for Mission: The Story of the Sisters of Our Lady of the Missions 1861–2011* (Auckland, NZ: David Ling Publishing, 2012).

6 Quentin Skinner, "Meaning and Understanding in the History of Ideas," *History and Theory* 81, no. 1 (1969): 3–53; James Tully, "The Pen Is a Mighty Sword: Quentin Skinner's Analysis of Politics," in *Meaning and Context: Quentin Skinner and his Critics*, ed. James Tully (Cambridge: Polity Press, 1988), 7–25.

7 A concept taken from Charles Taylor; see Charles Taylor, *A Secular Age* (Cambridge, MA: Belknap Press, 2007), 171–2.

8 Pierre Bourdieu, *Language and Symbolic Power*, ed. and introduced by J.B. Thompson, trans. G. Raymond and M. Adamson (Cambridge, MA: Harvard University Press, 1991).

9 See Schüssler Fiorenza, *Congress of Wo/men*.

10 See, among others, Sheila Ross, "Faithful Companions of Jesus in the Field of Education in Brandon, Manitoba, 1883–1895," *CCHA Historical Studies* 71 (2005): 79–93; T. Mitchell, "Forging a New Protestant Ontario on the Agricultural Frontier: Public Schools in Brandon and the Origins of the Manitoba School Question, 1881–1890," in *Issues in the History of Education in Manitoba*, ed. Rosa Bruno-Jofré (Lewiston, NY: Edwin Mellen Press, 1993), 22–5; Heidi MacDonald, "Women Religious, Vatican II, Education, and the State in Atlantic Canada," in *Catholic Education in the Wake of Vatican II (1962–1965)*, ed. Rosa Bruno-Jofré and Jon Zaldívar (Toronto, ON: University of Toronto Press, 2017), 170–88; Elizabeth Smyth, "Gender, Religion and Higher Education: A Century of Catholic Women at the University of St. Michael's College, University of Toronto," *Paedagogica Historica* 49, no. 4 (2013): 547–61; Elizabeth Smyth, "Canadian Women Religious: Continuity and Change within the Sisters of St Joseph and the Loretto Sisters," in *Education, Identity and Women Religious, 1800–1950: Convents, Classrooms and Colleges*, ed. D. Rafferty and Elizabeth Smyth (London: Routledge, 2015), 43–59; M. Stanley, "Women and Education at St. Ann's Academy, Victoria, British Columbia," 2000, online publication, www.pc.gc.ca/dci/rf-ap/ph3/stann/stann_e.asp [no longer available]; Heidi MacDonald, "Transforming Catholic Women's Education in the Sixties: Sister Catherine Wallace's Feminist Leadership at Mount Saint Vincent University," *Encounters in Theory and History of Education* 18 (2017): 53–77; Jacqueline Gresko, "Mission and History: The Sisters of the Assumption and Japanese Students in Canada during World War II," *Paedagogica Historica* 49, no. 4 (2013): 531–45; Christine Lei, "The Educational Work of the Loretto Sisters in Ontario, 1847–1983," in *Changing Habits: Women Religious Orders in Canada*, ed. Elizabeth M. Smyth (Ottawa: Novalis, 2007), 172–90, among others.

1 Who Were the RNDMs?

1 Barbara Henley, RNDM, et al., "RNDM Poetry: These writings by Sisters of Our Lady of the Missions were gathered as part of the centennial celebration of the Birth into Fullness of Life of their Foundress Euphrasie Barbier 1893–1993" (RNDM, n.d.), 3.

2 Marie Bénédicte Ollivier, RNDM, *Missionary Beyond Boundaries: Euphrasie Barbier, 1820–1893*, trans. Beverley Grounds, RNDM (Rome: Istituto Salesiano Pio XI, 2007). This book is a non-hagiographical account of Euphrasie Barbier's life and a good historical account of the foundation of the congregation.

3 Ibid.

4 Unless mentioned otherwise, all uses of "Church" refer to the Catholic Church.

5 Ollivier, *Missionary Beyond Boundaries*, 50–1.

6 Marie Bénédicte Ollivier, RNDM, RNDM Documents, 10 June 1978, Centre du Patrimoine, Société Historique de Saint-Boniface, St Boniface, Manitoba (hereafter referred to as CPSHSB), box 12, file 10.

7 Joseph Bergin, *The Politics of Religion in Early Modern France* (New Haven, CT: Yale University Press, 2014). In the middle of the seventeenth century, the papacy condemned propositions contained in a theological treatise by the Flemish bishop Cornelius Jansen entitled "Augustinus" (1636). The controversy needs to be understood in the context of debates over the relationship between God's grace and human free will, which shook the foundations of Christendom during the time of the Reformation. In "Augustinus," Jansen intended to restate the fourth century Catholic position on Grace advanced by Saint Augustine. Jansen insisted on the crippling impact of Original Sin on human will, which needed to be motivated by Grace. The movement that emerged, which also contained modernist elements, was seen as a threat to both Rome and Versailles. See Alexander Sedgwick, "Jansen and the Jansenists," *History Today* 40, no. 7 (1990): 36. Jansenism is often conflated with moral rigorism. Contemporary authors have interpreted Jansenism as favouring the rights of the individual consciousness and advocating direct contact with the Bible, a major role for women, and the understanding of the Church as an assembly of the faithful. See Françoise Hildesheimer, *Le Jansénisme, L'histoire et l'heritage*, Collection petite encyclopédie moderne du christianisme (Paris: Desclée de Brouwer, 1992), 8–10.

8 Ollivier, *Missionary Beyond Boundaries*, chap. 1.

9 Marie Bénédicte Ollivier, RNDM, *Straight Is My Path: Spirituality of Euphrasie Barbier, Foundress of the Congregation of Our Lady of the Mission* (Rome: RNDM, 1978).

10 Ibid. There is limited information about this period of Euphrasie Barbier's life.

11 Ollivier noted that the Marist fathers initially referred to the novitiate as the novitiate of the Third Order Regular. (Third Order Regular designates laypeople affiliated to religious orders; "regular" meant that the women lived in convents and took vows.) However, very early on, Barbier named the congregation "Religieuses de Notre Dame des Missions." In fact, "on 26th December 1862, Euphrasie Barbier made her vow of Obedience and vowed to consecrate her life to the foreign missions, according to the Rule and Constitutions of the Sisters of Our Lady of the Missions." Ollivier, *Missionary Beyond Boundaries*, 150.

12 Ibid., 148–9.
13 Extract from "Constitutions from Our Lady of the Missions Prior to 1864," RNDM Documents, CPSHSB, B01-02, box 10, file 3.
14 Susan Smith, RNDM, ed., *Zeal for Mission: The Story of the Sisters of Our Lady of the Missions 1861–2011* (Auckland, NZ: David Ling Publishing, 2012), 20.
15 Ibid., 20–1.
16 Ibid., 17.
17 Second Vatican Council, "Decree on the Appropriate Renewal of the Religious Life (*Perfectae Caritatis*)," in *The Documents of Vatican II*, ed. Walter M. Abbott, SJ (New York: The American Press, 1965), 466–82.
18 Susan Smith, RNDM, *Call to Mission: The Story of the Mission Sisters of Aotearoa New Zealand and Samoa* (Auckland, NZ: David Ling Publishing, 2010), 274.
19 Ibid.
20 Mary of the Heart of Jesus, superior general, "Notes of the Conference Given by Mother Foundress in Lyon, The Constitutions, 14 January 1870," Letters, Translation of the Writings of Mother Mary of the Sacred Heart of Jesus, vol. 3, 1870–1872, General Archives of the RNDM, Rome.
21 Marie Bénédicte Ollivier, RNDM, "Spirituality of the Sisters of Our Lady of the Missions," RNDM Documents, CPSHSB, box 12, file 10.
22 María Vianney Lawless, "Our Lady and the Spirit of the Congregation," typed document prepared for the General Chapter of 1978, RNDM General Archives in Rome, Shelf 5, Section F., 1.
23 Claire Himbeault, RNDM, and Moira Ross, RNDM, "Introductory Papers," Provincial Pre-Chapter Assembly, Brandon, Manitoba, 7–9 October 1989, 1, RNDM UK-A/5c/9/1.
24 Extract from "Constitutions from Our Lady of the Missions Prior to 1864," CPSHSB, B01-02, box 10, file 3.
25 Mary of the Heart of Jesus, superior general of the Sisters of Our Lady of the Missions, "Notes on the Beginning of the Congregation of Our Lady of the Missions, Rome, 31 March 1869," Translation of the Writings of Mother Mary of the Sacred Heart of Jesus, Archive of the British Isles Province of the Sisters of Our Lady of the Missions, Sturry, England.
26 Claire Himbeault, RNDM, superior general, "Centenary Reflection on the Charism of Euphrasie Barbier," transcript of video, January 1994, CPSHSB, A02, box 3, file 5.
27 Himbeault and Ross, "Introductory Papers."
28 Euphrasie Barbier, in a letter to Father Bruno, 22 May 1890. See Ollivier, *Missionary Beyond Boundaries*, 568.
29 Himbeault, "Centenary Reflection."

30 Ibid., 2; The Constitutions. Notes of Conference given by Mother Foundress, in Lyon, 14 January 1870, Letters, Translation of the Writings of Mother Mary of the Heart of Jesus, vol. iii, 1870–72. Section A, shelf 6, Letters of Euphrasie, RNDM, General Archives, Rome.

31 Himbeault and Ross, "Introductory Papers." See also Maureen McBride, RNDM, "'Our Students Must Become Valiant Women!' Approaches to Education of Euphrasie Barbier 1829–1893, Foundress of Sisters of Our Lady of the Missions" (paper presented to RNDM Education Symposium, St Mary's College, Shillong, North-East India, 26 January 2006), 2.

32 Arthur Marwick, *The Sixties: Cultural Revolution in Britain, France, Italy and the United States, c. 1958–1974* (Oxford: Oxford University Press, 1998).

33 Himbeault, "Centenary Reflection."

34 Ollivier, *Missionary Beyond Boundaries*, chaps. 3 and 4.

35 Raf Vanderstraeten, "Religious Activism in a Secular World: The Rise and Fall of the Teaching Congregations of the Catholic Church," *Paedagogica Historica* 50 (2014): 494–513.

36 Pedro Chico Gonzales, *Institutos y Fundadores de Educación Cristiana*, 7 vols. (Valladolid: Centro Vocacional La Salle, 2000), quoted by Paulí Dávila Balsera, "Las Órdenes y Congregaciones Religiosas Francesas y su Impacto sobre la Educación en España. Siglos XIX y XX," in *Francia en la Educación de la España Contemporánea (1808–2008)*, ed. José María Hernández (Salamanca: Aquillafuente, Ediciones Universidad de Salamanca, 2011), 101–57.

37 Ibid.

38 Dorothy Ross, "Introduction: Modernism Reconsidered," in *Modernist Impulses in the Human Sciences 1870–1930*, ed. Dorothy Ross (Baltimore, MD: Johns Hopkins University Press, 1994), 1–25.

39 Eric J. Hobsbawm, *The Age of Empire, 1875–1914* (London: Weidenfeld and Nicolson, 1987), 56–83.

40 Susan Smith, *Call to Mission*, 22.

41 Hobsbawm, *The Age of Empire*, 16.

42 Drew Christensen, SJ, "Commentary on Pacem in Terris (Peace on Earth)," in *Modern Catholic Social Teaching*, ed. Kenneth Himes, OFM (Washington, DC: Georgetown University Press, 2005), 217–43.

43 Paul Misner, "Catholic Anti-Modernism: The Ecclesial Setting," in *Catholicism Contending with Modernity: Roman Catholic Modernism and Anti-Modernism in Historical Context*, ed. Darrell Jodock (Cambridge: Cambridge University Press, 2000), 56–88.

44 Gerald McCool, *Catholic Theology in the Nineteenth Century: The Quest for a Unitary Method* (New York: Crossroad, 1977), 21; Thomas Shannon, "Commentary on Rerum Novarum," in *Modern Catholic Social Teaching: Commentaries and Interpretations*, ed. Kenneth R. Himes, OFM (Washington,

DC: Georgetown University Press, 2005), 127–50. See also Alexander Sedgwick, "Jansen and the Jansenists," *History Today* 40, no. 7 (1990): 36–42.
45 Smith, *Zeal for Mission*, 32.
46 Marie de la Redemption, "À nos chères Soeurs du Noviciat, Echo de Notre
Dame des Missions, Monastère de Sts-Anges, Armentières, 8 May 1884."
Archive of the British Isles Province of the Sisters of Our Lady of the
Missions, Sturry, England. Provided by the archivist.
47 Shannon, "Commentary on Rerum Novarum," 127–50.
48 Ibid.
49 McBride, "'Our Students Must Become Valiant Women!'"
50 Smith, *Call to Mission*, 22.
51 "Development of the Sisters of Our Lady of the Missions," manuscript
provided by Veronica Dunne, provincial superior of the Canadian province, August 2011.
   Note: the quotation in the caption of figure 1.3, commenting on the
cover of *The Message* magazine, is taken from Rosa Bruno-Jofré and Ana
Jofré, "Reading the Lived Experience of Vatican II – Words and Images:
The Canadian Province of the Sisters of Our Lady of Missions in Peru,"
CCHA Historical Studies 81 (2015): 31–51; quotation at 46.
52 The Manitoba School Question refers to the school crisis between 1890 and
1896, when provincial legislation abolished confessional state-supported
schools following the Laurier-Greenway Compromise (an agreement between the federal and provincial governments). Subsequently, the Public
School Act was modified in 1897, setting the basis for the common school.
The Catholic Church could no longer have its own school districts under
its jurisdiction supported by public funding. However, the act read that
religious exercises were permitted when there were ten pupils belonging
to a faith in any school and also that, when ten pupils in any school spoke
French or any other language other than English as their native language,
the teaching of such pupils could be done in French or any other language
and English. The Manitoba School Question was a Catholic question but
also a French one, since the new legislation moved the Franco-Manitoban
minority to the margins of power by denying French-speaking Manitobans
the constitutional rights and privileges they had enjoyed earlier as members of a founding nation. In 1916, the Manitoba government abolished
the bilingual (multilingual) schools, which had voluntary attendance, and
replaced them with a secular, unilingual, and universal system of public
schooling, where private schools were allowed but had to follow the public school curriculum. See Robert Perin, *Rome in Canada: The Vatican and Canadian Affairs in the Late Victorian Age* (Toronto: University of Toronto Press,
1990), 127–57; Ken Osborne, "One Hundred Years of History Teaching in
Manitoba Schools, Part 1: 1897–1927," *Manitoba History* 36 (Autumn/
Winter 1998–99), 3–25.

53 See Gilbert Comeault, "The Politics of the Manitoba School Question and Its Impact on L.-P.-A. Langevin's Relations with Manitoba's Catholic Minority Groups, 1895–1915" (master's thesis, University of Manitoba, 1977).

54 Ian McKay, "The Liberal Order Framework: A Prospectus for a Reconnaissance of Canadian History," *The Canadian Historical Review* 81, no. 4 (2000): 617–45. For the debate around this approach, see Jean-François Constant and Michel Ducharme, eds., *Liberalism and Hegemony, Debating the Canadian Liberal Revolution* (Toronto: University of Toronto Press, 2010).

55 See, for example, J.Ad. Sabourin, DD, *La religion et la morale dans nos écoles* (St Boniface, Manitoba: Arthur, archbishop de Saint-Boniface, 1925).

56 I am adapting Raymond Williams's theoretical model that distinguishes dominant, residual, and emergent forms of both alternative and oppositional culture. This theoretical model will be useful in analysing the long 1960s. See Raymond Williams, *Problems in Materialism and Culture: Selected Essays* (London: Verso, 1982).

57 In 1910, the Diocese of Regina, Saskatchewan, was created, and in 1915 (after Langevin's death) the Diocese of Winnipeg.

58 Comeault, "The Politics of the Manitoba School Question."

59 Ibid.

60 Jean-Marie Taillefer, "Les franco-manitobains et l'éducation 1870–1970: Une étude quantitative" (PhD diss., University of Manitoba, 1987), 254.

61 Rosa Bruno-Jofré, *The Missionary Oblate Sisters: Vision and Mission* (Montreal: McGill-Queen's University Press, 2005), 27.

62 Rosa Bruno-Jofré, "The Missionary Oblate Sisters of the Sacred Heart and Mary Immaculate (MO) and the Sisters of Our Lady of the Missions (RNDM): The Intersection of Education, Spirituality, the Politics of Life, Faith and Language in the Canadian Prairies, 1898–1930," *Paedagogica Historica* 49, no. 4 (2013): 471–93.

63 Journal of Our Lady of Fourvière, Ste-Rose-du-Lac, Manitoba, 16 January 1906, CPSHSB, box 60, file 5.

64 *Petit historique de nos premières fondations au Canada 1898–1923* (Lyon, FR: Institut de Notre-Dame des Missions, Maison de Recrutement pour les Missions, 1926), 9; hereafter referred to as *Petit historique*. To note: the author sometimes compared the French version with a typed version in English, "Sisters of Our Lady of the Missions in Canada 1898–1923," trans. Sister Mary of the Holy Trinity, a typed manuscript commemorating the Silver Jubilee of the RNDM (undated). This manuscript was provided by then provincial superior Veronica Dunne.

65 Veronica Dunne, "Canada, 1898–2011," in *Zeal for Mission: The Story of the Sisters of Our Lady of the Missions 1861–2011*, ed. Susan Smith (Auckland, NZ: David Ling Publishing, 2012), 233–54.

66 *Petit historique*.

67 Ibid.

68 Ibid., 13.
69 Ibid., 13–14.
70 Ibid., 16.
71 Ibid., 17.
72 Ibid, 19.
73 Ibid.
74 Ibid., 20.
75 Ibid., 21.
76 Ibid.
77 Ibid., 22.
78 Donald A. Bailey, "The Métis Province and Its Social Tensions," in *The Political Economy of Manitoba*, ed. James Silver and Jeremy Hull (Regina: University of Regina, 1990), 51–72.
79 The five poems at the end of this and several other chapters (2, 8, 10, and 11) are taken from "RNDM Poetry: These writings by Sisters of Our Lady of the Missions were gathered as part of the centennial celebration of the Birth into the Fullness of Life of their foundress, Euphrasie Barbier, 1893–1993" (RNDM, 1993).

2 Foundational Thoughts on Education

1 John W. O'Malley, SJ, *The Jesuits: A History from Ignatius to the Present* (Lanham, MD: Rowman & Littlefield, 2014), 13.
2 See Laurence Lux-Sterritt and Carmen M. Mangion, "Introduction – Gender, Catholicism and Women's Spirituality over the *Longue Durée*," in *Gender, Catholicism and Spirituality: Women and the Roman Catholic Church in Britain and Europe, 1200–1900*, ed. Laurence Lux-Sterritt, and Carmen M. Mangion (London: Palgrave Macmillan, 2011), 1–19.
3 See O'Malley, *The Jesuits*, chap. 1.
4 Rosa Bruno-Jofré, "The Sisters of the Infant Jesus in Bembibre, León, Spain, during the Second Stage of Francoism (1957–1975): The School with No Doors," in *Catholic Education in the Wake of Vatican II*, ed. Rosa Bruno-Jofré and Jon Igelmo Zaldívar (Toronto: University of Toronto Press, 2017).
5 De La Salle schools have been well analysed. This is not the case with the Charitable Teachers. See Enrique García Ahumada, "350 años del natalicio de San Juan Bautista de La Salle," *Annuario de Historia de la Iglesia* 11 (2002): 375–81; José María Valladolid and Paulí Dávila, *Estudio crítico, notas y bibliografía a la edición en español de la Guía de las Escuelas* (Madrid: Biblioteca Nueva-Siglo XXI, 2012); Paulí Dávila, Luis M. Naya, and Hilario Murúa, "Tradition and Modernity of the De La Salle Schools: The Case of the

Basque Country in Franco's Spain (1937–1975)," *Paedagogica Historica* 49, no. 4 (2013): 562–76.

6 Marie Bénédicte Ollivier, RNDM, *Missionary Beyond Boundaries: Euphrasie Barbier, 1829–1893*, trans. Beverley Ground, RNDM (Roma: Istituto Salesiano Pio XI, 2007), 106. Ollivier and Ground refer to Mount Pleasant Teachers' College. During the twentieth century, the college changed its name to Notre Dame Training College and moved to St Catharine's College; it is now also part of Liverpool Hope University College. See also Kim Lowden, "Spirited Sisters: Anglican and Catholic Contributions to Women's Teacher Training in the Nineteenth Century" (PhD diss., University of Liverpool, 2000).

7 Mary Linscott, Sister Mary of the Holy Angels, *Quiet Revolution: The Educational Experience of Blessed Julie Billiart and the Sisters of Notre Dame de Namur* (Glasgow: John Burns & Sons, 1966), 36.

8 Two papers on the educational ideas of Euphrasie Barbier that consulted the original letters have guided my search in the archives: Maureen McBride, RNDM, "'Our Students Must Become Valiant Women!' Approaches to Education of Euphrasie Barbier 1829–1893, Foundress of Sisters of Our Lady of the Missions" (paper presented at the RNDM Education Symposium, St Mary's College, Shillong, North-East India, 26 January 2006); and Colleen Mader, "Mother Mary of the Heart of Jesus: Her Thoughts and Ideas on Education," CPSHSB, box 3, file 4.

9 Mary of the Heart of Jesus, Armentières, to M. M. St Gabriel, prioress, Christchurch, 14 June 1881, Translation of the Writings of Mother Mary of the Heart of Jesus, 2/2/458 0 RNDM UK, Archive of the British Isles Province of the Sisters of Our Lady of the Missions.

10 Susan Ellen Doreen Mumm, "Lady Guerrillas of Philanthropy: Anglican Sisterhoods in Victorian England" (PhD diss., University of Sussex, 1992), 172.

11 Daniel Tröhler, *Pestalozzi y la Educacionalización del Mundo* (Barcelona: Octaedro, 2014).

12 Ibid., 106.

13 Pope Pius XI, *Divini Illius Magistri: Encyclical of Pope Pius XI on Christian Education to the Patriarchs, Primates, Archbishops, Bishops, and Other Ordinaries in Peace and Communion with the Apostolic See and to All the Faithful of the Catholic World* (Vatican: The Holy See, 1929), article 9, http://w2.vatican.va/content/pius-xi/en/encyclicals/documents/hf_p-xi_enc_31121929_divini-illius-magistri.html.

14 Mother Mary of the Heart of Jesus, Lyon, to M. M. St Michael, Vicar, Nelson, 2 June 1878, UK A, 2/5/1293, RNDM UK, Archive of the British Isles Province of the Sisters of Our Lady of the Missions, Sturry, England.

15 McBride, "Our Students Must Become Valiant Women!" See also Mader, "Her Thoughts and Ideas on Education."

16 Mother Mary of the Heart of Jesus to Mother Mary of the Angels, 21 May 1870, Translation of the Writings of Mother Mary of the Heart of Jesus, 2/2/419 RNDM/UK, Archive of the British Isles Province of the Sisters of Our Lady of the Missions. See also Mother Mary of the Heart of Jesus to M. M. St Michael, Vicar, Nelson, 2 June 1878, Archive of the British Isles Province of the Sisters of Our Lady of the Missions, UK A 1F/2/5/1293.

17 Mader, "Her Thoughts and Ideas on Education." See also Mother Mary of the Heart of Jesus to M. M. St Michael, 2 June 1878, Translation of the Writings of Mother Mary of the Heart of Jesus, 1F/2/5/1293, UKA; McBride, "Our Students Must Become Valiant Women!"

18 Mère Marie du Coeur-de-Jésus to M. M. St Michael, Nelson, 2 juin 1878, Translation of the Writings of Mother Mary of the Heart of Jesus, 2/5/1293, Archive of the British Isles Province of the Sisters of Our Lady of the Missions, UK A.

19 Mader, "Her Thoughts and Ideas on Education."

20 Mother Mary of the Heart of Jesus to M. M. St Michael, 2 June 1878, Translation of the Writings of Mother Mary of the Heart of Jesus, 2/5/1293, RNDM UK A. See also Mother Mary of the Heart of Jesus to M. M. of the Angels, prioress and the Sisters in Wallis, 12 February 1877, 2/5/1048 RNDM UK A.

21 See chapter one of this volume.

22 Rosa Bruno-Jofré, *The Missionary Oblate Sisters: Vision and Mission* (Montreal: McGill-Queen's University Press, 2005), 103.

23 Ibid.

24 Adélard Langevin, Archevêque de Saint-Boniface à Soeur Supérieure des Soeurs de la Croix de Murinais, 29 décembre 1906, Fonds Corporation archiépiscopale catholique romaine de Saint-Boniface (CACRSB), L26435-L26436. See also Rosa Bruno-Jofré, "The Missionary Oblate Sister of the Sacred Heart of Mary Immaculate (MO) and the Sisters of Our Lady of the Missions (RNDM): The Intersection of Education, Spirituality, the Politics of Life, Faith and Language in the Canadian Prairies, 1898–1930," *Paedagogica Historica* 49, no. 4 (2013): 454–71.

25 Mother Mary of the Heart of Jesus to M. M. St Anne, 3 January 1882. Translation of the Writings of Mother Mary of the Heart of Jesus 2/7/1728, RNDM UK A.

26 Ibid., 9.

27 Ibid., 10.

28 Mader, "Her Thoughts and Ideas on Education."

29 Mother Mary of the Heart of Jesus to M. M. St Anne, 3 January 1882, Translation of the Writings of Mother Mary of the Heart of Jesus,

2/7/1728, RNDM UK A. See also Mader, "Her Thoughts and Ideas on Education," 10.

30 Mother Mary of the Heart of Jesus to Sr M. St Bernardine, 18 October 1885, Translation of the Writings of Mother Mary of the Heart of Jesus, 2/8/2136, RNDM UK A.

31 *Petit historique de nos premières fondations au Canada 1898–1923* (Lyon, FR: Institut de Notre-Dame des Missions, Maison de Recrutement pour les Missions, 1926), 9; hereafter referred to as *Petit historique*. To note: the author sometimes compared the French version with a typed version in English, "Sisters of Our Lady of the Missions in Canada 1898–1923," trans. Sister Mary of the Holy Trinity, a typed document commemorating the Silver Jubilee of the RNDM (undated). This manuscript was provided by then provincial Veronica Dunne.

32 Susan Smith, *Call to Mission: The Story of the Mission Sisters of Aotearoa New Zealand and Samoa* (Auckland, NZ: David Ling Publishing, 2010), 275.

33 Mother Mary of the Heart of Jesus to Mother M. St Thechla, 17 September 1890, Translation of the Writings of Mother Mary of the Sacred Heart, 2/10/2903, RNDM UK A.

34 There was indeed the "modernist crisis" at the beginning of the twentieth century, which was prompted by intellectuals who tried to integrate the historical-critical method. See Jürgen Mettepenningen, *Nouvelle Théologie – New Theology: Inheritor of Modernism, Precursor of Vatican II* (London: T & T Clark, 2010).

35 Ibid.

36 Procès-verbal du Chapitre Général de Notre Dame des Missions, Deal, England, 21 August 1925, manuscript in English, B01-08, CPSHSB, file 18.

37 Pope Pius XI, *Divini Illius Magistri*, article 14.

38 Ibid., article 15.

39 Ibid., article 18.

40 John Elias, "Whatever Happened to Catholic Philosophy of Education?" *Religious Education: The Official Journal of the Religious Education Association* 94, no. 1 (1999): 92–110.

41 Rosa Bruno-Jofré, "Our Lady of the Missions (RNDM) in Canada, the Long 1960s, and Vatican II: From Carving Spaces in the Educational State to Living the Radicality of the Gospel," in *Catholic Education in the Wake of Vatican II* (Toronto: University of Toronto Press, 2017).

42 Procès-verbal du Chapitre Général, Maison Généralice de Notre Dame des Missions, Deal, England, 17 August 1912, manuscript in English, CPSHSB, B01-08, box 14, file 14.

43 Procès-verbal du Chapitre Général de Notre Dame des Missions, Deal, England, October 1919, manuscript in French, CPSHSB, B01-08, box 14, file 15.

44 Procès-verbal du Chapitre Général de Notre Dame des Missions, Deal, England, 21 August 1925, manuscript in English, CPSHSB, B01-08, file 15.
45 Ibid., file 20.
46 Procès-verbal of the Council of the General Administration, Hastings, 29 April 1944. Sacred Heart Province, Canada, CPSHSB, B1-03, box 10, file 14.
47 Procès-verbal of the Council of the General Administration, Hastings, 26 June 1943, CPSHSB, B01-03, box 10, file 14.
48 Ibid.
49 Procès-verbal of the Council of the General Administration, Hastings, 8 September 1954, Sacred Heart Province, Canada, CPSHSB, B01-03, box 10, file 15.
50 For example, see Procès-verbal of the General Administration, Hastings, 11 June 1956, Saint Mary's Province, Canada, CPSHSB, B01-03, box 10, file 16.
51 The notion of field helps us to understand the Canadian province as a locus with its internal dynamic, history, logic, and spiritual and socio-political positioning and distribution of species of power. This character would condition the relations between the province and central administration. See Pierre Bourdieu, *Language and Symbolic Power*, ed. J.B. Thompson, trans. G. Raymond and M. Adamson (Cambridge, UK: Polity Press, 1991); Pierre Bourdieu and Loïc Wacquant, *An Invitation to Reflexive Sociology* (Chicago: University of Chicago Press, 1992), 97.
52 For a long time, the Church and Catholic educators reacted against pragmatist philosophies of education, notions of instrumental knowledge, and evidentialism. However, in the late 1920s and 1930s, when "nouvelle théologie" gained some intellectual space, although questioned by the Vatican, Catholic theologians with a strong interest in education such as Frans De Hovre – and, in particular, Chilean Jesuit Alberto Hurtado – examined Dewey. They tended to separate pragmatism as the philosophical foundation of Dewey's educational theory from his educational theory itself. See Frans de Hovre, *Essai de philosophie pédagogique* (Brussels: Librairie Albert Dewit, 1927); Alberto Hurtado, SJ, *Le système pédagogique de Dewey devant les exigences de la doctrine catholique* (Belgium: Université de Louvain, 1935). See also Rosa Bruno-Jofré and Gonzalo Jover, "The Readings of John Dewey's Work and the Intersection of Catholicism: The Cases of the Institución Libre de Enseñanza and the Thesis of Father Alberto Hurtado, S.J. on Dewey," in *The Global Reception of Dewey's Thought: Multiple Refractions Through Time and Space*, ed. Rosa Bruno-Jofré and Jürgen Schriewer (New York: Routledge, 2012), 23–42. It is important also to mention interpretations provided by Jacques Maritain and Etienne Gilson in the 1940s and 1950s. See John Elias, "Whatever Happened to Catholic Philosophy of Education?" *Religious Education* 94, no. 1 (Winter 1999), 92–110.

53 Gonzalo Jover, "Democracy and Education Then and Now: 'De-pragmatizing' and 'Ultra-Pragmatizing' Readings of John Dewey's Pedagogy," in *Dewey in Our Time: Learning from John Dewey for Transcultural Practice*, ed. Peter Cunningham and Ruth Heilbronn (London: UCL Institute of Education Press, University College, 2016), 40–55.

54 See George Barry Ford, *A Degree of Difference* (New York: Farrar, Straus & Giroux, 1969); "Parochial School Here Looked Upon as a Model: Corpus Christi School Subject of Article by Educational Authority," *The Catholic News*, 16 July 1938, 5–7.

55 Veronica Dunne, "Canada 1898–2011," in *Zeal for Mission: The Story of the Sisters of Our Lady of the Missions, 1861–2011*, ed. Susan Smith (Auckland, NZ: David Ling Publishing, 2012), 233–55.

56 Ibid.

Introduction to Part Two

1 Quentin Skinner, "Meaning and Understanding in the History of Ideas," *History and Theory* 8, no. 1 (1969): 3–53, esp. 45 and 46. See also James Tully, "The Pen Is a Mighty Sword: Quentin Skinner's Analysis of Politics," in *Meaning and Context: Quentin Skinner and His Critics*, ed. James Tully (Cambridge, UK: Polity Press, 1988), 7–25.

2 Skinner, "Meaning and Understanding," 35.

3 "I speak of 'social imaginary' here, rather than social theory, because there are important differences between the two. There are, in fact, several differences. I speak of 'imaginary' (i) because I am talking about the way ordinary people 'imagine' their social surroundings, and this is often not expressed in theoretical terms, it is carried in images, stories, legends, etc. But it is also the case that (ii) theory is often the possession of a small minority, whereas what is interesting in the social imaginary is that it is shared by large groups of people, if not the whole society. Which leads to a third difference: (iii) the social imaginary is that common understanding which makes possible common practices, and a widely shared sense of legitimacy." Charles Taylor, *A Secular Age* (Cambridge, MA: Belknap Press, 2007), 171–2. The notion of nested spaces came out of a conversation with James Scott Johnston.

4 Rosa Bruno-Jofré, *The Missionary Oblate Sisters: Vision and Mission* (Montreal: McGill-Queen's University Press, 2005); Rosa Bruno-Jofré, "The Process of Renewal of the Missionary Oblate Sisters, 1963–1989," in *Changing Habits: Women Religious Orders in Canada*, ed. Elizabeth M. Smyth (Ottawa: Novalis, 2007), 247–73.

5 Rosa Bruno-Jofré and Josh Cole, "'What the Dead Say to the Living': Time, Politics, and Teacher Preparation in English Canada's Long-1960s," in

Pädagogik und pädagogishes Wissen / Pedagogy and Educational Knowledge, ed. Andreas Hoffmann-Ocon and Rebekka Horlacher (Bad Heilbrunn, DE: Julius Klinkhardt, 2016), 247–64.

6 Ibid. See also Ian McKay, "The Canadian Passive Revolution, 1840–1950," *Capital and Class* 34 (2010): 363–83.

3 Manitoba in the Early Years

1 Rosa Bruno-Jofré, "Citizenship and Schooling in Manitoba, 1918–1945," *Manitoba History* 36 (Autumn/Winter 1998–99): 26–35.

2 Marcel Martel, *French Canada: An Account of Its Creation and Break-up, 1850–1967*, Canada's Ethnic Group Series 24 (Ottawa: Canadian Historical Association, 1998), 3–5. See also Marcel Martel, *Le deuil d'un pays imaginé: Rêves, luttes et déroute du Canada français: Les rapports entre le Québec et la francophonie canadienne, 1867–1975* (Ottawa: Les presses de l'Université d'Ottawa, 1997), 20.

3 Martel, *French Canada*, 4–5.

4 Ibid.

5 *Petit historique de nos premières fondations au Canada 1898–1923* (Lyon, FR: Institut de Notre-Dame des Missions, Maison de Recrutement pour les Missions, 1926), 111.

6 Jean-Marie Taillefer, "Les franco-manitobains et l'éducation 1870–1970: Une étude quantitative" (PhD diss., University of Manitoba, 1987), 262–3.

7 Martel, *Le deuil d'un pays imaginé*.

8 Taillefer, "Les franco-manitobains et l'éducation," 262–3.

9 *Petit historique*, 23.

10 Ibid.

11 Ibid., 24.

12 Ibid., 33–4.

13 Ibid., 39.

14 Ibid., 35.

15 Ibid., 39.

16 Ibid., 38.

17 Unless otherwise noted, all distances are current distances by highway.

18 *Petit historique*, 69–70. See also Anatole E. Théoret, *Sainte-Rose-du-Lac* (Winnipeg: Gerald C. Murray, 1948), 5.

19 *Petit historique*, 70.

20 Paulí Dávila Balsera, "Las órdenes y congregaciones religiosas francesas y su impacto sobre la educacin en España. Siglos XIX y XX," in *Francia en la Education de la España Contemporánea (1808–2008)*, ed. José María Hernández Diaz and José Louis Peset (Salamanca: Ediciones Universidad de

Salamanca, 2011), 101–57. See also José Orlandis, "Ciento veinticinco años de escuela laica en Francia," *Anuario de historia de la Iglesia* 14 (2005): 83–90.

21 Procès-verbal du Conseil du 14 septembre 1900, Ste Rose-du-Lac, CPSHSB, box 60, file 14.

22 Manitoba Public School Act, in *Acts of the Legislature of the Province of Manitoba*, 60 Vict., 2nd session, 9th Legislature, vol. 1, *Public Acts* (Winnipeg, MB: Queen's Printer, 1897), chap. 26.

23 Ste Rose Novitiate, Canonical Erection, CPSHSB, box 42, file 14.

24 RNDM Journal, 16 January 1914, CPSHSB, box 59, file 24.

25 "Visite de Monseigneur 23 Mai 1914," Journal Ste-Rose-du-Lac, Our Lady of Fourvière Convent, CPSHSB, box 59. The text in French is quite eloquent: "le moment approche – encore quelques minutes plus que quelques seconds avant l'arrivée de l'Époux. Enfin sa douce voix émue par chacune des vierges consacrées. Qui oserait méconnáitre la bonté d'un Dieu s'abaissant presqu'á sa pauvre créature pour l'élever à la dignité de son Épouse mais qui pourrait se rappelée sans trembler que ce Dieu si bon est un Dieu jaloux qui ne peut souffrir aucune affection étrangère dans sa créature privilégie."

26 Ibid.

27 *Petit historique*, 72.

28 Ibid., 73.

29 Théoret, *Sainte-Rose-du-Lac*, 84.

30 *Petit historique*, 75.

31 Théoret, *Sainte-Rose-du-Lac*, 93.

32 *Petit historique*, 81.

33 Ibid.

34 *Livre historique concernant le Monastère de Ste Madeleine à Saint Eustache*, Manitoba, CPSHSB, box 61, file 17, 1–2.

35 "Les maîtresses se montrent bien délicates en nous résillant leurs fonctions," in *Livre historique*, 3.

36 *Petit historique*, 85.

37 Ibid.

38 Adélard, O.M.I., Archbishop of St Boniface to Révérend Mère St Irénée, Provinciale de Soeur de N.D. Des Missions, May 1903. The letter provides instructions for the payment of the land and sets a limit of $5,000.00 for the cost of the building. See also J.F. Letourneau, St Eustache to Révérend Mère St Albert, 16 December 1902. The letter deals with the conditions for the selling of the land in the amount of $950.00. See also G. Cinq-Mars, Contracteur, St Boniface, Manitoba, to Monsieur l'Abbé Campeau, curé de St Eustache, 15 September 1902. The letter contains the initial estimate for the building of the convent: $8,780.00. See also specifications for "un

Couvent à St Eustache," addressed to Révérend Monsieur Campeau, curé de St Eustache, from both Father Campeau and G. Cinq-Mars (contracteur) for the sum of $5,345.29, 1 May 1903. CPSHSB, box 62, file 10.

39 *Livre historique*, 6.
40 *Petit historique*, 86.
41 *Livre historique*, 8–11.
42 Ibid., 10–11.
43 Procès-verbal du Conseil du 12 December 1912, recommandation 4, CPSHSB, box 60, file 14.
44 Ibid., article 7.
45 *Petit historique*, 86.
46 Ibid., 96–7.
47 *Livre historique*, 10.
48 See discussion in chapter one of this volume.
49 *Petit historique*, 98.
50 Ibid., 99.
51 Ibid.
52 Ibid., 100.
53 Ibid.
54 Ibid., 103.
55 *Petit historique*, 101.
56 Ibid., 102.
57 Ibid.
58 Ibid., 104–5.
59 Ibid.
60 Ibid.
61 *Livre historique* (suite), Virgo Fidelis Convent, Letellier, 2 December 1915, CPSHSB, box 63, file 6.
62 *Livre historique* (suite), Virgo Fidelis Convent, Letellier, 23 January 1917, CPSHSB, box 63, file 7.
63 Ibid., 26 October 1913.
64 Ibid., 13 June 1915.
65 "History of the Congregation in Canada," RNDM UK, Sturry, England, typed pages, section 6, box 2.
66 *Petit historique*, 138.
67 Ibid., 139.
68 Ibid.
69 Ibid., 138.
70 Ibid., 145.
71 Ibid., 148.
72 "Fondation de St Joseph, Historique," 1909, CPSHSB, box 71, file 2.
73 Ibid.

74 Ibid.
75 Rosa·Bruno-Jofré, "Citizenship and Schooling in Manitoba, 1918–1945," *Manitoba History* 36 (Autumn/Winter 1998–99): 26–37.
76 "Address of the Minister of Education," *The Western School Journal* 5 (May 1918): 185. Cited in Bruno-Jofré, "Citizenship and Schooling," 27.
77 Ibid.
78 John Herd Thompson, *The Harvest of War: The Prairie West, 1914–1918* (Toronto: McClelland & Stewart, 1981), 74.
79 Martel, *Le deuil d'un pays imaginé*, 30.
80 Taillefer, "Les franco-manitobains et l'éducation," 263–4.
81 *Letellier, 1936–1961*, 1 February 1959, CPSHSB, box 63, file 10.
82 *Livre historique concernât le Monastère de Sainte Madeleine à Saint Eustache*, Manitoba, 21 October 1915, CPSHSB, box 61, file 17.
83 "Observations, Council of St Eustache," 22 June 1941, CPSHSB, box 62, file 3.
84 "St Eustache, May 1959," manuscript, St Eustache, CPSHSB, box 63, file 10.
85 Rosa Bruno-Jofré, "The Missionary Oblate Sisters of the Sacred Heart and Mary Immaculate (MO) and the Sisters of Our Lady of the Missions (RNDM): The Intersection of Education, Spirituality, the Politics of Life, Faith and Language in the Canadian Prairies, 1898–1930," *Paedagogica Historica* 49 no. 4 (2013): 454–70.
86 Soeur Cécile Granger, "Les Religieuses de Notre Dame des Missions à Letellier," 10 January 1982, CPSHSB, box 63, file 14.
87 *Letellier, 1936–1961*, 14 December 1937, CPSHSB, box 63, file 10.
88 Hon. W.C. Miller, "The Minister Page: The Role of the Inspector of Schools," *Manitoba School Journal* 19 no. 2 (1957): 3. Cited in Rosa Bruno-Jofré and Colleen Ross, "Decoding the Subjective Image of Women Teachers in Rural Towns and Surrounding Areas in Southern Manitoba, 1947–1960," in *Issues in the History of Education in Manitoba: From the Construction of the Common School to the Politics of Voices*, ed. Rosa Bruno-Jofré (Lewiston, NY: Edwin Mellen Press, 1993), 569–93, quotation at 586.
89 Ruth W. Sandwell, *Canada's Rural Majority: Households, Environments, and Economies, 1870–1940* (Toronto: University of Toronto Press, 2016), 128.
90 "Observations. Council of St Eustache," 22 June 1941, CPSHSB, box 62, file 3.

4 English-Speaking Communities, Immigrants, and the Quest for Social Recognition in Manitoba

1 Journal, 1899, CPSHSB, box 54, file 22. The journal begins with a narration of the trip and the foundation in Brandon.
2 Sheila Ross, "Faithful Companions of Jesus in the Field of Education in Brandon, Manitoba, 1883–1895," *CCHA Historical Studies* 71 (2005): 79–93;

332 Notes to pages 84–9

T. Mitchell, "Forging a New Protestant Ontario on the Agricultural Frontier: Public Schools in Brandon and the Origins of the Manitoba School Question, 1881–1890," in *Issues in the History of Education in Manitoba*, ed. Rosa Bruno-Jofré (Lewiston, NY: Edwin Mellen Press, 1993), 22–5.

3 Errol Black and Tom Mitchell, *A Square Deal for All and No Railroading: Historical Essays on Labour in Brandon* (St John's, NL: Canadian Committee on Labour History, 2000), intro., 13.

4 Ibid.

5 Patrick J. O'Sullivan, K.C.S.G., *By Steps, Not Leaps: St Augustine of Canterbury Parish, Brandon, Manitoba, 1881–1981* (Brandon, MB: privately published, 1981), 17.

6 *Petit historique de nos premières fondations au Canada 1898–1923* (Lyon, FR: Institut de Notre-Dame des Missions, Maison de Recrutement pour les Missions, 1926), 51.

7 Ibid.

8 Ibid., 50.

9 Golden Jubilee Canada, RNDM, 18, RNDM-UK-A/2E/7/2/2/.

10 Journal, St Michael's Convent, St Augustine School, Brandon, Manitoba, 1 September 1899, CPSHSB, box 54, file 22. Notably, *Petit historique* (51) states that seventy-five boys and girls started at the school.

11 *Petit historique*, 51.

12 "The Convent on Victoria and Lorne, Brandon," manuscript, CPSHSB, box 54, file 17. There is a note saying that this text is the testimony of Sister Cecile Jordans, RNDM, and a second sister whose name is not legible.

13 O'Sullivan, *By Steps, Not Leaps*, 44.

14 "The Convent on Victoria and Lorne, Brandon," manuscript, CPSHSB, box 54, file 17.

15 "Convention," manuscript signed by Van de Steene, CSSR, and M. St Sindonis, RNDM, 30 July 1908, Brandon, Manitoba, CPSHSB, box 54, file 11.

16 Ibid.

17 Charles Taylor, *Multiculturalism and "The Politics of Recognition": An Essay* (Princeton, NJ: Princeton University Press, 1992), 36.

18 O'Sullivan, *By Steps, Not Leaps*, 59.

19 Ibid., 45; *Petit historique*, 54.

20 *Petit historique*, 54.

21 "The Convent on Victoria and Lorne, Brandon," manuscript, CPSHSB, box 54, file 17.

22 Reverend James Woodworth wrote *Strangers within Our Gates* in 1909. The Methodist reformist leader, although sympathetic to the plight of immigrants, was concerned with the need to assimilate them.

23 Rosa Bruno-Jofré, "The Situational Dimension of the Educational Apostolate and the Configuration of the Learner as a Cultural and Political

Subject: The Case of the Sisters of Our Lady of the Missions in the Canadian Prairies," in *Education, Identity and Women Religious, 1800–1950: Convents, Classrooms and Colleges*, ed. Deirdre Raftery and Elizabeth M. Smyth (London: Routledge, 2016), 160–83.

24 O'Sullivan, *By Steps, Not Leaps*, 99.

25 Ibid.

26 Ibid.

27 Ibid., 58.

28 Ibid.

29 St Michael's Convent, 1 September 1924, CPSHSB, box 54, file 22.

30 *Petit historique*, 152–7.

31 Convents of Our Lady of the Missions in Manitoba, October 1967, General Archives of the RNDM, Rome.

32 Terence J. Fay, *A History of Canadian Catholics* (Montreal: McGill-Queen's University Press, 2002), 187.

33 Gerald Friesen, *The Canadian Prairies: A History* (Toronto: University of Toronto Press, 1987), 242–3.

34 Rev. Gerritsma, pastor, St Edward's, Cor. Arlington and Notre Dame to Rev. Mother Provincial, Sisters of Our Lady of the Missions, Brandon, 21 July 1909, CPSHSB, box 99, file 1.

35 Ibid., 26 July 1909.

36 Ibid., 12 September 1910.

37 Ibid.

38 Ibid. Note written on the back of the priest's letter.

39 Historical Notes: St Edward's, 1993, CPSHSB, box 126, file 8.

40 *Petit historique*, 155.

41 *Petit historique*, 157.

42 Report, signed Mary Gertrude, superior general, 14 March 1970, CPSHSB, box 28, file 31.

43 *Petit historique*, 159–60.

44 Ibid., 161.

45 Ibid.

46 Ibid., 162.

47 Ibid., 164.

48 Ibid., 165.

49 Sr Marie, Canada, "In the Reformatory," *The Message of Notre-Dame des Missions* 1 no. 2 (1928): 9.

5 The RNDM in Saskatchewan

1   See J.R. Miller, *Shingwauk's Vision: A History of Native Residential Schools* (Toronto: University of Toronto Press, 1997).

2 *Petit historique de nos premières fondations au Canada 1898–1923* (Lyon, FR: Institut de Notre-Dame des Missions, Maison de Recrutement pour les Missions, 1926), 43; "The Sisters of Our Lady of the Missions received a warm welcome in Crooked Lake Mission, 14 December 1898," brochure celebrating the 95th anniversary of arriving in Canada and the sisters' second foundation at Crooked Lake Mission, CPSHSB, box 54, file 10; Rev. Théophile Campeau, OMI, to SA Grandeur Monseigneur Langevin, Archevêque de St-Boniface, Manitoba, 1 December 1898, Box 54, file 10, COSHSB.

3 *Petit historique*, 44.

4 Ibid.

5 *Petit historique,* 44; "Sister Mary of the Holy Trinity, Sisters of Our Lady of The Missions in Canada 1898–1923," 32, English typescript provided by Provincial Veronica Dunne.

6 *Petit historique*, 45.

7 Ibid., 43.

8 Ibid., 45.

9 Ibid., 46.

10 Ibid.

11 "Editorial," *Les Cloches de Saint-Boniface* 1, no. 1 (1902).

12 Gerald Friesen, *Citizens and Nation: An Essay on History, Communication, and Canada* (Toronto: University of Toronto Press, 2000), chap. 2, "Interpreting Aboriginal Cultures."

13 Paul Phillips, "Manitoba in the Agrarian Period," in *The Political Economy of Manitoba*, ed. Jim Silver and Jeremy Hull (Regina, SK: Canadian Plains Research Centre, University of Regina, 1990), 3–24.

14 *Petit historique*, 47.

15 Ibid.

16 *Petit historique*, 47; "Sister Mary of the Holy Trinity," 35.

17 Ibid.

18 Ibid.

19 Brian Noonan, "Saskatchewan Separate Schools," in *A History of Education in Saskatchewan. Selected Readings*, ed. Brian Noonan, Dianne Hallman, and Murray Scharf (Regina, SK: Canadian Plains Research Centre, University of Regina, 2006), 21–32.

20 Brian Noonan, *Saskatchewan Separate Schools*, 2nd ed. (Muenster, SK: St Peter's Press, 1998), chap. 2, 10–17.

21 *Petit historique*, 59–60.

22 Ibid., 60.

23 Ibid. For information about Métis families, see Jonathan Anuik and James Ostime, "Métis Families after 1885: A Literature Review of Existing Narratives," *Prairie Forum* no. 37 (Fall 2012), 27–56.

24 Brenda MacDougall, *One of the Family. Metis Culture in Nineteenth-Century Northwestern Saskatchewan* (Vancouver: UBC Press, 2010), chaps. 3 and 4.

25 *Petit historique*, 62.

26 Ibid., 63; Congregation of Our Lady of the Missions, Golden Jubilee, Canada, 1949, RNDM-UK A/2E/7/2/2 (i), 36–8.

27 *Petit historique*, 63.

28 Congregation of Our Lady of the Missions, Golden Jubilee, Canada, 1949, RNDM-UK A/2E/7/2/2 (i), 36–8.

29 *Petit historique*, 64.

30 Ibid., 67.

31 Anthony Appleblatt, "The School Question in the 1929 Saskatchewan Provincial Election," Canadian Catholic Historical Association, *Study Sessions* 43 (1976): 75–90; Raymond Huel, "The Anderson Amendments and the Secularization of Saskatchewan Public Schools," Canadian Catholic Historical Association, *Study Sessions* 44 (1977): 61–76; Noonan, "Saskatchewan Separate Schools," 21–32.

32 Congregation of Our Lady of the Missions, Golden Jubilee, Canada, 1949, RNDM-UK A/2E/7/2/2 (i), 36–8.

33 Ibid.

34 *Petit historique*, 115.

35 Ibid.; Journal of St Raphael (Wolseley), 1914–1935, CPSHSB, box 64, file 12.

36 *Petit historique*, 116.

37 Congregation of Our Lady of the Missions. Golden Jubilee, Canada, 1949, RNDM-UK A/2E/7/2/2 (i), 39.

38 See Gerald Friesen, *Canadian Prairies: A History* (Toronto: University of Toronto Press, 1987).

39 *Petit historique*, 121–2.

40 Ibid., 122.

41 Congregation of Our Lady of the Missions. Golden Jubilee, Canada, 1949. Archives RNDM-UK A/2E/7/2/2 (i).

42 Ibid.

43 *Petit historique*, 126.

44 Ibid.

45 *Petit historique*, 127; Sister Mary of the Holy Trinity, "Sisters of Our Lady of The Missions in Canada 1898–1923," 105, English typescript provided by Provincial Superior Veronica Dunne.

46 *Petit historique*, 128.

47 Ibid., 129.

48 Ibid., 132.

49 Ibid., 130.

50 The wise historical observations made by Caroline Bowden about seventeenth century convents are to an important extent applicable to a

semi-contemplative congregation like the RNDMs. See Caroline Bowden, "Community Space and Cultural Transmission: Formation and Schooling in English Enclosed Convents in the Seventeenth Century," *History of Education* 34, no. 4 (2005): 365–86.

51 *Petit historique*, 129–30.

52 Ibid., 133.

53 Ibid., 134.

54 Ibid., 135.

55 Joyce Goodman, "Social Change and Secondary Schooling for Girls in the 'Long 1920s': European Engagements," *History of Education* 36, nos. 4–5 (2007): 497–513.

56 Susan Smith, RNDM, *Call to Mission: The Story of the Mission Sisters of Aotearoa New Zealand and Samoa* (Auckland, NZ: David Ling Publishing, 2010), 89.

57 Regina Catholic Schools, CPSHSB, box 92, file 27.

58 In 1964, Campion was granted federation with the Regina campus of the University of Saskatchewan.

59 Congregation of Our Lady of the Missions, Golden Jubilee, Canada, 1949, RNDM-UK A/2E/7/2/2 (i), 35.

60 "The Sisters of Our Lady of the Missions in Canada 1898–1948," General Archives of the RNDM, Rome, Braveta 628, section D, shelf 5, green box, Canada 1949–1961, 45.

61 Ibid.; "Brief Historical Account of the Convent of Our Lady of the Missions, Canada, 1961, History of the Congregation," filing cabinet 5, folder Canada, RNDM General Archives, Rome.

62 Ken Osborne wrote: "The farmers' movement was similarly enthusiastic about the potential of schools, but critical of their actual practice, at times taking dead aim against the way history was commonly taught. The farmers wanted not a competitive, but a co-operative society, characterized by a good measure of equality and social justice. To achieve it, they called for a new and higher type of citizenship and a new political morality, and this, they believed, could be achieved in part through the schools." Ken Osborne, "One Hundred Years of History Teaching in Manitoba Schools. Part 1: 1897–1927," *Manitoba History* 36 (Autumn/Winter 1998–99): 3–26, quotation at 21. See also Rosa Bruno-Jofré, "Citizenship and Schooling in Manitoba, 1918–1945," *Manitoba History* 36 (Autumn/Winter 1998–99), 26–36.

63 Eckhardt Fuchs, "Educational Sciences, Morality and Politics: International Educational Congresses in the Early Twentieth Century," *Paedagogica Historica* 40, nos. 5–6 (2004): 757–8.

64 Procès-verbal du Chapitre Général, Maison Généralice des Religieuses de Notre Dame des Missions, 1919, CPSHSB, B01-08, 544/14/15.

65 Friesen, *The Canadian Prairies*, 313.
66 Danielle Juteau and Nicole Laurin, *Un métier et une vocation: Le travail des religieuses au Québec, de 1901 à 1971* (Montréal: Les Presses de l'Université Laval, 1979).
67 See Marta Danylewycs, *Taking the Veil: An Alternative to Marriage, Motherhood, and Spinsterhood in Quebec, 1840–1920* (Toronto: McClelland & Stewart, 1987).

6 The Dusty Years to the Post-War Years

  1 Anthony Appleblatt, "The School Question in the 1929 Saskatchewan Provincial Election," Canadian Catholic Historical Association, *Study Sessions* 43 (1976), 75–90. Appleblatt cites Raymond J. Huel, "L'Association Catholique Franco-Canadienne de la Saskatchewan: A Response to Cultural Assimilation 1912–1934" (master's thesis, University of Saskatchewan, Regina, 1960), 95.
  2 Raymond Huel, "The Anderson Amendments and the Secularization of Saskatchewan Public Schools," Canadian Catholic Historical Association, *Study Sessions* 44 (1977), 61–76.
  3 Appleblatt, "The School Question," 75–90.
  4 Ibid.
  5 Ibid.
  6 "The Sisters of Our Lady of the Missions in Canada 1898–1948," chapter 4. Section D, Shelf 5, RNDM General Archives, Rome.
  7 Brian Noonan, *Saskatchewan Separate Schools*, 2nd ed. (Muenster, SK: St Peter's Press, 1998), 28; Appleblatt, "The School Question," 75–90.
  8 "The Sisters of Our Lady of the Missions in Canada."
  9 Veronica Dunne, "Canada 1898–2011," in *Zeal for Mission: The Story of the Sisters of Our Lady of the Missions 1861–2011*, ed. Susan Smith (Auckland, NZ: David Ling Publishing, 2012), 233–54.
 10 Ruth Sandwell, *Canada's Rural Majority: Households, Environments, and Economies, 1870–1940* (Toronto: University of Toronto Press, 2016), 135–6.
 11 Ibid.
 12 "The Sisters of Our Lady of the Missions in Canada."
 13 S. H. A. & C. Alumnae Association, documents signed by E.M. Drake and Marie A. Malone, CPSHSB, box 103/ file 7.
 14 Congregation of Our Lady of the Missions, Golden Jubilee, Canada, RNDM-UK A/2E/7/2/2 (i), 41; Smith, *Zeal for Mission*, 41.
 15 Congregation of Our Lady of the Missions, Golden Jubilee, Canada, 1949, RNDM-UK A/2E/7/2/2 (i), 41.
 16 Ibid.
 17 "The Sisters of Our Lady of the Missions in Canada."

18 "Our Holiday in the Mission Field," *The Message of Notre-Dame des Missions* 6, no. 1 (1933): 14–16, quotation at 14, RNDM-UK– A/9M/1/21.
19 Ibid.
20 "Summer Vacation Schools in Saskatchewan and Manitoba (Canada)," *The Message of Notre-Dame des Missions* 8, no. 1 (1935): 15–16.
21 "The Sisters of Our Lady of the Missions in Canada."
22 "The Sisters of Our Lady of the Missions in Canada," 45; "Brief Historical Account of the Convents of Our Lady of the Missions, Canada, 1961," typed pages provided by Veronica Dunne, RNDM.
23 "The Sisters of Our Lady of the Missions in Canada."
24 Mother Mary St Basil, superior general, Procès-verbal of the Council of the General Administration, Hastings, 20 November 1945, CPSHSB, box 10, file 14.
25 See Marie St Remi, secretary, to Rev. Mother Provincial, Sacred Heart Province, Canada, Hastings, 8 December 1937, CPSHSB, box 10, file 14.
26 Livre historique du Monastère de Ste-Marthe, Elie, Manitoba, Canada, January 1942, CPSHSB, box 13, file 02.
27 "Sixty Years at Saint Michael's, Clarion 1959," Golden Jubilee, Canada 1949–1961, General Archives of the RNDM, Rome, section D, shelf 5, green box, braveta 628.
28 Mother Mary St Basil, superior general, Procès-verbal of the Council of the General Administration, Hastings, 20 November 1945, CPSHSB, box 10, file 14.
29 Smith, *Zeal for Mission*, 389–95. In practice, auxiliary sisters could become choir sisters in light of pressing needs in the field. This, for example, was the case of Marie de l'Eucharistie, who came to the first mission in Canada in Grande Clairière, Manitoba; in 1907, she became the local superior in Regina. She was sent to India as vicar-provincial in 1920 and to Vietnam as vice-provincial in 1924.
30 Peter Berger and Thomas Luckman, *The Social Construction of Reality: A Treatise in the Sociology of Knowledge* (Garden City, NY: Anchor Books, 1966).
31 Pope Pius XII, allocution, "Le premier congrès general des états de perfection," Rome, 8 December 1950.
32 *Rapport de la visite canonique des religieuses de langue française de l'archidiocèse de Winnipeg, Manitoba 1954*, CPSHSB, box 28, file 27, 9.
33 Heidi MacDonald, "Smaller Numbers, Stronger Voices: Women Religious Reposition Themselves through the Canadian Religious Conference, 1960s–80s," in Rosa Bruno-Jofré, Heidi MacDonald, and Elizabeth M. Smyth, *Vatican II and Beyond: The Changing Mission and Identity of Canadian Women Religious* (Montreal: McGill-Queen's University Press, 2017), 17–54.
34 Rosa Bruno-Jofré, "Schooling and the Struggles to Develop a Common Polity, 1919–1971," in *Papers on Contemporary Issues in Education Policy and*

Administration in Canada: A Foundations Perspective, Monographs in Education 23, ed. Rosa Bruno-Jofré and Lois Grieger (Winnipeg: University of Manitoba, 1996), 71–108.

35 Rosa Bruno-Jofré and Josh Cole, "To Serve and Yet Be Free: Historical Configurations and the Insertions of Faculties of Education in Ontario," in *Teacher Education in a Transnational World*, ed. Rosa Bruno-Jofré and James Scott Johnston (Toronto: University of Toronto Press, 2014), 71–95.

36 Hugh Stevenson, "Developing Public Education in Post-War Canada to 1960," in *Canadian Education: A History*, ed. J.D. Wilson, R.M. Stamp, and L.P. Audet (Scarborough, ON: Prentice-Hall, 1970), 386–415.

37 Mary Dominique Savio, superior general, Saskatoon, Hastings, "Brief Historical Account of the Convents of Our Lady of the Missions, Canada, 1961," RNDM-UK-A/2E/7/2/3 (iii), 10.

38 "Brief Historical Account of the Convents of Our Lady of the Missions, Canada, 1961," history of the congregation, typed version, General Archive of the RNDM, Rome, braveta 628, filing cabinet 5, folder Canada.

39 Ibid.

40 See Joe Stafford, "Catholic Secondary Religious Education, Learning from the Past" (paper presented at the Canadian History of Education Association, 30 October 2016, Waterloo, Ontario). The notion of language of education is taken from Daniel Trohler, *Languages of Education: Protestant Legacies, National Identities, and Global Aspirations* (New York: Routledge, 2011).

41 Pope Pius XI, *Divini Illius Magistri*, Encyclical on Christian Education (Vatican: The Holy See, 31 December 1929), http://w2.vatican.va/content/pius-xi/en/encyclicals/documents/hf_p-xi_enc_31121929_divini-illius-magistri.html.

42 Clarence E. Elwell, *Toward the Eternal Commencement*, Our Quest for Happiness 4 (Chicago: Mentzer, Bush, 1958).

43 See "Les Religieuses de Notre Dame des Missions à Letellier," CPSHSB, box 7, file 7.

44 Patrick J. O'Sullivan, *By Steps, Not Leaps: St Augustine of Canterbury Parish, Brandon, Manitoba, 1881–1981* (Brandon, MB: privately published, 1981), 158.

45 Editorial, *Stella Oriens*, 1942 Yearbook, Sacred Heart College, Saskatchewan, CPSHSB, box 99, file 13.

46 Sister Diane Bélisle, RNDM, interviewed by Sister Dora Tétrèault, MO, at Villa Aulneau, St Boniface, Manitoba, on 20 July 2011, when Sister Diane was seventy-five years old. The recorded tape is the property of the congregation. Author discussed the questions with Sister Dora Tétrèault.

47 Sister Hilda Lang, RNDM, St Boniface, Manitoba, circa 2011. The recorded tape is the property of the congregation. Author discussed the questions

with Sister Dora Tétrèault and Provincial Veronica Dunne, but data are missing.
48 Sister Cécile Granger, RNDM, interviewed by Sister Dora Tétrèault, MO, at Despins Residence, St Boniface, Manitoba, on 14 July 2011, when Sister Cécile was ninety years old. The recorded tape is the property of the congregation. Author discussed the questions with Sister Dora Tétrèault.
49 Anonymous testimony included in the collection of interviews and testimonies provided by Provincial Veronica Dunne in 2013.
50 Sister Cécile Granger, RNDM, interviewed by Sister Dora Tétrèault, MO, at Despins Residence, 2011.
51 *Rapport de la visite canonique des religieuses de langue française de l'archidiocese de Winnipeg, Manitoba, November 1954*, requested by Mgr Philip Francis Pocock, JCD, archbishop of Winnipeg, CPSHSB, box 28, file 27.

7 The Church and the Classroom before Vatican II

1 *Petit historique de nos premières fondations au Canada 1898–1923* (Lyon, FR: Institut de Notre-Dame des Missions, Maison de Recrutement pour les Missions, 1926), 124.
2 Ibid., 124–5.
3 Ibid.
4 Ibid., 132.
5 Sister Veronica Dunne, RNDM, provincial superior, interviewed by Sister Dora Tétrèalt, MO, December 2011, provided by the RNDM sisters.
6 Historical Notes, 1993, CPSHSB, box 126, file 8.
7 *Petit historique.*
8 Ibid., 162.
9 *The Message of Notre Dame des Missions* (October 1950): 4, RNDM UK A/9M.
10 "The Enthronement of the Sacred Heart," *The Message of Our Lady of the Missions* (October 1958): 16–18, RNDM UK A/9M.
11 Livre historique, Virgo Fidelis Convent, journal of the Convent, 7 January 1932, CPSHSB, box 63, file 9.
12 "Convent of Letellier," Council for the month of October, 8 November 1942, CPSHSB, box 64, file 1.
13 "Convent of Letellier," Council for the month of December 1945 held in December, CPSHSB, box 64, file 2.
14 "Convent of Letellier," Council for the month of January 1946, CPSHSB, box 64, file 2.
15 "The Sisters of Our Lady of the Missions in Canada 1898–1948," chapter iv, RNDM General Archives, Rome Section D, Shelf 5.
16 Congregation of Our Lady of the Missions, pamphlet, 1946, RNDM-UK A/2E/7/3/12.

17 "The Congregation of Our Lady of the Missions," booklet, RNDM-UK A/2E/7/3/13.

18 Anne Chapman and Tom O'Donoghue, "An Analysis of Recruitment Literature Used by Orders of Catholic Religious Teaching Brothers in Australia, 1930 to 1960: A Social Semiotic Analysis," *Paedagogica Historica* 49, no. 4 (2013): 592–606. Chapman and O'Donoghue conduct a thorough analysis of the use of recruitment agents and of the recruitment literature used in the English-speaking world by the De La Salle brothers, the Marist brothers, and the Irish Christian brothers.

19 Sister Hilda Lang, RNDM; information provided by the congregation on October 2011. She started teaching in the congregation in 1959. No other information was provided.

20 Sister Aileen Gleason, RNDM, interviewed by Sister Dora Tétrèault, 1 September 2011, St Boniface, Manitoba. Sister Gleason was eighty-seven at the time (she was born in Watson, Saskatchewan, in 1924). The recorded tape is the property of the congregation.

21 Sister Sheila Madden, RNDM, interviewed by Sister Dora Tétrèault, MO, 18 August 2011, St Boniface, Manitoba.

8 The 1960s

1 Arthur Marwick, *The Sixties: Cultural Revolution in Britain, France, Italy, and the United States, c. 1958–1974* (Oxford: Oxford University Press, 1998).

2 Rosa Bruno-Jofré and Josh Cole, "'What the Dead Say to the Living': Time, Politics, and Teacher Preparation in English Canada's Long 1960s," in *Päadagogik und Pädagogisches Wissen / Pedagogy and Educational Knowledge*, ed. Andreas Hoffmann-Ocon and Rebekka Horlacher (Bad Heilbrunn, DE: Julius Klinkhardt, 2016), 247–64.

3 Josh Cole and Ian McKay, "Commanding Heights, Levers of Power: A Reconnaissance of Post-War Education Reform," *Encounters in Theory and History of Education* 15 (November 2014): 23–41.

4 Ibid., quotation at 26.

5 Anne Rohstock and Daniel Tröhler, "From the Sacred Nation to the Unified Globe: Changing Leitmotifs in Teacher Training in the Western World, 1870–2010," in *Teacher Education in a Transnational World*, ed. Rosa Bruno-Jofré and James Scott Johnston (Toronto: University of Toronto Press, 2014), 111–31.

6 See, for example, Kenneth Stampp, *The Peculiar Institution: Slavery in the Ante-Bellum South* (New York: Alfred A. Knopf, 1956).

7 J.R. Miller, *Shingwauk's Vision: A History of Native Residential Schools* (Toronto: University of Toronto Press, 1997).

8 Brian Noonan, *Saskatchewan Separate Schools*, 2nd ed. (Muenster, SK: St Peter's Press, 1998).

9 Theodore W. Schultz, "Investment in Human Capital," *American Economic Review* 51, no. 1 (1961): 1–17.

10 Veronica Dunne, RNDM, typed version of a draft written for a congregational story, 5 December 2009, provided by the author.

11 Sacred Heart Academy, List of Teachers, 1966, CPSHSB, box 92, file 5.

12 Letter to Parents and Guardians, Regina Separate Schools, Graton R.C.S.S.D. No. 13 and Regina R.C.S. H.S.D. informing them of the closing of Sacred Heart Academy, CPSHSB, box 92, file 22.

13 J.P. Deis, secretary-treasurer, Graton R.C.S.S.D. No. 13 to Sister Mary Ignatius, superior, Sacred Heart Academy, 15 June 1967. In this letter and the response, the school board and the sisters are discussing the ending of the contract with the board. Letter to Parents and Guardians, Regina Separate Schools, Graton R.C.S.S.D. No. 13 and Regina R.C.S.H.S.D. informing them of the closing of the Sacred Heart Academy, CPSHSB, box 92, file 22.

14 Letter to Parents and Guardians, Regina Separate Schools, Graton R.C.S.S.D. No. 13 and Regina R.C.S. H.S.D. informing them of the closing of Sacred Heart Academy, CPSHSB, box 92, file 22.

15 Sister Sheila Madden, RNDM, interviewed by Sister Dora Tétrèault, MO, 11 August 2011, St Boniface, Winnipeg, Manitoba.

16 Marcel Martel, *French Canada: An Account of its Creation and Break-up, 1850–1967*, Canada's Ethnic Groups 24 (Ottawa: The Canadian Historical Association, 1998).

17 Jean-Marie Taillefer, "Les franco-manitobains et l'education 1870–1970: Une étude quantitative" (PhD diss., University of Manitoba, 1988), 375.

18 Ibid., 377.

19 Ibid.

20 See Carolyn I. Ainslie Lintott, "School Division Consolidation in Manitoba," in *Papers on Contemporary Issues in Education Policy and Administration in Canada: A Foundations Perspective*, Monographs in Education 23, ed. Lois Greiger and Rosa Bruno Jofré (Winnipeg: University of Manitoba, 1996), 155–200. See also Benjamin Levin, "The Struggle Over Modernization in Manitoba Education: 1924–1960," in *Issues in the History of Education in Manitoba: From the Construction of the Common School to the Politics of Voices*, ed. Rosa Bruno-Jofré (Lewiston, NY: Edwin Mellen Press, 1993), 73–96.

21 Journal, Virgo Fidelis Convent, Letellier, February and March 1959, CPSHSB, box 63, file 10.

22 Journal, Virgo Fidelis Convent, Letellier, September 1960 and June 1961, CPSHSB, box 63, file 3.

23 Mrs A. Delveaux, secretary-treasurer, School District Ste Rose du Lac, Manitoba, 30 April 1958 to Rev. Mother St Genevieve, Inst. Notre Dame des Missions, Winnipeg, Manitoba, CBSHSB, box 30, file 28. In this box there are several letters between the provincial superior and Mrs A. Delveaux.

24 "Manuscript with Memories," Sister Bérénice, CPSHSB, box 60, file 3.

25 Joe Stafford, "The Implementation of Strict Neo-Thomism in the Catholic High Schools of the Archdiocese of Toronto," *Historical Studies, Journal of the Canadian Catholic Historical Association* 83 (2017): 47–66.

26 Five truths were declared in the oath: God's existence can only be known by the light of divine reason; the miracles and prophecies were proof of the divine origin of Christianity; the dogmas constituted "the divine deposit of the faith"; faith was not connected to any sentiment of the heart but to a truth received from an external source. Stafford, "Strict Neo-Thomism," 51.

27 Pope Pius XI, *Divini Illius Magistri*, Encyclical on Christian Education (Vatican: The Holy See, 31 December 1929), http://w2.vatican.va/content/pius-xi/en/encyclicals/documents/hf_p-xi_enc_31121929_divini-illius-magistri.html.

28 "Views with Regard to the Separate School Question as Set Down by the Sisters of Our Lady of the Missions," 22 March 1964, CPSHSB, box 54, file 7.

29 Peter Berger and Thomas Luckmann, *The Social Construction of Reality: A Treatise on the Sociology of Knowledge* (Garden City, NY: Anchor Books, 1966).

9 The Setting That Framed the Reception of Vatican II

1 This attitude was supported by the Second Vatican Council, "Pastoral Constitution of the Church in the Modern World (*Gaudium et Spes*)," in *The Documents of Vatican II*, ed. Walter M. Abbott, SJ, trans. Msgr Joseph Gallagher (New York: America Press, 1966), 199–308. See also Daniel T. Rodgers, *Age of Fracture* (Cambridge, MA: Harvard University Press, 2011), 146; R. Tong, *Feminist Thought: A Comprehensive Introduction* (Boulder, CO: Westview Press, 1989); H. R. Ebaugh, "The Growth and Decline of Catholic Religious Orders of Women Worldwide: The Impact of Women's Opportunity Structures," *Journal for the Scientific Study of Religion* 32, no. 1 (1993): 68–75; Sue Morgan, ed., *The Feminist Reader* (London: Routledge, 2006).

2 John W. O'Malley, *What Happened at Vatican II* (Cambridge, MA: Harvard University Press, 2008), 291.

3 Gregory Baum, "Vatican Council II: A Turning Point in the Church's History," in *Vatican II: Canadian Experiences*, ed. Michael Attridge, Catherine Clifford, and Gilles Routhier (Ottawa: University of Ottawa Press, 2011).

4 Jerrold Seigle, *The Idea of the Self: Thought and Experience in Western Europe since the Seventeenth Century* (Cambridge: Cambridge University Press, 2005), chap. 1.

5 Marie Bénédicte Ollivier, RNDM, *Missionary Beyond Boundaries: Euphrasie Barbier, 1829–1893* (Rome: Istituto Salesiano Pio XI, 2007), 231–50.

6 Susan Smith, *Zeal for Mission: The Story of the Sisters of Our Lady of the Missions, 1861–2011* (Auckland, NZ: David Ling Publishing, 2012), 17.

7 Second Vatican Council, "Dogmatic Constitution on the Church (*Lumen Gentium*)," in *The Documents of Vatican II*, ed. Walter M. Abbott, SJ, trans. Msgr Joseph Gallagher (New York: America Press, 1966), 14–101.

8 Second Vatican Council, "Decree on the Appropriate Renewal of Religious Life (*Perfectae Caritatis*)," in *The Documents of Vatican II*, ed. Walter M. Abbott, SJ, trans. Msgr Joseph Gallagher (New York: America Press, 1966), 466–82.

9 Second Vatican Council, "Pastoral Constitution on the Church in the Modern World (*Gaudium et Spes*)," 199–309.

10 Paul VI, Apostolic Letter, *Ecclesiae Sanctae*, 6 August 1966, https://w2. vatican.va/content/paul-vi/en/motu_proprio/documents/hf_p-vi_ motu-proprio_19660806_ecclesiae-sanctae.html.

11 Pierre Bourdieu, *Language and Symbolic Power*, ed. John B. Thompson, trans. Gino Raymond and Matthew Adamson (Cambridge, MA: Harvard University Press, 1991).

12 Pierre Bourdieu defined habitus as "[a] system of lasting, transposable dispositions which, integrating past experiences, functions at every moment as a matrix of perceptions, appreciations, and actions and makes possible the achievement of infinitely diversified tasks, thanks to analogical transfers of schemes permitting the solution of similarly shaped problems." Pierre Bourdieu, *Outline of a Theory of Practice* (Cambridge: University Press, 1977), 82.

13 Superior General Mary Dominic Savio, Hastings, Sussex, England, in a letter to Our Dear Reverend Mothers and Sisters – Canadian Province, Hastings, Sussex, England, 1 May 1966, CPSHSB, box 14, file 17.

14 Ibid.

15 Ibid.

16 Ibid.

17 Ibid.

18 Ibid.

19 Superior General Mary Dominic Savio, Hastings, Sussex, England, in a circular letter to sister delegates to the General Chapter, July 1966, dated 1 May 1966, CPSHSB, RNDM documents, box 14, file 17.

20 Excerpt from the speech of His Eminence Cardinal Antoniutti to the Mothers General, 5 December 1965, attached to Superior General Mary Dominic

Savio's circular letter to Sister Delegates to the General Chapter, July 1966, dated 1 May 1966, CPSHSB, RNDM documents, box 14, file 17.

21 Ibid.

22 Ibid.

23 Ibid.

24 Ibid.

25 Ibid.

26 Ibid.

27 Sister Jeanne Roche, provincial superior, Canada, to Very Reverend Mother (superior general), 29 May 1966, CPSHSB, box 14, file 17. The letter does not have a signature.

28 Ibid.

29 Ibid.

30 Wenceslaus Sebastian, OFM, vicar delegate for religious, canonical visitation of the Sisters of Our Lady of the Missions, Regina, 29 June 1960, CPSHSB, box 28, file 35.

31 Sister Jeanne Roche, provincial superior, Canada, to Very Reverend Mother (superior general), 29 May 1966, CPSHSB, box 14, file 17. The letter does not have a signature.

32 Ibid.

33 Ibid.

34 Ibid.

35 Ibid.

36 Ibid.

37 Ibid.

38 Statuts du Chapitre General 1966, Congregation of Notre Dame des Missions, 1966, CPSHSB, RNDM documents, box 14, file 18.

39 Ibid.

40 Ibid.

41 Second Vatican Council, "Declaration on Christian Education (*Gravissimum Educationis*)," in *The Documents of Vatican II*, ed. Walter M. Abbott, SJ, trans. Msgr Joseph Gallagher (New York: America Press, 1966), 637–52.

42 Joe Stafford, "The Conditions for the Declaration on Christian Education: Secularization and the Educational State of Ontario," in *Catholic Education in the Wake of Vatican II*, ed. Rosa Bruno-Jofré and Jon Igelmo Zaldívar (Toronto: University of Toronto Press, 2017).

43 Statuts du Chapitre General 1966, Congregation of Notre Dame des Missions, 1966, CPSHSB, RNDM documents, box 14, file 18.

44 George. B. Flahiff, archbishop of Winnipeg, in a letter to Mother Marie Jean d'Ávila, provincial superior of the Congregation of Our Lady of the Missions, 5 July 1966, CPSHSB, box 30, file 15.

45 Mary Gertrude, BS, superior general, Convent of Our Lady of the Missions, Hastings, 25 April 1967. Copy provided by the archivist, Rome.

46 Superior General Mary Gertrude, BS, Dear Mothers and Sisters, The Mother House of Our Lady of the Missions, Old London Road, Hastings, 30 October 1966. Extra copy provided by the archivist in Rome, braveta 628.

47 Ibid.

48 Sacra Congregazione per i Religiosi e gli Instituti Secolari, Statement, April 1968, General Archives of the RNDM, Rome, section H, shelf 2, box 7.

49 Ibid.

50 Ibid.

51 Ibid.

52 Mother Mary Gertrude, superior general, to Our Dear Sister Superiors in Retreat, Via dei Laghi, 15, Castel Gandolfo, Rome, 9 April 1968, General Archives of the RNDM, Rome, section H, shelf 2, box 7.

53 Second Vatican Council, *The Documents of Vatican II*, 466–82.

54 Sister Cécile Granger, RNDM, interviewed by Sister Dora Tetreault at Despins Residence, St Boniface, Manitoba, 14 July 2011. The recorded tape is the property of the congregation. Later Claire Himbeault (provincial superior from 1971 to 1977) became qualified to offer the same courses and workshops.

55 *André Rochais: Founder of PRH, Fondation Personnalité et Relations Humaines*, special edition of PRH-France's 1991 Newsletter (Winnipeg, MN: D.W. Friesen, 1994).

56 Sisters of Our Lady of the Missions, Leadership Discussion, August 2012, group conversation organized by provincial superior of the Canadian province, Sister Veronica Dunne, Winnipeg, Manitoba, tape and transcription provided by Sister Veronica Dunne.

57 Heidi MacDonald, "Smaller Numbers, Stronger Voices: Women Religious Reposition Themselves through the Canadian Religious Conference," in Rosa Bruno-Jofré, Heidi MacDonald, and Elizabeth M. Smyth, *Vatican II and Beyond: The Changing Mission and Identity of Canadian Women Religious* (Montreal: McGill-Queen's University Press, 2017), 18.

58 Sisters of Our Lady of the Missions, Leadership Discussion, August 2012, group conversation organized by provincial superior of the Canadian province, Sister Veronica Dunne, Winnipeg, Manitoba, tape and transcription provided by Sister Veronica Dunne.

59 Callum G. Brown, "What Was the Religious Crisis of the 1960s?" *Journal of Religious History* 34, no. 4 (2010): 468–79.

60 Adrian Hasting, *A History of English Christianity 1920–1985* (London: Collins, 1986). Brown calls attention to Hasting's approach and points out that there was a growing alienation of the people from Christianity,

particularly the young, a separation of church and popular culture, and a
surge of the remnant Christian culture towards evangelism and fundamen-
talism. Brown, "What Was the Religious Crisis," 479.

61 Brown, "What Was the Religious Crisis," 479.

62 Peter Berger, *The Many Altars of Modernity: Toward a Paradigm for Religion
in a Pluralist Age* (Boston/Berlin: De Gruyter, 2014), ix.

63 Ibid.

64 Rosa Bruno-Jofré and Ana Jofré, "Reading the Lived Experience of Vatican II – Words and Images: The Canadian Province of the Sisters of Our
Lady of Missions in Peru," *CCHA Historical Studies* 81 (2015): 31–51.

65 Mary Gertrude, BS, superior general, to Dear Mothers and Sisters, Castel
Gandolfo, Rome, 2 August 1968, General Archives of the RNDM, Rome,
section H, shelf 3.

66 Ibid.

67 Mary Gertrude, BS, superior general, to Very Dear Mothers and Sisters,
Castel Gandolfo, Rome, 17 March 1968, General Archives of the RNDM,
Rome, section H, shelf 3.

68 "Silence," *The Small Candle* 1, no. 2 (1967): 4, RNDM-UK, A/2E/7/1/1.

69 Sr M. Loretto Warnke, "We, as Religious, Have Renounced the World,"
The Small Candle 1, no. 2 (1967): 5, RNDM-UK, A/2E/7/1/1.

70 M. Bernard Gropp, RNDM, "To Have or Not to Have," *The Small Candle* 1,
no. 2 (1967): 8, RNDM-UK A/2E/7/1/1.

71 Ibid.

72 Ibid.

73 M. Zita Bolingbroke, RNDM, "To Light a Candle," *The Small Candle* 1, no.
2 (1967): 19, RNDM-UK A/2E/7/1/1.

74 Ibid., 16.

75 Ibid., 17.

76 Ibid., 18.

77 Mary Gerald, RNDM, "We're Growing!" *The Small Candle* 2, no. 2 (1968):
7, RNDM-UK A/2E/7/1/2.

78 Provincial Superior Marie Emilia (Cécile Campeau), Winnipeg, MB, to
Dear Sisters, 19 February 1969, CPSHSB, RNDM documents, box 29,
file 11.

79 Ibid.

80 Provincial Superior Marie Emilia (Cécile Campeau), Winnipeg, MB, to
Dear Sisters, 24 April 1969, CPSHSB, RNDM documents, box 29, file 11.

81 Provincial Superior Marie Emilia (Cécile Campeau), Winnipeg, MB, to
Dear Sisters, 23 May 1969, CPSHSB, RNDM documents, box 29, file 11.

82 Provincial Superior Marie Emilia (Cécile Campeau), Winnipeg, MB, to
Dear Sisters, 10 February 1970, CPSHSB, RNDM documents, box 29,
file 11.

83 The quotation in the letter from the statutes of the Chapter – quoted in its entirety by the provincial superior – somewhat differs from the typed manuscript of the procès-verbal of the Chapter preserved by the congregation. The letter says: "Sisters in the Canadian Province wear the basic habit of the Congregation, and permission has been granted for the variations demonstrated at the General Chapter to be experimented with in blue, beige or black." Provincial Superior Marie Emilia (Cécile Campeau), Winnipeg, MB, to Dear Sisters, 10 February 1970, CPSHSB, RNDM documents, box 29, file 11.

84 Procès-verbal of the Provincial Chapter of the Province of the Sacred Hearts of Jesus and Mary, Canada, 29 December 1969, 12–13, copy provided by Sister Veronica Dunne.

85 Provincial Superior Marie Emilia (Cécile Campeau), Winnipeg, MB, to Dear Sisters, 10 February 1970, CPSHSB, RNDM documents, box 29, file 11.

86 Ibid.

87 Ibid.

88 Ibid.

89 Ibid.

90 Ibid.

91 Rosa Bruno-Jofré, "The Canadian Province of the Religieuses de Notre Dame des Missions: The Horizon of Reference and Reception of Vatican II: Moving toward a New Constellation of Meanings," in *Understanding the Consecrated Life in Canada: Critical Essays on Contemporary Trends*, ed. Jason Zuidema (Waterloo, ON: Wilfrid Laurier University Press, 2015), 125–42.

92 Address of Reverend Mother Mary Gertrude, superior general, to the delegates to the Special General Chapter, 19 July 1969, CPSHSB, RNDM documents, box 14, file 22.

93 Ibid.

94 Ibid. The superior cites Womanly Fulfilment – Donum Dei 1962.

95 Ibid.

96 Ibid.

97 Christian Smith, *The Emergence of Liberation Theology: Radical Religion and Social Movement Theory* (Chicago: University of Chicago Press, 1991), 39.

98 Jean Vanier School, CPSHSB, RNDM documents, box 92, file 24.

99 Experimentation with a Budget – 1969–1970, CPSHSB, RNDM documents, box 31, file 14.

100 Ibid.

101 Special General Chapter 1969, General Archives of the RNDM, Rome, section H, shelf 2, box 7.

102 Document in preparation for 1969 Chapter, 2–4 January 1968, CPSHSB, RNDM documents, box 14, file 23.

103 Minutes of Experimentation Commission Meeting, Provincial House, Winnipeg, MB, 18 April 1971, CPSHSB, box 31, file 14.

104 Procès-verbal of the General Administration, Rome, held 6–7 February 1969, General Council, Peru, General Archives of the RNDM, Rome, section H, shelf 3, box 6.

105 Rosa Bruno-Jofré, "The Sisters of Our Lady of the Missions in Canada, the Long 1960s, and Vatican II: From Carving Spaces in the Educational State to Living the Radicality of the Gospel," in *Catholic Education in the Wake of Vatican II*, ed. Rosa Bruno-Jofré and Jon Igelmo Zaldívar (Toronto: University of Toronto Press, 2017), 189–212.

106 Patricia Wittberg, *The Rise and Decline of Catholic Religious Orders: A Social Movement Perspective* (Albany, NY: SUNY Press, 1994).

107 Procès-verbal of the Provincial Chapter of the Province of the Sacred Hearts of Jesus and Mary, Canada, Sacred Heart College, Regina, Saskatchewan, 29 December 1969, 11, all provinces 1964–1969, General Archives of the RNDM, Rome, section G, shelf 2.

108 Zygmunt Bauman, *Liquid Modernity* (Cambridge, UK: Polity Press, 2012), 31.

109 Ibid., quotation at 31.

110 Experimentation with a Budget, CPSHSB, box 31, file 14.

111 The religious community was a central theme for the overall International Congregation, and each province mailed a questionnaire to explore the theme. It was designed and analysed by Graham M.S. Dann, Department of Sociology, University of Surrey, England. The archive has kept the 1974 Canadian report, which was based on eighty interviews conducted in the Canadian Province of the Congregation of Our Lady of the Missions during the summer of 1974 and compiled by the researchers in 1975. General Archives of the RNDM, Rome, Canadian Provincial Administration, section G, shelf 9, orange box.

112 Minutes of the Meeting of the Experimental Commission held at St Michael's Academy, Brandon, Manitoba, 17 January 1971, CPSHSB, RNDM documents, box 31, file 14.

113 Analysis of Experimentation, Canadian Province, from Minutes of Experimentation Commission Meeting, St Michael's Academy, Brandon, Manitoba, 3 October 1971, CPSHSB, box 31, file 14, 1.

114 Ibid., 2.

115 Analysis of Experimentation, Provincial File, Canadian Province, signed by Aileen Gleason, no date, CPSHSB, RNDM documents, box 31, file 14.

116 Sisters of Our Lady of the Missions, Leadership Discussion, taped by Veronica Dunne, RNDM, appendix, 277.

117 Congregation of Our Lady of the Missions, Constitutions, 8 December 1978, Sacra Congreatio Pro Religiosis et Institutis Saecularibus, Rome.

118 Mary of the Heart of Jesus, superior general of Our Lady of the Missions, 31 March 1869, "Notes on the Beginning of the Congregation of Our Lady of the Missions, Its Development, Its Present State and Its Special Aim," Translation of the Writings of Mother Mary of the Heart of Jesus, vol. 2, 1869, letter 261, General Archives of the RNDM, Rome, letters, section A, shelf 6.

119 Congregation of Our Lady of the Missions, Constitutions, 8 December 1978, Sacra Congregatio Pro Religiosis et Institutis Saecularibus, Rome.

120 M. Bénédicte Ollivier, superior general, Closing Speech, 11 December 1972, in Congregation of Our Lady of the Missions, Acts of the Twentieth General Chapter, Recreated in Hope, Rome, September–October 1972, General Archives of the RNDM, Rome, section H, shelf 3, blue box.

121 Congregation of Our Lady of the Missions, Acts of the Twentieth General Chapter, Recreated in Hope, Rome, September–October 1972, General Archives of the RNDM, Rome, section H, shelf 3, blue box.

122 Marie Bénédicte Ollivier, RNDM, Report of the Visit to the Canadian Province, Regina, Saskatchewan, 26 May 1973, CPSHSB, box 13, file 9.

123 Ibid.

124 Report of the Core Group to the Meeting of the Enlarged General Council, Study on Foundress, 1975, CPSHSB, box 17, file 8. See also Sister Marie Bénédicte Ollivier, RNDM, Spirituality of the Sisters of Our Lady of the Missions, Rome, 10 June 1978, CPSHSB, box 12, file 10.

125 General Chapter, Report from the Canadian Province on "Why Our Provincial Chapter Arrived at the Key Problem for the Province" as stated in Our Document, 19 July 1978, CPSHSB, box 16, file 1.

126 Ibid., 2.

127 Ibid.

128 Ibid.

129 Ibid., 3.

130 M. Bénédicte Ollivier, superior general, Congregation of Our Lady of the Missions, Rome, 13 October 1977, CPSHSB, box 12, file 10.

131 Father J. Beyer, SJ, First Session, July 1978, CPSHSB, box 16, file 1.

132 Imelda Grimes, provincial superior of the Canadian provinces, to Dear Sisters, Bangalore, India, Holy Saturday 1982, CPSHSB, box 17, file 12.

133 Ibid.

134 M. Bénédicte Ollivier, Letter of Convocation of the 1984 General Chapter, 3 May 1983, Marino, Italy, CPSHSB, box 16, file 7.

135 "Witnessing to the Gospel: Beyond All Frontiers," Twenty-Second General Chapter of the Congregation, B01–08, CPSHSB, box 16, file 12, 3.

136 Ibid., 9.

137 Ibid., 11.

138 Provincial Chapter 1984–1986, Canada, copy of the resolutions provided by Superior Veronica Dunne.

139 Claire Himbeault, superior general and Moira Ross, assistant, Reflections of the Visitation of the Canadian Province, September–November 1989, CPSHSB, box 12, file 14.

140 Ibid.

141 Renewal of Life and Mission in the Spirit of Our Constitutions, Provincial Assembly of the Canadian Province, Brandon, Manitoba, 7–9 October 1989, CPSHSB, box 37, file 13. At the provincial Pre-Chapter assembly, Claire Himbeault stated that, after ninety years and much research, the new constitutions of 1978 contained the full expression of the charism as "divine missions." The General Chapter of 1984 had set a new commitment and a new direction: "to live the preferential option for the poor and promote peace for the sake of the kingdom." Congregation of Our Lady of the Missions, Canada, Pre-Chapter Assembly and Provincial Chapter Renewal of Life and Mission in the Spirit of Our Constitutions, Brandon, Manitoba, 7–9 October 1989, RNDM-UK, A/5c/9/1.

142 Renewal of Life and Mission in The Spirit of Our Constitutions, Provincial Assembly of the Canadian Province, Brandon, Manitoba, 7–9 October 1989, CPSHSB, box 37, file 13.

143 Claire Himbeault, superior general, to Dear Sisters, Rome, 15 July 1990, General Chapter 1990, Vision Statement, CPSHSB, RNDM for Mission, box 16, file 21.

144 General Chapter 1990, RNDM for Mission, Facilitation for Mission, CPSHSB, box 16, file 19.

145 General Chapter 1990, Vision Statement, RNDM for Mission, CPSHSB, box 16, file 21.

146 Ibid.

147 There are no documents discussing this influence except for some references. However, in conversations with the sisters, the theme emerged quickly, and they showed great familiarity with feminist thea/o/*logy. See Rosemary Radford Ruether, *Religion and Sexism in Jewish and Christian Traditions* (New York: Simon and Schuster, 1974); Rosemary Radford Ruether, *Sexism and God-Talk: Toward a Feminist Theology* (Boston: Beacon Press, 1985); Mary Daly, *Beyond God the Father: Toward a Philosophy of Women's Liberation* (Boston: Beacon Press, 1973); Mary Daly, *The Church and the Second Sex* (New York: Harper and Row, 1968); Elisabeth Schüssler Fiorenza, *In Memory of Her: A Feminist Reconstruction of Christian Origins* (New York: Crossroad, 1987); Elisabeth Schüssler Fiorenza, "Breaking the Silence – Becoming Invisible," in *Women: Invisible in Church and Theology*, ed. Elisabeth Schüssler and Mary Coolins (Edinburgh: T.T. Clark, 1985);

Elizabeth Johnson, *Consider Jesus: Waves of Renewal in Christology* (New York: Crossroad, 1990); Sandra Schneiders, *Women and the Word* (New York: Paulist Press, 1986).

148 Report to the delegates of the 1990 General Chapter, CPSHSB, box 16, file 14.

149 Ibid., 17.

10 Resignifying Vision and Mission

1 RNDM, 24th General Gathering, Rome, 26 May–15 June 1996, CPSHSB, box 17, file 2.

2 Ibid., 5.

3 Ibid., 7.

4 Ibid., 8.

5 Canadian Province, "Seeds, Challenges to New Birth" (International Gathering '96), CPSHSB, box 30, file 9.

6 Minutes from Meeting 14–15 January 1999, St Charles Retreat House, Winnipeg, Manitoba; Together at the Door: A Time for Visitation, Personal Reflection 31 May 1999; Women at the Door 2000, an RNDM Summer Gathering, 28 June–1 July 1999, materials provided by then provincial superior Veronica Dunne.

7 Florence, "At the Door in Solidarity," presented at Women at the Door 2000, an RNDM Summer Gathering, 28 June–1 July 1999, provided by then provincial superior Veronica Dunne.

8 The printed email attached was a statement of New Ways Ministry, Hotmail inbox, dated 26 May 2000, no other information; it was received by the RNDM sisters.

9 Statement of Fr Robert Nugent, SDS, copy of the email sent 24 May 2000, provided by then provincial superior Veronica Dunne. This version is incomplete; one page is missing.

10 Statement of New Ministry, copy of email sent 26 May 2000, provided by then provincial superior Veronica Dunne.

11 See Mary Ann Beavis, with Elaine Guillemin and Barbara Pell, "Introduction," in *Feminist Theology with a Canadian Accent: Canadian Perspectives on Contextual Feminist Theology*, ed. Mary Ann Beavis, Elaine Guillemin, and Barbara Pell (Ottawa: Novalis, 2008), 23–38. See also Rosemary Radford Ruether, "Patriarchy," in *A to Z of Feminist Theology*, ed. Lisa Isherwood and Dorothea McEwan (Sheffield, UK: Sheffield Academic Press, 1996), 173–4; Rosemary Radford Ruether, *Women Healing the Earth: Third World Women on Ecology, Feminism, and Religion* (Maryknoll, NY: Orbis, 1996); Elizabeth Johnson, "Redeeming the Name of Christ," in *Freeing Theology:*

The Essentials of Theology in Feminist Perspective, ed. Catherine Mowry LaCugna (San Francisco: HarperCollins, 1993), 115–27. Fascinating work appeared in the 2000s, including Rosemary Radford Ruether, *Feminist Theologies: Legacy and Prospect* (Minneapolis, MN: Fortress, 2007); and Elisabeth Schüssler Fiorenza, *Empowering Memory and Movement: Thinking and Working across Borders* (Minneapolis, MN: Fortress, 2013). One of the most inspiring books is Elizabeth Schüssler Fiorenza's *Congress of Wo/men: Religion, Gender, and Kyriarchal Power* (Cambridge, MA: Feminist Studies in Religion Books, 2016).

12   RNDM 25th General Gathering, Pattaya, Thailand, 28 January–12 February 2002, CPSHSB, box 17, file 6.

13   RNDM, *Earth Story, Sacred Story, Nurturing an Ecological Spirituality.* Sourced from handout materials from the RNDM retreat for the sisters of the Canadian province, held at Villa Maria Retreat House in Winnipeg and led by Sister Judy Schachtel, SMS, 20–27 June 2003, provided by then provincial superior Veronica Dunne, August 2014.

14   Ibid.

15   Ibid.

16   Ibid; these characteristics are attributed in the handout as coming from Jay B. McDaniel; however, no specific source is cited.

17   Ibid; the minutes taken during the retreat indicate the following as their source for this summary of Dowd's thinking: Michael Dowd, *Earthspirit: A Handbook for Nurturing an Ecological Christianity* (New London, CT: Twenty-Third Publication, 1991).

18   RNDM, *Earth Story, Sacred Story.*

19   Ibid.

20   This quotation, found in the record, is from Brian Swimme and Thomas Berry, *The Universe Story: From the Primordial Flaring Forth to the Ecozoic Era, a Celebration of the Unfolding of the Cosmos* (New York: HarperCollins, 1994), 77.

21   RNDM, *Earth Story, Sacred Story.* The text is signed by Jane Blewett, director, The Earth Community Center, Laurel, MD. The suggested reading to accompany Blewett's text was Brian Swimme and Thomas Berry's book, *The Universe Story.*

22   RNDM Provincial Assembly – Visitation to Pentecost, 2006, 30 May–5 June 2006, St Michael's Retreat Centre, Lumsden, SK.

23   RNDM, 26th RNDM Congregational Chapter, Pattaya, Thailand, 18 January–15 February 2008, *RNDM Earth Community: We Are One, We Are Love,* 10, provided by then provincial superior Veronica Dunne.

24   Ibid., 19.

25   RNDM 25th General Gathering, Pattaya, Thailand, 28 January–12 February 2002, 7. CPSHSB, box 17, file 6.

11 The Mission in Peru

1 Sister Marilyn LeBlanc, "The Paschal Mystery of a Returned Missionary," document provided by Sister Marilyn LeBlanc. No date.

2 Acts of the General Chapter 1966, the last Chapter before aggiornamento, *Statutes du Chapitre General, 1966, Congregation de Notre Dame des Missions,* CPSHSB, B01-08, box 14, file 18, 11.

3 Address of Reverend Mother Mary Gertrude, superior general, to the delegates to the Special General Chapter, 19 July 1969, CPSHSB, B01-08, 14/22, 5.

4 Susan Smith, RNDM, *Call to Mission: The Story of the Mission Sisters of Aotearoa New Zealand and Samoa* (Auckland: NZ: David Ling Publishing, 2010), 304.

5 At the University of Notre Dame, Indiana, United States, Msgr Agostino Casaroli read the document from the Pontifical Commission calling on congregations and religious provinces to send, over ten years, 10 per cent of their membership as of 1961 on missions to Latin America. See Agostini Casaroli, "Appeal of the Pontifical Commission to North American Superiors," in Gerald M. Costello, *Mission to Latin America: The Successes and Failures of a Twentieth-Century Crusade* (Maryknoll, NY: Orbis Books, 1979), 273–81.

6 Sister Marilyn LeBlanc, email originally sent to Norah Tobin and forwarded to author, 15 June 2009.

7 Ibid.

8 Sister Marilyn LeBlanc, undated document entitled, "This Document Was Written by Sr Marilyn LeBlanc, and Speaks of the Initial Planning from Canada Regarding the Founding of the Peru Mission," provided to the author by Provincial Superior Veronica Dunne, September 2013.

9 Jeffrey Klaiber SJ, *La Iglesia en el Perú. Su Historia Social desde la Independencia* (Lima, PE: Pontificia Universidad Católica del Perú, Fondo Editorial, 1988), 358.

10 Susan Fitzpatrick-Behrens, *The Maryknoll Catholic Mission in Peru, 1943– 1989, Transnational Faith and Transformation* (Notre Dame, IN: University of Notre Dame Press, 2012), 140.

11 Ibid.

12 LeBlanc, "This Document Was Written by Sr Marilyn LeBlanc," 1–2.

13 Sister St Fanahan, assistant general, to Mothers and Sisters, 2 February 1969, Our Lady of the Missions, Rome, CPSHSB, box 01-04 12/8. It says: "Our Canadian Sisters have begun their new mission in Peru and very shortly our Australian Sisters will be leaving for New Guinea ... The Canadian Missionaries have been studying Spanish in Puerto Rico, preparatory to beginning their service among the poor, especially the women and children."

14 Sister Marilyn LeBlanc, RNDM, "Questions Relating to Canada and the Peruvian Mission," written in August 2012 in preparation for the book on the RNDM in Canada.

15 Inter-American Economic and Social Council, 1961, "The Charter of Punta Del Este: Alliance for Progress: Official Documents," in Jeffery Taffet, *Foreign Aid as Foreign Policy: The Alliance for Progress in Latin America* (New York: Routledge, 2007), 205–23.

16 Ivan Illich, "The Seamy Side of Charity," *America* (21 January 1967): 88–91.

17 Rosa Bruno-Jofré and Jon Igelmo, "The Center for Intercultural Formation, Cuernavaca, Mexico, Its Reports (1962–1967) and Illich's Critical Understanding of Mission in Latin America," *Hispania Sacra* 66, no. 2 (2014): 457–87.

18 Ibid. See also François Houtard, "L'Histoire du CELAM ou l'oubli des origines," *Archives de sciences sociales des religions* 31e année, 62, no. 1 (1986): 93–105.

19 Hugo Assman, "La Desilusión que los Hizo Madurar (sugerencias de autocritica para los cristianos comprometidos)," La Tercera Conferencia del CELAM, *Documentación Política* 7, ALAI and Centre de Documentation d'Amerique Latine – SUCO (October 1974): 127–9. Reproduced from *Cristianismo y Sociedad, XII, segunda época* (Buenos Aires: Tierra Nueva, 1978), 40–1.

20 Ibid.

21 Fitzpatrick-Behrens, *The Maryknoll Catholic Mission in Peru*, 146.

22 Juan Velasco Alvarado, "Mensaje a la nación dirigido por el señor general de división, don Juan Velasco Alvarado, presidente de la República del Perú en el 1480 aniversario de la independencia nacional," *Revista Mexicana de Sociologia* 32, no. 5, Memorias del IX Congreso Latinoamericano de Sociologia 6 (September–October 1970): 1353–68, http://www.jstor.org/stable/3539555.

23 Ibid.

24 Fitzpatrick-Behrens, *The Maryknoll Catholic Mission in Peru*, 147.

25 Ibid.

26 Deborah Barndt, *Education and Social Change: A Photographic Study of Peru* (Dubuque, IA: Kendall/Hunt, 1980), 64–6.

27 Sr Marilyn LeBlanc, RNDM, "Questions Relating to Canada and the Peruvian Mission," written in August 2012 in preparation for the book on the RNDM in Canada.

28 "History Project. Questions Relating to Canada and the Peruvian Mission," manuscript provided to the author by Provincial Superior Veronica Dune, August 2012.

29 Dennis Gilbert, "The End of the Peruvian Revolution: A Class Analysis," *Studies in Comparative International Development* 15, no. 1 (1980): 15–98, quotation at 15.

30 Ibid., 16.
31 Ibid., 17.
32 "Theology of Liberation and RNDM Missionary Endeavour in Peru," document provided by Sr Marilyn LeBlanc, RNDM. Typewritten internal document.
33 Rosa Bruno-Jofré, "Popular Education in Latin America in the 1970s and 1980s: Mapping its Political and Pedagogical Meanings," *Bildungsgeschichte: International Journal for the Historiography of Education* 1, no. 1 (2011): 23–39.
34 Loretta Bonokoski, *Origins, Bethlehem Home, Hogar Belén, Moquegua, Perú*, pamphlet published in the early 2000s. The address of Hogar Belén is indicated as Prolongación Daniel Becerra Ocampo 509, CPM San Francisco, Apartado 89, Moquegua, Peru; for a tax receipt, donations could be sent to Franciscan Missionary Union c/o Father Adam Sebastian, OFM.
35 Moquegua Mission report, undated, but from the text circa 1982, General Archives of the RNDM, Rome, Latin America, Peru, filing cabinet J.
36 Bonokoski, *Origins, Bethlehem Home.*
37 Sister Marilyn LeBlanc, "Hogar Belén/Bethlehem Home," typed notes provided to the author in August 2012.
38 Bonokoski, *Origins, Bethlehem Home.*
39 Sister Marilyn LeBlanc, email sent to the author, 28 June 2014.
40 Moquegua Mission report, 2.
41 Bonokoski, *Origins, Bethlehem Home.*
42 Ibid.
43 News from Peru, 16 May 1977, Ilo, Peru, signed by Sr M. Monica (Irene), RNDM, Peru, Provincial Administration, Bulletins, Provincial News, orange box, section G, shelf 9.
44 Peruanito, no date or signature, but the text suggests it was written in the early 1970s, General Archives of the RNDM, Rome, Latin America, Peru, filing cabinet J.
45 News from Peru, 16 May 1977, Ilo, Peru.
46 "Theology of Liberation and RNDM Missionary Endeavour in Peru," manuscript provided to the author by Sister Marilyn LeBlanc.
47 Typed report, no date or other information, General Archives of the RNDM, Rome, Latin America, Peru, filing cabinet J.
48 Ibid.
49 "Theology of Liberation and RNDM Missionary Endeavour in Peru," 1.
50 "Letter to Dear Sisters and Friends," Ilo, Peru, 13 April 1984, RNDM General Archive, Orange Box, Section G, Shelf 9
51 Hugo Latorre Cabal, *La Revolución de la Iglesia Latinoamericana* (México DF: Editorial Joaquín Mortiz, 1969), 25–7.

52 A good analysis can be found in Kimba Allie Tichenor, *Religious Crisis and Civic Transformation: How Conflicts over Gender and Sexuality Changed the West German Catholic Church* (Waltham, MA: Brandeis University Press, 2016), 115–23.

53 Ibid., 30. The Colombian Episcopal Committee, presided over by Bishop Aníbal Muñoz Duque, replied to McNamara, saying that foreign imposition of restriction to population growth violates independence. The statement denounced the suggestion that economic cooperation be subordinated to contraceptive campaigns, which violate the most sacred of human consciousness.

54 Letter from Sister Kathleen, RNDM, to Dear Sisters, dated in Ilo, 23 September 1984, General Archives of the RNDM, Rome, Peru, Provincial Administration, Bulletins, orange box, section G, shelf 9.

55 "Theology of Liberation and RNDM Missionary Endeavour in Peru."

56 "Entrevistas," *La Voz del Pueblo, Boletin Parroquial S. Jan Bautista, Candarave* 1, no. 8 (1983), mimeo 8A3125, RNDM, General Administration, Rome, Peru, Provincial Administration, Bulletins, Provincial News, orange box, section G, shelf 9.

57 Ibid.

58 Ibid.

59 "History Project. Questions Relating to Canada and the Peruvian Mission."

60 "The Reality, Candarave," dated by the archivist September 1986, RNDM, General Administration, Rome, Peru, Provincial Administration, Bulletins, Provincial News, orange box, section G, shelf 9.

61 "The Reality, Candarave," RNDM, General Administration, Rome.

62 "History Project. Questions Relating to Canada and the Peruvian Mission."

63 Ibid.

64 Ibid.

65 "The Candarave Diary," 1983, Peru. RNDM, General Administration, Rome, Peru, Provincial Administration, Bulletins, Provincial News, orange box, section G, shelf 9.

66 Ibid.

67 "Witnessing to the Gospel: Beyond All Frontiers," CPSHSB, RNDM documents, B01-8, box 16–12, 1.

68 Ibid., 5.

69 Euphrasie Barbier, *Constitutions of the Daughters of Notre Dame des Missions* (Hastings: Institute de Notre Dame des Missions, 1936), no. 3, cited in Smith, *Call to Mission*, 304.

70 "Euphrasie's Personality," manuscript for the 1993 centennial activities, 1991–1993, CPSHSB, RNDM documents, C01-05, box 28, folder 45.

71 *RNDM 1979 Constitutions*, approved by Rome in 1979, no. 2 (Rome: Congregation of Our Lady of the Missions, 1980), 22.

72 Smith, *Call to Mission*, 304. See also Claire Himbeault, "Letter to the Congregation: General Chapter, 1990 Vision Statement," in *RNDM for Mission* (Rome: Congregation of Our Lady of the Missions, 1990), copy provided by the congregation in Winnipeg. See also, "Report to the Delegates of the 1990 General Chapters," CPSHSB, RNDM documents, box 16, file 14.
73 See Smith, *Call to Mission*, 304.
74 *General Gathering*, 26 May–15 June 1996, Rome, Congregation of Our Lady of the Missions, 1996, article 4a, copy provided by then provincial superior Veronica Dunne.

Conclusion

1 John W. O'Malley, *What Happened at Vatican II* (Cambridge, MA: The Elknap Press of Harvard University Press, 2008).
2 Jürgen Mettepenningen, *Nouvelle Théologie – New Theology: Inheritor of Modernism, Precursor of Vatican II* (London: T & T Clark International, 2010).
3 Pope Pius XI, *Divini Illius Magistri*, Encyclical on Christian Education (Vatican: The Holy See, 31 December 1929), http://w2.vatican.va/content/pius-xi/en/encyclicals/documents/hf_p-xi_enc_31121929_divini-illius-magistri.html.
4 Gregory Baum, "Vatican Council II: A Turning Point in the Church's History," in *Vatican II: Canadian Experiences*, ed. Michael Attridge, Catherine E. Clifford, and Gilles Routhier (Ottawa: University of Ottawa Press, 2011).
5 Peter L. Berger, *The Many Altars of Modernity: Toward a Paradigm for Religion in a Pluralist Age* (Berlin: de Gruyter, 2014).
6 Pierre Bourdieu, *Language and Symbolic Power*, ed. John B. Thompson, trans. Gino Raymond and Matthew Adamson (Cambridge, MA: Harvard University Press, 1991).

Appendix A

1 Paul Ricouer, "Memory-Forgetting-History," in *Meaning and Representation in History*, ed. Jörn Rüsen (New York and Oxford: Berghahn Books, 2006), 9–19.
2 Reinhold Niebuhr, *The Irony of American History* (New York: Charles Scribner's Sons, 1952), 63.
3 The text distributed to the sisters to prepare for the meeting was provided to the author by Sister Veronica Dunne.
4 Ruben Alves, *Tomorrow's Child: Imagination, Creativity, and the Rebirth of Culture* (New York: Harper & Row, 1972), 62ff.
5 Sister Veronica's note: Pablo was a Filipino man whom the sisters got to know. When he was going to be deported, the sisters gave him sanctuary

and then fought to halt his deportation. Pablo was allowed to stay in Canada.

6 The Gospel Way was a month-long retreat that nine sisters made together at Lake of the Woods.

7 Tertianship was a year-long formation program held at the motherhouse in Rome for any professed sisters from the various provinces who wished to attend and applied for it.

Index

French concours, 55, 63, 79–81, 120, 129

French Redemptorists (CSSRs), 87

French-speaking settlers, 6, 9, 50, 78, 101

Froebel, Friedrich, 4, 37

Gaire, Father Jean: bringing of RNDM sisters to Manitoba, 29–31; building of first RNDM convent, Canada, 55, 57; founding of Grande Clairière, 27; request for RNDM sisters, 28; visit to Armentières, 28. *See also* Canadian Province – RNDM

Gaudium et Spes, 155

gay and lesbian Catholics, 193. *See also* homosexual persons; New Ways Ministry

General Chapter of Aggiornamento. *See* 1969 Chapter of Aggiornamento

General Chapter of 1984, 186–7, 233–4, 351n141

General Council: General Chapter of Aggiornamento (1969), 170–8; letter censoring decision on habit, 174–5

Gérin-Lajoie, Marie Lacoste, 116

Grande Clairière, 27–8, 30–2, **32**, 64, 83, 85, 96, 102; first RNDM school, 50, 53, 55–9. *See also* Our Lady of the Snows Convent (Grande Clairière, Saskatchewan)

grassroots communities, 221, 243

Great Depression, 94, 117, 120, 136–7, 242; RNDM recruitment during, 136–42

Grimes, Sister Imelda. *See* Leadership Discussion, RNDM former provincials

habit, 30, 139, 140; Barbier's design of RNDM, 16–17; Cardinal Antoniutti's views on, 158, 160, 171–2; changes to the Canadian RNDM, 45, 106, 119, 156, 160, 164–7, 169, 177, 181–2, 249, 251, 264, 272–5, 278, 348n83; symbol of change in Canadian province, 243, 245; as symbol of poverty, 158; third order, 126

habit (holy), 74

Hastings, England, 24, 125, 139, **165**, 170, 173

Himbeault, Sister Claire, 18–19, 169, 184, 188, 351n141. *See also* Leadership Discussion, RNDM former provincials

Hobsbawm, Eric, 21

Hogar Belén (Bethlehem Home), **208**, **215**, **216**, 221

holistic cosmology, 195

Holy Heart of Mary Convent (Lac Croche). *See* Lac Croche, Assiniboia (Saskatchewan)

Holy Rosary Parish School (Regina), 62, 111–12

Holy See, 16, 130, 164, 166, 243; anti-liberal, 3, 22; anti-modernist, 3, 7, 21–2; involvement with US policies, Latin America, 211; neo-scholastic framework, 7, 42; non-acceptance of divine missions, 18, 240; RNDM loyalty to, 234; rules for apostolic women's congregations, 36; rules of interaction, 62. *See also* Vatican

Holy Spirit, 18–19, 159, 186, 240, 287–8, 299

homosexual persons: Church prohibition of ministry to, 193

Humanae Vitae (encyclical), 227, 234

Hurtado, Alberto, 326n52